FORTRAN
For Business People

FORTRAN
For Business People

Rich Didday

Rex Page

Roger Hayen

Mark Wayne

WEST PUBLISHING CO.
St. Paul • New York • Boston
Los Angeles • San Francisco

COPYRIGHT © 1978 By WEST PUBLISHING CO.
               50 West Kellogg Boulevard
               P.O. Box 3526
               St. Paul, Minnesota 55165
Library of Congress Cataloging in Publication Data
Main entry under title:
FORTRAN for business people.

    Includes indexes.
      1.   FORTRAN (Computer program languages)
2. Business—Data processing. I. Didday,
Richard L.
HF5548.5.F2F16   001.6'424   77–12345
ISBN 0–8299–0101–9

PREFACE

This book is designed for a first course in computer programming for business people. It illustrates general principles of programming practice by detailing solutions to a wide range of business oriented problems, using the Fortran language (as defined in American National Standards Institute document ANSI X3.9-1966 and subsequent clarifications).

The purpose of the text is to introduce students to Fortran so they (1) have knowledge and appreciation of a programming language, (2) can communicate with professional programmers in business or organizations, (3) have a better idea of how to use the computer as an effective management tool, and (4) can apply the computer to the solution of a variety of problems in other business courses using either their own programs or canned programs. A strict adherence to ANSI standards is followed throughout the book. Our experience has shown that use of ANSI Fortran avoids many pitfalls for students who will use Fortran on different computer systems. As you may have experienced, even on the same computer an updated version of a Fortran compiler may raise havoc with a non-ANSI program. Only a few very widely accepted deviations from the ANSI standards are used in the text, and when they are, they are clearly identified as non-ANSI.

There is a substantial amount of material in the book—more than can be covered in a one-quarter or semester undergraduate course. This is deliberate, for it allows the instructor to tailor the course to the particular needs and desires of the students by judicious selection of topics. The selection of topics also allows an instructor to use this text as a supplementary programming text for an introductory course in computers and data processing for business students. The depth of coverage is easily varied to meet the needs of the course.

We have arranged the material in the order which we feel is the most pedagogically sound. In many cases this means introducing restricted versions of certain statements a chapter or two ahead of the more general versions—a spiral approach. This makes it easier to vary the depth of coverage. But it does have an unfortunate side effect: it makes the text a little more difficult to use as a reference. To alleviate this difficulty we have prepared an extensive alphabetical index with multiple references to each discussion in the text. Important definitions and general versions of statements have page references in boldface type. This makes it easier for students to find what they need. Optional sections are included on some advanced topics in relevant chapters, keeping similar material together for easy reference.

> *Boxes throughout the text summarize important points and provide additional information.*

DO-loops are introduced in Chapter 7. We feel it is best to delay their introduction until the student is well versed in the construction of all kinds of loops; otherwise, there is a tendency to terminate loops with counters when other termination conditions would be more appropriate. However, Chapter 7 doesn't depend on any material beyond assignments, expressions, and arrays, and can therefore be covered quite early in the course. In fact, the first section of the chapter introduces the notion of a DO-loop without mentioning arrays, so that DO loops could be introduced in the course simultaneously with Chapter 3 without having to deviate from the text in any important way.

Chapter 10 is devoted to on-line programming. The first two sections of this chapter can be covered concurrently with Chapter 2 if programs are run from a terminal. Section 3 in Chapter 10 can be assigned simultaneously with Chapter 4 without any additional explanation from the instructor. With a few words of preparation from the instructor, it could also be assigned as early as Chapter 2.

This text is intended for an introductory course in programming. Accordingly, it emphasizes algorithm design, program organization, and clarity of expression more than statement syntax and semantic detail. The syntax and semantics are all there, but we spend more time discussing ideas that are more difficult to learn. We have tried, by example more than by essay, to emphasize internal program documentation (proper commenting, indentation, and the like). Such things are, to some extent, a matter of taste and style, but we think it is crucial that the student develop a feeling for the importance of good program design and documentation.

For the student who wants to know more about Fortran than is covered in this text, the related text *Fortran for Humans*, Second Edition, West Publishing Company, 1977, provides a more thorough coverage of Fortran. However, the problems and orientation are more general, not focused on business as in this text.

We hope that students will come away from their contact with this book with some of the spirit of discovery, creation, and satisfaction which we find in programming and using computers to solve problems in business.

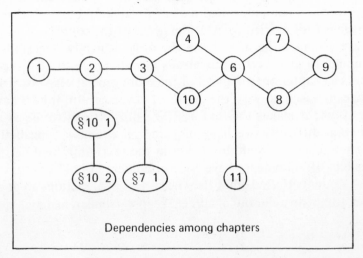

Dependencies among chapters

CONTENTS

* May be skipped without loss of continuity.

* May be skipped without loss of continuity.

†

1 BASIC IDEAS

Chapter Objectives: After studying this chapter, you should be able to:
- Define and discuss Fortran as a computer language.
- Describe a process of developing computer programs.
- Discuss top-down design and modular programming.
- Understand and write verbal descriptions of algorithms.
- Draw flowcharts of algorithms.
- Identify and discuss the three main parts of a computer.
- Describe the use of memory cells or locations.
- Use an algorithm to compute compound interest.

Section 1 1

Advice to You Who Are about to Learn Fortran

You will probably find learning to program a new kind of experience. Insofar as programming is like planning a task, it is a familiar process. What makes it difficult is that the planning must be much more complete than most people are used to.

For example, suppose a carpenter decides to write a set of directions for hanging a door. The difficulty of his task would depend to a large extent on his audience. It would be much easier for him to write a set of directions addressed to another carpenter than it would be to write directions addressed to the general public. For the public the directions would have to be much more complete because most people know little about carpentry. In fact, a layman who happened to know how to hang a door would probably write better instructions for the general public than would the expert carpenter. While the carpenter might be tempted to say "rout strike box in jamb," the layman would realize that he would have to explain what a door jamb is, what the strike of a lock is, and what routing is before he could make any such statement.

It is usually the case that the programmer, like the carpenter, knows much more than his audience, the computer, about the process he is trying to describe. The computer does know some things in the sense that it can perform certain operations, but it is up to the programmer to describe the process in the computer's terms. If a computer system accepts Fortran, then it already can perform all the operations of Fortran. It is up to the programmer to describe the process using only those operations.

To learn to do this is not easy for most people. However, it seems easier once you get the hang of it. It is also fun. Since it is easy and fun for those who know, you will no doubt have lots of friends who want to help you learn to program. Most of them will help you by writing a program which solves the problem you are working on. It should be fairly obvious that this does *not* help you learn to program. You can't learn to swim by having your friend do it for you. But it may not be so obvious that this form of help is often detrimental rather than merely unhelpful. It is detrimental primarily because your helper is likely to use statements you have never seen before. (It might be interesting for you to keep track of the number of times someone says to you: "Oh, that's no good. Why don't you do it this way?") These things you've never seen before will fall into one of four categories:

1 (OK) They are described in the text and you will learn them soon.
2 (POOR) They are advanced constructions and shouldn't be used until you know more about the basics.
3 (BAD) They are outmoded ways of doing things which are holdovers from more primitive languages.
4 (FREQUENT) They don't exist at all.

We offer this advice: Listen politely to friends who want to help, but always try to write the program yourself using techniques you know about from the part of the text you have read.

The exercises at the end of each section should help you confirm that you understand the material in the section. Answers for virtually all the exercises appear at the end of the book.

Although the first few chapters contain many new concepts, you will probably be able to grasp them quickly. Later chapters contain more and more complex combinations of these basic concepts and will probably require more thought. You can't learn to program in a day. It will take lots of thought and practice, but we think you will find it an enjoyable experience.

---

blanks: Although people rarely draw attention to them, blank characters are very important in written communications. A blank serves as an unobtrusive separator.

////Imagine/reading/a/sentence/like/this.////
Oronewithnoseparatorsatalllikethis.

You may not be used to thinking of a blank character as the same sort of thing as an a or a b or a ! But on a line printer (as on a typewriter) it takes a definite action to produce a blank just as it requires a definite action to produce an a.

One of the reasons we have numbered sections the way we have in this book is to draw attention to the blank as a legitimate character.

A typical usage is "Figure 8 4 1," read "figure eight four one," identifying the first figure in the fourth section of Chapter 8.

Section 1 2

Background

This book is intended to help you learn to program computers using the programming language Fortran. In practice, the only way to learn to program is to do it, so this book is really only an aid to reduce the number of errors in your trial-and-error learning process.

Fortran is a **computer language**, a language with which to communicate commands to a computer. **A computer** is a machine that manipulates symbols by following the instructions in a computer program (written in a computer language, of course). Humans may interpret these symbols as they please. For example, a person might want to interpret a certain set of

> *computer:* a machine which can perform arithmetic operations, make logical decisions, and perform many other symbol manipulation tasks automatically by following the instructions in a computer program

symbols as the results of a number of questionnaires, and he might write a program (a sequence of commands) in Fortran which would cause some of the symbols to be matched up in pairs. He might then call this process "computer dating" and make a lot of money.

Motivation for development of computers comes from efforts to mechanize symbol manipulation tasks. An adding machine is a familiar

> *program:* a sequence of instructions

device which manipulates symbols and, in so doing, winds up with symbols that we call the sum of the symbols we put in. Early computers were little more than assemblages of devices which added, multiplied, divided, and so on, and could do these operations in sequence. Thus, a person who wanted to add a large list of numbers, then divide the sum by another number, then subtract this from yet another number, could write down a series of commands which would be *stored in the machine* and carried out in order automatically. The key word here is *stored*. The instructions which the computer is to follow are stored in the machine, and they can be changed by the user of the computer, the programmer.

> *machine language:* a set of commands which a computer is built to perform. Different computers have different machine languages. A machine language program runs with no need for translation. Most machine languages bear little similarity to human languages.

In the early days, one of the programmer's biggest problems was keeping up with changes in computers. There was, and still is, a continuing introduction of newer, faster, different computers. In the early fifties a group of programmers began an attempt to get around this problem. It had become apparent that if something weren't done, programmers would be spending large portions of their lives just learning the language for one new computer after another. Since the process of learning new languages was both gruesome and time-consuming, they designed a computer language closer to English than typical machine languages. They called their new language **Fortran**. It was a higher-level language. They wanted Fortran to provide a way of giving commands to computers that was easy for programmers to learn, general enough to handle a great variety of problems, and designed so that the commands would be meaningful in terms of any computer's internal workings. Hopefully, manufacturers of new computers would provide machine language programs for translating Fortran programs into commands for their new machines. Programmers, then, wouldn't have to learn too much about the new machine to be able to program it and could continue to write their programs in Fortran, relying on the company's translation program to convert Fortran statements to machine commands.

> *higher-level language: a computer language which appears more like a human language than a machine language and is designed to be used on many different brands of computers*

Even though the new language wasn't really much like English, it was a big improvement over machine languages. It was concerned largely with arithmetic computing, and it promised to bring the use of the computer within reach of a large number of technically oriented people who would not have been willing to write programs before. Although the first version of Fortran was never widely available, Fortran II (introduced in 1958) became the first popular, commercially available higher-level language.

Through the years, as people have become more and more familiar with what is involved in programming, they have found certain types of statements more useful than others. *Higher-level languages have evolved.* Fortran IV, the language you will be learning, was introduced in 1962. It is available at virtually all computing installations and is defined by a set of standards maintained by the American National Standards Institute.

Most Fortran systems have some extra features which extend the standard (ANSI) language in one way or another. Since these extensions are different on different systems, we'll stick with the ANSI version in this text—it's the same everywhere. You can learn about extensions available on your system from the reference manual which describes it or from a local expert. However, our experience tells us that it is better to stick with standard Fortran. In the past we have been lured by the apparent convenience of some non-ANSI statements. The programs we wrote worked beautifully for a while, but when the computing system was "slightly" modified, our programs quit working properly. If we had stuck with ANSI Fortran in the first place, the programs would have continued to work. It wouldn't have been any harder to write them either, if we had been thinking in ANSI mode when we coded them. (For a description of standard Fortran, see *Fortran,* ANSI X3.9–1966, American National Standards Institute, Inc., 1430 Broadway, New York, New York 10018.)

Many higher-level languages in addition to Fortran have been designed and used, and it is probable that sooner or later Fortran will no longer be so popular— a more modern language will take its place. At this time, however, Fortran is very widely used, and computer companies have spent a lot of time and effort making programs which translate Fortran into their machine languages. These programs are called **compilers**, perhaps because they work by compiling a long list of machine commands which will do just what your Fortran statements ask. Of all the compilers available at your computer center, it is likely that the

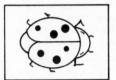

Fortran compiler is the most reliable and the most convenient to use. As you learn more about computer programming, you will see why there are likely to be mistakes (or **bugs** as they are called) in any large computer program, including a compiler. It is hard enough to write programs without having to worry about bugs in the compiler, so it is important to use a language whose compiler is as accurate as possible. Since this language will, on most computer systems, be Fortran, it is a valuable language to know.

> *compiler: a program which translates a higher-level language into machine language*

It is important to understand what it is that you are to learn about programming. We are not going to try to teach you to "think in Fortran"—in fact, this is undesirable. What you are encouraged to learn is first, how to analyze a problem from the real world and divide it into subproblems each of which you know how to solve, and second, how to communicate the results of your analysis to a computer in terms of a Fortran program. Figure 1 2 1 illustrates the process.

Phases 2 and 3 of Figure 1 2 1 are the most important to learn—and if you do learn them, you will be in a much better position to understand what can be done with computers. Unfortunately, they are virtually impossible to learn out of context. You will have to learn about reasonable analogies between real world processes and computer processes by learning about computers through programming.

Let's apply the scheme shown in Figure 1 2 1 to a specific problem. Figure 1 2 2 suggests a concrete example of a case in which it is very easy to make appropriate analogies. We don't expect you to understand all the details of the program, just the general idea.

Phase 1 You decide you want to know the average
price per pound of laundry detergent.

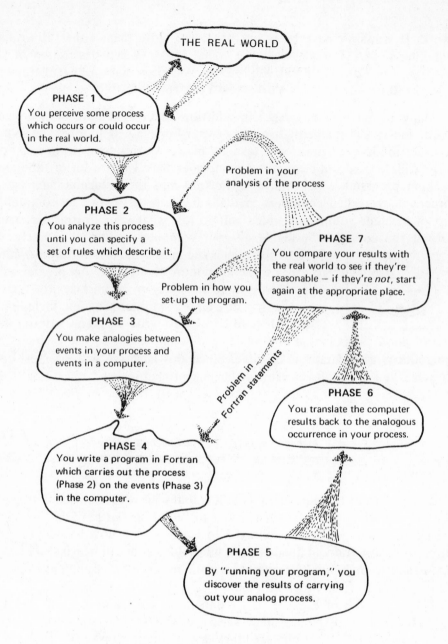

Figure 1 2 1 The Big Picture

Phase 2 The process you wish to carry out is to sum the individual brand prices and divide by the total number of brands.

$$\text{Average price} = \frac{\text{sum of prices}}{\text{total number of brands}}$$

Phase 3   You decide to let data locations in the computer represent the price per pound for each brand and the number of brands, and to use the addition and division operations to carry out your process.

Phase 4

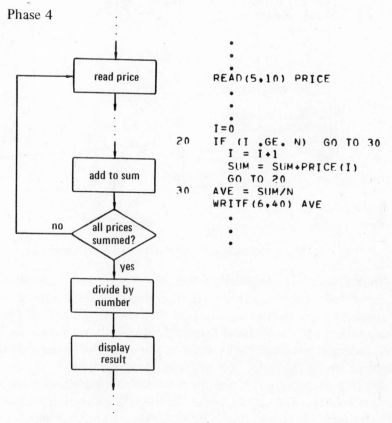

```
        READ(5,10) PRICE
        .
        .
        .
        I = 0
20      IF (I .GE. N)  GO TO 30
        I = I+1
        SUM = SUM+PRICE(I)
        GO TO 20
30      AVE = SUM/N
        WRITE(6,40) AVE
        .
        .
        .
```

Phase 5   You run your program and get the computed value.

Phase 6   That value should be the average price per pound.

Phase 7   If that number seems reasonable, accept it. If it doesn't, try to see where the problem lies, and start in again at the appropriate place.

Of course the statements shown in Phase 4 are unfamiliar to you. Perhaps, however, you can detect some of their meaning by just glancing at them. They include such actions as reading data (the detergent prices must be entered into the computation), computing the average price by first counting up the total and then dividing by N (the number of different brands), and finally, printing the result.

Figure 1 2 2   Selecting a Laundry Detergent

In this simple example, Phases 2 and 3 were relatively simple. But in more complicated problems, these are the most difficult phases. As you progress through this course, you should find that you spend most of your time analyzing the problem to be solved and gradually making your solution look more and more like processes you can easily code in Fortran. The better you lay your plans in Phases 2 and 3, the easier the coding in Phase 4 will be.

Writing programs and using the results of computations is (or should be) a very logical process. The stories about credit card foul-ups, statements like "we have student numbers because that's easier for the computer," and the assumptions that computers are like people, only dumber and faster, show that unfortunately, many people don't understand the BIG PICTURE. As you go through this book, recalling the ideas in Figure 1 2 1 may help you to keep your perspective.

While the process of using the computer is basically logical, Phase 4, in which your ideas are translated into Fortran commands, may not seem to be. Don't worry if certain requirements in Fortran don't seem rational to you—they're probably not. Don't forget that Fortran was designed before anyone had used higher-level languages. Since then, committees and special-interest groups have added parts, usually trying to keep the new version enough like the old so that old programs will run on new compilers. Such an evolution is bound to produce some clumsy appendages. In this book we are trying to protect you from as many idiosyncrasies as possible; in fact, we will occasionally lie to you. That is, initially we will leave certain details out of the language we describe. But these will be only little white lies, and we think that they're for your own good (the details often add little but confusion at first). We fill in details when it becomes necessary so that by the end of the text you have the whole picture.

By the way, you might consider that English, which was developed by a *huge* committee, isn't exactly logical either.

EXERCISES 1 2

1 Write down some of your current opinions about computers and how they work, what they do, what they will be able to do, how they affect the life of the average person, etc. Attach what you've written to the last page of this book so that when you've finished the book you can see in what ways your ideas about computers have changed.

2 Read more about the history of Fortran in the chapter on Fortran in *Programming Languages: History and Fundamentals* by Jean E. Sammet, New York, Prentice-Hall, 1969, pp. 143–172.

Section 1 3

Algorithms

Algorithm is a word used by the computing community to mean a rule, procedure, or sequence of instructions for performing a task. In an algorithm (a description of how to do some task), each step of the description, while incompletely specified, is understood by the person or machine which is to perform the task. Each step will always be incompletely specified simply because it's impossible to describe anything *completely*. You just hope to be understood most of the time. Our first example of an algorithm is so incompletely specified that one important instruction is totally left out. Look at Figure 1 3 1 and see if you can discover what is missing.

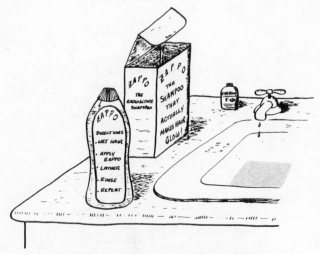

Figure 1 3 1   The ZAPPO Algorithm

Since the ZAPPO instructions fail to tell you when to stop, you would wash your hair forever if you followed them unswervingly. There is little doubt that sometime, someone you know, maybe even (perish the thought) *you,* will write a program for the computer which acts like the ZAPPO directions in Figure 1 3 1. Saying "but that isn't what I *meant*" will get you sympathy but not results. Fear not, however; your program will not run forever. The infinite loop is a universal problem, and for that reason all programs are given some time limit. They run just so long, then they are thrown out whether they seem to be finished or not.

> *infinite loop: a list of instructions which cannot be performed in a finite amount of time*

The most important things to notice in the ZAPPO algorithm are:

1 When performed in order, the instructions lead you through the process of "washing your hair with ZAPPO"–presumably this is a difficult task which must be explained.

2 Each instruction is incompletely specified–if you don't know how to "lather," this algorithm is of no use to you.

3 Each step within the algorithm seems reasonable, but the overall effect is not reasonable. Technically, it's not a true algorithm because it never stops; it doesn't tell you how to complete the task.

A popular and useful way of depicting algorithms is **flowcharting**. Writing a flowchart helps people visualize how the individual parts of an algorithm fit together.

> *flowchart: a pictorial presentation of an algorithm*

Figure 1 3 2 shows a flowchart of the ZAPPO algorithm.

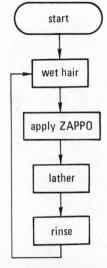

Figure 1 3 2

You will note that instruction 5 ("repeat") is not written out in the flowchart, and if you think about it a bit, you will realize that it is a different kind of instruction from the other four. Instructions 1 through 4 tell you to perform a specific act, whereas number 5 tells you where to get your next instruction. In a flowchart, arrows are used to indicate where to go next. We also added an oval-shaped box with *start* in it. If we read directions on a bottle, we assume we start at the top. In flowcharts this isn't always true.

So that you will be more comfortable thinking in terms of algorithms, we'll show you a few more examples. In each case we'll present a verbal description and a flowchart of the algorithm involved. Try to see how one relates to the other and see which is easier for you to use. Probably you'll want to use a combination of the two techniques.

The verbal description in the knitting algorithm may look strange to you, especially if you don't know that *sts.* means "stitches" and that *K2, P2* means "knit 2, purl 2," but this is a characteristic of programming languages—they contain symbols which mean precise things to the person or computer being instructed.

Knitting a Scarf

VERBAL DESCRIPTION

Starting at lower edge, cast on 116 sts. 1st row: *K2, P2. Repeat from * across. Repeat 1st row until total length is 60 inches.

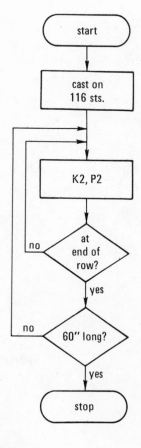

Figure 1 3 3   Knitting a Scarf

You will notice that a symbol (*) is used to identify a place to repeat from and that the "repeat from * across" instruction has become an arrow in the flowchart. Also, you will notice that, unlike the ZAPPO algorithm, the commands to "repeat" are conditional. You don't repeat forever; you repeat to the end of the row ("across"), or until the total length is 60 inches.

The flowchart for the knitting algorithm is relatively complicated, yet it is easy to understand. You probably won't write a program as complicated as this flowchart until you have read Chapter 3.

Get a Job (sha nana na sha nanananana)

Suppose you were out of work and wanted to get a job. One scheme would be:

VERBAL DESCRIPTION

START: Get the help wanted section of the newspaper and look at the first listing.

DECIDE: If you couldn't stand the job, proceed from the instruction called LOOP. If you could stand the job, call the people who placed the ad. If they seem reluctant to talk to you, try to convince them how great you would be at that job and check their response again. If they agree to talk to you, set up an appointment. In any case, proceed to the next step.

LOOP: Repeat the DECIDE instruction unless there are no more help wanted ads.

FINISH UP: If you've made some appointments, be hopeful. If not, be bitter, complain about the economy, and file for unemployment.

It may seem silly to you to write down an elaborate set of instructions for getting a job–after all, "everybody knows how to do that." That may be, but the point is most computer languages have been designed to do one fairly simple thing at a time, based on very little information, so when you are writing a computer

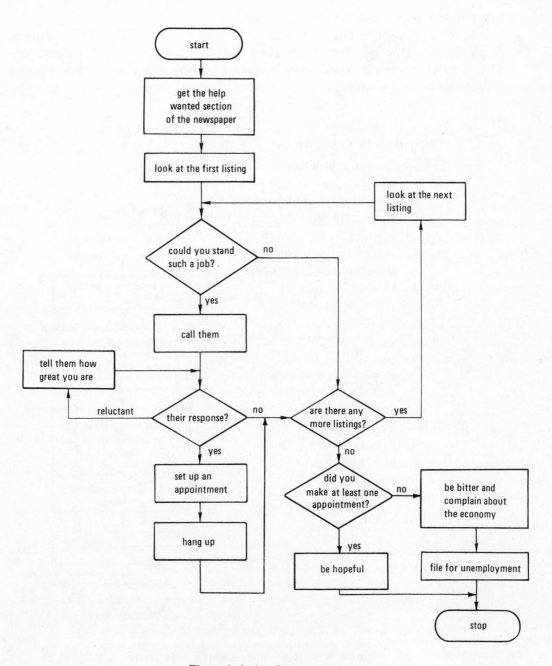

Figure 1 3 4 Getting a Job

program it is *you* who must figure out how to fit a number of basic instructions together to do a useful overall task. You will have to learn to describe the things you want done in simple terms. If you start thinking about all the little things you have to know to accomplish everyday tasks, it will give you some idea of the level of detail needed in computer programs.

Computing Compound Interest

Suppose you want to put some money in a savings account, and you want to decide whether it would be better to get 5 percent interest compounded quarterly or 4.85 percent interest compounded weekly. One way to find out which is better is to compute your interest for one year at each rate and then compare the results.

VERBAL DESCRIPTION

SETUP: Compute how many times a year you will receive interest (4 times with quarterly interest, 52 for weekly compounding). Call the number of times N.

UPDATE: Update the current principal by multiplying it by

$$1 + \frac{\text{interest rate}}{100 \times N}$$

Repeat this updating step until you have done it N times.

PROFIT: Subtract the initial deposit from the final principal to get the interest received.

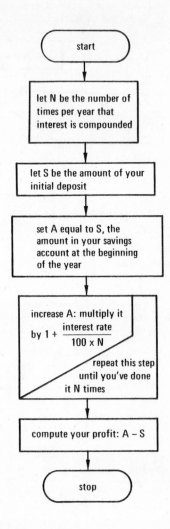

Figure 1 3 5 Computing Compound Interest

This compound interest algorithm, like the get a job algorithm, has a characteristic which is common to many algorithms—it repeats one of its statements several times. Computers are often used to perform difficult tasks by repeating many simple tasks, as in this example. Possibly this is where the characterization of computers as "high-speed idiots" comes from. This seems a little unfair since the computer *is* able to perform its program, and this is all we expect of it. Perhaps the *program* could be characterized as intelligent or idiotic, but the terms don't apply to the computer itself.

The algorithms explored so far have been relatively simple. What happens when things get really complicated? Since the human mind can't comprehend all the details of a complex algorithm simultaneously, the best approach is to divide a complex algorithm into a few more manageable pieces and attack each piece separately. Each chunk or **module** of the algorithm is then viewed as a problem in its own right. Complicated modules are divided into still simpler submodules, and so on, until the problem is solved. Thus, a modular approach makes it possible for people to solve complex problems like developing management information systems and exploring Mars by remote control. It is to make sure *all* the modules of the algorithm have been considered that this **top-down approach** of dividing the problem into subproblems is used. This is an organized way to solve a problem. You look at the whole problem from the top, identify a collection of modules which, when solved and put together, will solve the whole problem, and then proceed on down each submodule until the algorithm which solves the whole problem is finally finished. You may have to remind yourself to take this approach. It's easy to fall into the trap of working on an interesting piece of the algorithm before you have determined all the necessary modules. But this often leads to wasted effort because the process isn't usually a smooth one. You don't always divide the problem into modules in a fruitful way on the first crack, and you have to go back and divide the problem in a different way. This can be discouraging if you've spent a great deal of time on a module you have to throw away.

How about an example? You are in the middle of a modular approach to an education. As you strive to attain an education, you take a series of courses. Each course is a module. By using top-down design, you combine the right modules to obtain a degree in your chosen field. It would be very difficult for you to get a degree if you tried to learn everything in a degree program at one time, or if you tried to take the courses in a helter-skelter sequence. Not only are your courses modular, they are also **structured**. By structured we mean that there is only one point at which you can enter the course and only one point at which you can successfully complete the course. When algorithms are divided into structured modules, it is easier for you to comprehend what the algorithm does. Although there are more specific rules for writing structured programs which we haven't discussed here, you can think of structured programs as programs whose modules have only one entrance and only one exit. Top-down design provides the master plan for putting the structured modules together. So, when you encounter a large, complex problem, divide and conquer.

EXERCISES 1 3

1 Match each term on the left with the appropriate definition on the right.

algorithm (a) a graphic description of an algorithm

compiler (b) a manageable subpart of a complex algorithm

flowchart (c) a computer language

Fortran (d) a sequence of instructions telling how to perform a specific task

module (e) a program which translates statements in a higher-level language into an equivalent machine language program

2 Write a verbal description of and a flowchart for one or two of the following:

making a dessert (following a recipe)

making a desert (altering an ecosystem)

fixing a flat rear tire on a bicycle

computing your income tax

writing a haiku verse

buying a pair of shoes

figuring your grade-point average

getting a driver's license

Section 1 4

Machine Ideas

You will recall from Section 2 that Fortran was designed for use on many different computers. Fortran assumes that every computer has certain characteristics. These assumed characteristics can be described in simple terms and are helpful to know. The Fortran statements you will soon be learning will make sense if you visualize them as affecting the various parts of the **conceptual computer** shown in Figure 1 4 1.

The conceptual computer has three parts, a **controller** which carries out the commands which make up your program, a **memory** which stores your program and any values it may use or produce, and **input/output devices** through which values are fed in and printed out. We'll describe each part in concrete terms.

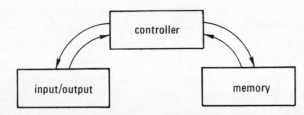

Figure 1 4 1 The Conceptual Computer

The **memory** consists of some number of words or **cells**. A **memory cell** is a collection of two-state elements. At any point in time each element is in one or the other state. These two states are commonly named "1" and "0" by machine designers, and although we'll rarely think of memory cells in these terms, the size of a memory cell is invariably given in **bits** (**binary digits**), the number of two-state elements making up the cell.

> *memory: the part of a computer which stores programs and data*

Each cell in memory has an **address** (denoting where it is) and a **value** (the particular pattern of 1's and 0's that it contains). In Fortran programs we give a **name** to each memory cell we wish to use; the name can be thought of as the address of the memory cell. We can issue commands which will copy the value from a particular memory cell into another part of the machine by using the

> *We use the terms* word, cell, memory word, memory location, *and* memory cell *interchangeably.*

name of that memory cell. As the term *copy* implies, doing this does not disturb the value in the memory cell. We will also be able to store values in memory cells, and since there is only a fixed storage capacity (a fixed number of bits) in a cell, the value that used to be there is destroyed when a new value is stored.

The **controller** is the central coordinator of the conceptual computer. Your program, when stored in the memory, is really just a bunch of values (patterns of 1's and 0's) in a bunch of memory cells. The values that make up your program are examined by the controller, and the 1's and 0's work like electrical switches turning on the various subunits required to carry out the command. We're not trying to say that a computer is just a lot of 1's and 0's. That would be a vast oversimplification. But we want to emphasize that

> *controller: the part of a computer which carries out commands from a program*

the controller simply carries out the instructions or commands specified by bit patterns in memory cells. The controller can get values from memory cells, can manipulate them, can put new values back in memory, and can supervise the input and output devices.

Input and output devices (**I/O devices**) are the means of communication between human users and the machine. You will probably punch commands to the computer on cards, and these cards will be "read" by a **card reader,** an input device. The other I/O device you will use frequently is the **printer**, which will print your program and its results. TV and movie scenes involving computers always seem to focus on card readers, line printers, magnetic tape devices, or card sorters. The

> *input/output: the parts of a computer which allow communication between users and the computer*

first three are I/O devices often used to help communicate with a computer. A card sorter, on the other hand, stands alone, not connected to a computer. It can do several information processing tasks, but it cannot be considered a general-purpose computer. Probably these devices are shown because they move at a spectacular rate of speed. In the controller and the memory, on the other hand, nothing moves at all except electrons, and they're hard to see.

There are other types of I/O devices, but until you know more about computers, you'll be able to get by with just a card reader and a line printer. If you think we're being elusive, look at the manual describing the computer you will be using. Then you'll think we're as clear as Frank Zappa is weird.

Anyway, lest you think a card reader can actually *read,* let us emphasize that a card reader converts the holes in the card into electrical signals. These signals are put into the memory by the controller. Hence they become values stored in specific memory cells.

The card reader is commanded to "read" a card by the controller (when the controller has been so instructed by your program). Similarly, the controller can send values to the printer and direct the printer to print them.

EXERCISES 1 4

1 Tour the computer you will be using and look at the various I/O devices, the controller (or **processor**), the various types of memory, etc.
2 Find out something about the machine you will be using—the number of bits per word, the number of words in the memory, the brand and model number, the price, the color, what it smells like, etc.
3 List the parts of the "conceptual computer" and their functions.
4 What is the difference between the name of a memory cell and its value?

Section 1 5
A Program for the Conceptual Computer

To get an idea of how computers operate, it will be helpful for you to simulate a computer running a program. The idea is to play the roles of the various parts of the conceptual computer as it goes through the steps of a program. This is a realistic simulation. Every command is directly analogous to a Fortran statement, and all of the parts of the conceptual computer are used. The program calculates the future value of $1 by raising 1.0 plus the interest rate to the power designated by the number of years [i.e., $(1 + i)^n$] using repeated multiplication. If the interest rate is 6 percent for 4 years, for example, the program will eventually arrive at the result $1.26 (1.06 times 1.06 times 1.06 times 1.06).

Begin as follows:
1 Get a stack of cards and label ten of them with the names STATEMENT 1, STATEMENT 2, . . ., STATEMENT 10. Label three more with the names INTEREST, YEARS, and AMOUNT. These thirteen cards represent the memory. Spread them out so you can see them all at once, or at least so you can get to them easily.

2 Get a piece of paper and a pencil to use to write the output sent to the "printer."

3 Take four more cards and write

.06   4   on the first card

.07   0   on the second

.05 −1   on the third

and .08   2   on the fourth.

Place these cards face up on a stack with the first card on top for use by the "card reader."

4 Write the instructions (program statements) below on the cards labeled STATEMENT 1 through STATEMENT 10.

COMMENT: This program computes the future value of $1 after a given number of years at a specified interest rate.

STATEMENT 1   Remove the top card on the card reader stack, copy the first number on it into memory cell INTEREST, copy the second number into memory cell YEARS, and then throw the card away.

STATEMENT 2   Send the message THE VALUE OF $1 IN to the printer. Look at the value in memory cell YEARS and send it to the printer followed by the phrase YEARS AT, then send the value of INTEREST to the printer, and finally send the phrase PERCENT INTEREST IS.

STATEMENT 3   Look at the value in INTEREST. Add the value 1 to the value stored in INTEREST and store it back in INTEREST, erasing the old value.

STATEMENT 4   Store the value 1 in memory cell AMOUNT.

STATEMENT 5   Look at the value in memory cell YEARS. If it is zero, take your next instruction from STATEMENT 9, otherwise go on to STATEMENT 6.

STATEMENT 6   Look at the values in memory cells AMOUNT and INTEREST, multiply them together, and store the result in AMOUNT, erasing the old value.

STATEMENT 7   Take the value from memory cell YEARS, subtract one from it, and place the new value back in YEARS, erasing the old value.

STATEMENT 8   Get your next instruction from STATEMENT 5.

STATEMENT 9   Look at the value in memory cell AMOUNT and send it to the printer.

STATEMENT 10 Get your next instruction from STATEMENT 1. T 1.

The program you will carry out does a fairly simple task. It reads in two numbers, INTEREST and YEARS, adds 1 to INTEREST, and then multiplies INTEREST by itself YEARS times. Figure 1 5 1 is a flowchart for the process.

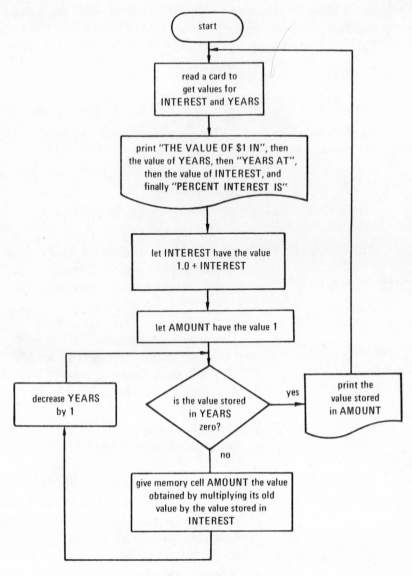

Figure 1 5 1

In order to carry out the program, simply start with the instruction in memory cell STATEMENT 1, do exactly what it says, and then proceed to the next memory cell in sequence (i.e., to STATEMENT 2, and so on). Some of the instructions say to break the sequence. In this case, you again proceed sequentially after starting from the new STATEMENT. Go!

$$\text{\textit{exponentiation:} } \textit{to compute } a^b, \textit{multiply}$$
$$\underbrace{a \times a \times \ldots \times a}_{b \textit{ factors}}$$

There are a great many things to be learned from what you just did (assuming that you did the above simulation). The STATEMENTs that you (simulating the controller) carried out are very similar to the commands which can be written as statements in Fortran, so you now have a feeling for the degree of explicitness required to write programs. In addition, the algorithm we used has an unfortunate but altogether too common property—it works fine for some input values, and lousy for others. Hope you didn't go on too long with the third pair of input values before you realized that something was desperately wrong. To be realistic, we should have given you a time limit, after which you (the controller) would stop executing the program whether you were finished or not. Because of this difficulty, you never reached the fourth pair of values. When something goes wrong, there's no guarantee that all your data will be used.

The exercises below will give you a little more practice in choosing and expressing commands.

EXERCISES 1 5

1 Add another command into the interest rate program so that it will just stop if the value for memory cell YEARS is negative.

2 Write a program for the conceptual computer which computes the average of a bunch of numbers.

3 Write a program which finds the longest name in a list of names. Write a bunch of your friends' names on cards, and simulate a computer executing the program to find the longest name.

4 Write a program to find your take-home pay from your gross pay.

2 SIMPLE PROGRAMS

Chapter Objectives: After studying this chapter, you should be able to:
- Write memory cell names.
- Identify and discuss REAL and INTEGER constants.
- Declare the use of memory cells to be either REAL or INTEGER.
- Identify, discuss and use
  - the ASSIGNMENT statement
  - the WRITE statement
  - the READ statement
  - the FORMAT statement
  - the STOP statement
  - the END statement
- Enter Fortran statements on cards for processing by the Fortran compiler.
- Draw input and output designs using card layout and print charts.
- Write a program to calculate your checking account balance.

Section 2 1

Memory Cells

Of the three parts of the conceptual computer, the memory is probably the most confusing. The I/O apparatus's purpose is straightforward; the **controller** carries out commands, some of which you can imagine from your class simulation; and the **memory** is used to store values. This seems simple enough, but confusion seems to arise from the fact that each memory cell has a name. Because of the way computer programs are written, many people tend to confuse the name of a memory cell with the value stored in it, a mistake similar to confusing a box with its contents. Try to keep in mind that a memory cell is a container for a value.

We've said a number of things about memory already (that it's made up of cells, each of which has an address or name and a value, and that both your program and data are stored there). In this chapter we'll make these ideas more concrete and begin to get some ideas of how we use the computer's memory.

In order to use the memory in the Fortran language, you need a name for each memory cell you intend to use. The language is very considerate in that it allows you to name the memory cells in any way you like, as long as you follow a few rules.

> *rules for naming memory cells*
> - *start with a letter*
> - *use only letters and numerals*
> - *use no more than six characters*

As long as you follow these rules you have *complete freedom*! For example, you may name a memory cell DRAT, if you like, or any other four-letter word, or POT or CELL12 or COFFEE. But you may not name a memory cell MARI-JUANA or ASPIRINS because these names have too many characters, nor can you name one D--N because two of the characters in that name are neither letters nor numerals. However, for improved clarity and easier debugging, use names that represent the data contained in the memory cell.

Once you have named a memory cell, the natural question arises: "What can you do with it?" The answer is that you can store any kind of information you want in it, as long as you can devise a way to represent the information.

By the time you get through this book, you will be able to create representations for whatever types of information you want to deal with. However, certain features of Fortran make it easier to deal with a few specific types of information. So, for a while we'll use only those types. In fact, in this chapter you'll see only two of those **data types**, as they are called.

> *data type: a collection of items of information organized in a standardized manner. A computer system or the programmer associates a special representation with each data type. Since a particular item of information, when stored in the computer's memory, is actually a string of 1's and 0's, this associated representation is essential for correct interpretation of the information item. Two different items of information may be stored in the computer's memory as the same string of 1's and 0's when the items have different data types. In this case the difference between them is determined solely by the difference in their associated representations.*

When you want to use a memory cell in a Fortran program, you must decide what kind of information it will contain; that is, you must choose its **type**. Within a program you may use many memory cells containing many different types of information, but any *one* memory cell is allowed to contain only *one* kind of information. That is, you will associate *one* name and *one* data type with each memory cell you use.

> FORTRAN *is not a legal memory cell name.*

There are several data types available in Fortran, but in this chapter we'll deal with only two of them: INTEGERs and REALs.

INTEGERs are whole numbers, like 1, 2, 3, 7, 11, −4, −1, and 0; numbers with no fractional parts. REALs are numbers with fractional parts and are always written with a decimal point, as in 137.9, 4932.1, 32.00, and −17.472. You might think it very picky to distinguish between whole numbers and numbers containing decimal fractions, especially if the two numbers happen to be 32, an INTEGER, and 32.00, a REAL. It *is* picky. But Fortran deals with the two numbers in vastly different ways, and the type you choose will seriously affect the result of a computation, so you may as well get used to the distinction. Numbers containing decimal points are REALs even if there is no fraction after the decimal point. Numbers without decimal points are INTEGERs.

> *In Fortran programs, numbers containing decimal points are* **REAL** *numbers. Thus, a REAL number is a sequence of digits with a decimal point located somewhere in the sequence. In addition, the sequence may be preceded by a plus or a minus sign.*
>
> | REALs | unREALs |
> |---|---|
> | 1497.3 | 1,497.3 |
> | +83.0 | +83 |
> | −983.25 | −983¼ |
> | 1.0 | 1 |
> | 0.5 | ½ |

> *In Fortran programs, each* INTEGER *constant must be written as a series of digits which may be preceded by a plus or a minus sign:*
>
> 1492
> +83
> −194
> +0047
>
> *A Fortran* INTEGER *may not contain any other kinds of symbols.*
>
> *1,492 won't work.*
> *+83.0 won't work either.*

At the beginning of each Fortran program we use **declaration statements** to name the memory cells we intend to use and we say what type of information we intend to store in them. For example, the declaration statement

`INTEGER TWO, M1, COUNT, A`

gives names to four memory cells whose contents will be INTEGERs. On the other hand, the declaration statement

`REAL X, Y, Z`

gives names to three memory cells, X, Y, and Z, and decrees that each will be used to store REAL numbers. A memory cell must always contain the same kind of information. It can't contain an INTEGER value at one point and a REAL value at another point.

EXERCISES 2 1

1 Which of the following are legal names for memory locations? If not, why not?

```
23SKIDOO
SKIDOO23
SALE3
TORQUE
FLIMFLAM
JUICE
TONY THE TIGER
FORTRAN
```

2 Which of the following are legal declaration statements?

```
INTEGER A
INTEGER A, B
INTEGER VERYLONG
INTERGER Q
REAL J, Z, BETA
REAL HIGH,LOW
REAL A, 149.2
```

3 Write a Fortran statement which declares that we want to use two memory cells, AJAX and FOAM, to store INTEGERs.

4 Circle the INTEGERs and place a check mark by the REALs.

41.7

349

692.0

81

−49

−896.721

0

Section 2 2

The Assignment Statement

The question of how to get information into the memory cells you have named still remains. There are two ways. One is to assign values to the cells directly in the program; the other is to get their values from some source of data such as punched cards. Each method has its advantages in different contexts.

An **assignment statement** gives values to memory cells directly in the program. The general form of the assignment statement is a memory cell name followed by the assignment operator (the equal sign, =), followed by the value which you wish to place into the memory cell. The assignment operator transfers the value on its right into the memory cell named on its left.

The assignment statement confuses many people, perhaps because the assignment operator (=) is a familiar sign, but the operation it designates is *not* familiar. The action in an assignment statement proceeds from *right to left:* the value on the right is placed into the memory cell named on the left. This is an important thing to remember, so important that you should probably read this paragraph again.

> = *Remember! In Fortran the equal sign does not mean equals in the mathematical sense. A statement like* A = B *places the value in the memory cell* B *into the memory cell* A. *It is true that immediately after the statement is executed the values in* A *and* B *are the same, but at some later time the values in the two memory cells may be different. For example, the next statement in the program may assign a different value to* B. *This won't affect the value of* A, *so at that point* A's *value will be different from* B's.

Examples

    TWO = 2

The value 2 is placed into the memory cell named TWO.

    THREE = -1

The value −1 is placed into the memory cell named THREE. (This is a lousy name for a cell containing the value −1, but Fortran doesn't care.)

    STUDNT = 3.982

The number 3.982 is placed into the memory cell named STUDNT.

    TRACK = -1.95

The number −1.95 is placed into the memory cell named TRACK.

These examples result in storing values in memory cells as shown below:

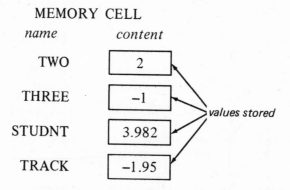

MEMORY CELL

name   *content*

TWO   [2]

THREE   [−1]

STUDNT   [3.982]   *values stored*

TRACK   [−1.95]

Of course, in order for the above assignment statements to work properly, the declaration statements

```
INTEGER TWO, THREE
REAL STUDNT, TRACK
```

must appear at the beginning of the program.

---

assignment statement

form
  $v = e$
  v is a memory cell name
  e is an expression

meaning
  computes the value of e and places it in v

examples
```
QUANT = 3
TAX = 19.27
COST = 3*AMOUNT + 47
```

It would soon get boring just writing programs that assigned values to a bunch of memory locations. Fortunately, the right-hand side of an assignment statement can be more complex than just a single number. It may be an **expression** involving some arithmetic computations. In Fortran, the familiar operations of addition, subtraction, multiplication, division, and exponentiation may be used in the usual ways (see Table).

operation	standard symbols	example	Fortran symbol	examples
addition	+	$a + b$	+	A+B 1+1
subtraction	–	$a - b$	–	A–B 3–2
multiplication	·	$a \times b \quad a \cdot b$	*	A*B 4*4
division	÷ — /	$a \div b \quad \dfrac{a}{b}$ a/b	/	A/B 10/2
exponentiation	superscript	a^b	**	A**B 2**10

The reason the multiplication and exponentiation symbols aren't the same as usual will become apparent if you look at a punched card. There would be no way of telling the multiplication sign X from the letter X, so an asterisk (*) is used instead. In addition, there's no way of punching superscript symbols, so we use ** instead.

Example

    A = 18427 - (14*639)

The value of the arithmetic expression above (namely 9481) is placed into the memory cell named A.

Expressions can be considerably more general than the ones you have seen so far, which have involved only constants. It is also permissible to use memory cell names in an expression. Thus, names of memory cells may appear on both sides of an assignment statement, but the names are used in very different ways. As you already know, the name on the *left* side tells where to *store* the value which results from the computation on the right side. Memory cell names on the *right* side mean "go to this place in memory, and use whatever value is stored there in the computation." It is important to realize that the values of memory cells on the right remain unchanged.

Example

    Q1 = (TWO*THREE) + (A - THREE)

The value of the arithmetic expression on the right is placed into the memory cell named Q1. To compute the value of the expression, the controller must first determine the contents of each of the memory cells TWO, THREE, and A, then execute the indicated arithmetic operations. If we assume the values of the memory cells TWO, THREE, and A haven't changed since the last time we used them in this chapter, then TWO has the value 2, THREE has the value −1, and A has the value 9481, so Q1 will be assigned the value 9480.

Example

```
Q1 = Q1 + 1
```

The value of the expression on the right is placed into the memory cell named Q1. This example may appear odd at first because the memory cell to be given a value is involved in the expression on the right. This is one time when it is especially important to remember that the action goes from right to left. First the computer looks up the current value of Q1; our last assignment made that value 9480. Adding 1 to 9480, the value of the expression is 9481, and this value is put into the memory cell Q1. This assignment destroys the old value of Q1, of course.

In most cases, writing arithmetic expressions to make computations is quite natural and the results fit in pretty well with your past experience. However, there is one big difference to keep in mind. Remember that each memory cell is made up of a fixed number of elements or symbols, 1's and 0's. That means that some numbers will be too long to fit. For example, INTEGER memory cells in IBM 360 and 370 computers cannot handle INTEGERs outside the range −2149531648 to +2149531647. This may not seem particularly restrictive, and usually it isn't, but it is important to realize that this doesn't include *all* integers. There are an infinite number of (mathematical) integers. If you are not careful, this restricted INTEGER range may cause you to get results you don't expect. If you multiply two big numbers together, the result may be too big to fit in one memory cell, and this will no doubt cause problems in your computation. (This type of error is known as an **overflow**.)

> **INTEGERs** *vs. integers: You have probably noticed that when we refer to Fortran values of type INTEGER, we write "IN-TEGER." When we want to refer to "counting numbers," i.e., mathematical numbers, we'll write "integers."*

Another problem arises in evaluating expressions like 29/7. The result certainly cannot be computed to infinite precision, but what value should be computed? Fortran settles this question by convention: the value of an arithmetic operation involving only INTEGERs must be an INTEGER. Therefore, if the number 4 1/7 comes up as the quotient of two INTEGERs, the fractional part is dropped. Hence 29/7 equals 4 (in Fortran). Similarly, 9/10 equals 0.

Arithmetic expressions will be dealt with in more detail later. For now, rely on your past experience with mathematics to guide you in using parentheses to denote groups of operations which are to be done before others. For example,

$1 + (7 * 3)$ is 22, but $(1 + 7) * 3$ is 24. You may also rely on the usual algebraic rules of precedence: exponentiations are performed first, then multiplications and divisions, then additions and subtractions. For example, $10 + 7**2/12$ equals $10 + ((7**2)/12)$, which is 14. When you are uncertain about how an expression will be evaluated, use parentheses to make it perfectly clear.

EXERCISES 2 2

1 At the end of the following program fragment, what are the values of A and B?

```
INTEGER A, B
B = 10
A = B
B = 2
```

2 What values would be stored in INTEGER memory cell B by these assignment statements?

```
B = 2*3*4
B = (2/1) + 1
B = -19*2
```

3 Which of these are legal assignment statements? If not, why not? (Assume all variable names have been declared to be INTEGERs.

```
A = A*A + A
BO = 2
-AT = 2
CAT + DOG = FIGHT
CAT + DOG-3
FIGHT = CAT + DOG
```

4 What value will be stored in INTEGER memory cell SOUP by these assignment statements?

```
SOUP = 1 + (7*4)/2
SOUP = 123/2
SOUP = (19/20) + 1
SOUP = (21/20) + 1
SOUP = (8/16)*1024
```

5 Write statements which will

a declare an INTEGER memory cell named FIRST and assign FIRST the value 2,

b assign FIRST its old value times 4, and

c assign FIRST its old value plus 1.

Section 2 3

The WRITE Statement

So far you have learned how to attach names to memory cells and to place values into them. You can also make the computer perform computations involving INTEGER numbers. Unfortunately, however, you have no way at this point of finding out the results of the computations. The WRITE statement will solve this problem, as the following example demonstrates.

Suppose you are buying a car, and you want to compute the total price, including an optional FM radio and supersport airfoil spoiler. The computation might proceed like this:

1 note the base price

2 note the price of the FM radio option

3 note the price of the airfoil spoiler option

4 add the above three figures to get a subtotal

5 compute 7 percent sales tax

6 add tax to subtotal to get total cost

The program below makes these computations. You should be able to understand everything in the program except, possibly, the WRITE, FORMAT, STOP, and END statements. We'll explain those after you've looked the program over carefully.

```
      REAL      BASEPR, RADIO, SPOILR
      REAL      SUBTOT, TAX, TOTAL
      BASEPR = 4127.00
      RADIO = 232.00
      SPOILR = 248.00
      SUBTOT = BASEPR + RADIO + SPOILR
      TAX = SUBTOT*0.07
      TOTAL = SUBTOT+TAX
      WRITE(6,1000) BASEPR
1000  FORMAT('1BASE PRICE      $',F7.2)
      WRITE(6,2000) RADIO
2000  FORMAT('       RADIO      $',F7.2)
      WRITE(6,3000) SPOILR
3000  FORMAT('     SPOILER      $',F7.2)
      WRITE(6,4000) SUBTOT
4000  FORMAT('0TOTAL PRICE      $',F7.2)
      WRITE(6,5000) TAX
5000  FORMAT('             TAX  $',F7.2)
      WRITE(6,6000) TOTAL
6000  FORMAT('0PLEASE PAY CASHIER     $',F7.2)
      STOP
      END
```

output

```
    BASE PRICE      $4127.00
        RADIO      $ 232.00
      SPOILER      $ 248.00

    TOTAL PRICE      $4607.00
            TAX  $ 322.49

    PLEASE PAY CASHIER      $4929.49
```

Each of the WRITE statements in the program instructs the controller to send one line to the printer. To understand how this works, you need to understand the various parts of a WRITE statement. First of all, most computers have several output devices attached to them, including line printers, magnetic tapes, disks, and so forth. To send output to the printer, the WRITE statement must select that particular device out of the whole collection of devices attached to the computer. That is the purpose of the "6" in the WRITE statements of the above program. On the computer system we were using, as on many others, I/O unit 6 is the line printer. (Your system may denote the printer with a different number, perhaps 3 or 2. Check with a local expert.)

Local Expert

In addition, the WRITE statement must refer to a FORMAT which describes the basic layout of the line, what kinds of values go where, where the line goes on the page, and so forth (more on this later). This is the purpose of the "1000" in the first WRITE statement; it tells the controller to use FORMAT number 1000 to determine the layout of the line. The FORMAT, however, doesn't specify all the information which goes on the line. Some of it comes from values stored in memory cells, and this is the purpose of BASEPR in the first WRITE statement. Thus, the first WRITE statement says to put the value of BASEPR on a line whose layout is described in FORMAT 1000 and send the line to unit 6, the printer.

The FORMAT statement must describe the layout of the line in several ways.

WRITE statement

form

WRITE (*u, f*) *list*

u is an INTEGER constant or INTEGER memory cell name

f is an INTEGER corresponding to the label on a FORMAT statement

list is a list of memory cell names, separated by commas (*list* may be omitted if the FORMAT completely specifies the line so that no values from memory are needed)

meaning

sends the line described in FORMAT *f*, filled in with values from the memory cells in *list*, to the designated I/O unit *u*

examples

```
WRITE(6,1030) A, B, C
WRITE(6,2019) Q
WRITE(3,3000)
WRITE(N,2042) A,C,T
```

First, it must say where to put the line on the page. There are several possible choices, but the most important are (1) on the next available line, (2) on the second line down from the current line, leaving a blank line in between, and (3) at the top of the next page, leaving the rest of the current page blank. The particular choice is indicated by a **carriage control character** in the FORMAT. Character strings in FORMATs (including the carriage control character) are distinguished from other types of information by enclosing them in **quote marks** (actually, they look more like apostrophes, but we call them quote marks because of the way they're used). Any character string in a FORMAT is copied (without the quote marks) onto the line being written. The carriage control character is simply the first character on the line.

In other words, the printer refuses to print the first character on any line sent to it by the controller. Instead, the printer uses the first character to select one of the three choices for line positioning. The character "blank" (' ') selects the next available line, the character "zero" ('0') selects the second line down from the current line, and the character "one" ('1') selects the top of the next page.

These character strings in FORMATs that are transmitted as is (less quote marks) to the output line are known as **literal descriptors** because they describe a part of a line *literally,* as it will stand. In order to leave a place in a line to insert values from memory, we use **data descriptors** in FORMATs. These data descriptors specify the type of information stored in memory which will be inserted at

---

literal descriptors

forms
> 'string'   non-ANSI
> nH*string*   ANSI standard
> *string* is a sequence of one or more characters (letters, digits, and/or special characters like periods, slashes, etc.)
> *n* is an INTEGER indicating the number of characters in *string*

meaning
> denotes the sequence of characters *string* to be copied literally onto an output line from a FORMAT

examples
```
 'ARCHETYPAL SYSTEMS INC.'
23HARCHETYPAL SYSTEMS INC.
 ','
 1H,
```

note
> We will use the nonstandard form in our programs because we feel it is easier to read. If your system will accept only the ANSI standard form, known as the **Hollerith notation**, or if you want to conform strictly to the standards, you should have no trouble converting our literal descriptors to yours. In fact, it won't be long before you'll be able to write a program to make the conversion for you.

carriage control characters

1H *or* • •	*(blank)*	*move down the page one line before printing*	*single space*
1H0 *or* •0•	*(zero)*	*move down the page two lines before printing*	*double space*
1H1 *or* •1•	*(one)*	*move to the top of the next page before printing*	*new page*

this point in the line (INTEGER or REAL), the number of character positions to use to print the value, and in the case of REALs, the number of digits to the right of the decimal point to print. Each data descriptor in a FORMAT will correspond to a memory cell in the *list* portion of the WRITE statement. The value from the first memory cell in the WRITE *list* goes into the spot on the line indicated by the first data descriptor in the FORMAT. The second memory cell in the WRITE *list* matches with the second data descriptor in the FORMAT, and so on.

For each type of value, there is a different kind of data descriptor. The Iw data descriptor is used for INTEGER values; I6, for example, leaves six spaces in the line for an INTEGER from memory to be inserted. The F$w.d$ data descriptor is used for REAL values; F7.2 leaves seven spaces in the line for a REAL value, rounded to two decimal places, to be inserted. It is essential in matching memory cells in the WRITE *list* with data descriptors in the FORMAT that the types of values in the memory cells be identical to the types of the data descriptors. If an INTEGER valued memory cell is matched with an F$w.d$ data descriptor, or if a REAL valued memory cell is matched with an Iw data descriptor, the results printed will be erroneous. If you are lucky, your computing system will detect the error. More likely a mysterious, erroneous result will be printed with no explanation given.

Since WRITE statements must reference FORMAT statements, FORMATs must have labels. As you can see in the box on Fortran statement layout, labels on statements must be placed in columns 1 through 5. A **label** is simply an unsigned INTEGER of one to five digits, not all zeros, with no sign. A FORMAT is a labeled statement consisting of the key word FORMAT followed by a parenthesized list of FORMAT descriptors (literal descriptors, data descriptors, and others we haven't covered yet).

data descriptors

forms

    Fw.d
    Iw

w and d are unsigned INTEGER constants (d must be smaller than w)

meaning

describes a field of width w (i.e., w character positions) to be filled with a REAL value expressed to d decimal places in the case of Fw.d, or an INTEGER value in the case of Iw. The values are always **right-justified** in the field (i.e., the number is placed as far to the right as possible in the field with spaces filling the unused portion on the left. If the value to be written is negative, the number is preceded by a minus sign (–) which takes up one of the w character positions. In REAL values, the decimal point occupies one of the w character positions and the decimal fraction takes up d positions, leaving $w - d - 1$ character positions for the rest of the number (and minus sign if needed).

examples

```
      INTEGER M
      REAL A, B
      A = 479.12
      B = -7.86
      M = 12
      WRITE(6,1000) A,B,M
 1000 FORMAT(' ', F10.2, F7.1, I4)
      WRITE(6,1001) M,B,A
 1001 FORMAT(' SALESMAN', I3, ' SALES $', F7.2,
     +          ' PERCENT CHANGE', F7.3)
```

printed lines

bbbb479.12bbb–7.9bb12   b means blank

SALESMANb12bSALESb$b479.12bPERCENTbCHANGEb–7.860

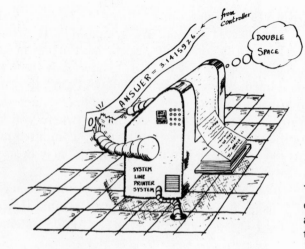

The printer rips off the first character on each line sent by the controller and uses it to decide how far to move the paper before printing.

Conventions concerning the physical appearance of Fortran state-ments are based on the assumption that the statements are punched on 80-column cards. Certain columns are used for certain purposes. There are four fields on a Fortran statement card:

1 *the label field (columns 1-5)*
2 *the continuation field (column 6)*
3 *the statement field (columns 7-72)*
4 *the identification field (columns 73-80)*

The identification field is completely ignored by the compiler but it is printed on your program listing and is often used for card numbering. In all fields, blanks are ignored; you should use blanks freely to make your program readable.

You write one statement on each card. However, if your statement is too long to fit in the statement field of one card, you may con-tinue it into the statement field of the next card by placing any mark (other than zero) in the continuation field (column 6) of the second card. (This doesn't work for comment statements.)

There is one additional convention: a C in column 1 will cause the compiler to ignore the entire card. Since the card will be printed on the program listing, you may use this convention to intersperse your program with comments.

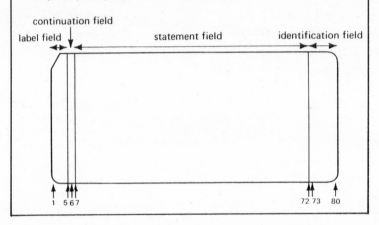

The whole notion of FORMATs, data descriptors, literal descriptors, and the like probably seems unduly complicated to you. We sympathize. It *is* unduly complicated. In fact, FORMATs are a major hurdle for novice Fortran program-mers. They're a real pain in the old wazoo. Figure 2 3 1 shows how the WRITE and FORMAT statements are related. When you write FORMATs, try to visualize the line to be printed. It often helps to write out a prototype line, then write the FORMAT to match the prototype, inserting literal descriptors where you know exactly what the line will look like and data descriptors where computed results will be inserted. A print chart like the one shown in Figure 2 3 2 may be used to assist you in constructing prototype lines.

If you look back at the program now, you should be able to understand how the WRITE statements work, using the FORMATs, to print results. However, you're still in the dark about the last two lines, the STOP and END statements.

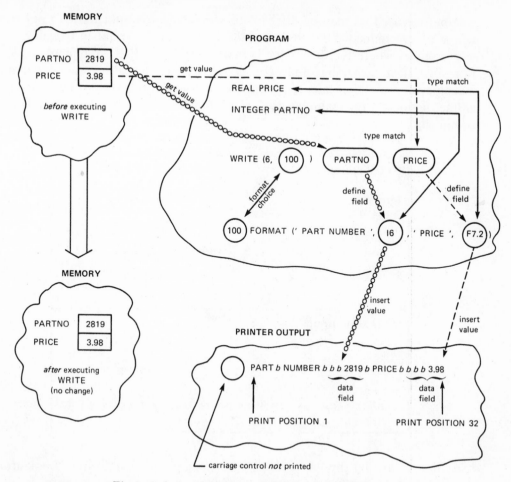

Figure 2 3 1 Getting the WRITE Statement Together

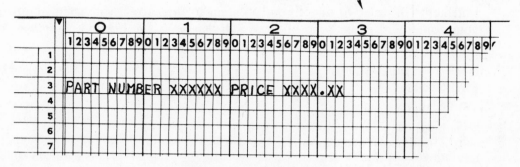

Figure 2 3 2 Print Chart

The STOP statement instructs the *controller* to stop executing your program and proceed to someone else's. The END statement instructs the *compiler* that there are no more statements in your program. The END statement must be, physically, the last card in your program, but the STOP statement may appear anywhere. Of course, after the STOP statement is executed, no other statement in your program will be executed. It may be difficult to see why you would want to put it any-where except immediately preceding the END statement, but in Chapter 3 we'll see examples where the difference between STOP and END statements is clearer. For now, just remember that the compiler, in translating your program to machine language, translates STOP into a command for the controller, but END is an instruction for the compiler itself and is not translated into a machine language command.

STOP statement

form
  STOP

meaning
  instructs controller to stop executing your program and to begin executing the next program

---

END statement

form
  END

meaning
  informs compiler that there are no more statements in your program

---

At this point you should be able to prepare a program and run it. Look around the computer center and find a sign describing the correct deck setup. It will in-clude some statements (known as job control statements) other than the Fortran statements in order to direct your program to the correct subsystems built into your computer system (one of these subsystems is the Fortran compiler). You might try the first problem at the end of this chapter for starters.

EXERCISES 2 3

1 Which of the following statements are legal?
```
WRITE(6,1000) X
WRITE(6,2000) X+Y, 21,72, 3*2
WRITE, A, B, C
WRITE(6,3000)
WRITE(6,3000),A
```

2 What would the following program fragment print?
```
      INTEGER M
      REAL A
      A = 2.0*35.2
      M = 3+9
      WRITE(6,1000) A,M
 1000 FORMAT(' ', F5.2, I4)
```

Section 2 4

The READ Statement

In most cases the most convenient and efficient way to place values into memory cells is to use the assignment statement which we have just discussed. There is, however, a second way to give values to memory cells which, in certain cases, makes a program easier to use. We are speaking of the READ statement. Its main advantage is that it allows you to change the data that the program uses in its computations without changing the program itself. The following example illustrates the point.

Suppose you are tired of balancing your checkbook each month, especially since your balance often disagrees with the bank's. You know the bank uses a computer to figure your balance, so maybe if you use a computer too, you will have a better chance of agreeing with the bank. Let's try to think of a way to write a program to compute your bank balance.

Basically, the program must assign the old balance and amounts of the month's transactions to memory cells, compute the new balance, and print the result. One approach to writing such a program is described below:

1 declare one memory cell to store the amount for each check you wrote

2 declare one memory cell to store the amount for each deposit you made

3 declare a memory cell to store the old balance and one to store the new balance

4 assign values for the old balance and all the checks and deposits, using assignment statements

5 write an expression which computes the new balance and assign its value to the memory cell to be used for that purpose

6 print the new balance

The big disadvantage to a program like this one is that it must be changed every month. Each month you will write a different number of checks for different amounts, make a different number of deposits, and have a different old balance. Therefore, you will have to declare a different number of memory cells in each month's program and assign them different values.

A second approach would be to keep a running balance rather than to do all the totaling at the end. Then, instead of needing a memory cell for each check and deposit, you need only one cell for the current transaction (check or deposit) and one cell for the current balance. This approach is shown in Figure 2 4 1.

Although this approach is closer to what we want, there is still a problem: there is no way to stop and print out the final balance. The program just keeps going. You will learn a way to exit the loop to print results in Chapter 3, but for now we'll try another approach.

We are trying to avoid changing the program each month. Of course it is clear that something must be changed, since the amounts of the transactions will be

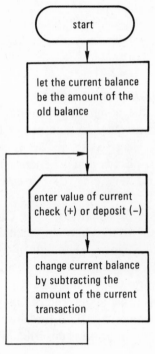

Figure 2 4 1

different each month, but it would be nice to have some way to give the program this information without having to change the program itself. To give data to the program from an outside source, in other words. This can be accomplished by using the READ statement.

The READ statement directs the controller to get values from the card reader and place them into memory cells. The card reader gets these values from **data cards**, which are not part of the program itself. A READ statement consists of the word READ followed by a unit number and FORMAT label in parentheses, followed by a list of memory cell names known as the **input list**. The memory cell names in the list must be separated by commas, just as they were in the WRITE statements you saw in Section 2 3. For many systems, the unit number associated with the card reader is 5, but as with the printer's unit number, you'll have to check with local experts to determine the correct number for your system.

The READ statement places a value into each memory cell in the input list, getting these values from a data card following your program. Just as output lines must be described by FORMATs, so must data cards be described by FORMATs. The READ statement refers to a FORMAT and matches each memory cell in the input list sequentially with the data descriptors in the FORMAT. The data descriptors specify the type of value which will be on the card and where the values will be. To look at it another way, the FORMAT divides the characters on columns on the data card into fields, one for each data descriptor, and the READ statement takes values for the memory cells in its input list from these fields. The value from the first field goes into the first memory cell in the input list, and so on down to the last memory cell in the input list.

Each card is called a record. A **record** is a collection of related data fields. A data card has 80 columns or character positions. A group of adjacent columns are combined to form a **field**. Then, several fields are combined on one card, resulting in a record.

FORMAT statement (restricted form)

form
> FORMAT (*spec*)
> *spec* is a list of FORMAT descriptors separated by commas

meaning
> describes an output line or data card

note
> Every FORMAT must be labeled.

examples
```
1001 FORMAT('0BALANCE=',F10.2)
2000 FORMAT(I7, F10.0)
2001 FORMAT(I10, I10, F8.0, I3)
```

As with WRITE statements, it is extremely important that the field types (REAL or INTEGER) match the types of the corresponding memory cells in the input list. If an F$w.d$ (REAL) data descriptor gets paired with an INTEGER type memory cell, the results can be a disaster, often without warning. Of course, pairing an Iw descriptor with a REAL type memory cell causes similar problems. Unlike FORMATs associated with WRITE statements, input FORMATs don't need carriage control characters; each time a READ statement is performed, a

---

READ statement

form
> READ(u,f) *list*
> u is an unsigned INTEGER constant or an INTEGER memory cell name
> f is a FORMAT statement label
> *list*, an input list, is a list of memory cell names separated by commas

meaning
> places values into the memory cells in *list*, taking the values from fields on a data card. The fields on the data card are described in FORMAT f and the data cards lie on unit u.

examples
```
READ(5,1000)A, B, C
READ(5,2000)X
```

---

new data card is used (you can't back up). In fact, literal descriptors won't be of any use to us in FORMATs associated with READ statements, but the F$w.d$ and Iw descriptors are used to describe REAL and INTEGER fields of w characters on the data card. If a FORMAT contains several data descriptors, the corresponding fields on the data card lie one after the other, left to right across the card. Figure 2 4 2 illustrates the relationship between the READ and FORMAT statements.

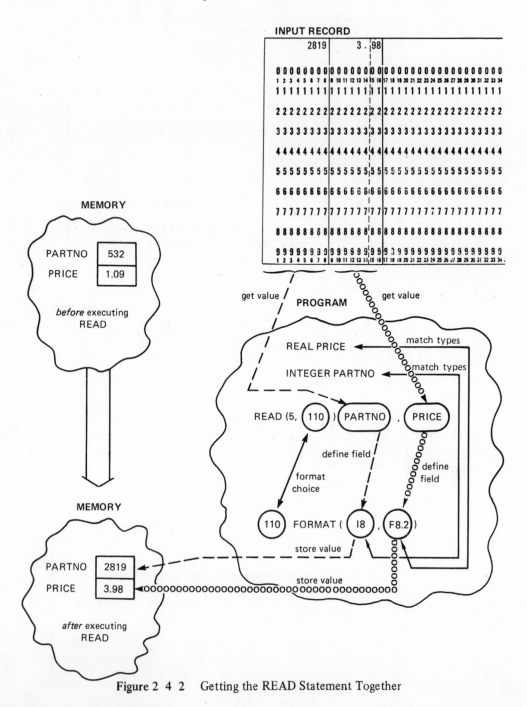

Figure 2 4 2 Getting the READ Statement Together

When you write FORMATs for the READ, it is useful to develop a prototype of the location of the data on a card, then write the FORMAT to match your prototype sketch. A card layout form is often used to aid programmers in this task. Figure 2 4 3 is an example prototype on a card layout form. The dashed line indicates the location of the decimal point for the F$w.d$ descriptor in the event you didn't punch the decimal in the number. Sometimes this is called an implied decimal.

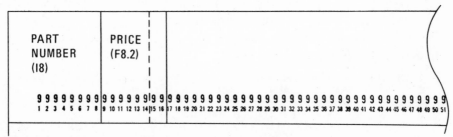

Figure 2 4 3 Data Card Layout

You may recall that in Chapter 1, when you were simulating a computer, the controller executed some statements similar to READ. It was a two-step process: first the controller told the card reader to read a card, and then it told certain memory cells to remember the values on that card. The Fortran READ statement is executed in the same way.

> **data cards:** *cards with values punched on them which follow your program. They are not statements in your program, but they contain values to be stored in memory cells used by your program.*

Data cards are placed after a special card put after the end of your program. This card varies from one computer system to the next, and again, you'll have to look around the computer center for a poster describing deck setup or consult a local expert on how to make up the card which separates your program from the data cards.

Now let's see how we can use the READ statement to solve the bank balance problem. Recall that we wanted to write the program in such a way that we could use it every month without change. Thus, the program itself can depend neither on the actual amounts of the checks and deposits nor on the number of transactions. This calls for careful planning, and we will take several stabs at the problem before coming up with a complete solution.

> *Since data cards come after your program and are not part of it, their use is not bound by the rules for punching Fortran statements. You may use any or all of the 80 columns available. Careful! Make sure you don't describe more than 80 columns in your FORMAT.*

> *No data card can be read twice. Each time a* READ *statement is performed, it starts at the beginning of a new card.*

Our first approach is to READ the amounts of the transactions one by one and keep a running total representing the current balance. Our program will assume that there are no more than 5 transactions in any one month. If you are a heavy check writer, you can easily change the program so that it will handle 25 or 50 transactions, but this dependence on a maximum number of checks is an objectionable feature which we will remove later in an improved version of the program. Read the program carefully, and try to understand what it does. We'll describe it in detail after you've read through it.

```
COMMENT:  THIS PROGRAM CALCULATES A NEW BANK BALANCE GIVEN
C         THE OLD BALANCE AND TRANSACTIONS.
C         TO USE THE PROGRAM, PUNCH SIX DATA CARDS.
C             CARD  1  :  OLD BALANCE
C             CARDS 2-6:  TRANSACTIONS (POSITIVE FOR CHECKS AND
C                                       NEGATIVE FOR DEPOSITS)
      REAL BALNCE, TRANS
      READ(5,1000) BALNCE
 1000 FORMAT(F6.0)
      READ(5,1000) TRANS
      BALNCE = BALNCE - TRANS
      READ(5,1000) TRANS
      BALNCE = BALNCE - TRANS
      READ(5,1000) TRANS
      BALNCE = BALNCE - TRANS
      READ(5,1000) TRANS
      BALNCE = BALNCE - TRANS
      READ(5,1000) TRANS
      BALNCE = BALNCE - TRANS
      WRITE(6,2000) BALNCE
 2000 FORMAT(' NEW BALANCE IS $', F7.2)
      STOP
      END
```

data
```
    456.03
     78.36
    -25.39
     45.25
     45.22
    -75.42
```

output
```
    NEW BALANCE IS $ 388.01
```

There are several important things to notice about the above program. For one thing, the data descriptor F6.0 in FORMAT 1000 describes a data card with a REAL number in columns 1 through 6. The *d* part of an F*w.d* data descriptor is ignored by the READ statement as long as there is a decimal point in the REAL number on the data card. For this reason, we normally let *d* be zero and always include the decimal point in a REAL number on a data card. If the decimal point is omitted, then the controller inserts one *d* places from the right-hand side of an F*w.d* field.

> *numeric fields and blanks:* On a data card, fields covered by an
> Fw.d. or Iw data descriptor are known as numeric fields. Numeric
> fields may contain blanks, but the blanks are interpreted as zeros.
> This will cause problems if a number with no decimal point does
> not extend all the way to the rightmost field position. Effectively,
> enough zeros are tagged onto the end of the number to fill out
> the field. Unless programmers do this intentionally, aware of the
> results, they end up with much larger numbers than they
> intended.

The second important thing to notice about the program is the high degree of
redundancy. The statements READ(5,1000) TRANS and BALNCE = BALNCE
– TRANS are repeated over and over again. There are always ways to avoid repeating the same statements over and over again, and you will learn one in the
next chapter, but for now this will have to suffice.

The third important feature is the technique of computing the sum of the transactions using a single memory cell in which the running sum builds up. In this
case, that memory cell is called BALNCE. First we put the amount of the old
balance into BALNCE. This step is called **initialization**. Each time the computer
gets the amount of a new transaction from a data card, it changes BALNCE by
that amount. This technique, called **accumulating a sum**, is very common in computer programming. You will see it again and again. In this case the sum accumu-
lates one term at a time in the memory cell BALNCE.

EXERCISES 2 4

1 Given that each input record is an 80-column card, what is the maximum
number of
  a character positions per record?
  b fields per card?
  c character positions per field?
  d records in a deck of cards?

2 Prepare some data cards for the above program, assuming that you wrote
four checks in the amounts $4.27, $27.92, $132.00, and $9.42, made one
deposit in the amount of $237.26, and had an old balance of $1.25. What
results would be printed if the program were executed with these data
cards?

3 Which of the following are legal Fortran I/O statements? If a statement is
not legal, explain why.

```
READ(5,1000) A, B, D
WRITE(6,2000) A, B, D
READ(5,3000) A, A+B, 2
WRITE(6,4000),A
WRITE(6,5000)
READ(5,7000)X
```

4 Write a program which READs four INTEGERs from a card and WRITEs
their sum.

PROBLEMS 2

1 Write a program to print your name and assign the result of a computation to an INTEGER memory cell [e.g., N = 1 – 3 + (4*5) /2] and print the value of this memory cell below your name. Make up three other expressions and WRITE their values.

2 Write a program to print your ID number, AGE, HEIGHT, and WEIGHT.

Input Design:

Output Design:

3 After bowling, you decide to let the computer figure your total score for the three lines you bowled and your average score as well. READ in the three scores, then WRITE them out along with the three-game total and the average score for the three games.

input		output				
columns	field	GAME 1	GAME 2	GAME 3	TOTAL	AVERAGE
1–3	score 1	125	135	130	390	130
4–6	score 2					
7–9	score 3					

4 Write a program to compute the interest on $1000 at 5 percent for 3 years. (Just in case you have an extra grand lying around!) Try another amount at a different rate for a different time period by changing the data card and running your program again.

input		output
columns	field	PRINCIPAL $1000
1–5	principal	INTEREST RATE .05
6–7	interest rate	TIME 36 MONTHS
8–10	time (months)	ACCUMULATED INTEREST $150.00

5 Write a program to compute gas mileage based on data submitted by drivers.

Input Design:

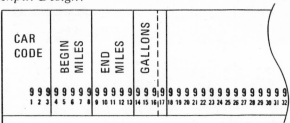

Output Design:

	0	1	2	3	4
	1234567890	1234567890	1234567890	1234567890	1234567890 12
1					
2					
3			MILEAGE REPORT		
4					
5			MILES		AVERAGE
6		CAR	TRAVELED	GALLONS	MPG
7					
8		XXX	XXX.X	XXX.X	XX.X
9					
10					

6 You are about to paint your house. Why not write a program to compute the amount of paint you need? The front-to-back measurement of the house is 62 feet, side-to-side is 85 feet. The house is 12 feet high, and all sides are rectangular. There are 240 square feet of windows on the front and back of the house and 188 square feet of window space on the sides. Assume that you can cover 200 square feet with a gallon of paint. In addition to computing the amount of paint you need, compute the time it'll take you to paint the house, assuming that you can apply a gallon of paint in two hours.

output

AREA		GALLONS	TIME
FRONT/BACK	SIDES	USED	EXPENDED
XXXX	XXXX	XX	XX

Complete the exact prototype design for the output using a print chart. Design your input cards as needed.

3 LOOPS

Chapter Objectives: After studying this chapter, you should be able to:

- Discuss the use of loops in programming.
- Identify, discuss and use
  - a GO TO statement
  - an IF statement
- Write Fortran programs containing loops.
- Discuss the use of pre-test and post-test loops.
- Describe and write programs containing nested loops.
- Write a program using loops to calculate your friends' checking account balances.

Section 3 1

Introduction

By now you know enough to write programs which perform numerical computations and print out the results. You also know that the numbers used in the computations can either be written within the program itself or obtained from data cards outside the program. Thus you are able to use a computer to do computations similar to those you can do on a desk calculator. In some cases it might actually be more convenient to use a computer to do these calculations, but most of the time it would be easier to use the desk calculator. In one case, the numbers and arithmetic operation symbols are punched on cards; in the other case, they are entered directly into the machine through its keyboard—about the same amount of work. The computer might have a slight advantage if the expression is written with lots of parentheses which make it hard to untangle, and the calculator might have a slight advantage in simply totaling up a list of numbers (as in our checking account problem) since the procedure is simple enough to be remembered without being written down in the form of a program. Thus, the computer may not seem particularly useful to you right now, but by the end of this chapter you will begin to see how useful it can be.

Totaling a list of numbers on a calculator is a very repetitious task: enter a number, punch the add key, enter a number, punch the add key, and so forth.

The program we wrote in Section 2 4 to total a list of numbers was also very repetitious:

```
        .
        .
        .
    READ(5,1000) TRANS
    BALNCE = BALNCE - TRANS
        .
        .
        .
```

It turns out that a repetitious program can always be written in a much more compact way using a program structure known as a **loop**. Instead of writing the same statements over and over, we tell the computer to repeat the statements. In order to tell the computer to repeat, we need to know a new kind of statement.

loop:

Section 3 2

Transfer of Control

If we come to a point in a program where we want to repeat a previous statement instead of proceeding in the usual sequence to the next statement, we must have some way of telling the controller where to begin that repetition. In Fortran this is done by placing a **label** on the statement to be repeated and refer- ring to that label to initiate the repeat. To tell the controller to repeat from the statement whose label is s, we write

GO TO s

The label s is an unsigned INTEGER between 1 and 99999. The statement to be repeated will have the number s in its label field, columns 1 through 5 (see the box on page 36 describing the statement card format). Almost any statement may be labeled, but it is wise to put a label on a statement only if it is necessary to refer to the statement from some other point in the program.

> *The only statements we've seen so far which may not be labeled are the declaration statements*
> INTEGER *list*
> REAL *list*
> *and the* END *statement.*
> *These are commands to the* compiler, *not to the controller.*

Examine the following rewritten version of Section 2 4's bank balancing pro- gram.

column 7

```
        INTEGER BALNCE, TRANS
        READ(5,1000) BALNCE
 1000 FORMAT(F6.0)
   20   READ(5,1000) TRANS
          BALNCE = BALNCE - TRANS
          GO TO 20
        END
```

This version avoids having to rewrite statements in the program. Instead, the GO TO statement causes them to be repeated. Unfortunately, the program suffers from the same malady as the flowchart in Figure 2 4 1: it never stops to print the final balance.

We need some way to avoid repeating the important steps in the program indefinitely. We want to add a new transaction to the balance only if we haven't already finished adding all of this month's transactions. In other words, instead of always returning to statement 20, we want to return only under certain *conditions*. A conditional GO TO would solve the problem. You may recall that in Section 1 3 we had a similar problem with the ZAPPO algorithm, but there was no problem with the knitting algorithm because it had a conditional repeat.

Fortunately, Fortran provides a way to construct a **conditional statement**: the IF statement. For our current purposes, the **IF statement** has the form

$$\text{If } (e_1 \; rel \; e_2) \text{ GO TO } s$$

where s is a statement label, e_1 and e_2 are arithmetic expressions like the right-hand side of an assignment statement, and *rel* expresses a relation between e_1 and e_2. The six possibilities for *rel* are shown below.

relation	usual symbol	Fortran symbol
less than	$<$	.LT.
less than or equal to	$\leqslant$	.LE.
equal to	$=$	.EQ.
not equal to	$\neq$	.NE.
greater than or equal to	$\geqslant$	.GE.
greater than	$>$	.GT.

(Actually the IF statement can be more general than this, but we'll get to that later.) If $e_2 \; rel \; e_2$ is true, then the controller proceeds to statement s; otherwise, the controller continues from the statement following the IF statement in the usual sequence. For instance, the IF statement below

```
IF (TRANS .NE. 0.0)  GO TO 20
```

means "IF the value of memory cell TRANS is not equal to 0, then GO TO statement 20; otherwise, just go on to the next statement."

IF statement (restricted version)

form

    IF (e_1 *rel* e_2) GO TO *s*

e_1 and e_2 are arithmetic expressions
rel is a relational operator
s is a statement label

meaning

instructs the controller to decide whether or not the expressed relationship between the arithmetic expressions is true; if so, the controller proceeds from statement *s*; otherwise it continues from the next statement as usual

examples

```
IF (A+B .GT. 0)  GO TO 130
IF (TOTAL*TAXRTE .GT. AMT)   GO TO 500
```

Now let's see how we can use the IF statement to fix our program. We want to say:

> "If the last transaction has not yet been added
> to the balance, repeat from statement 20."

There is no way to say this directly using the IF statement, so we will have to find a way to say it in the language we have available. To do this we need some way to tell when we have reached the last transaction. Of course, we have no way of knowing in advance exactly what the amount of the last transaction will be, but with a little thought we realize that we know something the last transaction won't be: it will *not* be zero. How can we use this fact?

Suppose that, after punching all of the month's transactions on cards, we punch one more card containing the transaction *zero*. When we come to a card containing zero, we will know that it must be the last transaction. Our program can use that fact to determine whether or not to continue the loop.

```
      REAL BALNCE, TRANS
      READ(5,1000) BALNCE
1000  FORMAT(F6.0)
20    READ(5,1000) TRANS
      BALNCE = BALNCE - TRANS
      IF (TRANS .NE. 0.0)  GO TO 20
      WRITE(6,2000) BALNCE
2000  FORMAT(' NEW BALANCE IS $', F7.2)
      STOP
      END
```

> Note that we've indented the statements that make up the loop.

```
data
   456.03
    78.36
   -25.39
    45.25
    45.22
   -75.42
     0.0
```

output
NEW BALANCE IS $ 388.01

The program places the beginning balance in memory cell BALNCE, then adds each transaction into the balance until it reaches the last transaction (zero). At that point, instead of returning to statement 20 to add in another transaction, it prints the final balance and stops.

Perhaps we should note that the program actually adds the phony zero transaction into the balance. Since zero doesn't change a sum, it doesn't affect the result, but that is really a fortunate coincidence. It would be better not to add the phony transaction into the balance at all. Can you think of a way to change the program so that it doesn't add the phony transaction (see Exercise 3 2 3)?

Simple as it may seem, the IF statement you have just learned about adds a great deal of power to the language. In fact, there is a mathematical theorem which says that any computation which can be done at all, no matter how complicated, can be programmed using statements you already know: the assignment statement, the WRITE statement, the GO TO statement, and the IF statement. The rest of the Fortran statements you will learn won't make the language any more powerful, but they will help you write programs in a more concise, efficient, and readable way than you could using only what you know now. Nevertheless, using only the statements you know now, you can program the computer to do a large variety of useful tasks, and these programs can be both efficient and clearly expressed. We hope this will give you some confidence when you attack the problems at the end of this chapter.

EXERCISES 3 2

1 What is the Fortran equivalent of the * which appears in the knitting algorithm of Section 1 3?

2 Which of the following IF statements are illegal?
```
IF (X .GT. Y)  GO TO 35
IF (X*2 +17 .LE. Y**2)  GO TO 100
IF (14 .EG. 2)  GO TO 10
IF (X .SGT. A)  GO TO 15
IF Y .EQ. 0, GO TO 20
```

3 Rewrite the bank balancing program so that it doesn't add in the phony transaction. (Hint: You will need to move the IF statement, change its GO TO statement, add another GO TO statement in the place where the IF now stands, and put a label on the WRITE statement.)

Section 3 3

Loops

To become more familiar with the IF statement, let's try to write a program to do the computations of the laundry detergent problem of Figure 1 2 2. In that problem we wanted to average the price per pound of a number of laundry detergents. Imagine that you have a bunch of cards and each card contains the price and weight of a different brand of detergent. The flowchart in Figure 3 3 1 shows what we want to do. Briefly, we want to accumulate a sum of prices, counting the number of terms in the sum as we go along, and divide the total by the number of terms to get the average price. You are already aware of a technique for accumulating a sum, so the part of the program which computes the sum of the prices should be easy to follow.

VERBAL
DESCRIPTION

Count number of detergents surveyed while accumulating sum of unit prices.

Divide sum of unit prices by number of detergents surveyed to get the average price.

Print results.

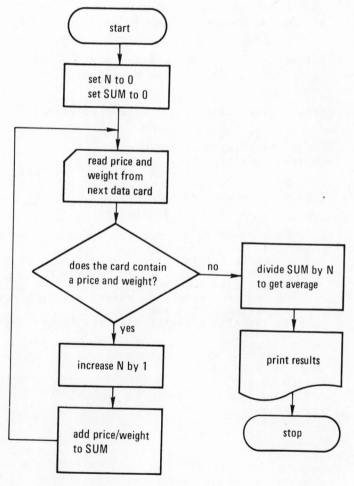

Figure 3 3 1   Computing the Average Price of a Laundry Detergent

Follow the flowchart in Figure 3 3 1 and try to see what it does. If you don't
quite get it, make up some data cards and follow the instructions, performing the
computations as you go. Once you understand the flowchart, try to see how
you can convert each part of it to Fortran statements. Hopefully the only place
you'll have any trouble at all is in translating the statement "does the card contain
a price and weight?"

How can the program know what is a price and weight and what isn't? The
method we used in the check balancing program was to put a data card containing
a phony value after the data cards containing legitimate values and testing for the
phony value in the program. We can do the same thing here. We know that no
company is going to pay you to take their detergent, so no brand will have a
negative price. Thus, we can put a data card indicating a negative price at the end
of the cards with legitimate prices. Then, to see if the card we just READ is the
last card, we simply test to see if the value we READ is less than zero.

Follow through this program and convince yourself that it does what we want.

```
COMMENT:  FIND THE AVERAGE COST OF LAUNDRY DETERGENT
      REAL PRICE, WGT, SUM, N, AVG
C
C     GET PRICES AND WEIGHTS, KEEPING TRACK OF TOTAL UNIT
C     COSTS AND NUMBER OF BRANDS SAMPLED.
      N = 0.0
      SUM = 0.00
 10   READ(5,1000) PRICE,WGT
 1000 FORMAT(F5.0,F5.0)
C         HERE'S WHERE WE TEST FOR THE TERMINATION CARD
          IF (PRICE .LT. 0.00)  GO TO 20
C         AVERAGE IN THIS BRAND
          SUM = SUM + (PRICE/WGT)
          N = N+1.0
          GO TO 10
C
C     WE'VE GOT THE TOTAL UNIT COST.  NOW COMPUTE AVERAGE.
 20   AVG = SUM/N
      WRITE(6,2000) N
 2000 FORMAT(' NUMBER OF BRANDS SURVEYED:',F6.0)
      WRITE(6,2001) AVG
 2001 FORMAT(' AVERAGE PRICE PER POUND:    $',F4.2)
      STOP
      END
```

data
```
   4.49 15.0
   1.47  3.1
   2.96  4.7
   6.95 18.3
   5.36 15.8
  -1.1  0.00
```

output
```
NUMBER OF BRANDS SURVEYED:    5.
AVERAGE PRICE PER POUND:   $ .42
```

loop writing

one entry, one exit

In general, a loop should be entered only at the top. That is, there should not be any jump (GO TO) from outside the loop to a statement in the middle of a loop. One reason for this is that, when writing a loop, you will tend to make many assumptions about the values of the memory cells involved in the loop. A jump into the middle of the loop often makes these assumptions unjustified. Similarly, exits from the loop should be jumps to the first statement following the loop. Following this rule tends to keep the program more straightforward.

pre-test, post-test

In general, there should be only one statement in a loop which can terminate the loop, and this statement should be either at the very beginning of the loop (pre-test) or at the very end (post-test). Jumps out of the middle of a loop, especially if there are more than one of them, can lead to erroneous assumptions about the memory cells involved in the loop. Although the test in our detergent program is not the first statement of the loop, it is an inherent part of the first operation in the loop, namely the operation of obtaining a new piece of legitimate data. In a sense, it is reasonable to think of the test for legitimate input as a part of the READ statement itself, the first statement in the loop.

In fact, many versions of Fortran make this idea explicit by allowing the following (nonstandard) form of READ statement.

END condition READ (non-ANSI)

form

READ(u, f, END = s) *list*

u is a unit number (usually 5)
f is the label of a FORMAT statement
s is the label of an executable statement
list is a list of memory cell names

meaning

stores values from unit u in the memory cells in *list*, according to FORMAT f. If an end of file is reached (i.e., if there are no more data cards to be read), transfer control to statement s.

examples

```
READ(5,5000,END=20) TAXRT
READ(5,1000,END=100) PRICE,WGT
```

Even without this specialized READ statement it is always possible to convert a loop into a version which satisfies a strict interpretation of the *pre-test* (or *post-test*) concept. But the idea is to produce clear, simple constructs. Bending over backwards to suit some supposed ideal can cause clutter itself.

Loops like the ones you have seen in the check balancing program and the detergent price program are an extremely important part of most computer programs. In fact, many programs would simply be impossible to write in Fortran without using loops. The loops you have seen so far have been quite simple, and you have probably had little difficulty in understanding what they do. but loops can get complicated quickly. (We'll show you a more complicated loop in the next section.) For this reason, it is advisable to construct loops carefully in an attempt to keep the program as well organized and straightforward as possible. Some rules to follow in writing loops are outlined in the accompanying box. We think that if you will keep these rules in mind when you write programs, you will be able to avoid many errors.

EXERCISES 3 3

1 Any value that could not possibly be a price for a detergent can be used to signal the end of the data cards. Rewrite the IF statement in the detergent price program so that the value 999.9 is the last card signal.

2 The algorithm for knitting a scarf (Figure 1 3 3) and the algorithm for computing compound interest (Figure 1 5 1) each include two loops. Do these loops conform to the suggested pre-test/post-test forms?

3 Write a program that counts by fives, printing the successive counts as it goes. Terminate the count when it reaches 100.

4 (optional) Rewrite the detergent price program so that its loop is in post-test form.

Section 3 4

Nested Loops

We have decided to provide a bank balance computing service for our friends. At the end of each month our friends will bring us a record of their checking account transactions in the form of a deck of punched cards. We could simply take the first deck, use the program in Section 3 2 to compute the new balance, then take the next deck, run it, and so on. We would have to repeat this process until we had completed each of our friends' new balances; that is, until we had no decks left to run. We might be at the computer center all day.

Alternatively, we could let the computer do more of the work by adding a few statements to the bank balance program so that it automatically starts the process over for each friend's account.

Let's consider what sorts of things we would need to do to convert our old program to this new, more useful form. First we would need some way of making the correspondence between the new account balances and the person who gave us those cards. One way to do that would be to ask our friends to place a card punched with their social security number on it at the front of their deck. Other than that, they need make no changes—just as before, they put the old account

> Our *friends would be somewhat offended by not being able to use their names instead of their social security number. We'll see how to do that in Chapter 4.*

balance on a card, follow it by their transactions for the month, and indicate the end of their deck by putting a card with a 0.0 on it at the end.

All we have to do now is add some statements to our program so that it repeats its computations once for each of our friends' accounts. It can tell when it is through with one deck by testing (just as before) for a 0.0 transaction card. But wait ... how can it tell when it has processed the last deck? After it completes the last deck, how is it to know that no deck follows?

So far we've imagined the program to have the form of Figure 3 4 1. After it has finished the last deck, it would just go back, expecting another name card. A

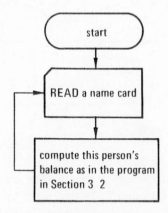

Figure 3 4 1

reasonable solution is for us to slap a special card at the very end—a card with a negative (hence impossible) social security number will do.

Our program will now have the form of Figure 3 4 2. It contains what is known as a **nested loop**, that is, a loop inside another loop. This structure is like that of the knitting algorithm in Section 1 3.

VERBAL DESCRIPTION

Get social security number of account holder.

Get old balance for this account.

Process transaction cards for this account.

Repeat.

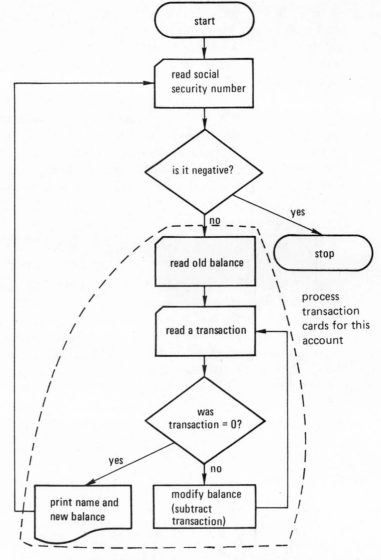

Figure 3 4 2

Our new program appears below. Although the general form of the program is familiar, some of the details are new. For example, it contains a new kind of IF statement. The statement to the right of the first IF statement is not a GO TO statement as it has always been before. It is a STOP statement instead. In general, any executable statement (READ, WRITE, assignment, or STOP) can be placed to the right of an IF. An exception is that an IF statement cannot be on the right of another IF. Of course, nonexecutable statements (e.g., compiler instructions like INTEGER A, REAL B, or END) cannot be objects of IF statements because that wouldn't make sense. In order to make sense of them, the compiler would have to check the value of the relational expression, but that can be done only when the controller executes the program.

IF statement (restricted form)

form
    IF (*rel*) *s*

    rel is a relational expression
    s is an executable statement other than an IF (*s* is the **object** of
       the IF)

meaning
    performs *s* if *rel* is true

examples
```
IF (TRANS .LT. 0.00)  STOP
IF (PRICE*QTY .EQ. AWARD) PRICE=PRICE*BONUS
IF (QUANT .EQ. ONHAND) WRITE(6,1000) BCKORD
```

```
COMMENT:  THIS PROGRAM COMPUTES BANK BALANCES FOR A NUMBER
C         OF PEOPLE.  THE DATA CARDS MUST BE ORGANIZED IN
C         GROUPS, EACH GROUP STARTING WITH A SOCIAL SECURITY
C         NUMBER WHICH IDENTIFIES THE PERSON WHOSE BALANCE
C         IS TO BE COMPUTED.  THE SECOND CARD IN EACH GROUP
C         MUST CONTAIN THE PERSON'S OLD BALANCE.  EACH
C         ADDITIONAL CARD MUST CONTAIN A TRANSACTION ON THE
C         ACCOUNT, POSITIVE VALUES FOR WITHDRAWALS AND
C         NEGATIVE ONES FOR DEPOSITS.  EACH GROUP TERMINATES
C         WITH A CARD CONTAINING 0.0, AND THE FINAL CARD
C         (FOLLOWING THE LAST GROUP) MUST CONTAIN A NEGATIVE
C         VALUE (AN ILLEGITIMATE SOCIAL SECURITY NUMBER).
          INTEGER SOCSEC
          REAL BALNCE, TRANS
100       READ(5,1000) SOCSEC
1000      FORMAT(I9)
          IF (SOCSEC .LT. 0)  STOP
          READ(5,2000) BALNCE
2000      FORMAT(F7.0)
200       READ(5,2000)TRANS
          IF (TRANS .EQ. 0.00)  GO TO 300
          BALNCE = BALNCE - TRANS
          GO TO 200
300       WRITE(6,3000) SOCSEC
3000      FORMAT('0SOCIAL SECURITY NUMBER:', I10)
          WRITE(6,4000) BALNCE
4000      FORMAT(' NEW BALANCE: $', F7.2)
          GO TO 100
          END
```

data

column 1

```
276407566
 456.32
  22.98
  33.54
-291.55
  54.39
   0.0
175504244
 332.53
  22.03
-329.41
  22.11
   0.0
        -1
```

output

```
SOCIAL SECURITY NUMBER: 276407566
NEW BALANCE: $ 636.96

SOCIAL SECURITY NUMBER: 175504244
NEW BALANCE: $ 617.80
```

EXERCISES 3 4

1 What parts of the knitting algorithm of Section 1 3 correspond to what parts of the program in this section?

2 Write one statement which has the same effect as the first two statements below.

```
      IF (PRICE*QTY .LT. LIMIT)  GO TO 200
        PRICE = PRICE*(1.0 - DSCNT)
  200 COST = PRICE*QTY
```

3 Modify the program in Section 3 4 so that it prints a record of transactions as well as a balance for each person. If you can, have the program print each transaction as a positive number (even though deposits are negative on data cards) with the word DEPOSIT beside each deposit.

PROBLEMS 3

1 You and five of your friends are going to Fiesta Lanes to have a weekend bowling festival. Each of you rolls three lines. Print the scores of each game, totals for each person, and averages of each game and total. The winner gets an autographed picture of Dick Weber.

	input	*output*			

columns	field	SCORES			
		GAME 1	GAME 2	GAME 3	TOTAL
1–5	ID#	100	150	175	425
6–8	score 1	192	183	175	550
9–11	score 2	200	100	50	350
12–14	score 3	100	200	300	600
		147	133	122	402
		90	80	70	240
	AVERAGES	138	141	149	428

2 Write out the ages, heights, and weights for ten of your friends. At the
end of the list, print the average age, height, and weight for all those in
the list.

Input Design:

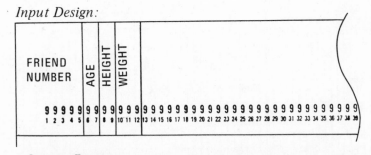

Output Design:

3   Print out at least five phone bills with the following assumptions: basic
    service costs $4.00 plus $1.25 for each extension phone; local calls are
    computed at the rate of 4.5¢ per message unit; local tax is 5 percent;
    federal tax is 10 percent. Be careful not to tax past-due balances or lo-
    cal calls.

Input Design:

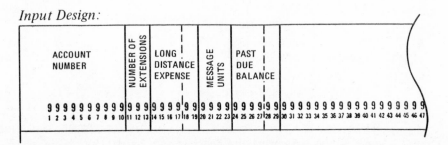

Output Design:

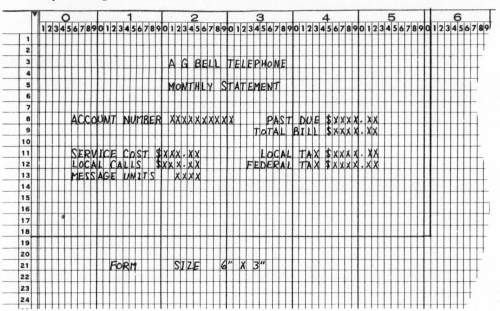

4 Archetypal Systems, Inc. has decided to modernize, and will promote you from stockroom worker to programmer if you write a program to analyze the inventory on hand. **Extended cost** is the amount on hand multiplied by its cost. Write YES under NEED REORDER if the amount on hand is less than the reorder point.

Input Design:

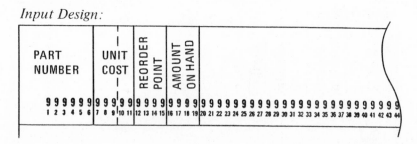

Output Design:

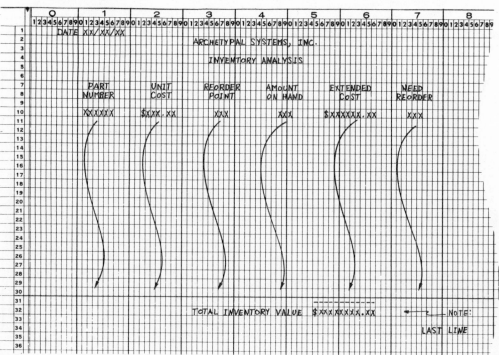

5 With the following input, compute the average miles per gallon. Write out the information only for "lightfoot" drivers who average 20 or more miles per gallon and travel at least 200 miles. Keep track of the number of lightfoot drivers and the number of them who drive small cars (car codes 055–099) and write out this percentage at the end.

Input Design:

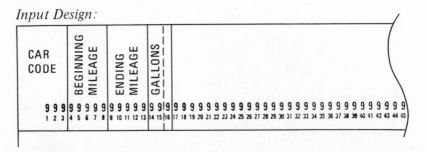

Output Design:

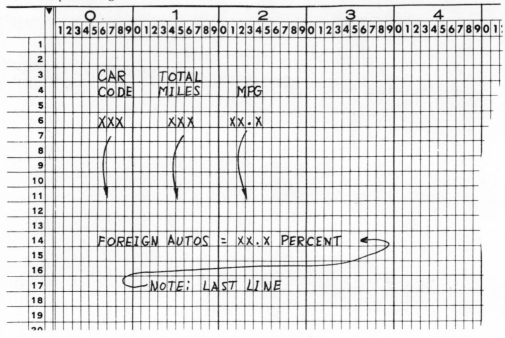

6 Since most large purchases involve loans and repayment schedules, write a program to print out the loan repayment schedule for a number of loans. Interest = principal × rate × time. (Use either 360 days per year ordinary time, or 365 days exact time.)

Input Design:

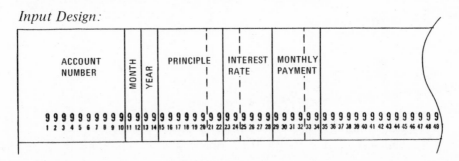

Output Design:

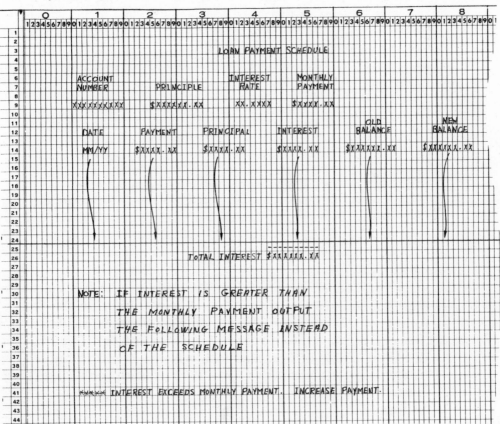

7 A good friend of yours needs a table of numbers to look up squares, cubes, and quads. You decide to help so that both of you can make it to the TGIF bash. Write the program to do the computation for the numbers 1 through 100. Arrange your output as follows.

NUMBER	SQUARE	CUBE	QUAD
1	1	1	1
2	4	8	16
3	9	27	81
.			
.			
.			

8 Cash Master, general manager of Thrifty Savings and Loan, has asked you to write a demonstration program that will help promote new savings accounts. The program should produce one page of output per customer showing the annual balance of a savings account at a series of interest rates for a period of five years. The demonstration should consider a customer who deposits $100 per month at the beginning of each month. Interest is compounded monthly.

The formula to determine the future value of a constant known payment (an annuity) made at the beginning of each period is

$$F = A(1 + r) \left(\frac{(1 + r)^n - 1}{r} \right)$$

where A = amount of annuity
    n = number of periods (in this case months)
    r = interest rate per period (in this case per month)
(Don't forget to divide the annual interest rate by 12 to get the monthly equivalent.) At 6 percent interest per year, the result at the end of year one would be $1,239.72 and at the end of year five would be $7,011.89.

Write a customer report showing the year-end values for interest rates of 5, 6, and 7 percent.

9 You have decided to take a job for the Christmas holidays and have negotiated an unusual pay scale. You will work for 1¢ for the first day (a paltry sum), 2¢ the second day, 4¢ the third, 8¢ the fourth (still not much money), and so on, with your pay doubling each day. This will go on for the entire month of December with only one day off—Christmas Day, of course. Use the computer to figure out how much you'll make. Is the old man a Scrooge or not?

output

```
$    .01    DEC.  1
$    .02    DEC.  2
$    .04    DEC.  3
$    .08    DEC.  4
        ⁙
TOTAL EARNINGS  -  $XXXXXXXXXX.XX
```

10 Bobby's mom gave him a new bike for his birthday. The gear ratios on his bike are

gear	ratio
1	3.3:1
2	2.02:1
3	1.52:1
4	1:1

and the speed of his bike is given by the formula

speed (miles per hour) = .02 * rpm/gear ratio

For example, his speed at 3300 rpm in low gear would be

.02 * 3300 * 1 / 3.3 = 20 mph

Write a program which READs data cards giving the rpm's where he shifts. For each shift point, have your program print out his top speed in each gear. If an rpm value over 6500 rpm comes in, print the message

BOBBY'S BIKE EXPLODED

and then STOP.

Bobby's New Bike

Read (5,100) RPM
100 FORMAT (F4.0)
     IF (

4 DETAILS ON EXPRESSIONS AND FORMATS

Chapter Objectives: After studying this chapter, you should be able to:

- Describe the characteristics of REAL and INTEGER constants.
- Interpret REAL numbers in E-notation.
- Write simple and complex arithmetic expressions and know how they are evaluated.
- Use integer arithmetic in scaling and counting data values.
- Write Fortran programs using library FUNCTIONs to save yourself programming effort.
- Create decision tables and use logical IF statements to implement these decisions in your program.
- Write programs which read, process, and print alphabetic data, such as names.
- Write programs with complex FORMATs.
- Use implicit typing of memory cells in writing programs

Section 4 1

Introduction

Recall that the computer's memory is made up of a number of cells and that we can place values into these cells as well as retrieve values placed there previously. We also mentioned that the interpretation of these values is pretty much up to us. In Fortran we can denote values of several different data types, and the system will automatically represent them as a pattern of 1's and 0's in memory cells. You're already familiar with the INTEGER and REAL data types. In this chapter we'll discuss other available data types and explain the rules for the evaluation of expressions. Also, we'll fill in the details about FORMATs so you will have more control over input and output operations.

Section 4 2
INTEGERs and REALs

Before jumping directly into the details of arithmetic expressions, we'd like to review the characteristics of their basic elements, numbers—REALs and INTEGERs. An **INTEGER constant** is a signed or unsigned string of digits. Since each memory cell has a finite capacity, some numbers may be too large (+ *or* −) to fit. The exact values INTEGERs may take depends on which computer system you are using.

INTEGER constant

form
   string of decimal digits which may be preceded by a plus or a minus sign

+1497
−392
−01124
33421

+1,497   *no commas allowed*
−392.0   *no decimal point allowed*
33,492.1

The Number of '54 Chevy's You've Seen
in Your Lifetime Is an INTEGER

For the same reason, REALs have a finite range. In practice, the limitations imposed by the finite range of REALs seldom come into play, but their finite accuracy does. We didn't have the accuracy problem with INTEGERs because they are represented exactly. REAL numbers, on the other hand, are represented to some number of digits of accuracy (again, the exact number depends on which computer system you are using).

REAL constants are usually written as signed or unsigned strings of decimal digits containing a decimal point. But there is an additional possibility. For writing super-big numbers like the national debt or super-small numbers like the diameter of the chlorine atom, Fortran provides a version of the widely used "scientific notation." In this form a decimal point shift factor (which is an E followed by an INTEGER constant) follows the number. The decimal point shift factor in a REAL constant indicates how far to move the decimal point in the number that precedes the E. Positive shifts indicate shifts to the right, negative shifts to the left.

This E-notation for REALs is something like the way the numbers are represented in the computer. The 1's and 0's in a REAL valued memory cell are divided into two parts, the fraction, or "mantissa," and the point shifter, or "exponent." If a computation results in a number with an exponent which is too large, an **overflow** occurs. On the other hand, computations may result in numbers whose exponent parts are too large in the negative direction to fit in the reserved space. Such a condition is called an **underflow** since the number is too small to be represented.

How do you know when an overflow has occurred? Most systems will print an error message when the overflow occurs. Others will represent the result in a special internal encoding and store it in memory. When you print the result you get an indication that something went wrong printed in the field where you expected to see the number. (For example, you may get *'s or #'s or an R for "out of range" printed in the field.)

REAL constants

form
    x
    xEs
    x is a signed or unsigned string of decimal digits containing a decimal point
    s is an INTEGER constant

meaning
    specifies a number indicated by x with its decimal point shifted s places (positive s indicates right shift; negative s, left shift)

If You Measure a Pizza, You Get a REAL Number

examples of REAL constants

form		*meaning*
1.00		
−7.7254		
+.000137		
.472E5	LEGAL	47200.
+7.21E−2		.0721
−1.22E−12		−.00000000000122
5.763E+11		national debt ceiling
.002E3		Avis's Number
1,482.5	ILLEGAL	invalid, no comma allowed
723		invalid, needs decimal point
−4.18732E−.5		invalid, shift factor must be INTEGER

Overflows and underflows occasionally occur, but they don't cause nearly as many problems as the restricted accuracy in the mantissa. Limited accuracy makes it impossible to represent a number like

$$1./3. = .33333333333 \ldots$$

Any digits beyond those that fit into the memory word simply get lost. This can occasionally cause some embarrassing situations, because in Fortran

$$1./3. + 1./3. + 1./3.$$

doesn't quite equal 1.0! The errors due to this effect are called **roundoff errors**. In certain applications, roundoff errors, each one seemingly insignificant, can add up to make a final answer completely wrong. This is a serious problem, and numerical analysts have spent enormous effort trying to understand how to avoid getting such erroneous results.

EXERCISES 4 2

1 Which are legal INTEGER constants; which are not? If not, why not?

1	4*2
1.0	12.75
−12	−127.5
−134794	1275
12 + 2	−0

2 Which are legal REAL constants? If not, why not?

2	5.67
+2	5.67E0
+2.00	300E30.0
−2.01E3.2	−22.E+30
−2.1E3	−.0000021
−2.22E−22	

3 Write the REAL value +1.0 in five different legal ways.

Section 4 3

Arithmetic Expressions

You have already seen many examples of arithmetic expressions. They were used as the right-hand side of assignment statements and in relational expressions in IF statements. We purposely kept those expressions quite simple in order to defer a detailed explanation of the rules of evaluation until now.

Arithmetic expressions are formed of memory cell names and arithmetic constants separated by arithmetic operators (+, −, *, /, **). In addition, parentheses may be used to force the controller to perform the operations in the desired order.

Consider the following examples of arithmetic expressions:

```
COUNT+1
```

Find value of COUNT and add 1 to it.

```
(1+BRATE-DRATE)*POPUL
```

Find value of BRATE, add it to 1, subtract the value of DRATE, and multiply the result by the value of POPUL.

```
PRIN*(RATE*1.06)
```

Raise the value of RATE to the power 1.06 and multiply the result by the value of PRIN.

In each of these examples the meaning of the expression is not hard to see, but consider a more complicated expression like

```
SUMXSQ/(N-1.0) - SUMX**2/(N*(N-1.0))
```

In this case the expression appears ambiguous because it is not clear which operations should be performed first. Should we proceed from left to right, from right to left, or by some other set of rules? Surely we should perform the operations grouped by the parentheses first, but after that there is still ambiguity. Are we to raise SUMX to the power 2 or to the power 2/(N*(N − 1.0))? Do we divide SUMXSQ by (N − 1.0) or by (N − 1.0) − SUMX? The expression would be easier to interpret if we didn't have to write it all on one line, but Fortran requires us to do so.

> in normal algebraic notation the expression is
>
> $$\frac{sumxsq}{n-1} - \frac{sumx^2}{n(n-1)}$$

In Fortran the order of operations proceeds according to the following rules of precedence, which are the same as those used in ordinary algebra.

( )   First   compute the expressions within parentheses
**   Second   perform exponentiations
*, / Third   perform multiplications and divisions
+, – Fourth   perform additions and subtractions
→   Tiebreaker   perform adjacent additive operations
      (non-ANSI)   (+, −) from left to right
                    perform adjacent multiplicative operations
                    (*, /) from left to right
                    perform adjacent exponentiations
                    (**) from right to left

Now no ambiguity remains. The expression is equivalent to

```
(SUMXSQ/(N-1.0)) - ((SUMX**2)/(N*(N-1.0)))
```

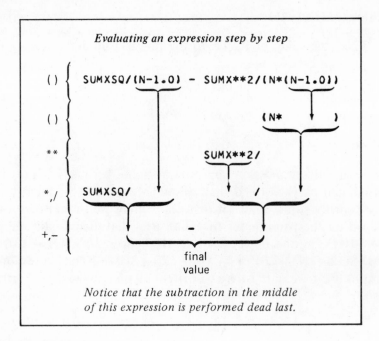

Evaluating an expression step by step

Notice that the subtraction in the middle of this expression is performed dead last.

Consider this expression:

$$A/B*C - D + E$$

The rules of precedence tell us to perform multiplications and divisions before additions and subtractions. Therefore $A/B*C$ must be evaluated first. But does that mean $(A/B)*C$ or $A/(B*C)$? Using the tiebreaker rule, $(A/B)*C$ would be the correct interpretation.

> *tiebreaker: On most Fortran systems, adjacent operations of equal precedence are performed as follows:*
>
> | | | |
> |---|---|---|
> | $A - B + C$ | *means* | $(A - B) + C$ |
> | $A/B*C$ | *means* | $(A/B)*C$ |
> | $A**B**C$ | *means* | $A**(B**C)$ |
>
> *However, this is not required by the ANSI standards, and some compilers will use other procedures. When in doubt, use parentheses.*

Arithmetic operators may be used with either REALs or INTEGERs, so that both 2/4 and 2.0/4.0 are legal expressions, which yield the values 0 and 0.5 respectively. But how should something like 2/4.0 be interpreted? The first value is an INTEGER constant, the second a REAL. The ANSI standards solve this problem by forbidding it. Such an expression, which combines values (or memory cells) of differing types, is said to be **mixed mode**. Versions of Fortran which adhere strongly to the standards will issue an error message and refuse to run the program. Most versions of Fortran are more lenient, however. Unfortunately, since such situations are not covered in the standards, different versions of Fortran make different assumptions about what the programmer means by the expression. This makes it advantageous to avoid mixed mode expressions altogether.

One exception is in the case of exponentiation. Here is one place where it is desirable to mix REAL and INTEGER in the same expression, and so this *is* permitted by the standards. For example, the expression 4.73**8 means to form a product containing eight factors, 4.73 times itself eight times. The result of this computation is a REAL number, of course.

It is also possible to raise a REAL to a REAL power, but the computation which is performed is very different. For example, 4.73**1.79256 clearly cannot mean to multiply 4.73 times itself 1.79256 times. In order to make this computation, the controller first computes the logarithm of the base in the exponentiation, multiplies that by the exponent, getting a product p, and finally raises $e = 2.7182818\ldots$ to the power p. Since logarithms of negative numbers do not generally result in REAL values, *it is illegal to raise a negative number to a REAL power.* No logarithms are involved in raising a number to an INTEGER power, however, so there is nothing wrong with an expression like (−4.73)**8 even though the expression (−4.73)**8.0 would be illegal. Use INTEGERs for exponents whenever you can. There is one other thing that can cause trouble. We said that INTEGER constants could be numbers like −2 or 3 and that you could use an arithmetic operator between two constants; however, 3*−2 is illegal in Fortran. In addition to the rules for forming arithmetic expressions that you've seen so far, there is the rule that *no two operator symbols (*, /, +, −, **) may come in a row,* no matter what they're used for. The expression 3*−2 can be written as 3*(−2).

---

arithmetic expressions

form
> basic arithmetic elements (numeric memory cells, unsigned numeric constants, or parenthesized subexpressions) separated by arithmetic operators (+, −, *, /, or **) with an optional sign (+ or −) at the beginning of the expression

meaning
> specifies a numeric value, namely the value obtained by following the rules of precedence and carrying out the operations denoted by the arithmetic operators

examples

```
X**(-2)
COL*(COL-1)/2 + ROW
DVN-3*QUO
Z**3/3.0
4*(-3)
-4*A
```

```
X***2
DVN-3*
A*-4
```

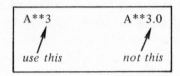

Now that we know how to create and interpret arithmetic expressions, let's return to the assignment statement. Recall that an assignment statement is a memory cell name followed by the assignment operator (=) followed by an expression. The assignment statement tells the controller to evaluate the expression and store the result in the memory cell named to the left of the assignment operator. In this way the controller gives the cell a new value. For example, if we had made the declarations

```
INTEGER PURCH1, PURCH2, TOTAL, CENTS
REAL DOLARS
```

then these assignment statements

```
PURCH1 = 75
PURCH2 = 50
TOTAL = PURCH1 + PURCH2
CENTS = 125
DOLARS = 125.0/100.0
```

would leave the memory cells with these values:

PURCH1	75
PURCH2	50
TOTAL	125
CENTS	125
DOLARS	1.25

Everything was nice and easy—each expression on the right was of the same type as the memory cell named on the left, so it was obvious what to store. But what if a statement like

```
CENTS = DOLARS*100.00
```

has appeared? The memory cell named on the left is an INTEGER: the expression on the right is REAL. A very important rule about assignment statements takes care of this situation. (Notice that this is *not* an example of a mixed mode expression. The expression on the right involves the multiplication of two REAL values.)

The rule is that *the expression to the right* of the replacement operator *is evaluated first* without any concern for the memory location named on the left. After the expression has been evaluated, a check is made to see if the type of the result agrees with the type of the memory cell where the result is to be stored. If it does not agree, then *the value stored in the memory cell is the value of the expression after being converted to the data type required by the memory cell.*

So, in the example above, first DOLARS * 100.0 is evaluated to get the REAL value 125.0, and then, since CENTS is declared to be an INTEGER, the corresponding INTEGER value 125 is stored in CENTS.

This is a very important rule to understand. Let's see it in action again.

Suppose at some point in a program we need to compute a term N/M. Since we've been counting with M and N, they are declared INTEGERs, but the use we make of the term requires it to be REAL. Knowing that INTEGER division involves truncation, it's not hard to guess that some problems arise in computing the ratio N/M. Can you see why these two program fragments produce different results?

```
INTEGER M,N              INTEGER M,N
REAL TERM,FRAC,NUM       REAL TERM,NUM,DENOM
N=2                      N=2
M=3                      M=3
NUM=N                    NUM=N
FRAC=1/M                 DENOM=M
TERM=NUM*FRAC            TERM=NUM/DENOM
```

M | 3 | M | 3 |

N | 2 | N | 2 |

NUM | 2.0 | NUM | 2.0 |

FRAC | 0.0 | DENOM | 3.0 |

TERM | 0.0 | TERM | 0.666666 |

The key difference is caused by the statement

```
FRAC = 1/M
```

The INTEGER expression 1/M is evaluated first (giving the INTEGER value 0). Then (and only then) the value computed is converted to REAL (0.0), and stored in FRAC.

EXERCISES 4 3

1 Rewrite each expression into an equivalent, parenthesis-free form, if possible. Assume all variables are REAL.

   a   PRINC*(RATE**1.06)

   b   (CAR/(FEA*NUT))*TER

   c   1.0/(N+1.0)

   d   (COST*(1.0+STAX+FEDTAX)) - BRIBE

2 Using the precedence rules, compute the value of the expression (−1**2).

3 As it stands, the expression 6 + 2/8/4 has the value 6 (right?). By inserting parentheses, but leaving everything else the same, you can create expressions with four different values. What are those values?

4 This program is supposed to compute the average of the first N numbers, but it doesn't work very well. What's wrong, and how could you fix it?

```
COMMENT   THIS PROGRAM COMPUTES THE AVERAGE OF THE
C             NUMBERS 1, 2, 3, ... UP THROUGH "N"
          INTEGER N, SUM, NUMBR
          REAL AVERGE
          READ(5,1000) N
 1000 FORMAT(I5)
C                                       ADD UP THE FIRST "N" NUMBERS
          SUM=0
          NUMBR=1
  100 IF (NUMBR .GT. N)  GO TO 200
          SUM = SUM + NUMER
          NUMER = NUMBR+1
          GO TO 100
C                                       DIVIDE THE SUM BY "N"
  200   AVERGE = (1/N)*SUM
          WRITE(6,2000) N, AVERGE
 2000 FORMAT(' THE AVERAGE OF THE FIRST',I6,
      +           ' NUMBERS IS', F10.3)
          STOP
          END
```

Section 4 4

Other Operators

Many people write programs which involve finding the logarithm of some value. Although not as many people use the logarithm operation as, say, addition, it still would be a terrible waste for each person to have to rediscover his own algorithm for computing logarithms. Fortran provides a number of additional commonly used operators which may be used in expressions. The following program uses two of these operators: ALOG for logarithms and SQRT for square root.

```
          REAL X, T, SQRX, SQRT, ALOG
          X = 144.0
          SQRX = SQRT(X)
          WRITE(6,1000) SQRX
 1000 FORMAT(' SQUARE ROOT OF 144=',F5.2)
          T = ALOG(X/12.0)
          WRITE(6,2000) T
 2000 FORMAT(' LOGARITHM OF 144/12=',F5.2)
          STOP
          END
```

output

```
 SQUARE ROOT OF 144=12.00
 LOGARITHM OF 144/12= 2.48
```

Notice that the operators appear just before the expression (yes, *expression*) we wish them to operate on, and that that expression is enclosed in parentheses. Also notice that we have declared that the operators will yield REAL values by listing their names in a type statement.

The expression enclosed in parentheses after an operator is called its **argument**. Probably this term is familiar to you from algebra. Some operators have more than one argument, and in that case the arguments are separated by commas. In fact, some built-in operators may be given a different number of arguments at different times (MIN0, for example, which yields the minimum value of all its arguments, no matter how many there may be).

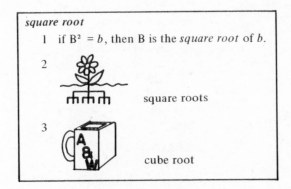

square root
1 if B² = *b*, then B is the *square root* of *b*.

2 square roots

3 cube root

infix operator: an operator which is written between its arguments	prefix operator: an operator which appears before its arguments
examples	**examples**
+, −, *, /, **	SQRT
as in	MIN0
A + 375	ABS
	as in
	MIN0 (I, N)

A number of commonly used operators (or built-in FUNCTIONs, as they are often called) are shown in Figure 4 4 1. To find the rest of the built-in FUNCTIONs look in the Fortran manual for your computer system.

Let's look at an example of a how a built-in FUNCTION could be useful to you in solving a compound interest problem. You are aware of annual, semi-annual, quarterly, monthly, and daily compounding of interest. Some financial institutions even have *continuous* compounding. The equation

$$F_n = P \times e^{r \times n}$$

can be used to determine the value of $100 (P = 100) placed in a savings account for three years (*n* = 3) at 6 percent interest (*r* = .06) *compounded continuously.*

Some useful built-in FUNCTIONs

The argument should be REAL valued if shown as r and INTEGER if shown as i.

FUNCTION	value computed	type of result
SQRT(r)	$\sqrt{r}$	REAL
ALOG10(r)	log to the base 10 of r	REAL
ALOG(r)	natural logarithm of r	REAL
EXP(r)	e^r, where e is the base of natural logarithms	REAL
SIN(r)	trigonometric sine of r radians	REAL
COS(r)	cosine of r radians	REAL
ATAN(r)	the angle $\left(-\frac{\pi}{2} \text{ to } \frac{\pi}{2} \right)$ whose tangent is r	REAL
ABS(r)	the absolute value of r $\|r\|$	REAL
IABS(i)	$\|i\|$	INTEGER
FLOAT(i)	REAL version of i FLOAT(2) is 2.0	REAL
INT(r)	INTEGER version of r INT(−3.7) is −3	INTEGER
MAX0($i_1, i_2, \ldots, i_n$)	largest value of $i_1, i_2, \ldots, i_n; n \geqslant 2$	INTEGER
MIN0($i_1, i_2, \ldots, i_n$)	smallest value of $i_1, i_2, \ldots, i_n, n \geqslant 2$	INTEGER
AMAX1($r_1, r_2, \ldots, r_n$)	largest value of $r_1, r_2, \ldots, r_n; n \geqslant 2$	REAL
AMIN1($r_1, r_2, \ldots, r_n$)	smallest value of $r_1, r_2, \ldots, r_n; n \geqslant 2$	REAL
RANF (r)	generates a pseudorandom number between 0.0 and 1.0 (non-ANSI)	REAL

Figure 4 4 1   Built-in FUNCTIONs

This program performs the calculation and shows an application of the EXP operation, a built-in FUNCTION which computes powers of $e = 2.71828 \ldots$

```
      REAL RATE, YEARS, PRINC, FUTURE
      READ(5,1000) PRINC, RATE, YEARS
 1000 FORMAT(F10.2, F5.3, F5.2)
      FUTURE = PRINC*EXP((RATE/100.0)*YEARS)
      WRITE(6,2000) PRINC, RATE, YEARS, FUTURE
 2000 FORMAT(' $',F7.2,' AT',F6.3,'% INTEREST FOR',
     +        F5.2,' YEARS IS $',F7.2)
      STOP
      END
```

data
```
 1000.00    6.0    5.0
```

output
```
 $1000.00 AT 6.000% INTEREST FOR 5.00 YEARS IS $1349.86
```

You have seen FUNCTIONs used in several expressions, and you have seen expressions form the arguments in FUNCTION references. An interesting question is: can FUNCTIONs be used in the argument of another FUNCTION? That is to say, is the following statement okay?

```
 A = EXP(R*FLOAT(N))
```

Yes, it is. However, it's best not to get carried away with functions of functions. Take a look at the indecipherable statement below, and you'll see why.

```
 F=P*AMAX1(EXP((RATE1/100.0)*FLOAT(N)),
+          (1.0+RATE2/1200.0)**(FLOAT(N)*12.0))
```

To avoid statements like this, it's best to break the computation into small pieces and put them together using a sequence of statements, as shown below.

```
C                             CONTINUOUS COMPOUNDING AT RATE1
       YEARS = FLOAT(N)
       RATEYR = RATE1/100.0
       AYR = EXP(RATEYR*YEARS)
C                             MONTHLY COMPOUNDING AT RATE2
       TMNTHS = 12.0*YEARS
       RATEMN = RATE2/1200.0
       AMN = (1.0+RATEMN)**TMNTHS
C                             MAKE THE BETTER INVESTMENT
       A = AMAX1(AYR,AMN)
       F = P*A
```

You will probably find most of the functions familiar even if their names seem a little strange. The reason some of the names have extra letters stuck in front of them (ALOG, AMIN1, IABS. . .) is because of the Fortran implicit typing convention, which is covered in Section 4 9. The reason the minimum and maximum functions have numbers tacked on the end (AMIN1, MAX0) is to identify the type of arguments each takes (0 for INTEGER, 1 for REAL). Actually, it's a good thing the FUNCTION names are strange. It helps avoid conflicts with memory cell names which you make up.

EXERCISES 4 4

1 What values do these expressions have?
```
SQRT(4.0)
MIN0(-1,-2,-2,4,7)
INT(3.1415926)
ABS(AMAX1(-1.0,-3.0,-2.5))
ABS(AMIN1(-1.0,-3.0,-2.5))
FLOAT(3*7)
```

2 There is no operator for the trigonometric tangent function in ANSI Fortran. Is this a gross oversight?

Section 4 5 *

Using Truncation

This section may be skipped without loss of continuity.

You are probably wondering why Fortran chooses to deal with two different kinds of numbers instead of sticking with one kind as we normally do in our hand computations. The answer probably lies in the fact that experience has shown that integers and numbers with fractional parts are used in basically different ways in most computations. It is also true that the difference allows for greater flexibility in our programs. For example, INTEGER division, with its truncation property, can often be used to advantage. The following question can be dealt with easily in Fortran because INTEGER division drops the remainder.

Question: Is the INTEGER value stored in N evenly divisible by 2?

Answer: If $(N/2)*2$ is equal to N, then yes, otherwise no.

Explanation: If N is evenly divisible by 2, then $N/2$ will not have any fractional part to lose, so $(N/2)*2$ will equal N. If, however, N is not even, then the division will lose a fractional part and $(N/2)*2$ will be different from N.

Examples: If N = 6, then
             $(N/2) = 3$ and $3*2$ is equal to 6.
             If N = 7, then
             $(N/2) = 3$ and $3*2$ is not equal to 7.

There are many other ways in which the differences between INTEGERs and REALs are useful. Our next example uses the fact that if an assignment statement has a REAL on the right-hand side and an INTEGER memory cell on the left, an INTEGER version of the right-hand side is stored in the cell. Another way of saying this is that the fractional part is truncated or **chopped** so that the value can be expressed as an INTEGER.

A bar graph is a popular way to summarize data. Figure 4 5 2 is a bar graph summarizing the data pictured in Figure 4 5 1.

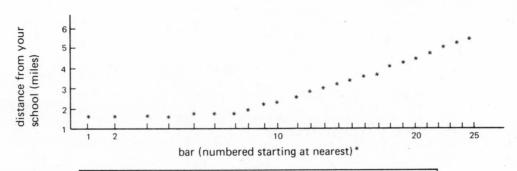

*Bars are numbered rather than named to avoid giving free publicity to Maynards of Pacific Beach.

Figure 4 5 1

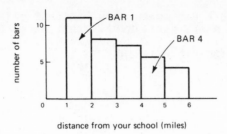

distance from your school (miles)

Figure 4 5 2

How might we convert our data from the first form (REAL) to the second (INTEGER)? Basically what our program will do is to read information about one bar at a time and decide which data summary, BAR0, BAR1, BAR2, BAR3, BAR4, or BAR5, the information should be added to. For example, if we find an establishment 3.27 miles from school, we would count it in BAR3, since the height of BAR3 indicates the number of establishments between 3.00 and 4.00 miles away. Bars exactly 3 miles away go into BAR3; those exactly 4 miles away go into BAR4. A flowchart for the program which organizes the data in this way is shown in Figure 4 5 3.

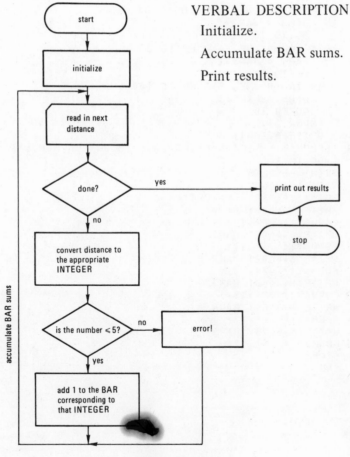

VERBAL DESCRIPTION
Initialize.
Accumulate BAR sums.
Print results.

Figure 4 5 3

```
COMMENT:  MAKE A BAR GRAPH FROM DISTANCE DATA.
        INTEGER BAR0, BAR1, BAR2, BAR3, BAR4, BAR5, NUMB
        REAL DIST
C       INITIALIZE BAR HEIGHTHS
        BAR0=0
        BAR1=0
        BAR2=0
        BAR3=0
        BAR4=0
        BAR5=0
C       READ DISTANCES AND ACCUMULATE BAR SUMS
   10   READ(5,1000) DIST
 1000   FORMAT(F10.0)
        IF (DIST .LT. 0.0)  GO TO 200
C       DROP FRACTIONAL PART TO DETERMINE BAR SUM AFFECTED
   18   NUMB = DIST
C       FIGURE OUT WHICH BAR IT FITS IN
        IF (NUMB .NE. 0)  GO TO 20
            BAR0 = BAR0+1
            GO TO 10
   20   IF (NUMB .NE. 1)  GO TO 30
            BAR1 = BAR1+1
            GO TO 10
   30   IF (NUMB .NE. 2)  GO TO 40
            BAR2 = BAR2+1
            GO TO 10
   40   IF (NUMB .NE. 3)  GO TO 50
            BAR3 = BAR3+1
            GO TO 10
   50   IF (NUMB .NE. 4)  GO TO 60
            BAR4 = BAR4+1
            GO TO 10
   60   IF (NUMB .NE. 5)  GO TO 100
            BAR5 = BAR5+1
            GO TO 10
C       ERROR ...
  100   WRITE(6,1001) DIST
 1001   FORMAT(' DISTANCE',F12.2,' IS OUT OF RANGE')
        GO TO 10
C       PRINT RESULTS
  200   WRITE(6,2000)
 2000   FORMAT('1BAR    HEIGHT')
        WRITE(6,4000) BAR0
 4000   FORMAT('  0',I7)
        WRITE(6,4001) BAR1
 4001   FORMAT('  1',I7)
        WRITE(6,4002) BAR2
 4002   FORMAT('  2',I7)
        WRITE(6,4003) BAR3
 4003   FORMAT('  3',I7)
        WRITE(6,4004) BAR4
 4004   FORMAT('  4',I7)
        WRITE(6,4005) BAR5
 4005   FORMAT('  5',I7)
        STOP
        END
```

Statement number 18 is the heart of the program. Let's see how it works. Suppose READ statement number 10 gives DIST the value 1.275. Then, since NUMB is an INTEGER, the assignment

```
18      NUMB = DIST
```

will *convert* the value 1.275 to an INTEGER before storing it in NUMB. So in this case, NUMB would be given the INTEGER value 1.

Given data corresponding to Figure 4 5 1

```
1.9
0.4
0.9
3.9
17.5
2.8
4.5
4.1
3.2
5.8
6.9
4.5
3.7
2.9
5.2
-1.0
```

our program would finally print out

```
DISTANCE        17.50 IS OUT OF RANGE
DISTANCE         6.90 IS OUT OF RANGE


BAR     HEIGHT
 0        2
 1        1
 2        2
 3        3
 4        3
 5        2
```

Using this information, we drew a bar graph like Figure 4 5 2.

EXERCISES 4 5

1 Write an assignment statement which computes the number of nickels in CENTS pennies.

2 What BARs do these values go in?

4.715	−2.98
3.2	496.1
0.96	

Section 4 6

LOGICAL Expressions

The IF statement you used in Chapter 3 in tests like

```
IF (TAX .GT. 2000.00)  GO TO 100
```

is the simplest form of the "logical IF" statement. The expression TAX .GT. 2000.00 is a **relational expression** and is either true or false. Relational expressions are simple examples of a more general type of expression known as a LOGICAL expression. Typically, a LOGICAL expression is a combination of two, or possibly more, relational expressions connected by "and" or "or" conditions. But no matter how complex they become, LOGICAL expressions always produce one of only two possibilities—true or false. Therefore, they may be used in IF statements to make decisions in the same way as simple relational expressions.

Learning about arithmetic expressions was pretty easy because you were already familiar with the arithmetic operators (+, -, *, /, and **), and you were accustomed to writing them in various combinations. LOGICAL operators (.AND., .OR., and .NOT.) are also familiar. You use them in thinking and speaking, but you rarely write them down in formal expressions. For this reason you may have to study them more carefully than arithmetic expressions. The trick is not to be confused by their simplicity. They are, in a sense, simpler than arithmetic expressions because they cannot take a wide range of values—1.3, −492.45, 1984.498, and so forth. The value of a LOGICAL expression must be one of only two possibilities—.TRUE. or .FALSE. . And only one at a time, of course. A LOGICAL expression can't be true-or-false. It must be *either* true *or* false.

Using LOGICAL expressions extends the kinds of tests you can make in IF statements. Before, you could make only one test; now you will be able to combine several tests in one statement. Let's begin by describing the LOGICAL operators .AND., .OR., and .NOT. .

The .AND. operator serves to combine two relational expressions. The resulting combination is a LOGICAL expression which is true if *both* of the relational expressions are true. If either one (or both) of them is false, then the entire LOGICAL expression becomes false.

The .OR. operator also serves to combine two relational expressions. If either of the relations is true (or if both are true), the combined LOGICAL expression is true. The .OR. combination is false only when *both* of the relational expressions are false.

The .NOT. operator serves to reverse the value of a *single* relational expression. If a relation is true, the expression becomes false when modified by a .NOT. operator. Similarly, if a relational expression is false, the .NOT. operator makes the LOGICAL expression true. Some examples of familiar situations should help you in understanding the use of LOGICAL operators.

> *If you aren't familiar with formal logic or Boolean algebra, you may become confused by trying to see too deep an analogy between the symbols .TRUE. and .FALSE. and the familiar philosophical, ethical, moral concepts "true" and "false." Try to keep firmly in your mind that a LOGICAL memory cell always has exactly one value at a given point in time (just as an INTEGER variable may have only one value at a time). That value is either .TRUE. or .FALSE.. There are no in-betweens. No LOGICAL value is partly true and partly false. This isn't much like real life, and perhaps that makes it confusing, but LOGICAL expressions are used to tell the controller exactly what to do. Fortran instructions are precise, not "maybe do this" or "maybe do that," so LOGICAL values are always either .TRUE. or .FALSE., never both.*

Examples

.AND.

"[It is raining] and [the sun is shining.]"
    A   B

The statement is true if both A *and* B are true.

.OR.

"[He is heavy] or [he's wearing a pillow around his waist.]"
   A   B

The statement is true if either A *or* B (or both) is true.

.NOT.

"He is not [pregnant]."
             A

The statement is true if A is *not* true.

The above examples are, of course, not Fortran but English. The "basic logical elements" in the sentences are bracketed. Two of the logical operators, *and* and *or*, are *conjunctions*; they connect two statements (or "basic logical elements," as we have called them). In Fortran the LOGICAL operators .AND. and .OR. are also conjunctions—they connect two basic LOGICAL elements. The third LOGICAL operator, .NOT., is different. In the English example, the word *not* applies only to *pregnant* rather than to two parts of a sentence. Similarly, .NOT. operates on *one* basic LOGICAL element. For this reason .AND. and .OR. are called **binary operators** (operating on two things), and .NOT. is called a **unary operator** (operating on *one* thing).

Now that we've explained the three LOGICAL operators, let's discuss the basic LOGICAL elements which make up LOGICAL expressions.

> **LOGICAL**: *a data type with only two possible values—.TRUE. and .FALSE.—corresponding to Boolean (two-valued) logic*

A LOGICAL expression is formed of basic LOGICAL elements separated by LOGICAL operators (.AND. , .OR., or .NOT.) and grouped by parentheses. A **basic LOGICAL element** can be one of three things:

1 a relational expression (like those we've seen in IF statements)
2 the name of a memory cell which has been declared to have type LOGICAL
3 a LOGICAL constant (.TRUE. or .FALSE.)

Of these three possibilities, relational expressions are by far the most common. We'll focus on using LOGICAL expressions in IF statements, and we'll not have any need for LOGICAL constants. Just for the sake of completeness, we'll say that the two LOGICAL constants are written .TRUE. and .FALSE. in Fortran.

The relational expression states a relation between two arithmetic expressions. A relational expression is true when the stated relation is true.

As you may recall from Chapter 3, relations are stated using the six relational operators.

.EQ.	meaning equals
.NE.	meaning not equal to
.LT.	meaning less than
.LE.	meaning less than or equal to
.GE.	meaning greater than or equal to
.GT.	meaning greater than

The results of the comparisons (relational expressions) we used in Chapter 3, then, are LOGICAL values. For example, the relational expression

```
(A**2 + B**2) .EQ. C**2
```

has the value .TRUE. if the square of the value of C is the same as the sum of the squares of the values of A and B; otherwise, its value is .FALSE..

The six operators above are the *only* relational operators that are defined in Fortran. Other natural relations like .EG. ("equal to or greater than") or .SGT. ("slightly greater than") will not be accepted. However, you can use LOGICAL operators to make combinations of relational expressions.

Notice the difference between *relations* (like .EQ. or .GT.) and LOGICAL *operators* (like .AND. or .NOT.). Relations compare two *arithmetic* expressions and the result of the comparison is either .TRUE. or .FALSE.. LOGICAL operators operate on *LOGICAL* expressions, and again the result is .TRUE. or .FALSE.. Since a relational expression results in a LOGICAL value, it is a special case of the general class of LOGICAL expressions.

The most common use of LOGICAL expressions is in IF statements. You already know how to write IF tests like

```
IF (SALES .GT. 200.00) WRITE(6,1000) AWARD
```

Now, using the LOGICAL operators, you can write all sorts of elaborate tests. For example,

```
IF ((BONUS.GT.0.00).AND.(BONUS.LT.10.00))COMIS=1000.00
```

will cause the program to set the commission equal to 1000 if the bonus lies between 0 and 10.

Like arithmetic operators, LOGICAL operators have a hierarchy of precedence: .NOT. is performed first, then .AND., and finally .OR. operations are performed. Of course, parentheses may be used to override this hierarchy. When in doubt, use parentheses.

IF statement

form

   IF (*b*) *stmt*

   b is a LOGICAL expression

   stmt is an executable statement other than an IF or DO (DO statements are covered in Chapter 8)

meaning

   executes statement *stmt* if the expression *b* has the value .TRUE. In any case, proceed from the next statement unless the execution of statement *stmt* transfers control to another part of the program (as in a GO TO).

examples

```
IF (PAY .LE. 0.00)  GO TO 27
IF (.NOT.(TAX .GT. 200.00  .OR. INCOME .LT. MAX))
+                    TAX = (INCOME-MAX)*IRATE
IF(TAX.GT.AMT .AND. RATE.LT.HIGH)WRITE(6,1000)TAX,RATE
```

WARNING!

Don't do this:

```
IF (QUANT .GT. 0.0  .AND.  .LT. 100.0) STOP
```

Do this instead:

```
IF (QUANT .GT. 0.0  .AND.  QUANT .LT. 100.0) STOP
```

Remember! LOGICAL *operators can operate only on* LOGICAL *values, and*

```
.LT. 100.0
```

is not a LOGICAL *value.*

A common use of LOGICAL expressions in IF statements is to implement decision tables. Decision tables provide a way to describe, in a tabular form, the logic of decision processes. They are most effective when you have the problem of selecting one or more alternatives from a collection of possibilities. The selection should be based on some condition or some series of conditions. All the conditions which can occur are listed in the decision table along with possible actions. Once you have determined which conditions hold in a particular case, you can look up the appropriate action in the decision table. The same information can be displayed in a flowchart, but many people find that decision tables make it easier to be sure that all the possibilities are covered. After a decision process has been reduced to a decision table, the decision process can be carried out by a computer following a Fortran program containing a number of IF statements.

Figure 4 6 1 illustrates the basic format of a decision table. The condition stub contains a separate statement for each decision condition which might possibly occur. All the possible actions are listed in the action stub. Taken together, the conditions and actions form an IF-THEN relationship. IF the condition(s) occurs, THEN take the appropriate action. The condition entry and the action entry are the parts of the table that tell you which action(s) to take for the occurrence of which condition(s). The condition entry is used to record those conditions which apply and those which don't apply. Each combination of possible conditions is called a **rule**. There are as many rules as there are possible combinations of conditions. If a condition applies, a "Y" or "yes" is entered in the grid. If it doesn't apply, an "N" or "no" is entered in the grid. When any of the possible actions is to be used for a combination of conditions (a rule), an "X" is placed in the action grid to indicate the required action(s) for that rule. In applying the decision table, you examine the conditions. Then you find a combination of those conditions which apply (a rule). From this, you proceed to the action stub and find out which action(s) is to be followed. The arrows in Figure 4 6 1 show you how you move around the decision table to use it manually.

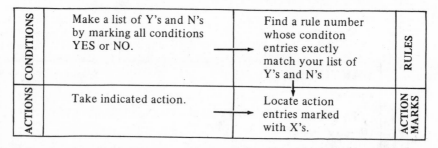

Figure 4 6 1   Decision Table Basic Format

Let's look at how we can team up the decision table and the IF statement by considering an example. The personnel director of Archetypal Systems, Inc., has developed a decision table to determine the cost to employees of health insurance under the company's four options. These options are (1) single, (2) married, (3) family, and (4) major medical. "Single" insurance costs $10 per month, "married" costs $17, and "family" costs $25. Major medical for "single" costs $2 per month extra, major medical for "married" costs $3 extra, and major medical for "family" also costs $3 extra. The decision table for determining the employee contribution to health insurance coverage is shown in Figure 4 6 2.

The "Y" and "N" indicate *yes* or true, and *no* or false. The "X's" tell you which action to take for the conditions which occur for each rule in the condition entry. To use the decision table, you would first look at the conditions and find the one which applies. Suppose "family" is the right condition. Read

Condition (IF):	1	2	3	4	5	6	7	8	9
Single	Y	N	N	Y	N	N	N	Y	–
Married	N	Y	N	N	Y	N	N	Y	Y
Family	N	N	Y	N	N	Y	N	–	Y
Major Medical	N	N	N	Y	Y	Y	–	–	–
Action (THEN):									
Deduct $10	X			X		X			
Deduct $17		X							
Deduct $25			X						
Deduct $2				X					
Deduct $3					X	X			
Error							X	X	X

Figure 4 6 2   Decision Table for Finding Employee
Contribution to Health Insurance Plan

across the table to the rules. Any rule which is marked "Y" for that condition applies to the condition. Now read down this rule column to the action entry row where an "X" is located. You will use that action. Read the action listed for the "X." The action that goes with family is "deduct $25." What does all this mean? It says: IF the type of insurance is family, THEN deduct $25 for health insurance. IF "single" and "major medical" are the conditions, THEN you would take two actions: deduct $10 and deduct $2. What would you do for "married"? What would you do if none of the conditions applied? (The table covers the possibility of errors, too.) A program which would read an employee number, a code for health insurance, and a code for major medical and then write out the employee number with his or her insurance cost could be constructed using our decision table. A decision table like this is one of several that would be required in a complete payroll program.

Compare the decision table and the program below. You should be able to see that the decision table is built into the program. Decision tables are independent of programming languages like Fortran. In fact, they are independent of the whole process of programming. Business managers can use them to write Fortran programs as we have just done, or to communicate the decision process to someone else who will write the program for them, or even to describe the process to someone who will make the decisions without the aid of a computer.

```
COMMENT: PROGRAM TO DETERMINE THE COST  OF
C          HEALTH INSURANCE FOR AN EMPLOYEE OF
C          ARCHETYPAL SYSTEMS, INC.
        INTEGER EMPNO, HEALTH, MAJOR
        REAL INSUR
   900  READ(5,1000) EMPNO, HEALTH, MAJOR
  1000  FORMAT(I10,2I1)
          IF (EMPNO.EQ.0) STOP
```

```
C                                              HERE'S THE DECISION TABLE
          INSUR=0.0
          IF (HEALTH.EQ.1) INSUR=10.00
          IF (HEALTH.EQ.2) INSUR=17.00
          IF (HEALTH.EQ.3) INSUR=25.00
C                                              CHECK FOR ERROR
          IF (INSUR.EQ.0.0) GOTO 1200
C
          IF (HEALTH.EQ.1.AND.MAJOR.EQ.1) INSUR=INSUR+2.00
          IF (HEALTH.EQ.2.AND.MAJOR.EQ.2) INSUR=INSUR+3.00
          IF (HEALTH.EQ.3.AND.MAJOR.EQ.3) INSUR=INSUR+3.00
          WRITE(6,1100) EMPNO, INSUR
 1100     FORMAT(' EMPLOYEE ',I10,' INSURANCE ',F6.2)
          GOTO 900
 1200     WRITE(6,1300) EMPNO
 1300     FORMAT(' EMPLOYEE ',I10,' INCORRECT INSURANCE CLASS.')
          GOTO 900
       END
```

data

```
001293678433
010093876222
029300756440
069438179210
076957321430
083647531320
091128974200
093658321811
000000000000
```

output

```
EMPLOYEE    12936784 INSURANCE   28.00
EMPLOYEE   100938762 INSURANCE   20.00
EMPLOYEE   293007564 INCORRECT  INSURANCE CLASS.
EMPLOYEE   694381792 INSURANCE   10.00
EMPLOYEE   769573214 INSURANCE   25.00
EMPLOYEE   836475313 INSURANCE   17.00
EMPLOYEE   911289742 INCORRECT  INSURANCE CLASS.
EMPLOYEE   936583218 INSURANCE   12.00
```

EXERCISE 4 6

1 Write one IF statement which will have the same effect as the statements below.

```
       IF (TOTAL .GT. 0)  GO TO 20
          GO TO 30
 20       IF (TOTAL .LT. 10)  STOP
 30       ...
```

2 Again, as in 1 above.

```
       IF (TOTAL .GT. 10)  GO TO 20
       IF (TOTAL .LT. 0)  GO TO 20
          GO TO 30
 20       STOP
```

3 Alter the health insurance program so it implements this decision table.

	Rule									
Condition (IF):	1	2	3	4	5	6	7	8	9	10
Single	Y	N	N	Y	N	N	Y	N	N	N
Married	N	Y	N	N	Y	N	N	Y	N	N
Family	N	N	Y	N	N	Y	N	N	Y	N
Maternity	N	N	N	Y	Y	Y	Y	Y	Y	–
Major Medical	N	N	N	N	N	N	Y	Y	Y	–
Action (THEN):										
Deduct $10	X			X			X			
Deduct $17		X			X			X		
Deduct $25			X			X			X	
Deduct $2							X			
Deduct $3								X	X	
Deduct $4				X			X			
Deduct $5					X	X		X	X	
Error										X

Draw a flowchart for this decision table and compare the two. Which one makes it easier for you to compare all the conditions and actions?

Section 4 7

Characters

If Fortran could handle nothing but numeric and logical values, only dyed-in-the-wool technical people would use it. Fortunately, Fortran can be used to manipulate most of the symbols we ordinarily use in writing. Unfortunately, the current ANSI standards do not provide a separate data type for values which are neither numeric nor LOGICAL, and we must sneak in through the back door.

The data descriptors (so far we've seen just I*w* and F*w.d*) which appear in a FORMAT associated with a READ statement specify how the symbols which appear on the data card are to be interpreted. Thus, symbols interpreted under an I*w* data descriptor are converted into the pattern appropriate for storing INTEGERs, and symbols interpreted under an F*w.d* data descriptor are converted into REALs. By altering the data descriptor, we can alter the interpretation of the symbols appearing on the data card.

To specify that we wish the symbols interpreted as **characters** (i.e., letters of the alphabet, parentheses, punctuation marks, digits, etc.) we use the A*w* data descriptor. The A stands for **alphameric**, which for our purposes means any character you can find on the keyboard.

We can also use the A*w* descriptor for output. In that case the value in the memory cell named in the WRITE statement is interpreted as a sequence of *characters* to be printed.

Just as the size of the memory cells limits the size of allowable INTEGERs and REALs, so it determines the number of characters which will fit in one memory cell. In our examples, we'll assume that four characters will fit in a cell, but it may be different on your computer. Usually we'll want to deal with words containing more than four letters. In that case we'll just use more than one memory cell. Here's a simple program that reads one person's name (or the first 16 characters of the name) and then prints it.

> *nonstandard characters:* The characters available in ANSI Fortran are the letters (A–Z), the digits (0–9), and the special characters (+ – * / = . ( ) , $ and blank). The other characters on your keypunch might not correspond exactly to the characters on your printer. Therefore, they may not be printed in the way you expect. In fact, some computer systems will replace certain nonstandard characters with blanks before printing them.

```
      INTEGER NAME1, NAME2, NAME3, NAME4
      READ(5,1000) NAME1, NAME2, NAME3, NAME4
 1000 FORMAT(A4,A4,A4,A4)
      WRITE(6,2000) NAME1, NAME2, NAME3, NAME4
 2000 FORMAT(' THE PERSON IS ', A4, A4, A4, A4)
      STOP
      END
```

data

```
HEINRICH HAMKER
```

output

```
THE PERSON IS HEINRICH HAMKER
```

After the READ is performed, the memory cells look like this:

NAME1	HEIN
NAME2	RICH
NAME3	*b*HAM
NAME4	KER*b*

Remember that the content of a memory cell is a pattern of 1's and 0's. Since we told the compiler that NAME1, NAME2, and so on, contain INTEGERs, the controller doesn't know (or care) that we're thinking of the bit patterns in the memory cells as a person's name. This has an important implication: we can *compare* characters by using relational expressions. The bit patterns corresponding to characters are deliberately chosen so that we can tell if one group of characters is in alphabetical order with respect to another by using the .LE. relation. Suppose that the memory cells NAME1 and NAME2 contain these characters:

NAME 1   ATOM

NAME2   BONG

Then the relational expression

    NAME1 .LT. NAME2

has the value .TRUE. because ATOM comes before BONG alphabetically. Later we will see how to use this property to put lists of people's names in alphabetical order.

collating sequence: The ANSI standards don't require that letters be represented so that they'll be in alphabetical order when compared as INTEGERs, but we don't know of any system where they're in a different order.

Suppose that we want to write a program which will READ a number of people's last names and count the number of times the common last names Brown, Smith, and Nerdly appear. Since we know how to READ the names, and we know how to make comparisons, we might plunge right in. But wait! We need to check each name to see if it is Brown, Smith, or Nerdly. How do we do that? The answer is a little unpleasant, but it can be done. To ease our way in, first we'll show a method which, while not conforming to the ANSI standard, is allowed by many versions of Fortran. This involves using the Hollerith constant notation, as in these statements.

```
IF (NAME1 .EQ. 4HBROW  .AND.  NAME2 .EQ. 1HN) B=B+1
IF (NAME1 .EQ. 4HSMIT  .AND.  NAME2 .EQ. 1HH) S=S+1
IF (NAME1 .EQ. 4HNERD  .AND.  NAME2 .EQ. 2HLY) N=N+1
```

While this may be awkward and hard to read (especially if there are any very long names to be checked) at least it is fairly similar to the sorts of tests we've made many times before.

To make the test using only ANSI standard statements, we must introduce a restricted form of a new statement, the DATA statement. The DATA statement is a nonexecutable statement, that is, an instruction to the compiler. It tells the compiler to place values in memory cells before execution of the program begins, thus allowing us to give memory cells initial values. The standards allow these initial values to be Hollerith constants.

DATA statement (restricted form)

form
  DATA $m_1/c_1/,m_2/c_2/, \ldots , m_n/c_n/$
  the m_i's are memory cell names
  the c_i's are constants

meaning
  instructs the compiler to place each constant c_i into the corresponding memory cell m_i

examples
```
DATA FLAG/2H**/, INSECT/3HANT/, BLANK/1H /
DATA FINIS/4HEND /
DATA YES/3HYES/
```

At last we can write our program to count common last names.

```
COMMENT: THIS PROGRAM READS A LIST OF LAST NAMES AND COUNTS
C        THE NUMBER OF OCCURRENCES OF THE NAMES "SMITH,"
C        "BROWN," AND "NERDLY."
C        THE LAST CARD CONTAINS "****"
         INTEGER B, S, N,  W1,W2,  NAMEB1,NAMEB2,NAMES1,NAMES2,
        +                          NAMEN1,NAMEN2,  FINIS
C        STORE THE NAMES WE SEEK
         DATA NAMEB1/4HBROW/, NAMEB2/1HN/
         DATA NAMES1/4HSMIT/, NAMES2/1HH/
         DATA NAMEN1/4HNERD/, NAMEN2/2HLY/
         DATA FINIS/4H****/
```

```
C       INITIALIZE
        B=0
        S=0
        N=0
C       READ DATA AND ACCUMULATE SUMS
  10    READ(5,1000) W1,W2
1000    FORMAT(A4,A4)
        IF (W1 .EQ. FINIS)  GO TO 20
        IF (W1 .EQ. NAMEB1  .AND.  W2 .EQ. NAMEB2)  B=B+1
        IF (W1 .EQ. NAMES1  .AND.  W2 .EQ. NAMES2)  S=S+1
        IF (W1 .EQ. NAMEN1  .AND.  W2 .EQ. NAMEN2)  N=N+1
        GO TO 10
C       REACHED END OF LIST
  20    WRITE(6,2000) B, S, N
2000    FORMAT(' THERE WERE', I3, ' BROWNS,',
       +          I3, ' SMITHS, AND ', I3, ' NERDLYS')
        STOP
        END
```

data
```
    JIMENEZ
    DEREMER
    BROWN
    BROWNING
    NERDLY
    VALTEAU
    DROVOS
    SMITH
    BROWN
    RODRIGEZ
    NERDLY
    ****
```

output
```
 THERE WERE  2 BROWNS,  1 SMITHS, AND   2 NERDLYS
```

With a little more effort, we could alter our program so that it accepts full names and searches for BROWN, SMITH, and NERDLY, ignoring the rest of the name.

> *Although it is legal to use memory cells of any numeric type (INTEGER or REAL) to store characters, it is far safer to use INTEGERs. Since manipulation of REALs is not an exact process, some odd conditions can arise which can cause unexpected results when values are stored in REAL memory cells.*

EXERCISES 4 7

1 What would we have to change in our program to make it look for JONES instead of SMITH?

2 Write Fortran statements which will READ a data card and search the first five columns for a dollar sign.

Section 4 8

More on FORMATs

In Chapter 2 we introduced two kinds of FORMAT descriptors: literal descriptors and data descriptors. In this section we'll discuss several more types of descriptors which may be used in FORMATs.

You recall that Iw data descriptors were used with INTEGERs and Fw.d data descriptors with REALs. In addition to data descriptors and literal descriptors, FORMATs may contain spacing descriptors. The nX descriptor tells the controller to skip the next n character positions on a data card or output line.

```
        WRITE(6,1000)
 1000 FORMAT(' STE', 10X, 'REO')

output
 STE bbbbbbbbbb REO
```

```
        READ(5,2000)CH
 2000 FORMAT(8X,A1)
data
 RACQUET BALLS
result
 CH        'B'
```

b: In picturing printed lines or punched cards where spacing is critical, we'll use the symbol b for the blank character.

Fortran Charlie prepares to learn FORMATs (It's a whole 'nother language)

You've learned how to use the Fw.d data descriptors for REALs. We'd like to introduce you to the *Ew.d* descriptor, which is used with REALs expressed in scientific notation (remember, the E-notation for REALs you learned about earlier). This notation is useful with those really big or really small numbers.

input

The effect of Ew.d on input is the same as Fw.d if the external value (the one you are READing) isn't written in scientific notation. If it is written in scientific notation, then the decimal point shift factor (see E-notation, Section 4 2) must be right-justified in the field; otherwise, the blanks following it will be interpreted as zeros, thus increasing the shift by factors of ten. If a sign is included with the decimal point shift factors, as in 1.7E–6, and 4.932E+8, then the E may be omitted to save room in the data field. In addition, the decimal point may be omitted from the number, but if so, it is implicitly placed d places to the left of the decimal point shift factor. The following examples should clarify the myriad cases.

external	E7.2	internal
bb3.141		3.141
bbb3.14		3.14
bbbb314		3.14
3.14E00		3.14
3.14E–2		.0314
b314E–2		.0314
bb314–2		.0314
314b+2b		$31.40*10^{20}$

output

When you use Ew.d for output, the REAL value in the corresponding memory cell is printed in scientific notation, rounded to d significant digits. The rightmost four spaces in the output field of width w are used for the decimal point shift factor printed in the form E+xx or E–xx, where each x is a single digit. The number is printed in the $d + 3$ spaces to the left of the decimal point shift factor in the form b0.f or –0.f where f is a d digit unsigned INTEGER. The leftmost $w - (d + 7)$ spaces are left blank. As you can see, w should be at least as large as $d + 7$ to allow enough room for the number.

internal	E10.2	external
3.168		bb0.32E+01
$492.1*10^{-23}$		bb0.49E–21
–3987.12		b–0.40E+04
3749		illegal

In addition to the data descriptors we've discussed, there are some others: Dw.d and Gw.d and the sP scaling factor descriptors. If the ones we've described to you won't give you the output or accuracy you need, then consult a Fortran manual or your local expert to find out about these descriptors. They're useful in certain situations, but you won't need them for most types of business problems.

Now that we've described the various data descriptors, let's look in more depth at how we can combine them to perform the input or produce the output we might desire.

Formatted records, whether they are lines or cards, often have a very regular structure. In a number of examples we've had several *identical* data descriptors in a row. For example, suppose our data cards contain ten numbers in fields of width eight. One way to describe such a card is with FORMAT 1000 below:

```
1000 FORMAT(F8.0,F8.0,F8.0,F8.0,F8.0,
     +         F8.0,F8.0,F8.0,F8.0,F8.0)
```

Fortunately, we don't need to write so many identical descriptors. Instead, we can place a **repeat specification** in front of one descriptor. The effect is then the same as if the data descriptor is repeated the number of times indicated by the repeat specification. Thus, FORMAT 2000 below is equivalent to FORMAT 1000 above.

```
2000 FORMAT(10F8.0)
```

The repeat specification is an unsigned INTEGER constant *r* which appears in front of a FORMAT descriptor.

> **repeat specification:** *an unsigned nonzero INTEGER constant r placed in front of data descriptor or group to indicate that the group is to be repeated r times*

If the same pattern of FORMAT descriptors is repeated several times, as in FORMAT 3000 below, then that *pattern* may be grouped by parentheses and a repeat specification placed in front of the group, as in the equivalent FORMAT 4000 below.

```
3000 FORMAT(' ',F11.4,' AND',I10,20X,
     +         F11.4,' AND',I10,20X,I15)

4000 FORMAT(' ',2(F11.4,' AND',I10,20X),I15)
```

> **group:** *a parenthesized sublist of* FORMAT *descriptors. It may be preceded by an explicit repeat specification. Groups may be nested to a depth of two.*

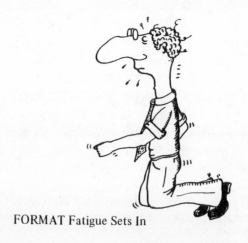

FORMAT Fatigue Sets In

Any list of FORMAT descriptors can become a group, and groups may be nested two deep, but no deeper. Usually a group is preceded by a repeat specification, but it doesn't have to be. If the repeat specification is omitted, it is taken to be one. Even a group with no explicit repeat factor affects the meaning of a FORMAT in the aberrant (but legal) case when a READ or WRITE list includes more values than the FORMAT appears equipped to handle. We'll ignore that possibility for a while. Then these two FORMATs are equivalent:

```
5000 FORMAT(A5, A5, I3, I3, 1X, A1, 1X, A1,
    +              I3, I3, 1X, A1, 1X, A1,
    +              I3, I3, 1X, A1, 1X, A1, A8, A8, A8)

6000 FORMAT(2A5, 3(2I3,2(1X, A1)), 3A8)
```

Most FORMATs describe a single line or a single card. In other words, they describe one I/O **record**. The length of a formatted I/O record is measured in characters. For example, the length of a record for the 80-column card reader is 80

> record: the basic unit of I/O. Different I/O devices have different types of records. The card reader record is one card (usually 80 characters). The printer record is one line. Different printers have different line lengths; 132 is the line length for many printers.

characters. No FORMAT should describe a record longer than the record length for the intended I/O device. However, it is possible for a FORMAT to describe more than one record. For example, the following statement prints two records (i.e., two lines) as a heading on a page.

```
    WRITE(6,1000)
1000 FORMAT('1', 5X, 'SCREWS'/ ' ', 'SIZE', 4X, 'PRICE')
```

carriage control character

The slash (/) in the FORMAT separates the descriptions of the two records. (Note that each record, being a printed line, has a carriage control character.) In general, a FORMAT may describe many records, with each record separated from the next by a slash. For example, the following READ statement will read three cards. Two values will be taken from the first card, one value from the second, and two from the third.

```
    READ(5,2000)A,B,C,D,E
2000 FORMAT(2F10.0/F30.0/2F15.0)
```

Two consecutive slashes imply a blank record in between. The printer will skip a line because the implied blank line includes a blank character for carriage control. The reader will skip one card when given a // specification.

An I/O statement may process several records even if the FORMAT describes only one. Here's how that can happen. The WRITE statement below has more values in its list than there are data descriptors in the FORMAT. The computer

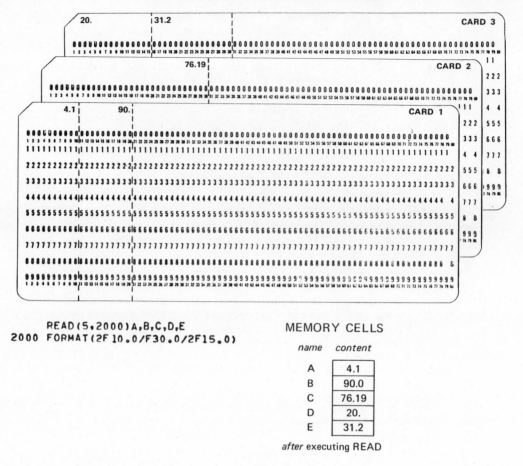

```
     READ(5,2000)A,B,C,D,E
2000 FORMAT(2F 10.0/F30.0/2F15.0)
```

MEMORY CELLS

name	content
A	4.1
B	90.0
C	76.19
D	20.
E	31.2

after executing READ

must print all the values listed, so it simply uses the FORMAT over again, starting a new record when it comes to the end of the specification.

```
      INTEGER A, BEE, SEA, D
      A = 110
      B = 60
      SEA = 950
      D = SEA - 5*A
      WRITE(6,1000) A, BEE, SEA, D
 1000 FORMAT(' ', 2I6)
```

results

*bbb*110*bbbb*60
*bbb*950*bbb*400

In general, if an I/O statement is not completed when it runs out of data descriptors in the FORMAT, it starts a new record and uses the FORMAT over again. This is a relatively simple and useful idea. It lets you describe one record or even several records that you're thinking of as one logical unit and lets you use that description over and over to input or ouptut several sets of data. The following FORMAT describes a pair of data cards, one containing a car name and the other a REAL and an INTEGER (price and mileage). The READ statement READs three pairs of cards, using the FORMAT three times.

```
      INTEGER CAR1A, CAR1B
      INTEGER CAR2A, CAR2B
      INTEGER CAR3A, CAR3B
      INTEGER M1, M2, M3
      REAL PRICE1, PRICE2, PRICE3
      READ(5,1000) CAR1A,CAR1B,PRICE1,M1,
     +             CAR2A,CAR2B,PRICE2,M2,
     +             CAR3A,CAR3B,PRICE3,M3
 1000 FORMAT(2A4/F7.0,I7)
```

data
> RABBIT*bb*
> 3300.00*bbbbb*41
> FOX*bbbbb*
> 5000.00*bbbbb*37
> DASHER*bb*
> 4500.00*bbbbb*38

The repeated use of the FORMAT gets a little more complicated if the FORMAT contains groups of descriptors. In this case, the repetition starts from the last top-level group or from the repeat factor preceding it, if it has one. The following WRITE statement illustrates this feature. It assumes the memory cells have the values they were given by the READ statement above.

```
      WRITE(6,2000) CAR1A,CAR1B, PRICE1, M1,
     +              CAR2A,CAR2B, PRICE2, M2
     +              CAR3A,CAR3B, PRICE3, M3
 2000 FORMAT('  CAR         PRICE     EPA MILEAGE'/
     +        (1X,2A4, F9.2, I8))
```

output
```
   CAR         PRICE     EPA MILEAGE
   RABBIT      3300.00        41
   FOX         5000.00        37
   DASHER      4500.00        38
```

> *last top-level group:* the group in a FORMAT *which is terminated by the first right parenthesis to the left of the right parenthesis which closes the* FORMAT. *Got that?*

Now you know what happens if an I/O list includes more memory cell names than the associated FORMAT has data descriptors. There is yet another possibility, believe it or not. What if there are fewer memory cells to be dealt with than there are data descriptors left in the FORMAT? Perhaps the answer "the remaining data descriptors are ignored" is obvious. But what's *not* obvious is what happens if there is a slash or a literal descriptor after the last data descriptor that was used but before a data descriptor which is not needed. Do we ignore those too, or not? Well, it's not hard to imagine cases in which you would want them to be used, nor is it difficult to imagine cases in which you wouldn't want them. Verbosity won out, as illustrated below:

```
      INTEGER X, WN1,WN2
      DATA WN1/4HMILL/, WN2/2HER/
      X=2
      WRITE(6,1200) X, WN1,WN2
      X=0
      WRITE(6,1200) X
 1200 FORMAT(' THERE WERE', I2, ' PRIZE WINNERS.  ',
     +          2A4, ' CAME IN FIRST')
      STOP
      END
```

output

```
 THERE WERE 2 PRIZE WINNERS.  MILLER   CAME IN FIRST
 THERE WERE 0 PRIZE WINNERS.
```

The second WRITE statement doesn't have list elements to match with the 2A4 data descriptor. Hence, all the literal descriptors in the FORMAT, up to the 2A4 data descriptor, are printed; everything else is ignored.

FORMAT

form

FORMAT (*spec*)

spec is a list of FORMAT descriptors (i.e., data descriptors, literal descriptors, spacing descriptors, slashes, or groups of these) separated by commas. Slashes serve as delimiters, so commas should be omitted around slashes. Every FORMAT must have a statement label.

meaning

A FORMAT describes the layout of an I/O record or records.

examples

```
1000 FORMAT(I10,A20,F11.4)
2000 FORMAT(5F10.0)
3000 FORMAT(' ',20('*****',F5.2))
4000 FORMAT('1',3F4.2//' ',6(3F5.2,I5))
```

> *group: A group of* FORMAT *descriptors is a parenthesized sublist of descriptors in* **spec**. *It may be preceded by an explicit repeat specification.* FORMAT *4000 above contains the group 6(3F5.2,I5).*

Let's face it. This has been a hard, unpleasant section. You might feel that just as you were starting to learn Fortran, all of a sudden an entirely foreign language called FORMATs was pushed on you. You'd be right. Unless you are using a version of Fortran which allows some form of format-free I/O (for which there are no standards), you simply have to put up with the baroque details of FORMATs.

Now that you've learned the language for controlling the interaction of your program with input and output devices, we can get back to the more interesting (to us at least) parts of computing.

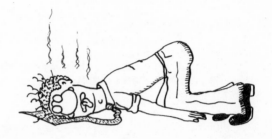

EXERCISES 4 8

1 Which data type and corresponding data descriptor would be most appropriate if you were printing out
    a   baseball batting averages
    b   the number of olives in a martini
    c   a list of people's names
    d   the national debt

2 Below are some pairs of FORMAT statements. Which have the same effect? Which are different?

```
1000 FORMAT(' ', I3, I3, I3, F12.2)
1001 FORMAT(' ', 3(I3,F12.2))

2000 FORMAT(' ', I3, I3, A2, I3, I3, A2)
2001 FORMAT(' ', 2(2I3, A2))

3000 FORMAT('0', F10.2)
3001 FORMAT(/' ', F10.2)

4000 FORMAT(13(' '), I10)
4001 FORMAT(13X, I10)

5000 FORMAT(' ', 10X, ' A=', I5)
5001 FORMAT(12X, 'A=', I5)
```

3 If the following READ FORMAT is used, where should the REAL number be put on the data card?
```
1000 FORMAT(F80.0)
```

4 What is wrong with the following FORMAT?
```
     READ(5,1000) A,B,C,D,E,F
1000 FORMAT(6F20.0)
```

5 How should the data be punched on cards for the following READ statement?
```
     READ(5,2000) A,B,C,D,E,F
2000 FORMAT(2F10.0)
```

6 Write a FORMAT describing a card with the following layout:

      col 1–2, alphameric
      col 21–30, REAL
      col 41–50, REAL
      col 61–70, REAL

7 What values will be placed in A and B?

```
     REAL A, B
      READ(5,1000) A,B
1000 FORMAT(2E9.1)
        .
        .
        .
```

data
```
 +6.02E+23+602E+23
```

8 What will be printed?

```
     REAL A
     A = 1.234E+5
     WRITE(6,1000) A,A,A
1000 FORMAT('bbA=',    F10.1, 'bbA=', E9.3, 'bbA=', E9.1)
     STOP
     END
```

9 Write one WRITE and one FORMAT statement which will print the line FORMAT IS A TRICKY LANGUAGE 100 times, starting at the top of a page. (Careful! Don't print it at the top of 100 separate pages. You might upset your local expert.)

10 What will be produced by

```
     INTEGER X, WN1,WN2
     DATA WN1/2HBO/, WN2/2HMO/
     X = 2
     WRITE(6,1350) WN1, X, WN2
1350 FORMAT('0IN FIRST PLACE WAS ',A2/
    +        ' THERE WERE', I2, ' TIED FOR IT')
     STOP
     END
```

Section 4 9

Implicit Typing

Fortran does not require memory cell names to be listed in type statements. If a memory cell name is not explicitly given a type, Fortran makes an assumption. The convention is, if the memory cell name starts with I, J, K, L, M, or N, it is assigned the type INTEGER; otherwise, the type assigned is REAL.

This has one side effect which may have already brought you grief. If you make a keypunching mistake and misspell a memory cell name, the compiler won't print an error message. Instead, it assumes you want to have a memory cell of that name and assigns it a type according to the convention. The result is a program which may look like it works, but produces incorrect results.

The question of whether or not to explicitly type INTEGER and REAL variables can lead to heated debate (believe it or not). Here are some arguments.

pro: It's crucial for the programmer to be aware of the use he or she intends to make of each memory cell. Explicitly naming the type ensures that the programmer is conscious of each memory cell, its name, and its type.

con: If you don't follow the naming rules, you have to look all the way up to the top of the program to see what type a given memory cell is. That takes your mind off what you're doing.

pro: It's important to choose memory cell names which are strongly suggestive of the use made of the cell. Often six letters are inadequate to the task, and further restricting the choice of the first letter to fit the implicit typing convention becomes unbearable.

con: There's too big a deal made of using fancy memory cell names. People see a memory cell named IDEAS and think that the program does something significant. It's better to use names like A, B, and C—they don't mislead anyone about what the computer is actually doing.

pro: You have to use type statements for all the Fortran data types besides INTEGERs and REALs—why not be consistent and do it for all of them?

con: Consistency is the hemoglobin of small minds. Besides, it's just a waste of time to punch the type statements. Let the compiler figure out what types the memory cells have.

.
.
.

> *I–N are INtegers*

PROBLEMS 4

1 Write and run a program which will use input values for A, B, C, and D and will compute and output the values of each of the variables below. Use the values A = 3, B = 4, C = 7, and D = 6.

$UA = A(B + C)D$

$UB = (AB + CD)D$

$UC = ABC + ACD$

$VA = (A - B)^3 + (A + B)^3$

$VB = 2A^3 + 6AB^2$

$VC = 2A(A^2 + 3B^2)$

$WA = \dfrac{C}{B} + \dfrac{C}{D}$

$WB = \dfrac{CD + BC}{BD}$

$WC = \dfrac{C}{BD}(D + B)$

$XA = A^2 - 2AB + B^2$

$XB = (A - B)^2$

$XC = B^2 + A^2 - 2AB$

$YA = A \div B - A$

$YB = C + B - C$

$YC = D + B - D$

$ZA = (A + B)(C + D)^C$

$ZB = (A + C)(B + D)^D$

$ZC = (A + D)(B + C)^D$

2 Use a series of WRITE statements to print a giant version of the letter(s) of your choice in the middle of the page. You might want to sketch out your design on a print chart to assist you in getting the right spacing.

```
Z Z Z Z Z
Z Z Z Z Z
        Z Z
      Z Z
    Z Z
  Z Z
Z Z Z Z Z
Z Z Z Z Z
```

3 Write a program which READs in the cost of an item of merchandise and then computes the change from a $5 bill. If an item costs $1.27 then the change is $3.73 and the input and output should be as shown below.

Input Design:

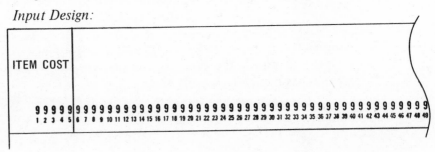

Output Sketch:

COST	$1B	H	Q	D	N	P	CHANGE
$1.27	3	1	0	2	0	3	$3.73

Create at least 10 data cards using values of items costing from 1¢ to $5. You may want to lay out your completed output design on a print chart to aid you in spacing.

4 In statistics, you will frequently need to calculate the mean (average), standard deviation, and range of a set of data values. You are to write a program which calculates these statistics for data on the age, height, and weight of a group of your friends. The method of calculating each statistic is

$$\text{range} = \text{highest value} - \text{lowest value}$$

$$\text{mean average} = \text{sum of values/number of values}$$

$$\text{standard deviation} = \frac{\text{sums of (values)}^2 - \dfrac{\text{(sum of values)}^2}{\text{no. of values}}}{\text{no. of values} - 1}$$

The "sum of (values)^2" is each data-value squared and then added together, while the "(sum of values)^2" is the result of adding the values together and then squaring the sum.

Input Data Items:

data	description
name	20 alpha
age	2 numeric
height	3 numeric
weight	3 numeric

Output Sketch:

	AGE	HEIGHT	WEIGHT
RANGE	35–17	82–50	229–98
MEAN	22.3	62.7	173.4
STANDARD DEVIATION	2.0	4.9	11.3

Complete your input design with a card layout, finish the output design with a print chart, prepare a program flowchart, and write the program. After running the program, make sure the results correspond to your print chart.

5 The Solar Power Company, Inc., has designed and built several test houses to determine the efficiency of their Sunshine Heater. The temperature is recorded periodically in degrees centigrade in each house. You have been assigned the task of writing a program which will summarize the test data. The output report which has been sketched by the Chief of Testing is shown below. The report is to include headings and page numbers. The very last page contains the summary temperature information. Each page contains *40* detail lines, excluding the heading. As you can see from the sketch, it is necessary to convert the centigrade temperature to Fahrenheit. The formula for converting to Fahrenheit is $F = (9/5)C + 32$. The mean temperature is the average calculated by

$$\text{mean temperature} = \frac{\text{sum of temperatures}}{\text{number of temperatures}}$$

Input Data Items:

data	description
house number	3 numeric
time: hours	2 numeric
minutes	2 numeric
centigrade temperature	5 numeric

Output Sketch:

TEMPERATURE

HOUSE NUMBER	TIME	CENTIGRADE	FAHRENHEIT	PAGE 1
XXX	XX:XX	XXX.X	XXX.X	
XXX	XX:XX	XXX.X	XXX.X	
XXX	XX:XX	XXX.X	XXX.X	
XXX	XX:XX	XXX.X	XXX.X	

TEMPERATURE

HOUSE NUMBER	TIME	CENTIGRADE	FAHRENHEIT	PAGE 2
XXX	XX:XX	XXX.X	XXX.X	
XXX	XX:XX	XXX.X	XXX.X	
XXX	XX:XX	XXX.X	XXX.X	
XXX	XX:XX	XXX.X	XXX.X	

	CENTIGRADE	FAHRENHEIT	PAGE 3
MEAN TEMPERATURE	XXX.X	XXX.X	

Complete input and output designs, prepare a flowchart, and write and execute the program.

6 Programmit Company hires you as a consultant to solve their payroll problem. The previous programmer botched the job so badly that she was bent, folded, stapled, mutilated, and fired. The information concerning each employee is already punched in cards, one card per employee, as follows.

data	columns
social security number	1–9
employee name	10–20
hours worked	21–24
rate of pay per hour	25–28
tax rate	29–30
health plan	31

The health plan is coded as follows:

> N — doesn't belong
> S — $5.34 per week deduction
> F — $10.74 per week deduction

The output from the program is to be, for each employee:

a A paycheck listing gross pay and deductions (tax, health plan, social security, and pension) as well as take home pay.

b After all the paychecks have been printed, a list giving total gross pay, total tax deduction, total health plan, total social security, and total pension so that the company knows "where the money went."

The output can be computed as follows:

$$gross\ pay = hours\ worked * rate\ of\ pay$$
$$tax = gross\ pay * tax\ rate$$
$$health\ plan = \$0,\ \$5.34,\ or\ \$10.74\ depending\ on\ plan$$
$$type\ none,\ single,\ or\ family,\ respectively$$
$$social\ security = 6.75\%\ of\ gross\ pay$$
$$pension = 6\%\ of\ gross\ pay$$
$$take\ home\ pay = gross\ pay - tax - health\ plan - social$$
$$security - pension$$

Run your program with the following test data. Your output should be designed and printed to look like a paycheck (i.e., bank name, address, date, etc.).

532402221	FIELDS	WC	3421	0253	09	S
427556677	RAKE	HIHO	1477	1317	16	F
363407210	FIGMO	FRED	0925	0215	08	N
939721471	CRAFTER	IMA	7500	0876	10	S
874661193	BIG	BUCK	8275	1545	12	F
369452546	DYMO	DINA	4350	0990	11	S

Develop an output design, prepare a flowchart, and write and execute the program.

7 As tax time draws near, depreciation figures are needed. Of course, the idea behind depreciating an asset is to show its value as long as the item is used. The declining balance method is one way to calculate depreciation. An item bought the first half of the month in January would be depreciated the entire year; an item bought the last half of January would have only 11 months' depreciation. Use the 1st through the 15th and the 16th through the last day of the month for determining depreciation for that month. The rate is found by taking the useful life (e.g., 5 years), dividing it into 1 and getting a decimal answer (e.g., 1/5 = .20), and then doubling the rate (e.g., .20 × 2 = .40). If the item is used instead of new, use 1½ times the rate (e.g., .20 × 1½ = .30).

Input Data Items:

data	columns	notes
accounting code	1–4	
description	5–30	
date acquired	31–36	Yr Mo Da
useful life	37–38	# years
cost	39–43	dollars only
type	44	new/used

Output Sketch:

YEAR	COST	ACCUMULATED DEPRECIATION AT BEGINNING OF YEAR	BOOK VALUE AT BEGINNING OF YEAR	RATE	DEPRE-CIATION FOR YEAR	BOOK VALUE AT END OF YEAR
1975	$10,000	----	$10,000.00	40%	$4,000.00	$6,000.00
1976		$4,000	6,000.00		2,400.00	3,600.00
1977		6,400	3,600.00		1,400.00	2,160.00
1978		7,840	2,160.00		864.00	1,296.00
1979		8,704	1,296.00		518.40	777.60

Complete the output design, prepare a flowchart, and write and execute the program to calculate depreciation.

8 Straight-line is another depreciation method. Use the same format for input as the declining balance problem above. Design your output from the report sketch shown below. You may find it helpful to use a print chart.

Output Sketch:

ACCOUNT-ING CODE	ITEM DESCRIP-TION	DATE ACQUIRED	LIFE	COST	THIS YEAR'S DEPRECIA-TION	MONTHLY DEPRE-CIATION	YEARLY DEPRE-CIATION	SPECIAL REMARKS
XXX	XX	XX-XX-XX	XX	$XXXXX	$XXXXX	$XXXXX	$XXXXX	

Total depreciation this year	$XXXX.XX	
Average monthly depreciation	$XXX.XX	
Average yearly depreciation	$XXX.XX	
Total investment tax credit	$XXX.XX	Note: Print only if bought in 1975; see below.

Possibilities include:

1 Assets acquired prior to 1975

    a that are fully depreciated: print $00 for this year's depreciation and "remove this item"

    b where this is the last year to take depreciation: print the amount of depreciation and "fully depreciated"

    c where more years are left: take a full year's depreciation

2 Asset acquired in 1975

Depreciate only number of months the asset was actually held (days between the 1st and 15th are part of the current month;

days between the 16th and 31st are in with the next month). The government allows a 10 percent investment tax credit on certain capital items bought in 1975. Print the investment tax credit as indicated on the sketch above.

9 Fair Weather Forecasts, Inc., prepares a report for the "magical prognostications" of TV and radio stations in several states. To improve the accuracy of their forecasts, the company's managers have decided to develop a computer system to analyze and report the daily temperature information. You are to write a program which produces the output shown in the sketch from the input data. Your program should indicate if a new record has been set as shown in the output sketch.

Input Data:

data	description
date	MMDDYY (i.e., Month, Day, Year)
high temperature for the day	XXX
low temperature for the day	XXX
year record high set	XXXX
record high temperature	XXX
year record low set	XXXX
record low temperature	XXX

Output Sketch:

10/23/78	High Today	52
	Low Today	23
10/24/78	High Today	71*
	Low Today	38

* (Beats Record of 70 Set in 1906)

10/25/78	High Today	73*
	Low Today	−10**

* (Beats Record of 68 Set in 1932)
** (Beats Record of −8 Set in 1918)

10/26/78	High Today	22
	Low Today	−18*

* (Beats Record of −12 Set in 1890)

Prepare the input and output designs, draw the flowchart, and write and execute the program.

10 Write a program which simulates fleas on a dog, using the equations below. Perform the simulation of several different values of the parameters and see what happens (for some values the fleas die out, for some they over- -

whelm the poor dog, for some they reach an uncomfortable compromise with the dog). For each set of parameter values, print out the flea population each minute for a total of 60 simulated minutes.

memory cell	meaning	typical value
FLEAS	The total number of fleas on the dog this minute.	50
SCRACH	The number of scratches the dog makes this minute.	10
SCRATE	The number of scratches the dog makes per minute per flea.	.1
TIRED	The maximum number of scratches the dog can make each minute.	20
NEWFLE	The fraction of fleas born or hopping on the dog each minute.	.2
DEATHf	The fraction of fleas which die or jump off the dog each minute.	.1

Equations:

$$\text{SCRACH} = (\text{SCRATE} * \text{FLEAS}) \text{ or TIRED, whichever is less}$$

$$\text{FLEAS (next minute)} = \text{FLEAS} + \text{NEWFLE} * \text{FLEAS} - \text{DEATHF} * \text{FLEAS} - \text{SCRATCH}$$

5 DEBUGGING YOUR PROGRAMS

Chapter Objectives: After studying this chapter, you should be able to:

- Design programs in a four-step process.
- Recognize three main causes of program failure.
- Debug programs in a three-step process.
- Apply mirror printing, write statements and walkthroughs to locate errors.

Section 5 1

Introduction

So far it must seem that we think if you read this book you'll be able to write programs that contain no errors. After all, all our examples have involved programs that work properly. Probably you are spending most of your time rewriting programs that *don't* work. As you know, the often laborious task of getting a program to run the way you want is called **debugging**. This chapter gives hints about how to proceed.

The best course, obviously, would be to avoid errors in the first place. By using verbal descriptions and flowcharts, and by designing your program carefully before you write down anything in Fortran, you can avoid an amazing number of bugs. By using comment statements in your program, you can make it much easier to follow the logic of the troublesome parts of your program. By taking your | **debug:** *to remove the errors (bugs) from a program* | time and checking each card carefully after you punch it, you can eliminate a number of typing errors. Even if you do all these things, however, you will, no doubt, still have bugs in your programs. We certainly do.

What steps can you take to reduce your errors in writing programs? Think of designing programs as a four-step process: (1) problem statement, (2) input/output description, (3) stepwise refinement of the solution, and (4) Fortran coding. It won't always be possible to keep these steps completely separate. Sometimes you'll have to repeat parts of the process (see the Big Picture, Section 1 2 and review the last few pages of Section 1 3), but using this general approach can be very helpful. If you carefully follow steps 1 through 3, you will find that your debugging efforts in step 4 will be greatly reduced. It's very, very tempting to jump directly to step 4 and later wonder why it's so hard to get your program to run. The time spent on preparation will definitely reduce your suffering later.

---

steps in program design

1 *Problem Statement*
State the problem you are trying to solve as precisely as you can.

2 *Input/Output Description*
Describe in precise terms the input your program will accept and the output it will produce.

3 *Stepwise Refinement*
Describe the process your program is to perform in terminology you can understand. Refine each portion of the process into terminology closer to that which the computer can understand. Continue refining the language until you have something you can code directly into Fortran.

4 *Fortran Coding*
Translate the statements in your final refinement from Step 3 into Fortran.

Let's assume that you've done all you can beforehand, you've run your program, and it doesn't work right. There are three main ways your program can fail. First, it might be that you have written some illegal statements and the compiler couldn't figure out what you meant. We'll call such errors **compile-time errors** because they are detected in the process of translating your Fortran statements into machine language. Another possibility is that even though you've written a legal Fortran program, it has illegal consequences; for example, it might wind up dividing by a variable which has the value zero. We'll call such errors **execution-time errors** because they are detected while the machine language instructions corresponding to your program are being performed (executed). The third possibility is that while your program produces results, the results are wrong. For example, if your program was supposed to compute your checking account balance and it gave a very large number as the answer, you'd know right away that something was wrong. We'll call these kinds of errors **logic errors** because they are caused by flaws in the way you wrote your program, errors in your logic. Often, logic errors cause execution-time· errors, and we'll tend to lump the two together for that reason.

Section 5 2

Compile-time Errors

Compile-time errors are easy to find—the compiler itself will carefully mark where they occur and will supply an error message that usually has something to do with the problem. Keypunching mistakes often cause this sort of error. Things like accidentally leaving out the replacement operator (=), forgetting to mark column 6 on continuation cards, leaving out an asterisk (*), using too many letters in a memory cell name, not balancing parentheses, and forgetting statement labels are typical compile-time errors. If you're not absolutely certain of the form of a statement you want to use, look it up.

> *syntax: a tax for sin. Fortran makes you pay when you don't follow the rules.*

> *syntax error: an error caused by not following the rules for writing Fortran statements. These errors are detected at compile-time.*

You can think of program debugging as a three-step process. First, you must realize or detect that you have an error. Second, you must locate the statement(s) that caused the error. And third, you must correct the error(s). Sometimes the computer will help you detect and locate errors, but other times it won't and you'll have to hunt them down.

> *steps in debugging*
> *1 error detection*
> *2 error location*
> *3 error correction*

Sometimes one error can lead to lots of error messages. For example, if you use too many letters in a memory cell name, an error message will be printed each time the name appears in your program. The statement

`BALANCE = BALANCE + CHARGE`

might result in two error messages even though you know you made only one.

An example of a compile-time error is

`1100 UNDEFINED LABEL`

What does it mean? The "1100" would usually refer to a statement label. The message indicates you have used the label in a READ, WRITE, or GO TO statement, but it doesn't appear anywhere in columns 1–5 of any statement. If this occurs, you either forgot to number a statement or, more likely, you just used the wrong number. Your local expert should be able to refer you to a manual for your specific computer which explains most compile-time errors.

A statement such as

`COST + PRICE*QUANT`

when you really mean

`COST = PRICE*QUANT`

would most likely produce an error message such as

`UNRECOGNIZABLE STATEMENT`

Notice that the error message doesn't tell you that you put a + where you wanted an =, but only that it can't recognize the statement. This is very typical of the compile-time errors you will get if you have illegal syntax.

Another thing to watch for is this: if you have *two* errors in one expression, e.g.,

```
A = 2(1 + AARDOR))
```

sometimes only the *first* error is discovered by the compiler. If you don't look closely, you might correct the statement to read

```
A = 2*(1 + AARDOR))
```

only to discover another error message staring at you after your next run. There are too many right parentheses. Look over your statements carefully to find all the errors at once.

Compile-time Errors

Section 5 3

Execution-time Errors

We face a problem in writing this section—many errors that will occur are errors which are detected by the actual machine hardware, when the Fortran compiler isn't around to help you. This means that the details of the errors are machine-dependent and vary widely from one model to another (let alone the variations from manufacturer to manufacturer). What we'll do is go through an example and indicate the nature of the errors. Your instructor or local expert should be able to tell you exactly what the error messages will look like on your system.

To correct an error you need to know (1) where in your program the error occurred and (2) what caused it. To help locate the error, we'll describe three (increasingly difficult) ways to proceed. First, you may be fortunate and be provided with a message that tells you which line of your program the error occurred in or at least at which memory location in the machine it occurred. Second, by studying which of your WRITE statements were printed before the error occurred, you may be able to deduce in what part of your program the error occurred. This is a reason to put extra WRITE statements in programs you are debugging. (On some systems, with some types of errors, the last few WRITE statements' results may not appear even though they were executed, however.) Third, you may be able to infer where the error occurred from the nature of the error. For example, if your program exceeded its time limit, then it probably was in a loop at the time. If it tried to divide by zero, then obviously it was carrying out some statement which involved a division. If you absolutely cannot locate the error, you will have to insert additional WRITE statements in suspicious spots of your program and run it again.

> *diagnostic: a message which indicates that an error has occurred and the possible location of the error*

> *The precise nature of an execution-time error, that is, the error mentioned in the resulting error message, is often only the tip of the iceberg. You must deduce the underlying cause.*

To fix the error once it's located, you must determine its cause. If the error is for time limit, then the conditions for stopping a loop must not have been met for some reason. If it is an arithmetic sort of error (overflow, underflow, division by zero), then some variable is getting a value you didn't expect.

Many errors result from bad logic in the program which ultimately makes the instructions in your program impossible to perform, thus helping you detect the errors. However, some logic errors simply cause your program to produce incorrect results without asking the computer to perform impossible operations. These errors are often more difficult to fix—you simply may not notice that there is anything wrong. Just because something comes out of a computer doesn't mean it's right! It's a good idea to run a small test case in order to verify that your program really is working properly. If the small test doesn't work as you expect,

> *Test your program on simple data where you know the results before you assume it is producing correct results on more complicated data.*

you may be able to locate the trouble, or you may be forced to get more information by sprinkling your program with WRITE statements to give you partial results. Once the error is located and you know what caused it, alter the program and run it again. It is an *extremely* bad bet ever to assume that the error was a fluke and to run the program again hoping the error will go away by itself!

> *Print partial results to trace the execution of the program and find errors.*

Once you get the hang of it, debugging is almost fun. There's a Sherlock Holmes flavor to it. To illustrate, we'll run through an actual case from our programming diary.

Debugging Example

Recall the program we wrote in Section 3 3 which computed the average cost of laundry detergents. Look at the flowchart in Figure 3 3 1 to refresh your memory about how the program was organized. The program, in a prior, undebugged form, appears below.

Here's what we started with after drawing a flowchart, converting it to Fortran, punching up the deck, and removing the compile-time errors.

```
COMMENT:  FIND THE AVERAGE COST OF LAUNDRY DETERGENT
          REAL PRICE, WGT, SUM, N, AVG
C                        INITIALIZE COUNTER AND SUM ACCUMULATOR
          N = 0.0
          SUM = 0.00
C                                    READ UNIT PRICE AND WEIGHT
   10     READ(5,1000) PRICE,WGT
 1000     FORMAT(F5.0,F5.0)
C                                 ANOTHER BRAND TO AVERAGE IN
          N = N+1.0
C                            IF PRICE IS NEGATIVE, WE'RE DONE
          IF (PRICE .LT. 0.00)  GO TO 20
C                            ADD IN UNIT PRICE OF THIS BRAND
          SUM = SUM + (PRICE/WGT)
          GO TO 10
C                          GOT THEM ALL--COMPUTE AVERAGE
   20     AVG = SUM/N
          WRITE(6,2000) AVG
 2000     FORMAT(' THE AVERAGE PRICE PER POUND IS  $',F6.2)
          STOP
          END
```

We made up some data cards with a few easily computed values on them to test our program before turning it loose on our real data.

```
2.00   2.0
10.00  5.0
```

If our program had worked the way we wanted, it would have gotten the result $(2./2. + 10./5.)/2. = 1.5$. We ran it and, not only didn't we get 1.5, we didn't get anything at all except an error message telling us that an "end of file" had been reached on "unit 5." Needless to say, we were a little disappointed. The error message seemed a bit obscure, but since statement 10 is the only READ statement, and it, of course, refers to unit 5, we realized that the error must have occurred while the controller was carrying out statement 10. This set us to thinking . . . The program must not have stopped READing soon enough and must have gone on past what we intended to be our last card, looking for another card, finally READing the job control card at the end of our deck.

> *When eliminating complicated errors, especially in large programs, it helps to form a* hypothesis *about the malfunction, keeping notes on the hypotheses you have checked. Eventually you can deduce the roots of the problems.*

We checked our data and, sure enough, we'd forgotten to put a trailer card at the end of the data. We added a final card with −1.0 in the first field and tossed our program in to be run again. This, by the way, is a *mistake*. You should *never* correct just one error and assume there aren't others. If we had taken a little more time to go over our program carefully, we could have avoided the next round of errors.

This time we got no error messages, but the result was

```
THE AVERAGE PRICE PER POUND IS $   1.00
```

"What?" we said. "We expected a much higher average!" We stared at the statements for a while but didn't see anything wrong. We looked at the data cards carefully to see if we had mispunched any (wishing all the time that we had placed statements like

```
     WRITE(6,1100) PRICE,WGT
1100 FORMAT(' PRICE=',F6.2,' AND WEIGHT=',F6.2)
```

after the READ statement). Since we didn't find anything wrong, we began a time-honored process. We wrote down the names of all the memory cells we used in the program and drew a box beside each. Then we put one finger beside the

> *mirror printing: It is usually a good idea, especially in the debugging stage of writing a program, to print values obtained by READ statements immediately after READing. This is called mirror printing. It helps discover errors in the program which cause the data to be misinterpreted.*

first statement of the program, keeping one hand free to write values into the 'memory cells' as necessary. We analyzed the effect of the statement our finger was on. If it altered a memory cell value, we crossed out any old value we had for that cell and wrote in the new one. If it was a control statement like

```
GO TO 10
```

we moved our finger appropriately. After a while we found the problem. By the time we got to statement 20, N had the value 3.0. even though there were only two brands of detergent in the data. Our program was counting the end-of-data card!

> **walkthrough:** *checking the logic of a program by "playing computer" and going through the program one statement at a time recording the results of executing the statements. This is used to locate errors in program logic.*

Tracking Down Errors

Now that our attention was drawn to it, we were embarrassed to discover that our loop wasn't even one of the recommended forms (pre-test or post-test). We made the loop a pre-test READ loop by moving the statement

```
N = N+1.0
```

and its associated comment so that they appeared immediately *after* the IF test, not before. This had the twin benefits of making the loop into a pre-test form and of allowing 1.0 to be added to N only when the data represented a legitimate detergent price and weight.

We looked our program over carefully, decided to add another WRITE statement

```
WRITE(6,3000) N
3000 FORMAT(' ', F5.0,' BRANDS WERE IN THE SURVEY')
```

and ran it again. Notice that if we'd been awake enough to use this more informative WRITE statement to begin with, we would have been able to find the problem more quickly.

The computer is a "great humbler." It seems that no matter how careful you are, there will always be bugs in your programs. Some large business programs run for years with undetected bugs in them only to "bomb out" at the least expected moment. Learning to avoid bugs requires great patience and great self-control. Like a master craftsman, a good programmer produces well-thought-out, finely finished work.

> *For a number of good ideas about how to improve your programs, make them more readable, more easily debugged, more efficient, and so forth, see the little book Elements of Programming Style by B. W. Kernighan and P. J. Plauger, McGraw-Hill, 1974.*

PROBLEMS 5

There are no problems provided for you to debug since you will get *plenty* of experience in the problems of other chapters.

6 ARRAYS

Chapter Objectives: After studying this chapter, you should be able to:

- Describe how arrays are named and how values are stored in and retrieved from the memory cells of an array.
- Describe how arrays allow you to write programs which would be unmanageable in size without them.
- Write programs using one-, two-, and three-dimensional arrays.
- Debug programs which contain arrays.
- Read and write arrays using implied do lists.
- Perform a simple business simulation with the computer.

Section 6 1

Using Arrays

You already have a repertoire of Fortran instructions sufficient to describe all possible computations. Many computations, however, would require programs of unmanageable size if you used only your present stock of instructions. For this reason, all programming languages incorporate some way of referring to a large number of memory cells simply and concisely. In Fortran, **arrays** are provided for this purpose. The following problem is one in which the use of arrays leads to great simplification.

Let's suppose we have written to the governors of 11 western states inquiring about sales tax. While we are waiting for replies, we will prepare a program to analyze the data we hope to receive. Given 11 data cards, each of which contains the name of a state and its sales tax rate, we want our program to list those states where the sales tax is below average.

We can compute the average from the data easily enough. The problem arises from the necessity to print certain parts of the data after the average is computed and, therefore, after the data cards have all been read. Since there is no standard way to reread the cards, we must save the information in memory cells. Figure 6 1 1 describes our general strategy. Our program appears below.

VERBAL DESCRIPTION

Get sales tax data.

Compute average.

Print states with below average
sales tax.

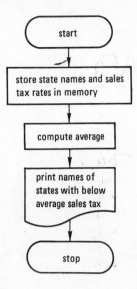

Figure 6 1 1

```
COMMENT--PROGRAM TO LIST THE WESTERN STATES WITH
C        BELOW AVERAGE SALES TAX RATES.
      INTEGER S1,S2,S3,S4,S5,S6,S7,S8,S9,S10,S11
      REAL T1,T2,T3,T4,T5,T6,T7,T8,T9,T10,T11,AVE
C     STORE DATA
      READ(5,1000) S1 ,T1
      READ(5,1000) S2 ,T2
      READ(5,1000) S3 ,T3
      READ(5,1000) S4 ,T4
      READ(5,1000) S5 ,T5
      READ(5,1000) S6 ,T6
      READ(5,1000) S7 ,T7
      READ(5,1000) S8 ,T8
      READ(5,1000) S9 ,T9
      READ(5,1000) S10,T10
      READ(5,1000) S11,T11
 1000 FORMAT(A2,F7.0)
C
      AVE=(T1+T2+T3+T4+T5+T6+T7+T8+T9+T10+T11)/11.0
C
      WRITE(6,2000)
 2000 FORMAT('1STATES WITH BELOW AVERAGE SALES TAX'/)
      IF (T1  .LE. AVE) WRITE(6,3000) S1
      IF (T2  .LE. AVE) WRITE(6,3000) S2
      IF (T3  .LE. AVE) WRITE(6,3000) S3
      IF (T4  .LE. AVE) WRITE(6,3000) S4
      IF (T5  .LE. AVE) WRITE(6,3000) S5
      IF (T6  .LE. AVE) WRITE(6,3000) S6
      IF (T7  .LE. AVE) WRITE(6,3000) S7
      IF (T8  .LE. AVE) WRITE(6,3000) S8
      IF (T9  .LE. AVE) WRITE(6,3000) S9
      IF (T10 .LE. AVE) WRITE(6,3000) S10
      IF (T11 .LE. AVE) WRITE(6,3000) S11
 3000 FORMAT(' ',A2)
      STOP
      END
```

data

```
WA  0.045
ID  0.03
MT  0.00
OR  0.04
WY  0.03
CA  0.06
NV  0.03
UT  0.04
CO  0.03
AZ  0.04
NM  0.04
```

output

```
STATES WITH BELOW AVERAGE SALES TAX

ID
MT
WY
NV
CO
```

As you can see, the program's input section has 11 almost identical statements. So does the output section. Normally we'd like to make a loop out of such a section, but in this case we have no way of making the statements identical so that we can replace them with a loop. To do so, we'd have to refer to the same memory cells in each READ, and this would continually wipe out previously recorded information. We'd wind up with only one state's sales tax rate in memory. What we need is some way to change the memory cell used by the READ statement without changing the READ statement itself. We can do this by using arrays.

An **array** is a group of memory cells which all have the same name. They are distinguished by a **subscript** or **index** which is associated with the name. In a program the name and the subscript are associated by enclosing the subscript in parentheses to the right of the name. In our example we will need two arrays, each of which is a group of 11 memory cells, one group for the names of the states, and the other for the taxes. Then, instead of dealing with the 11 separate memory cells S1, S2, S3 and so on, we will use the array S and refer to S(1), S(2), S(3), and so on.

S1 [ ]	S
S2 [ ]	S(1)
S3 [ ]	S(2)
S4 [ ]	S(3)
S5 [ ]	S(4)
S6 [ ]	S(5)
S7 [ ]	S(6)
S8 [ ]	S(7)
S9 [ ]	S(8)
S10 [ ]	S(9)
S11 [ ]	S(10)
	S(11)

Of course, if our only option were to write S(5) instead of S5 or S(7) instead of S7, nothing would be gained. The advantage is that we can write the subscript as an *arithmetic expression* whose value can change from time to time as the program runs. Instead of writing

```
READ(5,1000) S1,T1
```

we will write

```
READ(5,1000) S(N),T(N)
```

where N is an INTEGER memory cell whose value will be 1 the first time the computer executes the READ statement, 2 the second time, and so on.

Arrays used in a program must be declared at the beginning of the program. Like memory cell declarations, **array declarations** establish the name and the type of information the array will contain—INTEGER, REAL, or whatever. (An array may contain only one type of data; no single array can contain both INTEGER and REAL numbers, for example.) In addition, an array declaration must specify the number of memory cells in the array by placing that number in parentheses after the array name. This part of an array declaration is known as the **length declarator** and should not be confused with a subscript. A subscript designates a particular memory cell in an array. A length declarator establishes the *number* of memory cells in the entire array.

---

array declarator

form
> name (*len*)
> *name* is a Fortran identifier (up to six characters)
> *len* is an unsigned INTEGER constant (but not zero)

meaning
> establishes an array named *name* with *len* memory cells

example
```
INTEGER QUANT(100), PARTNO(100), BACKOR
REAL PRICE(100), TOTAL, COST
```

These statements establish three arrays to contain various kinds of information. In addition, the types of three simple memory cells are established. Array declarators and memory cell declarators may be mixed in the same declaration statement.

Together, the name and length declarator make up an **array declarator**. Array declarators are placed in type statements (INTEGER statements, REAL statements, and the like) either interspersed with ordinary memory cell declarations or alone.

An **array element** (a memory cell in an array) is used in the same ways that other memory cells are used, but each reference to an array element must include both the array name and the subscript. The elements are always numbered starting

> *array element: a memory cell in an array*

from 1. The last element's subscript, therefore, is the same as the number of elements in the array.

Using arrays, we can rewrite our sales tax program in a simpler way still following the plan of Figure 6 1 1.

```
COMMENT--PROGRAM TO LIST THE WESTERN STATES WITH
C       BELOW AVERAGE SALES TAX RATES.
        INTEGER S(11)
        REAL T(11), AVE
        INTEGER N
C VARIABLES:
C       S--ARRAY OF STATE ABBREVIATIONS
C       T--ARRAY OF SALES TAX PERCENTAGES
C       STORE DATA
        N=1
 100    READ(5,1000) S(N),T(N)
 1000   FORMAT(A2,F7.0)
        N=N+1
        IF (N .LE. 11) GO TO 100
C
        AVE=(T(1) + T(2) + T(3) + T(4) + T(5) + T(6) +
     +      T(7) + T(8) + T(9) + T(10) + T(11))/11.0
C
        WRITE(6,2000)
 2000   FORMAT('1STATES WITH BELOW AVERAGE SALES TAX'/)
        N=1
 300    IF (T(N) .LE. AVE) WRITE(6,3000) S(N)
 3000   FORMAT(' ',A2)
        N = N+1
        IF (N .LE. 11) GO TO 300
        STOP
        END
```

data

```
WA 0.045
ID 0.03
MT 0.00
OR 0.04
WY 0.03
CA 0.06
NV 0.03
UT 0.04
CO 0.03
AZ 0.04
NM 0.04
```

output

`STATES WITH BELOW AVERAGE SALES TAX`

```
ID
MT
WY
NV
CO
```

---

subscripts

Many Fortran compilers will accept any INTEGER *valued expression as an array subscript. However, some compilers will accept only ANSI standard subscripts made up of constants and simple* INTEGER *variables in the following forms.*

k

v *c and k are unsigned*

$v - k$ INTEGER *constants*

$v + k$

$c*v$ *v is an unsubscripted*

$c*v - k$ INTEGER *memory cell name*

$c*v + k$

Arrays may have their types established *implicitly* in the same way memory cells may be implicitly typed. In this situation, we still need to establish the size of our array. The DIMENSION statement provides us with a way to declare an array. It is used primarily with implicit typing since it declares an array without naming the type. We could, however, declare the type only in a mode declaration and then use a DIMENSION to set up the array.

DIMENSION statement

form

    DIMENSION *list*

    list is a list of array declarators like those which may be used in type statements.

meaning

    Establishes array with names and lengths declared in *list*. Implicit types are assumed unless they have been established by previous declaration.

restriction

    Array length declarators can't appear more than once in a program unit.

examples

```
DIMENSION AB(10), C(3), P(12)
DIMENSION SALES(37)
```

```
REAL SALES              INTEGER PART(100)
DIMENSION SALES(100)    DIMENSION PART(100)
```

EXERCISES 6 1

1 Which of the following are legal declarations?
```
REAL A(10)
INTEGER A(13-2)
INTEGER A(I)
REAL A(150) , BOK(3472)
REAL X(15.0)
```

2 Under what conditions would B(I) and B(J) refer to the same element of array B?

3 Assuming that B is an array of ten elements and I and J are memory cells with the values 3 and 7 respectively, which of the following statements are legal? If not, why not?
```
B(3) = B(I)
B(1) = B(I-1)
B(J) = B(2*I)
B(4) = B(J-1) + B(I*J-21)
B(2*I) = B(J+4)
B(1.7) = 0
```

4 Suppose that, instead of wanting to list only the states whose sales tax is below average, we had wanted to make a list of the states and their sales taxes and print the average sales tax at the end of the listings. If the data provided were the same as that of this section, would we need to use arrays to write the program?

Section 6 2

A More Useful Solution

We were probably not being realistic when we wrote the program of Section 6 1 because we assumed that all 11 governors would reply to our letter. A program which would still work with only a partial response would be more useful. Fortunately, such a program is easy to write now that we know about arrays. (Without arrays the program becomes much more difficult—see the exercises.)

The main problem we face is that we can no longer compute the average by summing and dividing by 11.0. The program itself will have to keep track of the number of responses so that it can divide the sum by the appropriate number. So the program can recognize the end of the input loop, we'll add a special data card containing the characters **.

Figure 6 2 1 depicts the general plan of our revised program. With the exception that it keeps track of the number of data items, our new plan doesn't differ much from the old one in Figure 6 1 1.

Study the new program carefully; it is typical of many that you will write in the future. An important point to notice is that the memory cell N is used to count the number of state governors who responded to our question. The com-

VERBAL DESCRIPTION

Store data in memory, keeping track of the number of data items.

Compute average.

Print states with below average sales tax.

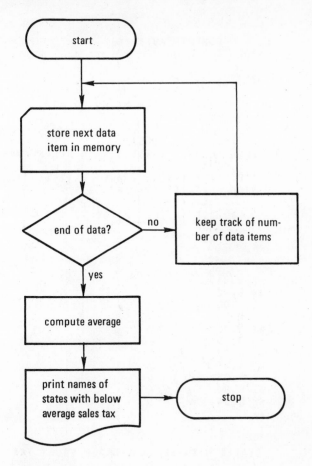

Figure 6 2 1

puter performs the READ statement (statement 100) many times, but it is always true that just prior to a time when the READ statement is performed, the value of N is the number of governors' responses which have already been read. In addition, since N is not increased until after the test for the end of the data, the value of N when the computer reaches statement 200 is the total number of governors' responses. Thus the count N does not include the special "**" card; it counts only response cards. This section's exercises help explain other details of the program.

```
COMMENT--PROGRAM TO LIST STATES WITH BELOW AVERAGE SALES TAX
        INTEGER S(12),N,K,FIN
        REAL T(12),AVE,SUM
      . DATA FIN/2H**/
C
C       STORE DATA
        N=0
  100   READ(5,1000) S(N+1),T(N+1)
  1000    FORMAT(A2,F7.0)
          IF (S(N+1) .EQ. FIN) GO TO 200
          N=N+1
          GO TO 100
```

```
C
C     COMPUTE AVERAGE
 200  SUM=0.0
      K=1
 210  SUM=SUM+T(K)
        K=K+1
        IF (K .LE. N) GO TO 210
      AVE=SUM/N
C
      WRITE(6,2000)
2000  FORMAT('1STATES WITH BELOW AVERAGE SALES TAX'/)
      K=1
 310  IF (T(K) .LE. AVE) WRITE(6,3100) S(K),T(K)
3100  FORMAT(' ',A2,F7.3)
        K=K+1
        IF (K .LE. N) GO TO 310
      STOP
      END
```

data
```
   WA 0.045
   ID 0.03
   MT 0.00
   OR 0.04
   WY 0.03
   CA 0.06
   NV 0.03
   UT 0.04
   CO 0.03
   AZ 0.04
   NM 0.04
   **
```

output
```
      STATES WITH BELOW AVERAGE SALES TAX

   ID    .030
   MT   0.000
   WY    .030
   NV    .030
   CO    .030
```

EXERCISES 6 2

1 Why did we allocate 12 memory cells to the arrays instead of 11?

2 Show how the running sum could be incorporated into the input loop to avoid the loop in the section where the average is computed.

3 If none of the governors respond and we run our program with only the "**" card, something bad will happen. What?

4 What changes need to be made in the program to allow all 50 states to be included in the data?

5 Suppose, by some fluke, we give the program more than 11 response cards. What will happen? How can we change the program to avoid this problem? (This is a very important way of making the program more robust.)

> *robust: a program is more robust if it functions properly given a wider range of input values*

6 Write a program which does the same thing as the one in this section without using arrays. (Note: This is a lot of work. Why not just look at the answer?)

7 Rewrite the program of Section 4 5 so that it uses an array in place of the memory cells BAR0, BAR1, BAR2, BAR3, BAR4, and BAR5.

Section 6 3*

Some Misconceptions to Avoid

> This section may be skipped without loss of continuity.

Arrays confuse many novice programmers. The following list may help you avoid some common mistakes.

1 Don't confuse the subscript value with the array element value. The value of the element A(5) usually has nothing to do with the number 5.

	A
A(1)	−4.7
A(2)	192.1
A(3)	3.9
A(4)	485.3
A(5)	−19.1
A(6)	0.00

2 When a memory cell name is used in a subscript, it is only the *value* of that memory cell which is important; its name is irrelevant. At one point in a program, we may refer to A(I), and at another point in the same program we may refer to A(J). In each case we are dealing with the same array. In fact, we may even be referencing the same element of the array depending on what values I and J have at the times of the array references.

3 For the same reason, a program may reference both A(I) and B(I). That is, the same memory cell may be used as a subscript in referencing two (or more) different arrays. Again it is the value of the subscript which counts, not its name.

4 Don't use arrays when you don't need them. Profligate use often results in unclear, inefficient programs.

5 In general, Fortran can deal with only one element of an array at a time. For example if A is an array of ten elements, then the statement

```
IF ( A .NE. 0 ) GO TO 100
```

does not test all ten elements of A. In fact, it isn't even a legal statement. If the intention is to transfer to statement 100 in case some element of A is nonzero, then each element must be tested individually as in the loop below.

```
      I = 1
10    IF (A(I) .NE. 0)  GO TO 100
      I = I+1
      IF (I .LE. 10)  GO TO 10
```

6   Remember: In Fortran, the number of memory cells in an array may not be changed in your program at execution time. If you don't know exactly how much room you will need (as we didn't in Section 6 2), you must declare the array larger than you will actually need, and let your program keep track of how many memory cells it is using.

Section 6 4

Debugging Arrays

One lousy bug in an array can create a mountain of errors before you know it. When you use arrays in your program, you can greatly reduce the number of statements required to write the program. This feature tends to work in the exact opposite direction when it comes to creating error messages. One simple error can cause pages of error messages. **Error cascade**, which you learned about in Chapter 5, is particularly prevalent among array errors. For example, an error in a type declaration statement such as

```
INTEGER QUANT(200, SHIP
```

which was supposed to set the size of the array will result in an error message each time (yes, each time) you use the array name in your program. At *compile-time*, the compiler won't know that QUANT is supposed to be an array. The one simple mistake in your declaration causes this cascade of errors. Fortunately, it is likely that some of the error messages in this cascade caused by the erroneous declaration will suggest the possibility of an undeclared array, a good hint toward what went wrong. In our example, there is a good chance your computer would write an error message something like

```
ILLEGAL SYNTAX
```

or

```
RIGHT PARENTHESIS MISSING
```

or

```
ILLEGAL VARIABLE SUBSCRIPT
```

If your computer gives you an error message such as

```
UNDEFINED ARRAY
```

or

`MISSING SUBSCRIPT`

you have a pretty good clue to your error. An error message which may really throw you is

`UNDEFINED FUNCTION`

How can this be an array error? You will recall from Chapter 4 that we wrote FUNCTION references like EXP(X) and IABS(N-10). They look like arrays. The argument is very similar to our subscript for an array. In Chapter 8, you will learn more about FUNCTIONs and understand still further how the compiler could get confused. For now, just remember that the *undefined FUNCTION* error message could mean you somehow failed to set up an array in your declaration statement, and you don't have an error in a FUNCTION at all. Although the error messages we have described depend on your particular computer, most systems produce similar error messages.

An execution-time error which you might encounter in using arrays is

`SUBSCRIPT OUT OF RANGE`

This indicates that a subscript you calculated in your program is either too large (i.e., bigger than the declared length of the array) or is zero or negative. You've either made a mistake in calculating the subscript or you didn't declare a long enough array. If this should occur, you might try inserting WRITE statements to print out the value of the *subscript* just before the statements using the array in your program.

Arrays are not immune to the error conditions described in Chapter 5. The conditions and examples described above are things that can happen to arrays *in addition to* those discussed in the previous chapter. Don't let this disillusion you with arrays. All you need to do is be careful with them when you use them, and they will save you a great deal of effort in writing your programs.

Section 6 5

Using Arrays in Simulation

Arrays provide a convenient way to keep track of the occurrence of events in simulating various business processes. Let's suppose you have just taken a job as manager of the Golden Flick Drive-In Movie Theater. You are considering making Wednesday night Dollar-a-Car night. Before you make this decision, you would like to analyze the potential number of people who would attend your Wednesday night showing. You talk with several people and decide you will try to analyze attendance using simulation. After some discussion with your cashier, you determine that the number of people arriving in each car would be from one to six. You also conclude that the chance a car would have one person in it is the same as if two, three, four, five, or six people were in the car. That is, the chance or probability of a car having one through six people in it is the same. Figure 6 5 1 indicates the chance or probability (on a scale from 0 to 1) of the number of people in each car.

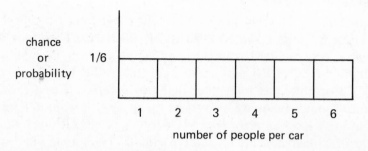

Figure 6 5 1

You expect about one hundred cars to show up for your Dollar-a-Car night. What you would like to know is how many cars have one person, two people, three people and so on. In simulating the arrival of one hundred cars, you need to simulate the arrival of each car individually. The number of people in an individual car would be a number from one to six. The result for that car can then be added or tallied into the total for all the cars with that number of people in them. An array makes a great place to tally these results. To clarify our simulation, let's set up the array PEOPLE.

PEOPLE(1)

PEOPLE(2)

PEOPLE(3)

PEOPLE(4)

PEOPLE(5)

PEOPLE(6)

Now, PEOPLE(1) will contain a number which is the sum of the number of cars which have arrived containing one person. If we simulate the arrival of 100 cars the sum of PEOPLE(1) through PEOPLE(6) would be 100.

Let's consider how we'll conduct our simulation. A car arrives and we count the number of people in it and record that number in the corresponding location. The next car arrives and we repeat the process. We continue until the arrivals of 100 cars have been simulated.

How might you perform this simulation manually? You could take six slips of paper and number them 1 through 6. Then you could put them in a hat. For each arrival you would pull a slip out of the hat, record the result, and put the slip back in the hat. Or you could get a die and roll it. Whatever number came up would represent the number of people in the car.

Figure 6 5 2 depicts the general plan for a program that would keep track of each car and simulate the arrival of 100 cars.

VERBAL DESCRIPTION
Initialize the array to zero, since no cars have arrived.

Loop: A car arrives and the number of people in it is determined.

Tally the people.

Check to see if 100 cars have arrived. Repeat loop if necessary.

Print the results for 100 cars.

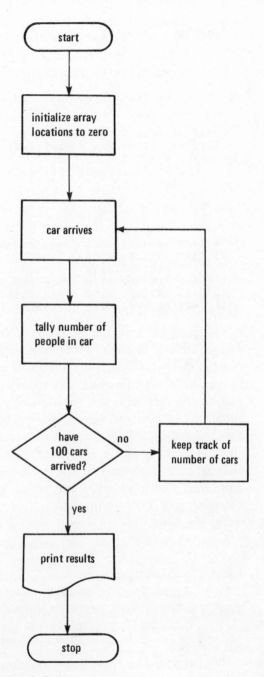

Figure 6 5 2

```
COMMENT:   PROGRAM TO SIMULATE THE ARRIVAL OF 100 CARS
C          ON DOLLAR-A-CAR NIGHT
       INTEGER PEOPLE(6), CARS, N
C                                              INITIALIZE COUNTERS
       N = 1
100    PEOPLE(N) = 0
       N = N+1
       IF (N .LE. 6)  GO TO 100
C                                              SIMULATE ARRIVALS
       CARS = 1
200    N = INT(RANF(0.0)*6.0) + 1
C                                              A CAR WITH
C                                     "N" PEOPLE HAS ARRIVED
       PEOPLE(N) = PEOPLE(N) + 1
       CARS = CARS + 1
       IF (CARS .LE. 100)  GO TO 200
C                                              PRINT RESULTS
       N = 1
300    WRITE(6,3000) PEOPLE(N), N
3000   FORMAT(1X,I3, ' CARS ARRIVED WITH', I2, ' PERSON(S)')
       N = N+1
       IF (N .LE. 6)  GO TO 300
       STOP
       END
```

output

```
14 CARS ARRIVED WITH 1 PERSON(S)
16 CARS ARRIVED WITH 2 PERSON(S)
15 CARS ARRIVED WITH 3 PERSON(S)
21 CARS ARRIVED WITH 4 PERSON(S)
16 CARS ARRIVED WITH 5 PERSON(S)
18 CARS ARRIVED WITH 6 PERSON(S)
```

The program uses the built-in FUNCTION RANF to simulate the number of people arriving in a car. You might notice how we used it to obtain an INTEGER number from 1 through 6. You could use the same scheme for any other range of integer numbers you would like to create. Look again at how we kept track of the number of cars with their respective number of people. There are many similar situations in business where you might want to develop a simulation. Some of these would include the arrival of customers at a bank, supermarket, or hospital. Or, you might consider the arrival of ships, barges, trucks, trains, or airplanes. The chances or probabilities of the different occurrences may not be equal. It may be more likely that two ships will arrive than that three will arrive. In that case, the outcome is a little more difficult to determine but the tallying of the results works the same.

EXERCISES 6 5

1 If you allow vans and station wagons on Dollar-a-Car night, they may have more than six people in them. Change the program so it would simulate 1 through 12 people per vehicle with the chance or probability of each equal, as in our present program.

2 How could you change the program for an equal chance of 0 through 6 people in each car? What problem does this present in tallying results in your array?

Section 6 6

Arrays with Two Subscripts

t	w	o							a	y
							r			
d	i	m	e	n	s		r			
				i	a					
				o						
				n	a	l				

There are situations in which it is convenient to have arrays with more than one subscript. For instance, imagine that you work for a politician and you want to analyze patterns of support for your candidate. You have block-by-block results of preliminary polls taken by your volunteers and would like to store your data in a convenient form. An array with two subscripts works beautifully here since you can let the value of the first subscript represent the north-south position of the block, the second subscript represent the east-west position, and the value stored in each memory cell be the percent of positive responses in that block (see Figure 6 6 1).

An array with two subscripts is usually called a **two-dimensional array**. The name of a memory cell in a two-dimensional array is simply the array name followed by a parenthesized list of two subscripts separated by a comma. The memory cells with the names POLL(2,4) and POLL(6,5) are indicated in Figure 6 6 1. Just as with one-dimensional arrays, dimensions must be given at the beginning of our program. The lowest legal value of a subscript is 1, so all we need in the declaration is the maximum subscript value. In our case the declaration

```
REAL POLL(7,5)
```

would be appropriate since we want to be able to use all memory cells from POLL(1,1) (the top left memory cell in Figure 6 6 1) to POLL(7,5) (the bottom right memory cell). We'll give a precise summary of all types of array declarations in Section 6 8. Until then, we will make do with this informal description.

It is often convenient to think of a two-dimensional array as a grid of boxes arranged in rows and columns, as we have pictured the array POLL in Figure 6 6 1. The first subscript is customarily thought of as the row number and the second as the column number. Thus the declaration says how many rows and columns the array has. (We should emphasize, however, that this is only a custom. You can think of subscripts in any arrangement you like.) Arrays in which the number of rows is the same as the number of columns are thought of as **square arrays**. Those like the one we're using here in our polling problem, in which the numbers of rows and columns are different, can be visualized as **rectangular arrays**.

Storing our poll data in a two-dimensional array makes it easy to analyze the data in a number of different ways. For instance, let's compute the average

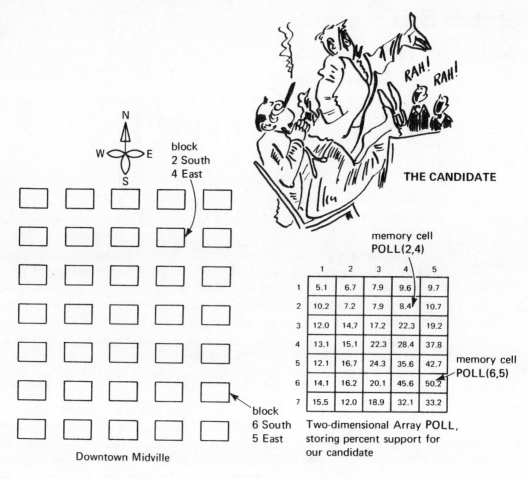

block
2 South
4 East

memory cell
POLL(2,4)

THE CANDIDATE

RAH! RAH!

	1	2	3	4	5
1	5.1	6.7	7.9	9.6	9.7
2	10.2	7.2	7.9	8.4	10.7
3	12.0	14.7	17.2	22.3	19.2
4	13.1	15.1	22.3	28.4	37.8
5	12.1	16.7	24.3	35.6	42.7
6	14.1	16.2	20.1	45.6	50.2
7	15.5	12.0	18.9	32.1	33.2

memory cell
POLL(6,5)

Downtown Midville

block
6 South
5 East

Two-dimensional Array POLL,
storing percent support for
our candidate

Figure 6 6 1

support for our candidate in the eastern blocks as opposed to his support in the west. This amounts to looking at the average of the numbers in each column of the array. To compute these averages, we will use a loop which cycles across the columns. For each column we have to sum the elements, and to do this we'll use another loop nested inside the column loop which scans down a column. Figure 6 6 2 shows the overall plan. We've left out the details of computing the sum for two reasons: it makes the plan easier to follow, and you are already familiar with the process of computing sums. The program follows.

If an array has ROW rows and COLUMN columns, then the number of elements in each row is COLUMN and the number of elements in each column is ROW.

VERBAL DESCRIPTION

Store results of poll in memory.

Compute and print average along each north-south street.

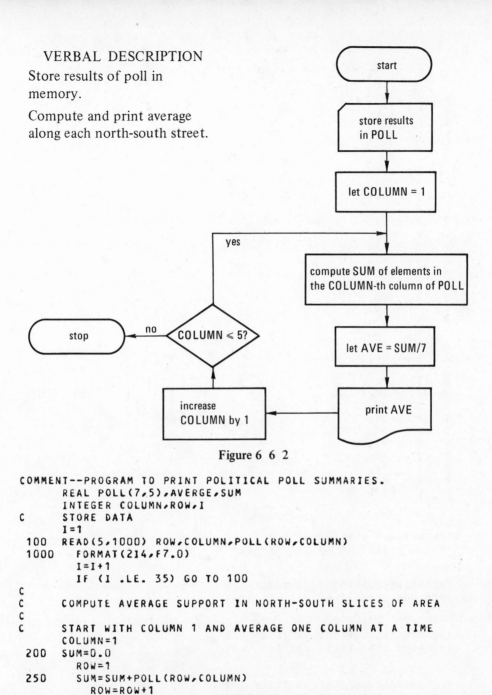

Figure 6 6 2

```
COMMENT--PROGRAM TO PRINT POLITICAL POLL SUMMARIES.
      REAL POLL(7,5),AVERGE,SUM
      INTEGER COLUMN,ROW,I
C     STORE DATA
      I=1
 100  READ(5,1000) ROW,COLUMN,POLL(ROW,COLUMN)
 1000    FORMAT(2I4,F7.0)
      I=I+1
      IF (I .LE. 35) GO TO 100
C
C     COMPUTE AVERAGE SUPPORT IN NORTH-SOUTH SLICES OF AREA
C
C     START WITH COLUMN 1 AND AVERAGE ONE COLUMN AT A TIME
      COLUMN=1
 200  SUM=0.0
      ROW=1
 250  SUM=SUM+POLL(ROW,COLUMN)
      ROW=ROW+1
      IF (ROW .LE. 7) GO TO 250
C     FINISHED SUMMING COLUMN--COMPUTE AVERAGE
      AVERGE=SUM/7.0
      WRITE(6,2000) COLUMN
 2000    FORMAT(' THE AVERAGE SUPPORT IN SLICE ',I3)
      WRITE(6,3000) AVERGE
 3000    FORMAT(' FROM THE WEST IS',F7.3,' PER CENT'//)
      COLUMN=COLUMN+1
      IF (COLUMN .LE. 5) GO TO 200
      STOP
      END
```

data

```
1    1     7.
1    2    40.
1    3    91.
1    4    18.
5    4    25.
5    5    24.
2    3    44.
3    4    75.
3    5    28.
6    1    93.
6    2    94.
2    4    99.
4    1    27.
4    2    12.
6    3    45.
6    4    40.
6    5    57.
4    5     1.
4    3    88.
4    4    79.
1    5    81.
2    5    52.
7    1    33.
2    1    88.
3    1    44.
5    1    24.
3    2    79.
5    2    82.
3    3    31.
7    2    90.
5    3    52.
2    2    68.
7    3    74.
7    4    86.
7    5    37.
```

output

```
THE AVERAGE SUPPORT IN SLICE    1
FROM THE WEST IS 45.143 PER CENT


THE AVERAGE SUPPORT IN SLICE    2
FROM THE WEST IS 66.429 PER CENT


THE AVERAGE SUPPORT IN SLICE    3
FROM THE WEST IS 60.714 PER CENT


THE AVERAGE SUPPORT IN SLICE    4
FROM THE WEST IS 60.286 PER CENT


THE AVERAGE SUPPORT IN SLICE    5
FROM THE WEST IS 40.000 PER CENT
```

As you can see, the way the results are organized in the two-dimensional array POLL makes all kinds of regional analysis of the data easy.

1   Which of the following are legal declarations?

```
INTEGER A(100,3), B(3,100), I
REAL QRT(3,49)
REAL X(N,100)
```

2   Assuming the declarations of exercise 1 have been made, mark the statements below which are not legal.

```
A(4,2) = 0
B(4,2) = 0
A(3,50) = 0
I = 10
```

3   The political poll summary program has a bad feature—suppose one of the data cards gets left out by accident! Revise the data entry part of the flowchart so that if a data value doesn't appear for a particular block the value 0.0 is used and so that if a block appears twice (due to a typing error, for example) the program prints a warning.

Section 6 7

Input and Output of Arrays

By now you have had a fair amount of experience printing out arrays. Perhaps you have noticed that in each WRITE statement, you had to know, while writing the program, exactly how many elements of an array you wanted to print. If the number of array elements you wanted to print depended on a computation in the program, you had to write a loop and print one element at a time until you had printed all the appropriate elements (as in the example in Section 6 2). This doesn't cause any particular problems if you want each element on a separate line, but if you want them on the same line, you're in for a lot of work. To eliminate this extra effort, there is an alternative form of the I/O list.

Previously we said that the list in a READ or WRITE statement must be made up of variable names separated by commas. Until now we haven't really needed anything else. However, the list can be slightly more complicated. In addition to variable names, it can also contain repetitive lists called **implied do lists**.

An implied do list is a list of variable names (possibly subscripted) followed by indexing information which specifies how many times to repeat the variables in the implied do list (that is, how many times to "do" the list) and what values of the index to use in these repetitions. Before we describe the exact form of an implied do list, let's look at an example or two.

Suppose we want to print out all the values in the array A from A(1) to A(N), where N is a memory cell containing some INTEGER. Instead of writing a loop:

```
        I=1
50   WRITE(5,1000) A(I)
        I=I+1
        IF (I .LE. N) GO TO 50
```

we can simply put

```
WRITE(5,1000) (A(I), I=1,N)
```

This is not only shorter to write and easier to read but has the added benefit of commanding the computer to try to put all the values on one line. If there are too many to fit on one line, the computer will automatically go on to the next (see Section 4 8). In the case of the loop, each value goes on a separate line because each time the computer performs a WRITE statement, it begins on a new line.

An implied do list doesn't have to be exactly like the one we have written above. The list section can contain more than one element and the indexing section doesn't have to start the index at 1 and increase by 1 each time; it can start at any positive INTEGER value and increase at each stage by any positive INTEGER value. What's more, these starting and increment values can be specified by variables instead of constants. For example, the following WRITE statement's implied do list is legal.

```
WRITE(5,7000) (L,A(L),B(L), L=M,N,K)
```

It says to set L equal to M, print out the value of L, then the value of A(L), then B(L), and then to increase L by K and print L, A(L), B(L), and so on. It keeps repeating as long as L isn't larger than N. If we had known while writing the program that M would be 2, N would be 7, and K would be 3, we could have gotten the same result by writing

```
I1=2
I2=5
WRITE(5,7000) I1,A(2),B(2),I2,A(5),B(5)
```

---

implied do list

forms
  ($list$, $v = s, b$)
  ($list$, $v = s, b, i$)

  $list$ is any legal I/O list
  v is an unsubscripted INTEGER memory cell name
  s, b, and i are nonzero unsigned INTEGER constants or unsubscripted INTEGER memory cell names (with positive values)

meaning
  describes an I/O list consisting of consecutive repetitions of *list*
  for each value of v starting at s and incrementing by i as long
  as v doesn't exceed b (the increment is 1 if i is omitted)

examples
```
READ(5,1000)  (WAGE(I),  I=1,10,3)
WRITE(6,3050) (EMPNO(K-1),  K=2,N)
WRITE(6,2000) (PART,COST(PART,FCOST),  PART=1,NPARTS)
```

What happens if the upper bound in the indexing section is smaller than the starting value? The ANSI standards simply call it illegal and leave it at that. Most versions of Fortran will accept it and do this: print the list section for the starting value of the index, and that's all. This isn't a case you should worry about excessively, but it might happen and it pays to be vaguely aware of the consequences.

Note that the general form allows **nesting** of implied do lists. That is, one implied do list can be inside another. The effect of nesting is to cause the inside implied do list to be completely repeated with every repetition of the outside implied do list. The following examples should help clarify the effects of this nesting.

```
WRITE(6,1000) C, (B, (A, I=1,3), J=1,2), D
                is equivalent to
WRITE(6,1000) C,  B, A,A,A,  B, A,A,A,  D


WRITE(6,2000) ((A(I,J),J=1,3),I=1,2)
                is equivalent to
WRITE(6,2000)A(1,1),A(1,2),A(1,3),A(2,1),A(2,2),A(2,3)
```

As you can see in the first example, the *list* section of an implied do list does not need to involve the index. It may or it may not, at your option.

---

array transmission: Entire arrays may be transmitted to output or filled from data cards by placing the array name alone, without subscripts, in an I/O list. The order of transmission is the order in which the array's memory cells are stored in the machine.

```
INTEGER AGE,SEX,NAME(3)
READ(5,1000) AGE,SEX,NAME
```

is
equivalent
to

```
INTEGER AGE,SEX,NAME(3)
READ(5,1000) AGE,SEX,NAME(1),NAME(2),NAME(3)
```

Implied do lists may also be used in READ statements. They order input variables in the same way that they order output variables. You will get a chance to use some implied do lists in READ statements in the exercises. Here's one last example using implied do lists.

In the bar graph example (Section 4 5) our program printed out the size of each bar, but didn't print the bar graph itself. Implied do lists make it very easy to print bar graphs with the bars going across the page because a bar can be "drawn" by repeatedly printing some character.

The program in Section 4 5 READs in distances, figures out which bar to record the occurrence of each distance in, and eventually leaves the totals for each bar in memory cells BAR0, BAR1, BAR2, . . ., BAR5. These statements:

```
      INTEGER COUNT, XCH
      DATA XCH/1HX/
         •
         •
         •
      WRITE(6,5000) (XCH,COUNT=1,BAR0)
 5000 FORMAT(' BAR0:', 100A1)
```

will print BAR0 (the number of distances assigned to that bar) copies of X across
the page. However, we will have a problem if BAR0 has no entries in it. Then,
because of the way implied do lists work, the WRITE statement would be illegal
and the results unpredictable. (On most Fortran systems exactly one X would be
printed.) We'll have to test for the missing bar case separately and execute a different WRITE statement in that case.

```
      IF (BAR0 .LE. 0)  GO TO 510
         WRITE(6,5000) (XCH, COUNT=1,BAR0)
 5000    FORMAT(' BAR0:',100A1)
         GO TO 600
 510     WRITE(6,5000)
 600     •
         •
         •
```

We could insert a sequence of such statements for each of BAR0, BAR1, BAR2,
. . ., BAR 5 in the program of Section 4 5, but that would require a lot of work.
Instead we'll alter the much shorter bar graph program which uses arrays (see
exercise 6 2 7 and answer).

```
COMMENT: MAKE A BAR GRAPH FROM DISTANCE DATA.
         INTEGER BAR(6),NUMB
         REAL DIST
         INTEGER COUNT,XCH,THISB
         DATA XCH/1HX/
C        INITIALIZE BAR HEIGHTS.
         NUMB=1
 10      BAR(NUMB)=0
            NUMB=NUMB+1
            IF (NUMB .LE. 6) GO TO 10
C        READ IN A DISTANCE.  IF IT'S NEGATIVE, THEN
C        THERE ARE NO MORE DISTANCES IN THE DATA.
 20      READ(5,2000) DIST
 2000 FORMAT(F7.0)
         IF (DIST .LT. 0.0) GO TO 200
C        CONVERT THE DISTANCE INTO AN INTEGER (DROP FRACTION)
         NUMB=DIST
C        INCREMENT BAR COUNTER.
         IF (NUMB .LE. 5) GO TO 30
            WRITE(6,2010) DIST
 2010    FORMAT(' DISTANCE ',F7.1,' IS OUT OF RANGE.')
            GO TO 20
 30         BAR(NUMB+1)=BAR(NUMB+1) + 1
            GO TO 20
```

```
C
C     PLOT A BAR GRAPH.
200   NUMB=0
300   THISB=BAR(NUMB+1)
      IF (THISB .LE. 0) GO TO 310
      WRITE(6,3000) NUMB,(XCH,COUNT=1,THISB)
3000  FORMAT(' BAR',I1,':',100A1)
      GO TO 400
310   WRITE(6,3000) NUMB
400   NUMB=NUMB+1
      IF (NUMB .LE. 5) GO TO 300
      STOP
      END
```

data

```
3.9
0.4
5.4
0.9
3.9
17.5
5.6
2.8
4.5
5.8
3.2
5.8
6.9
4.5
3.7
2.9
5.2
-1.0
```

output

```
DISTANCE     17.5 IS OUT OF RANGE.
DISTANCE      6.9 IS OUT OF RANGE.
BAR0:XX
BAR1:
BAR2:XX
BAR3:XXXX
BAR4:XX
BAR5:XXXXX
```

EXERCISES 6 7

1 Without using implied do lists, write I/O statements equivalent to the
   following ones, assuming that M, N, and K have the values 4, 12, and 2
   respectively.

```
READ(5,5000)  (A(J),  J=1,4)
WRITE(6,1000)  (A(J),  J=M,N,K)
WRITE(6,3000)  (A(J),  J=K,N,M)
READ(5,2000)  ( (B(I,J),I=1,M), J=1,K )
WRITE(6,4000)Q,R,(S,B(3,J),A(J),J=1,K),BC,(A(J),J=1,4)
```

2   Using implied do lists, write I/O statements equivalent to the following ones.

```
WRITE (6,1000) A(1), A(2), A(3), A(4), A(5)
WRITE (6,1000) A(2), A(4), A(6), A(8), A(10)
READ (5,2000) B(2,1),B(3,1),B(2,2),B(3,2),B(2,3),B(3,3)
```

3   What is illegal in the following I/O statements?

```
WRITE (6,2000) (A(J), J=1,N-1)
READ (5,7000) (J, A(J), J=1,N)
WRITE (6,1000) (A(J), J=1,C(N))
```

4   What will happen in the bar graph routine if there are more than 100 items in a bar?

5   Suppose that instead of using X's to make bars, you wanted to use numbers—0's for bar 0, 1's for bar 1, etc. What would you change?

Section 6 8

Three-D Arrays

ANSI Fortran arrays may have one, two, or three subscripts. Some versions of Fortran allow more. Problems where arrays with several subscripts are handy come up occasionally, but since you are already familiar with one- and two-dimensional arrays, you should have no problem applying your knowledge to arrays with higher dimensions. Just for fun, we include the following example, in which a three-dimensional array is useful.

The Longlife Insurance Company sells insurance based on an applicant's age, sex, and job classification. The premium per $1,000 of life insurance is organized in a rate table. When you want to know the insurance rate for a particular applicant, you look it up in the table. Insurance rates change from time to time and the table is updated to reflect these changes.

Let's suppose Longlife has hired us to develop a program which will look up the insurance rate and calculate the total premium for an applicant.

The approach we'll take is to use a three-dimensional array to store the rate table. We'll READ in the table each time we want to calculate premiums for a batch of applicants. It is desirable to READ in the rate table so that when a rate change takes place, all we need to do is change the input data and we don't have to make any changes to our program. Each entry in the table will be for a specific age group, sex, and job classification. We'll store the rate table in the array RATE.

Our array RATE will have three subscripts used as follows:

subscript 1 indicates age:

1 for age 18–24
2 for age 25–29
3 for age 30–34
4 for age 35–39
5 for age 40–44
6 for age 45–49
7 for age 50–54
8 for age 55–59

subscript 2 indicates sex:

1 for male
2 for female

subscript 3 indicates job class:

1 for class A
2 for class B
3 for class C

Using this scheme, RATE(6,2,3) would contain the insurance rate per $1,000 for age 45–49 year-old females in job class C. What will RATE(8,1,1) contain?

---

array declarator

form

　　a (*size*)

　　a is an array name
　　size is a list of up to three unsigned INTEGER constants sepa-
　　rated by commas. The declarator appears as an element in the
　　list of a type statement.

meaning

　　Used in a type statement, it declares an array *a*. The array will
　　have as many subscripts as there are elements in the list *size*;
　　each subscript will have a range starting at 1 and running up to
　　the corresponding element of *size*.

examples

```
INTEGER CUSTNO(100), SALES(10,40), NAME(100,3)
REAL PRICE(40,10,2), COST(37)
```

The current rate table for Longlife is:

	MEN			WOMEN		
AGE	CLASS A	CLASS B	CLASS C	CLASS A	CLASS B	CLASS C
18–24	21.00	22.00	24.00	19.00	20.00	22.00
25–29	21.50	22.75	25.00	19.00	20.00	22.50
30–34	22.50	23.75	26.00	20.00	21.25	23.75
35–39	24.00	25.50	28.00	21.50	22.75	25.25
40–44	25.50	27.00	29.50	23.00	24.50	27.00
45–49	27.50	29.50	33.00	25.00	26.50	29.25
50–54	30.00	32.00	35.00	27.50	29.50	32.50
55–59	33.00	35.00	38.00	30.50	32.50	35.50

This rate table is punched into eight cards using the following format.

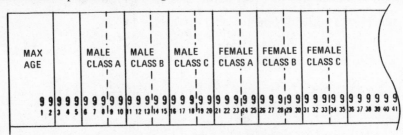

The card for each applicant is entered in the following format.

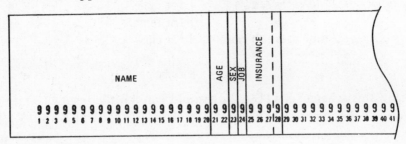

Sex is entered as the code M or F. Job class is A, B, or C. Insurance is entered in thousands of dollars to the nearest tenth (i.e., insurance will be computed in one-hundred-dollar increments).

The following program reads and stores the rate table. Then it reads each applicant card, looks up the insurance rate, calculates the insurance premium, and prints out the name, age, sex, job class, amount of insurance, and insurance premium. After all applicants are processed, the rate table is printed.

```
COMMENT--THIS PROGRAM CALCULATES INSURANCE PREMIUMS BY
C          LOOKING UP AN INSURANCE RATE IN A TABLE
       INTEGER M,F,A,B,C,MAXAGE(8),IAGE,JSEX,KJOB,NAME(5)
       INTEGER AGE,SEX,JOB
       REAL RATE(8,2,3),INSUR,AMOUNT,PREM
       DATA M,F,A,B,C/1HM,1HF,1HA,1HB,1HC/
C                                    READ AND STORE RATE TABLE
       READ(5,1000) (MAXAGE(IAGE),((RATE(IAGE,JSEX,KJOB),
      +              KJOB=1,3),JSEX=1,2),IAGE=1,8)
 1000 FORMAT(I2,3X,6F5.2)
C                                    PRINT REPORT HEADINGS
       WRITE(6,1100)
 1100 FORMAT(1H1,8X,4HNAME,10X,3HAGE,2X,3HSEX,2X,3HJOB,
      +      4X,4HRATE,6X,9HINSURANCE,6X,7HPREMIUM   /)
C                                    READ APPLICANT
  100 READ(5,1200) (NAME(I),I=1,5),AGE,SEX,JOB,INSUR
 1200 FORMAT(5A4,I2,2A1,F4.1)
       IF (AGE.EQ.99) GOTO 600
C                     CHECK APPLICANT'S AGE FOR INSURABILITY
       IF ((AGE.GE.18).AND.(AGE.LE.59)) GOTO 200
       WRITE(6,1300) (NAME(I),I=1,5),AGE
 1300 FORMAT(1X,5A4,3X,I2,35X,11HUNINSURABLE )
       GOTO 100
C                     FIND AGE SUBSCRIPT FOR RATE TABLE
  200 IAGE=0
  300 IAGE=IAGE+1
       IF (MAXAGE(IAGE).LT.AGE) GOTO 300
```

```
C                                           CHECK SEX AND JOB CLASS CODE
        IF ((SEX.EQ.M).OR.(SEX.EQ.F)) GOTO 400
        WRITE(6,1400) (NAME(I),I=1,5)
 1400   FORMAT(1X,5A4,8X,9HSEX ERROR )
        GOTO 100
  400   IF ((JOB.EQ.A).OR.(JOB.EQ.B).OR.(JOB.EQ.C)) GOTO 500
        WRITE(6,1500) (NAME(I),I=1,5)
 1500   FORMAT(1X,5A4,8X,15HJOB CLASS ERROR )
        GOTO 100
C                              FIND SEX SUBSCRIPT FOR RATE TABLE
  500   IF (SEX.EQ.M) JSEX=1
        IF (SEX.EQ.F) JSEX=2
C                         FIND JOB CLASS SUBSCRIPT FOR RATE TABLE
        IF (JOB.EQ.A) KJOB=1
        IF (JOB.EQ.B) KJOB=2
        IF (JOB.EQ.C) KJOB=3
C                                          CALCULATE PREMIUM
        PREM=INSUR*RATE(IAGE,JSEX,KJOB)
C                              CALCULATE INSURANCE IN DOLLARS
        AMOUNT=INSUR*1000.
C                                     PRINT DATA FOR APPLICANT
        WRITE(6,1600) (NAME(I),I=1,5),AGE,SEX,JOB,
       +               RATE(IAGE,JSEX,KJOB),AMOUNT,PREM
 1600   FORMAT(1X,5A4,3X,I2,3X,A1,4X,A1,3X,1H$,F6.2,5X,1H$,
       +        F8.0,5X,1H$,F7.2)
        GOTO 100
C                                          PRINT RATE TABLE
  600 WRITE(6,1700) (MAXAGE(IAGE),((RATE(IAGE,JSEX,KJOB),
       +             KJOB=1,3),JSEX=1,2),IAGE=1,8)
 1700 FORMAT(1H1,//,19X,32HLONGLIFE INSURANCE COMPANY, INC.,
       +        //,30X,10HRATE TABLE,///,12X,
       +        27H------------MEN------------,3X,
       +        27H-----------WOMEN-----------,//,3X,3HAGE,
       +        6X,7HCLASS A,3X,7HCLASS B,3X,7HCLASS C,3X,
       +        7HCLASS A,3X,7HCLASS B,3X,7HCLASS C,//,
       +        (I6,2X,6F10.2,/))
C                                          END OF JOB
        WRITE(6,1800)
 1800 FORMAT(1H1,10HEND OF JOB )
        STOP
        END
```

data

```
   24    21.0022.0024.0019.0020.0022.00
   29    21.5022.7525.0019.0020.0022.50
   34    22.5023.7526.0020.0021.2523.75
   39    24.0025.5028.0021.5022.7525.25
   44    25.5027.0029.5023.0024.5027.00
   49    27.5029.5033.0025.0026.5029.25
   54    30.0032.0035.0027.5029.5032.50
   59    33.0035.0038.0030.5032.5035.50
JOHN Q. SMITH       48MB16.4
PAUL B. BUNYON      24MC20.0
CLARA P. MONROE     55FA 6.0
DUSTY O. RHODE      31MD24.5
JANE G. DOWNS       42FB11.9
JIMMY P. STARTER    52MC40.0
CANDY A. SWEET      26UC12.4
JAMES C. MOORE      36MA50.0
BILLIE T. KIDD      19FA15.0
CHEVY C. FORD       62MA20.0
JUNIOR S. FRYE      15MA 5.0
                    99
```

output

NAME	AGE	SEX	JOB	RATE	INSURANCE	PREMIUM
JOHN Q. SMITH	48	M	B	$ 29.50	$ 16400.	$ 483.80
PAUL B. BUNYON	24	M	C	$ 24.00	$ 20000.	$ 480.00
CLARA P. MONROE	55	F	A	$ 30.50	$ 6000.	$ 183.00
DUSTY O. RHODE			JOB CLASS ERROR			
JANE G. DOWNS	42	F	B	$ 24.50	$ 11900.	$ 291.55
JIMMY P. STARTER	52	M	C	$ 35.00	$ 40000.	$1400.00
CANDY A. SWEET			SEX ERROR			
JAMES C. MOORE	36	M	A	$ 24.00	$ 50000.	$1200.00
BILLIE T. KIDD	19	F	A	$ 19.00	$ 15000.	$ 285.00
CHEVY C. FORD	62					UNINSURABLE
JUNIOR S. FRYE	15					UNINSURABLE

LONGLIFE INSURANCE COMPANY, INC.

RATE TABLE

AGE	----------MEN----------			----------WOMEN----------		
	CLASS A	CLASS B	CLASS C	CLASS A	CLASS B	CLASS C
24	21.00	22.00	24.00	19.00	20.00	22.00
29	21.50	22.75	25.00	19.00	20.00	22.50
34	22.50	23.75	26.00	20.00	21.25	23.75
39	24.00	25.50	28.00	21.50	22.75	25.25
44	25.50	27.00	29.50	23.00	24.50	27.00
49	27.50	29.50	33.00	25.00	26.50	29.25
54	30.00	32.00	35.00	27.50	29.50	32.50
59	33.00	35.00	38.00	30.50	32.50	35.50

END OF JOB

EXERCISES 6 8

1 Add a section to the program which counts the number of applicants and prints a report of the total number, the number insurable, and the number uninsurable.

2 Revise the program, so that if sex and job class are both coded incorrectly, this will be detected and the applicant's name will be printed only once.

3 Add a section to the program which sums the total insurance and calculates the average amount of insurance and the average rate.

PROBLEMS 6

1 Your company, the Super-Duper Department Store, has ten central warehouses throughout the nation in which it stores a wide variety of items sold in its retail stores. An inventory is kept for each stock item telling

how many of that item is stored in each of the ten warehouses. The input record format is shown below.

input:

columns	field
1–5	stock number (numeric field)
6–25	item description (alphameric field)
26–30	quantity of this item in Warehouse 1 (numeric field)
31–35	quantity of this item in Warehouse 2 (numeric field)
.	
.	
.	
71–75	quantity of this item in Warehouse 10 (numeric field)

Your goal is to print a report listing each item, the quantity stored in each of the ten warehouses, and the total quantity in inventory for each item.

After all of the input records have been listed, print the total number of items stored in each warehouse. Complete the necessary input and output designs to aid in your programming effort.

Output Sketch:

SUPER-DUPER DEPARTMENT STORE

WAREHOUSE INVENTORY REPORT

STOCK NUMBER	DESCRIPTION	WAREHOUSE NUMBER					ITEM TOTAL
		1	2	3	4	etc.	
XXXXX	X————X	XXXXX	XXXXX	XXXXX	XXXXX		XXXXXX

WAREHOUSE 01 TOTAL IS XXXXXXX

WAREHOUSE 02 TOTAL IS XXXXXXX

etc.

etc.

2 You have a file of instructor name cards as follows:

columns	field
1–6	instructor's code number (numeric field)
7–27	instructor's name (alphameric field)
28–35	instructor's department (alphameric field)

You also have a file of student record cards as follows:

columns	field
1–2	student's number (numeric field)
3–24	student's name (alphameric field)
25–26	student's age (numeric field)
27–35	faculty advisor's code number (numeric field)

Your goal is to coordinate the information in the two files to produce a list of students accompanied by the names of their respective advisors.

From the first file (instructors) build a table in central memory of instructors' names, code numbers, and departments. Assume there are no more than 350 instructors.

READing the student cards one at a time, match each student with his/her advisor by using the instructor's code number, then print the student's name followed by his/her number in the form XXX-XX-XXXX, his/her age, then his/her advisor's name, code number, and department. Use a print chart to design your report's format.

3 Write a computer program which will:

    a Read cards containing data as shown below.

    b Summarize the total income, average income, and average number of dependents for each city, and print the data as indicated below.

    c Summarize the average income and average number of dependents for each county.

    d Summarize the total income, average income, and average number of dependents for all cards.

City and county codes are as follows:

01 Fremont	06 San Lorenzo	11 San Ramon
02 Union City	07 San Leandro	12 Cowell
03 Pleasanton	08 Oakland	13 Drawbridge
04 Livermore	09 Clayton	20 Alameda County
05 Hayward	10 Concord	30 Contra Costa County

Input Data:

data	description
city code	XX
county code	XX
annual income	XXXXX
number of dependents	XX

Output Sketch:

CITY CODE	CITY CODE	AVERAGE INCOME	AVERAGE NUMBER OF DEPENDENTS	TOTAL INCOME	PAGE 1
~	~	$ ~.~	~	$ ~,~.~	
~	~	~.~	~	~,~.~	
~	~	~.~	~	~,~.~	
			ALAMEDA COUNTY	~	
			AVERAGE INCOME	$ ~.~	
			AVERAGE DEPENDENTS	~	
~	~	$ ~.~	~	$ ~,~.~	PAGE 2
~	~	~.~	~	~,~.~	
~	~	~.~	~	~,~.~	
			CONTRA COSTA COUNTY	~	
			AVERAGE INCOME	$ ~.~	
			AVERAGE DEPENDENTS	~	
			TOTALS	$ ~,~.~	
				~,~.~	
				~,~.~	

Complete the input and output designs, make up a set of test data, and run your program with the test data.

4 Write a program which READs from each data card
   a a student's name in columns 1–25
   b a student's grade points 26–29 and
   c units completed in columns 30–33.
   (The last card will be blank.)
   grade point average = grade points/units completed

The output from your program should include a list of all the students and their grade point averages, a list of those on the honor roll (grade point average above 3.299) under the heading HONOR ROLL, and a list of suspended students (grade point average below 1.7) under the heading SUSPENDED.

Design a report, make up a test data set which covers all possible conditions, and run the program with your test data.

5 Write a program to compute the sales price of an automobile given its base price and the prices of its optional equipment, if any. The data cards for the program will be in groups. Each group will describe one car and will be organized as follows.

Typical group of cards describing a car:

card 1:   car name (up to 24 characters)   base price (INTEGER)
0 to 25 more cards: name of option   price (INTEGER)
                        (up to 24 characters)

termination card: **NO MORE OPTIONS**

There may be from 0 to 25 option cards, making a group consisting of anywhere from 2 to 27 cards. Following all the groups of cards will be the termination card shown below.

NO MORE CARS

For each automobile described in the data cards, store the information about the car in memory, compute its total price by adding its base price, all its option prices, a $150 dealer preparation charge, and 6 percent sales tax, and print the results as shown in the output sketch.

Output Sketch:

line 1:   car name   base price   total price
                                                       (including
                                                       tax and
                                                       dealer prep)

0 to 25 more lines: name of option   price
last line: blank

Your program should make *no* assumptions about the number of cars described in the data cards.

6 Write a "grading program" which reads student numbers and scores for each student from cards, then computes the total score (sum of scores) for each student. Print out the input information, the total scores, and the average total score. You may assume that there are 100 or fewer students and that each student has 10 scores. Think up a special signal card to put at the end of the input cards so that you can count the number of students as you read their scores. Use a two-dimensional array to store the scores. Add a section to your program which computes and prints the largest total score and the smallest total score. Design your inputs and outputs and run the program with test data of your choice.

7 As racquetball commissioner, you want to mail out entry forms for the upcoming National Racquetball Association Tournament. Since you were donated 50 cases of address labels of the form shown below, set up your program output accordingly.

Name/Address Labels

Input:

Acct #	Name	St #	Street (P.O. Box)	Apt	City	St	Zip
1–4	5–28	29–33	34–50	51–54	56–72	73–74	75–79

Output:
Print labels form across
Actual label size (1½" × 4")

Acct #

```
xxxx




                                                    Name
                                                    Address
                                                    City, St., Zip
```

Note: Many printers print 6 lines vertically per inch and 10 characters horizontally per inch.

8 As part of a certification test, scientists record the potentials induced in a 10-by-10 sheet of polystyrene by the meditations of candidate gurus. If a candidate is able to cause some point on the sheet to have a voltage more than ten times the average voltage, he passes this phase of the test. Otherwise he is labeled a sham and sent away in disgrace.

Write a program which carries out the certification test on the voltages and issues an appropriate message. Make up some data, or make the measurements yourself on a guru of your acquaintance. (Hint: Finding the average of the values in a 10-by-10 two-dimensional array is similar to what was done in the political poll problem of Section 6 6.)

Aging Guru Radiates Potential

9 You are a programmer for the Bigdad Insurance Company. Every day your computer center receives thousands of copies of insurance policies that have been sold all over the nation. Your keypunch department punches one card for every policy as follows:

columns	field
1–9	customer number (numeric field)
10–31	customer name (alphameric field)
32–34	rate class (numeric field)
35–37	salesman number (numeric field)
38–39	sales district (numeric field)
40–42	face amount of policy in thousands of dollars (numeric field)

Notice that the premiums are not punched on the cards described above. Premiums will be computed using the customer's rate class and his policy's face amount.

A set of ten cards containing the 100 different types of policies sold by your company is described below.

columns	field
1	card code (numeric field)
1–3	rate class (numeric field, as above)
4–8	monthly premium per $1,000 of insurance for this rate class (numeric field, XX.XX)
9–16	rate class and monthly premium as above
73–80	rate class and monthly premium as above

In other words, the information on this set of ten cards tells you how to compute the monthly premium on a policy given the face amount and the rate class.

Write a program which creates a table in central memory of the rate class and premiums information on the set of ten cards. Then READ each customer data card produced by the keypunch department. For each of these cards, look up the monthly premium per $1,000 face amount in the table you created, and use this information to compute the monthly premium for the policy described on the data card. Then print a report for the files containing the information described below.

Customer — Customer number
Rate class
Premium per $1,000
Face amount of policy
Total monthly premium

10 You, the ace programmer of your school, Filmore Potts Tech., are asked to print a table (by state) of the average heights, weights, and ages of the students at your fine institution. There are 51 categories: 50 states plus foreign-born. You want to compute the averages for each category and compute the overall averages. Make sure your program takes into account the possibility that some of the states may not be represented in the student body. Don't print reports for categories which aren't represented.

Input:

columns	data
1–9	student number
10–31	student name
32–33	home state number
34–35	age
36–37	height in inches
38–40	weight in pounds
41	sex (male = 1, female = 2)
42	marital status (1 = single, 2 = married, 3 = divorced)

Output:

STATE NUMBER	AVG. AGE	AVG. HT.	AVG. WT.
01	19.7	67.3	139.2
02	21.3	62.7	149.7
05	18.5	69.8	144.4
{	{	{	}
51	23.7	70.1	207.9
TOTAL AVERAGE	21.0	69.2	159.7

11 The year is 1811 and the fame of the pirate Lafitte has spread throughout the islands of the Caribbean and the Gulf. In Havana there resides a wealthy soldier of fortune, Captain Hawkbill, who owns a fast gunship and can hire a large crew of tough sailors. He reasons that he can make a fortune if he can capture Lafitte and take his loot. His enterprise would bring him both fortune and favor because Lafitte is universally hated by honest, law-abiding people.

The Captain sails his ship into the Gulf of Mexico to a point 5 nautical miles south and 5 nautical miles east of New Orleans. Then, from his position, he sees Lafitte's ship 5 nautical miles due west. Fortunately for Hawkbill, Lafitte's crew has just finished robbing a large cargo of gold and furs from a British ship. Lafitte's ship is sailing straight north toward New Orleans at 9 knots. Hawkbill gives chase immediately. In today's wind his ship can travel at 13 knots, and he orders his crew to keep the ship at top speed and pointed directly at Lafitte's ship.

> **knot:** *a measure of speed, one nautical mile per hour*

Write a program that computes each ship's position at one-minute intervals in terms of nautical miles south and east of New Orleans. Assume that the chase is ended if Lafitte reaches New Orleans or is overtaken by Captain Hawkbill. Print out on the line printer a graphic display of the chase in a format similar to the following:

```
New Orleans
   X . . . . . . . . . . . . . . . . .
   .
   .
   .
   H
   .
   L
   .
   .
   .
   L
   .
   L      H
   .
   L          H
   .              H
   L                  H      H
```

Note that the chase is over if either Hawkbill's distance east of New Orleans or Lafitte's distance south of New Orleans becomes negative.

12 Suppose you own a travel service and your policy is to book your customers with a direct flight if possible. You have a stack of punched cards describing the direct flights for which you may schedule passengers. That is, each card contains a departure point and time, an arrival point and time, and the name of an airline, e.g.,

flight description card:

    KANSAS CITY   10:00AM   DENVER   11:00AM   TWA

You have a second stack of cards each of which contains the name of a customer, his point of departure and his destination, e.g.,

customer request card:

    CLIFFORD TREASE   CHICAGO   SAN FRANCISCO

You are to write a program which stores the flight descriptions in memory then tries to find a direct flight to fill each customer request. If the program finds a direct flight, it should print out the customer's name, departure point and time, arrival point and time, and airline. Otherwise print the customer's name and a message to the effect that there is no direct flight available for the customer between his requested departure and arrival points.

Your program may *not* assume that the cards have been counted, so you will need some sort of termination card at the end of each of the two stacks so that it can test to see when it has stored all the flight descriptions and when it has taken care of all the customers. You may assume that there are no more than 100 flight descriptions, but your program should not depend *in any way* upon the number of customers.

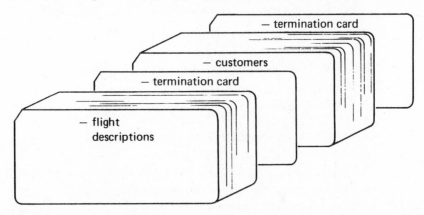

13 Write a program to make airline reservations. Assume that the airline you work for has seven flights with the number of seats given in the table below.

flight	seats available
101A	147
237	83
208	6
505	21
110	122
650	62
810B	3

Your program should reserve seats on these flights on a first come, first served basis. Each data card will contain a customer's name (up to 40 characters) and the number of the flight he wants (4 characters). The termination card will contain the phrase NO MORE CUSTOMERS in place of the name. Make no assumptions about the number of customers.

For each request, print the name of the customer and a message indicating whether or not his reservation is confirmed.

14 Write a program to solve a more general version of the previous problem. The program should first READ the flight information from data cards. Each flight description will be on a separate card with the flight number (4 characters) followed by the number of seats available (INTEGER). The termination card for the flight descriptions will be

◆◆◆◆   0

The rest of the data cards will be customer requests as in problem 12. As before, make no assumptions about the number of customers, but assume that the airline has no more than 100 flights.

The advantage of this version is that the airline can still use the program if it adds or deletes flights or changes to planes of different capacities.

7 DO-LOOPS

Chapter Objectives: After studying this chapter, you should be able to:

- Identify when a DO-loop may be used.
- Explain the operation of a DO-loop.
- Compare the simple loop to the DO-loop.
- Write programs using DO-loops.
- Construct programs using DO-loops to manipulate arrays.
- Use canned programs with variable FORMATs.
- Prepare a simple questionnaire analysis with the computer.
- Identify situations where the computed GO TO statement might be used.
- Write programs using the computed GO TO statement.

Section 7 1

The DO Statement

By now you have read enough programs to have noticed that GO TO statements make a program difficult to read because you have to hunt all over the program for the statement labels. In addition, GO TO statements used without discretion can lead to programs with extremely contorted logic. It would make programs easier to read if there were some way to write loops without using GO TO statements. Fortran provides a little help in this direction with a GO TO-less, though highly restricted, loop construction known as the DO-loop. The DO-loop can be used whenever the looping is controlled by an INTEGER variable which increases by uniform increments on each pass through the loop, and the loop terminates when the variable exceeds some upper bound. Such a loop may be called a **counting loop** since the control variable is counting from some initial value to some final value.

A surprisingly large proportion of program loops are counting loops. This makes the DO-loop very useful. However, many Fortran programmers try to force their loops to fit this category even when they could be more clearly written in some other way. By this point, however, you should be familiar enough with looping in general that you will be able to choose the most appropriate construction.

HI FRIENDS!
FRIENDLY FRANK THE STATEMENT SALESMAN HERE! HAVE I GOT A DEAL FOR YOU! TIRED OF USING COUNTERS AND HAVING TO INITIALIZE THEM? TIRED OF USING IF STATEMENTS TO STOP LOOPS? TRY THE NEW, IMPROVED, LEMON-FRESHENED DO STATEMENT.

Study the equivalent programs below.

A Program with a DO-Loop

```
COMMENT:  PRESENT VALUE TABLE
      INTEGER I, N
      REAL PV, RATE
      DATA RATE, N /0.08, 10/
C     PRINT HEADINGS
      WRITE(6,1000)
 1000 FORMAT('   $1 AT 8%'/
     + '0YEAR    PRESENT'/
     + '          VALUE')
COMMENT:  THE DO-LOOP
      DO 100 I=1,N
 10       PV=1.0/(1.0+RATE)**I
          WRITE(6,1001) I,PV
 1001     FORMAT(I4,F10.5)
 100      CONTINUE
      STOP
      END
```

output

```
   $1 AT 8%

YEAR    PRESENT
         VALUE
   1    .92593
   2    .85734
   3    .79383
   4    .73503
   5    .68058
   6    .63017
   7    .58349
   8    .54027
   9    .50025
  10    .46319
```

An Equivalent Program with an Ordinary Loop

```
COMMENT:  PRESENT VALUE TABLE
      INTEGER I, N
      REAL PV, RATE
      DATA RATE, N /0.08, 10/
C     PRINT HEADINGS
      WRITE(6,1000)
 1000 FORMAT('   $1 AT 8%'/
     + '0YEAR    PRESENT'/
     + '          VALUE')
COMMENT:  ORDINARY LOOP
      I=1
 10       PV=1.0/(1.0+RATE)**I
          WRITE(6,1001) I,PV
 1001     FORMAT(I4,F10.5)
 100      I=I+1
          IF (I .LE. N)GO TO 10
      STOP
      END
```

output

```
   $1 AT 8%

YEAR    PRESENT
         VALUE
   1    .92593
   2    .85734
   3    .79383
   4    .73503
   5    .68058
   6    .63017
   7    .58349
   8    .54027
   9    .50025
  10    .46319
```

You may be able to tell what's going on just by staring at the above programs and the output for a while. There are a number of formal rules about DO-loops, but before we look at the rules, let's see how a DO-loop works by looking at a flowchart. Figure 7 1 1 diagrams an ordinary counting loop and an equivalent DO-loop. Study the figure. Both loops perform the same computation. They both start with i equal to 1. Then they perform the statements in the loop. After those statements have been performed, i is increased by 1, and the statements in the loop are repeated.

This is continued until i is equal to n. Are the statements in both loops executed when i is exactly equal to n? For the DO-loop the answer is yes. And, if you look at the counting loop, you should be able to determine from our IF statement that this loop also is executed the final time for i exactly equal to n.

In the ordinary loop, three different statements are used to indicate the beginning value ($I = 1$), the increment ($I = I + 1$), and the ending value of the loop (IF

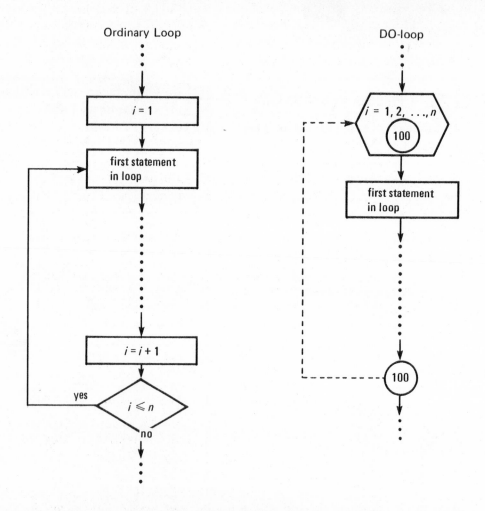

Figure 7 1 1 Loop Flowcharts

(I .LE. N) GO TO 10). In the DO-loop, this is all done in one statement. Each DO-loop starts with a statement called a **DO statement**, which specifies five things:

1 the control variable or **index**
2 the **starting value** of the index
3 the **upper bound** for the index
4 the **increment** for the index
5 the **range** of the DO-loop (that is, the statements which are part of the DO-loop)

Looking at the flowchart in Figure 7 1 1, you can see all these specified in the first box of our DO-loop program. The *index* is *i*. The *starting value* is 1. The *upper bound* is *n*. The *increment* (i.e., the difference between successive values of the index) is 1. The *range* of the DO is indicated by the statement label inside the circle. In this example, the last statement in the range has the label 100.

In a Fortran program, the index of a DO-loop must be an unsubscripted IN-TEGER variable. The starting value, upper bound, and increment must have positive INTEGER values. The range is specified by a statement label in the DO statement that indicates the last statement of the loop. Thus the loop includes all the executable statements *following* the DO statement up to and *including* the terminal statement. It is important to realize that the DO statement itself is *not* part of the loop; it merely sets up the loop. Nonexecutable statements, like FORMATs or DATA statements, may appear physically inside a DO-loop, but they are not part of the loop because they can't be executed.

Although it's not required, we'll use a CONTINUE statement as the last statement in our loop. This will help us find the end of the loop when we look at the program. The statements in the range of the DO-loop are repeated once for each value of the index, beginning with the starting value and increasing by the specified increment after each pass through the range until the upper bound is exceeded.

> **CONTINUE** *is an executable statement. Its (rather unusual) meaning is to* do nothing. *It is often used as the terminal statement in the range of a* DO-*loop. Its use in the* DO-*loop helps to avoid programming errors.*

Let's dissect the DO-loop in the example above to see how it fits the rules.

```
        DO-loop form                         non-DO-loop form

        DO 100 I=1,N                    I=1
10      PV=1.0/(1.0+RATE)**I    10     PV=1.0/(1.0+RATE)**I
        WRITE(6,1001) I,PV             WRITE(6,1001) I,PV
1001    FORMAT(I4,F10.5)        1001   FORMAT(I4,F10.5)
100     CONTINUE                100    I=I+1
                                       IF (I .LE. N)GO TO 10
```

The DO statement comes first and specifies the number of times the loop will be repeated, and the values the index will take. The statement label after the key word "DO" indicates the **range** of the loop. The range is all statements *after* the DO statement up to and including the indicated statement (the CONTINUE statement labeled 100 in our example). The memory cell called I serves as the index, and its value is changed on each pass through the loop. The index I is initialized to the value 1 (the **starting value**) and is increased by 1 (the **increment**) on each pass. The statements of the loop are repeated as long as the index is less than or equal to the value of N (the **upper bound**). Compare the DO-loop to the equivalent form using the conditional GO TO again. You'll probably agree that the DO statement is easier to read, once you understand the notation.

DO statement

forms

DO s $v = m_1 , m_2$

DO s $v = m_1 , m_2 , m_3$

s is a statement label

v is an unsubscripted INTEGER variable

m_j is an unsigned INTEGER constant or an unsubscripted INTEGER variable (which must have a positive value)

meaning

The range of the DO-loop includes all executable statements after the DO statement up to and including the statement labeled s, the **terminal statement** or **object** of the DO-loop. The index v is initialized to the **starting value** m_1 and increased by the **increment** m_3 after each pass through the statements in the range. (If m_3 is not present, it is assumed to be equal to 1.) The statements of the range are repeated as long as v is less than or equal to the **upper bound**; that is, as long as $v \leqslant m_2$.

examples

```
      DO 100 K=1,27
         SUM = SUM + A(K)
100      CONTINUE

      DO 200 PERIOD=LOW,HIGH,3
         PRICE = BASE+AMOUNT*PERIOD
         WRITE(6,1000) PRICE
200      CONTINUE
```

Let's look at another example. Suppose you want to compute a mortgage payment schedule for the villa you just purchased in the mountains. You had to borrow $50,000 from your friendly banker, who is charging you a mere 12 percent annual interest rate on a thirty-year mortgage. You want your mortgage payment schedule printed by the month for the first twelve months and then every twelfth month thereafter through year ten of the mortgage. This is a perfect situation for the DO-loop. You want to count through the months of the mortgage until you've finished the first year. Then you want to count through years two through ten figuring the repayment schedule on a monthly basis but printing it only once a year. There's a lot of counting going on here. We will need a loop counting the months one through twelve nested inside the loop counting the years two through ten. You are already familiar with nested loops written in the ordinary way. Here you'll see nested loops written with the DO statement.

```
COMMENT:  MORTGAGE PAYMENT SCHEDULE FOR MOUNTAIN VILLA
          INTEGER YEARS,Y, MONTHS,M
          REAL AMOUNT,BEGAMT,RATE,MRATE,INTRST,PAYMNT,PRINC
          DATA AMOUNT,RATE,YEARS/50000.00, 0.12, 30/
C                                          COMPUTE MONTHLY PARAMETERS
          MONTHS = YEARS*12
          MRATE = RATE/12.0
C                                          CALCUALTE MONTHLY PAYMENT
          PAYMNT=AMOUNT*(MRATE/(1.0 - 1.0/(1.0+MRATE)**MONTHS))
C                                                  PRINT HEADING
          WRITE(6,1000)
     1000 FORMAT('1',8X,'BEGINNING  MONTHLY',24X,'ENDING'/
         +      '  MONTH  MORTGAGE   PAYMENT  PRINCIPAL',
         +      '  INTEREST  MORTGAGE')
C                                          CALCULATE AND PRINT
C                                          FIRST TWELVE MONTHS
          DO 200 M=1,12
             INTRST = AMOUNT*MRATE
             PRINC = PAYMNT-INTRST
             BEGAMT = AMOUNT
             AMOUNT = AMOUNT-PRINC
             WRITE(6,2000) M,BEGAMT,PAYMNT,PRINC,INTRST,AMOUNT
     2000    FORMAT(1X,I4,F12.2,F10.2,F9.2,F11.2,F11.2)
      200    CONTINUE
C                                          CALCULATE MONTHLY BALANCES
C                                          PRINT EVERY 12-TH MONTH
          DO 320 Y=2,10
             DO 310 M=1,12
                INTRST = AMOUNT*MRATE
                PRINC = PAYMNT-INTRST
                BEGAMT = AMOUNT
                AMOUNT = AMOUNT-PRINC
      310       CONTINUE
             M = 12*Y
             WRITE(6,2000) M,BEGAMT,PAYMNT,PRINC,INTRST,AMOUNT
      320    CONTINUE
          STOP
          END
```

output

MONTH	BEGINNING MORTGAGE	MONTHLY PAYMENT	PRINCIPAL	INTEREST	ENDING MORTGAGE
1	50000.00	514.31	14.31	500.00	49985.69
2	49985.69	514.31	14.45	499.86	49971.24
3	49971.24	514.31	14.59	499.71	49956.65
4	49956.65	514.31	14.74	499.57	49941.91
5	49941.91	514.31	14.89	499.42	49927.02
6	49927.02	514.31	15.04	499.27	49911.99
7	49911.99	514.31	15.19	499.12	49896.80
8	49896.80	514.31	15.34	498.97	49881.46
9	49881.46	514.31	15.49	498.81	49865.97
10	49865.97	514.31	15.65	498.66	49850.32
11	49850.32	514.31	15.80	498.50	49834.52
12	49834.52	514.31	15.96	498.35	49818.56
24	49632.09	514.31	17.99	496.32	49614.11
36	49404.00	514.31	20.27	494.04	49383.73
48	49146.97	514.31	22.84	491.47	49124.13
60	48857.34	514.31	25.73	488.57	48831.61
72	48530.98	514.31	29.00	485.31	48501.99
84	48163.24	514.31	32.67	481.63	48130.56
96	47748.85	514.31	36.82	477.49	47712.03
108	47281.91	514.31	41.49	472.82	47240.42
120	46755.75	514.31	46.75	467.56	46709.00

Now that we've seen a couple of examples, let's look at a detailed description of the form and meaning of the DO statement.

There are lots of rules to remember about DO-loops.

1 The values of the DO-parameters (index, starting value, upper bound, and increment) may *not* be changed by any statement in the range.

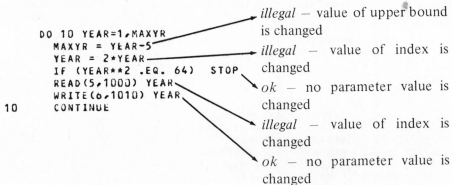

```
      DO 10 YEAR=1,MAXYR                    illegal — value of upper bound
         MAXYR = YEAR-5                     is changed
         YEAR = 2*YEAR                      illegal — value of index is
         IF (YEAR**2 .EQ. 64)    STOP       changed
         READ(5,1000) YEAR                  ok — no parameter value is
         WRITE(6,1010) YEAR                 changed
   10    CONTINUE
                                            illegal — value of index is
                                            changed

                                            ok — no parameter value is
                                            changed
```

2 No statement may cause a transfer into the range of a DO-loop from outside the range.

```
      GO TO 10                              illegal — transfers into DO-loop
      DO 10 IN = 1,25                       range
         IF ( (IN/2)*2 .EQ. NOW)  GO TO 20
         WRITE(6,1000) IN                   ok — transfers outside range
   10    CONTINUE
   20    ZOMBIE = 2.0*3.14159
```

3 The index of a DO-loop may be assumed to have a value only within the range of the DO-loop. Once the loop terminates the value is lost. The only exception is the case in which a transfer from inside the range to outside the range occurs before the loop has terminated normally.

```
      DO 100 IND=1,25
         IF ( (IND/3)*3 .EQ. NOW ) GO TO 200   ok — within loop, IND has a
         WRITE(6,1000) IND                     value
  100    CONTINUE
         WRITE(6,1000) IND                     illegal — the DO-loop has ter-
         GO TO 300                             minated so IND has no value
  200    WRITE(6,1000) IND
  300    ...                                   ok — transfer to this point
                                               occurs before DO-loop termi-
                                               nation
```

4 DO-loops may be nested. That is, the range of one DO-loop may be wholly inside the range of another. However, the ranges of two DO-loops may not overlap in any other way (see Figure 7 1 2).

```
      (LEGAL)                               (ILLEGAL)

      DO 20 HIT=1,142,2                     DO 10 HIT = 1,142,2
         DO 10 LUMP=1,57                    DO 20 LUMP=1,57
            WRITE(6,1000) HIT,LUMP          WRITE(6,2000) HIT,LUMP
   10       CONTINUE                     10 CONTINUE
         WRITE(6,4000)                       WRITE(6,4000)
   20    CONTINUE                         20 CONTINUE
```

Nested   Overlapping

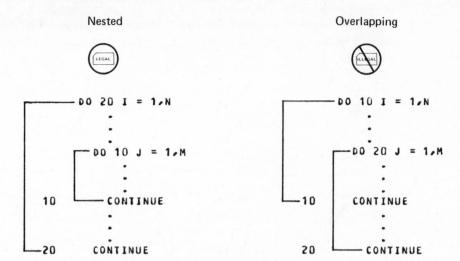

Multiple Nesting

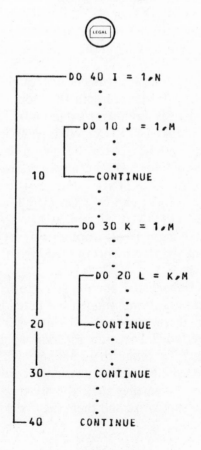

Figure 7 1 2   Nesting DO-loops

5 Nested DO-loops may have the same terminal statement, but if they do, then only the innermost DO-loop may include a transfer of control to the terminal statement.

```
DO 1U KATZ=1,142,2
   DO 1U LUMP=1,57
      IF(MIRE.GT.KATZ)GO TO 10
      WRITE(6,1000)KATZ,LUMP
      WRITE(6,2000)
10    CONTINUE
```

```
DO 10 KATZ=1,142,2
   IF (MIRE.GT.KATZ)GO TO 10
   DO 10 LUMP=1,57
      WRITE(6,2000)
10    CONTINUE
```

6 The terminal statement of a DO-loop must be executable and must *not* be a GO TO, STOP, DO, or RETURN statement, nor may it be an IF statement containing one of these. It may be a CALL statement though (CALL statements are described in the next chapter).

Look at rules 5 and 6 again. It is because of these rules that we have used the CONTINUE as the last statement in our DO-loop. It certainly avoids the difficulty of using one of the illegal statements listed under rule 6. If you use a CONTINUE with each DO (we call it a DO-CONTINUE pair), it avoids the problems indicated in rule 5. We strongly advise you to use such a DO-CONTINUE pair if you have any doubts about how your DO-loop might be executed. In addition to keeping you out of trouble, the CONTINUE statement improves the readability of your program. The DO statement and the CONTINUE act as a visual "bracket" for the DO-loop. And, the CONTINUE statement has no effect other than to act as a place to attach a statement label. Another way of improving readability in your programs is to indent the statements in the range of the DO-loop, as we have done in our examples.

With all the rules we've listed, there is still another situation we should consider. What happens when the *starting value* of the index is greater than the *upper bound* for the index? For an answer, look back at Figure 7 1 1. What happens in the case of the *ordinary loop*? The ordinary loop would be executed once since it's a post-test loop. Right? The same thing happens with the DO-loop on all the Fortran systems we are familiar with. However, according to the ANSI standards, the upper bound cannot be smaller than the starting value. Therefore the situation isn't covered by the standards, and there may be some Fortran systems where the results are unpredictable.

EXERCISES 7 1

1 Replace each program fragment with an equivalent sequence which includes a DO-loop.

a
```
        INTEGER FIVES
        FIVES = 0
10      FIVES = FIVES + 5
        WRITE(6,1000) FIVES
1000    FORMAT(I15)
        IF (FIVES .LT. 100)  GO TO 10
        .
        .
        .
```

b
```
        .
        .
        .
        I = 1
10      PV = 1.0/(1.0+RATE)**I
        WRITE(6,1001) I,PV
        I = 1+1
        IF (I .LE. N)  GO TO 10
        .
        .
        .
```

c
```
        .
        .
        .
        HOT = 99
100     IF (HOT .GT. 108)  GO TO 200
        BODYT = (HOT-BODYT)/BODYT + BODYT
        HOT = HOT + 1
        GO TO 100
        .
        .
        .
```

2 In the first DO-loop example program (in the box), what will be the output if N is initialized to 2 (instead of 1)?

3 In what way would the output of the first DO-loop example program be changed if the DO statement was changed to

$$DO\ 100\ I = 1, N, 1$$

4 What's wrong with this?

```
        .
        .
        .
        DO 200 INDEX = 1,10
100     N = N + I
200     WRITE(6,1100)  N, I
        IF (N .LT. 100)  GO TO 100
        .
        .
        .
```

5   How many lines will this bizarre and possibly senseless program print?

```
            INTEGER OUTER, INNER, MIDDLE
COMMENT:   THIS PROGRAM IS BIZARRE AND POSSIBLY SENSELESS.
C          READ IT AT YOUR OWN RISK.
        DO 100 OUTER = 2,8,2
          DO 100 MIDDLE = OUTER,2,1
            DO 100 INNER = 1,4,8
              WRITE(6,1000)
1000          FORMAT(' LINE')
100         CONTINUE
        STOP
        END
```

Section 7 2

DO-Loops and Arrays — A Great Team

Commonly the values stored in an array are related to each other and must be dealt with in a very similar way, but one at a time, of course. Such situations are great opportunities to use DO-loops, resulting in a more efficient program which is easier to read, hence easier to debug. Here's part of a program which locates the largest value in an array of numbers. We assume that an earlier section of the program has succeeded in READing N values into array positions SALES(1), SALES(2), . . . , SALES(N). Notice the use made of the CONTINUE statement in statement 300. It provides a convenient place to go when, under certain conditions, you want to skip some part of the DO-loop range. In this case we wanted to skip the statement MAXIM = SALES(HERE) unless we found a new maximum value.

```
        INTEGER SALES(1000), N, HERE, MAXIM
          .
          .
          .
COMMENT  FIND THE LARGEST VALUE IN THE ARRAY "SALES"
C                                FIRST ELEMENT IS LARGEST SO FAR
        MAXIM = SALES(1)
C                                SEARCH THE OTHER ELEMENTS
C                                       FOR LARGER ONES
        DO 300 HERE = 2,N
          IF (SALES(HERE) .LE. MAXIM) GO TO 300
C                                HERE IS A LARGER VALUE.  UPDATE
            MAXIM = SALES(HERE)
300       CONTINUE
C                                       PRINT MAXIMUM
        WRITE(6,4000) MAXIM
4000 FORMAT(' NO SALESMAN HAS MORE THAN $',F8.2,' SALES')
        STOP
        END
```

Nested DO-loops are convenient ways of dealing with two-dimensional arrays. To illustrate this, let's look again at the program that we saw in the first part of Section 6 6. That's where we first used two-dimensional arrays. We had an array which stored the results of a poll taken for our political candidate. We used the array REAL POLL(7,5) and we wanted to know the average value in each column. Using DO-loops our program would look like the one below.

```
      REAL POLL(7,5), AVERGE, SUM
      INTEGER COLUMN, ROW
         .
         .
         .
      DO 200 COLUMN = 1,5
        SUM = 0.0
        DO 100 ROW = 1,7
          SUM = SUM + POLL(ROW,COLUMN)
100       CONTINUE
        AVERGE = SUM/7.0
        WRITE(6,2000) COLUMN,AVERGE
2000    FORMAT(' THE AVERAGE SUPPORT IN COLUMN',I2,' IS',
     +              F5.1,' PER CENT')
200     CONTINUE
      STOP
      END
```

The nesting of DO-loops is limited by your ability to keep track of them. Figure 7 1 2 shows you how DO-loops may be nested. As you can see, you must be careful not to overlap any of your DO-loops since this will cause a compile-time error. Drawing brackets on your DO-loops like we've done in Figure 7 1 2 will help you track down an overlapping loop condition.

Where they are appropriate, DO-loops help by providing a concise notation for a specific sort of loop. You already know how to write any sort of loop you want, so if the restrictions on DO-loops make them inappropriate to your problem, you know what to do.

EXERCISES 7 2

1 Look at the examples in Chapters 3 and 6 and see which of the loops could be appropriately written as DO-loops and which of them couldn't.

2 Alter the example which finds the largest value in SALES so that it determines the smallest.

3 Alter the example which determines the largest value in SALES so that it also prints the number of memory cells in SALES which have the largest value, in case of ties.

Section 7 3 *

Questionnaire Analysis and Variable FORMATs

Skip this section
if you feel like it.

Businesses frequently engage in survey research to determine attitudes and buying habits of their customers. They also survey their employees to find out their feelings towards working conditions and management practices. We're sure you can think of a variety of business surveys. You may have been asked questions such as "Do you intend to buy a new car?" or "Have you shopped at the Super Colossal Shopping Center?" The analysis of the political poll described in Section 6 6 used summary survey data obtained from a poll.

How do we go about conducting a survey and summarizing its results? There are a number of different ways in which questionnaires can be designed and people selected to answer them. Our focus, however, will be on how to summarize the data once the questionnaire has been completed.

Let's look at the questionnaire we want to summarize.

CAR BUYER'S QUESTIONNAIRE

1. Your sex:
   _____ male
   _____ female

2. Your age:
   _____ under 20
   _____ 20–29
   _____ 30–39
   _____ 40–49
   _____ 50–59
   _____ 60–69
   _____ 70–79
   _____ 80 or over

3. Your marital status (check only one):
   _____ single
   _____ married
   _____ separated
   _____ divorced
   _____ living together
   _____ widowed

4. Your present occupation (check only one):
   _____ student
   _____ housewife
   _____ clerical
   _____ laborer
   _____ manager
   _____ professional

    _____ retired
    _____ between jobs
    _____ other

5. Do you have a driver's license?
   _____ yes
   _____ no

6. How many miles a year do you drive?
   _____ under 10,000
   _____ 10,000–19,999
   _____ 20,000–29,999
   _____ 30,000–39,999
   _____ 40,000–49,999
   _____ 50,000 or over

7. How often do you purchase a new car?
   _____ each year
   _____ every second year
   _____ every third year
   _____ every fourth or more years
   _____ never (purchase used cars)

8. When do you plan to buy your next new car?
   _____ within 1 month
   _____ within 1 year
   _____ within 2 years
   _____ over 2 years

---

9. If you were to buy a new car, from which of the following manufacturers would you buy it?

_____ American Motors

_____ Chrysler

_____ Ford

_____ General Motors

_____ Volkswagen

_____ Datsun

_____ Toyota

_____ other American

_____ other foreign

10. How much would you expect to pay for your new car?

_____ under $3,000

_____ $3,000–$3,999

_____ $4,000–$4,999

_____ $5,000–$5,999

_____ $6,000–$6,999

_____ $7,000–$7,999

_____ $8,000–$8,999

_____ $9,000–$9,999

_____ $10,000 or over

That's all the questions.

Thank you for your cooperation. Please keep the enclosed ballpoint pen as a token of our appreciation.

FIELD
SURVEY INC.
WE GET THE FACTS YOUR
BUSINESS LACKS

More questions could be added to the questionnaire, depending on the information you want to obtain by your survey. We'll let you do that since you can think of many other interesting questions. The ten questions we've listed are sufficient to show how to go about analyzing a questionnaire.

After you've prepared the questionnaire, you mail it out using the mailing labels in Problem 6 7. Unfortunately, of the 27 you mailed out, only 10 are sent back, so you decide to go downtown and interview some people on the street to fill out 10 more. Now, you're ready to summarize them. The first thing we need to do is code the questionnaire. We'll do that using the following codes.

Questionnaire Codes

1. Sex
    - 0 no response
    - 1 male
    - 2 female

2. Age
    - 0 no response
    - 1 under 20
    - 2 20–29
    - 3 30–39
    - 4 40–49
    - 5 50–59
    - 6 60–69
    - 7 70–79
    - 8 80 or over

3. Marital status
    - 0 no response
    - 1 single
    - 2 married
    - 3 separated
    - 4 divorced
    - 5 living together
    - 6 widowed

4. Present occupation
    - 0 no response
    - 1 student
    - 2 housewife
    - 3 clerical
    - 4 laborer
    - 5 manager
    - 6 professional
    - 7 retired
    - 8 between jobs
    - 9 other

5. Driver's license
    - 0 no response
    - 1 yes
    - 2 no

6. Miles driven
    - 0 no response
    - 1 under 10,000

- 2 10,000–19,999
- 3 20,000–29,999
- 4 30,000–39,999
- 5 40,000–49,999
- 6 50,000 or over

7. How often do you purchase
    - 0 no response
    - 1 each year
    - 2 every second year
    - 3 every third year
    - 4 every fourth or more years
    - 5 never

8. When do you plan to buy
    - 0 no response
    - 1 within month
    - 2 within year
    - 3 within two years
    - 4 over two years

9. Manufacturer
    - 0 no response
    - 1 American Motors
    - 2 Chrysler
    - 3 Ford
    - 4 General Motors
    - 5 Volkswagen
    - 6 Datsun
    - 7 Toyota
    - 8 other American
    - 9 other foreign

10. Expect to pay
    - 0 no response
    - 1 under $3,000
    - 2 $3,000–$3,999
    - 3 $4,000–$4,999
    - 4 $5,000–$5,999
    - 5 $6,000–$6,999
    - 6 $7,000–$7,999
    - 7 $8,000–$8,999
    - 8 $9,000–$9,999
    - 9 $10,000 or over

```
COMMENT:  QUESTIONNAIRE ANALYSIS
      INTEGER NQ,NUMBER,MXCODE(10),FMT(20),RESPON(10)
      INTEGER MAXRES,I,J,Q, TALLY(10,10), NUMRES(10)
      REAL PERCNT(10,10)
      DATA NQ, TALLY,NUMRES/10, 110*0/
C                                            READ DATA FORMAT
      READ(5,1000) FMT
 1000 FORMAT(20A4)
C                          READ CODE RANGE FOR EACH QUESTION
      READ(5,FMT) MXCODE
C                              READ NUMBER OF QUESTIONNAIRES
      READ(5,1010) NUMBER
 1010 FORMAT(I5)
C                          READ AND TALLY QUESTIONNAIRES
C                               FIRST, DO FREQUENCY COUNT
      DO 100 Q=1,NUMBER
        READ(5,FMT)   (RESPON(I),I=1,NQ)
        DO 100 I=1,NQ
        IF (RESPON(I) .EQ. 0  .OR.
     +        RESPON(I) .GT. MXCODE(I) )  GO TO 100
        J = RESPON(I)
        TALLY(I,J) = TALLY(I,J) + 1
  100   CONTINUE
C                          NOW, SUM RESPONSES TO EACH QUESTION
      DO 200 I=1,NQ
        MAXRES = MXCODE(I)
        DO 200 J=1,MAXRES
        NUMRES(I) = NUMRES(I) + TALLY(I,J)
  200   CONTINUE
C                          FINALLY, CALCULATE PERCENTAGES
      DO 300 I=1,NQ
        MAXRES = MXCODE(I)
        DO 300  J=1,MAXRES
        RATIO = FLOAT(TALLY(I,J))/FLOAT(NUMRES(I))
        PERCNT(I,J) = 100.0*RATIO
  300   CONTINUE
C                          PRINT QUESTIONNAIRE TABULATION
      WRITE(6,1020)
 1020 FORMAT('1',7X,'CAR BUYER QUESTIONNAIRE ANALYSIS'//
     +      ' QUESTION      CODE        FREQUENCY      PERCENT')
      DO 400 I=1,NQ
        WRITE(6,1030) I
 1030 FORMAT('0',I5)
        MAXRES = MXCODE(I)
        DO 400 J=1,MAXRES
        WRITE(6,1040) J,TALLY(I,J),PERCNT(I,J)
 1040   FORMAT(15X,I2,9X,I5,8X,F6.2)
  400   CONTINUE
      STOP
      END
```

data
```
   (1011)  ◄──────────────  here's our variable FORMAT
  2869265499
       20
  1314111221
  2213115134
  2423122215
  1121135349
  1025145356
  1111204471
  2211153361
  1566161181
  2657151299
  1426141263
  1727262372
  1666224015
  2857015426
  1259122337
  2332132141
  1448143248
  1445151249
  2352161235
  2222122424
  1534014316
```

output

CAR BUYER QUESTIONNAIRE ANALYSIS

QUESTION	CODE	FREQUENCY	PERCENT
1			
	1	12	60.00
	2	8	40.00
2			
	1	2	10.53
	2	4	21.05
	3	3	15.79
	4	4	21.05
	5	2	10.53
	6	2	10.53
	7	1	5.26
	8	1	5.26
3			
	1	4	20.00
	2	6	30.00
	3	2	10.00
	4	2	10.00
	5	4	20.00
	6	2	10.00
4			
	1	3	15.00
	2	3	15.00
	3	2	10.00
	4	2	10.00
	5	2	10.00
	6	3	15.00
	7	3	15.00
	8	1	5.00
	9	1	5.00

5			
	1	15	83.33
	2	3	16.67
6			
	1	4	21.05
	2	4	21.05
	3	2	10.53
	4	3	15.79
	5	3	15.79
	6	3	15.79
7			
	1	6	30.00
	2	5	25.00
	3	2	10.00
	4	3	15.00
	5	4	20.00
8			
	1	3	15.79
	2	7	36.84
	3	6	31.58
	4	3	15.79
9			
	1	3	15.00
	2	3	15.00
	3	3	15.00
	4	4	20.00
	5	1	5.00
	6	2	10.00
	7	2	10.00
	8	1	5.00
	9	1	5.00
10			
	1	5	25.00
	2	1	5.00
	3	1	5.00
	4	2	10.00
	5	3	15.00
	6	3	15.00
	7	1	5.00
	8	1	5.00
	9	3	15.00

Look at the program. You can easily see all the loops we've used. How would you like to try to follow the program if we hadn't used DO-loops? They sure make it easier, don't they?

Our program also shows you another FORMAT feature. You thought we'd covered *all* of them, didn't you? Well, here's another. This is what's known as a *variable FORMAT*. It's really nifty when you have a program you want to use with many different data files. By using the variable FORMAT, you enter the FORMAT on a *data card* (yes, a data card) each time your program is to be run. That way you don't have to modify your program to fit every data set. Many general-use statistical programs are already written and available to you which make use of this feature. So by learning about Fortran FORMATs, you are in a better position to use these "**canned**" programs.

> **canned program**: *a program which is already written and can be used by following the instructions or documentation for its use. Sometimes known as a packaged program. Since many businesses solve similar problems, there exists a great variety of "canned" programs for business applications.*

A **variable FORMAT** is an array containing a character string. That string must be a legal FORMAT specification. That is, it must be a string which could appear after the word FORMAT in a FORMAT statement, including the parentheses. The I/O statement using the variable FORMAT is exactly the same as if we had used a normal FORMAT except that the name of the array containing the variable FORMAT now replaces the usual FORMAT label.

> **variable FORMAT I/O statement**
>
> *forms*
>   READ (*u,f*) *list*
>   WRITE (*u,f*) *list*
>   WRITE (*u,f*)
>   *f* is the name of an array containing a character string of FORMAT specifications surrounded by parentheses
>
> *meaning*
>   same as with constant FORMAT

Where did we use the variable FORMAT? The first READ statement reads the FORMAT from our data deck. The second and fourth READ statements the read our data using that variable FORMAT. Look at our first data card and you can see how to write these variable FORMATs. They're the specifications we discussed in Chapters 2 and 4 enclosed in parentheses. From our example, you should be able to write all sorts of variable FORMATs.

EXERCISES 7 3

1 Change the variable FORMAT in the questionnaire analysis so Question 7 would be skipped. That is, our analysis would then be of Questions 1 through 6 and 8 through 10. (Assume the value of NQ is 9.)

2 Modify the questionnaire program so responses are tallied and results printed for females age 20 to 39.

3 Change the program so it tallies and prints results for professionals only.

> **CROSSTAB**: *A cross tabulation or crosstally is the analysis of questionnaire data for a specified question(s) and response(s). Exercises 2 and 3 above produce CROSSTABS.*

4 Alter the questionnaire program so that it prints an error message when it encounters a missing or invalid response.

Section 7 4

Asset Depreciation, DO-loops, and Multiple Branching

In the problems of Chapter 4, you were introduced to a couple of depreciation methods. There are three methods commonly used by businesses to calculate depreciation. These are straight-line, declining balance, and sum-of-the-years digits. A business might apply all three methods at the same time or in the same year for different assets. Therefore, it's necessary in calculating total depreciation for a company to first select the method and then calculate the depreciation.

As you know, we could use a series of IF statements to select the depreciation method. However, another statement, the **computed GO TO**, allows us to make such a selection using only one statement instead of three. Here's an example which uses the computed GO TO statement to select our depreciation method.

```
COMMENT: ASSET DEPRECIATION
        INTEGER YEAR,NUMBER,NAME(5),PURYR,METHOD,USEYRS,I
        REAL COST,SALV,LIFE,DEPREC,ACCUM,SOYD,TDEPR,TACCUM
C                                          READ CURRENT YEAR
        READ(5,100) YEAR
100 FORMAT(I5)
C                                          PRINT REPORT HEADING
        WRITE(6,110) YEAR, YEAR
110 FORMAT(1H1,//,45X,29HDEPRECIATION INDUSTRIES, INC.,//,
      +      42X,30HANNUAL DEPRECIATION REPORT FOR,I5,//,
      +      36X,4HYEAR,,53X,I5,7X,11HACCUMULATED,/,2X,
      +      6HNUMBER,10X,4HNAME,11X,9HPURCHASED,10X,
      +      4HLIFE,5X,4HCOST,5X,7HSALVAGE,5X,6HMETHOD,
      +      2X,12HDEPRECIATION,2X,12HDEPRECIATION,/)
C                                          READ ASSET
120 READ(5,130) NUMBER,NAME,PURYR,LIFE,COST,SALV,METHOD
130 FORMAT(I10,5A4,I5,F5.0,2F10.0,4X,I1)
        IF (PURYR.EQ.0) GOTO 150
        USEYRS=YEAR-PURYR
C                                          HERE'S THE COMPUTED GOTO
        GOTO (1000,2000,3000),METHOD
C                                          STRAIGHT LINE DEPRECIATION
1000    DEPREC=(COST-SALV)/LIFE
        ACCUM=DEPREC*USEYRS
        GOTO 4000
C                                          DECLINING BALANCE DEPRECIATION
2000    ACCUM=0.
        DO 2100 I=1,USEYRS
          DEPREC=2.0*(COST-ACCUM)/LIFE
          ACCUM=ACCUM+DEPREC
2100      CONTINUE
        GOTO 4000
```

```
C                          SUM-OF-THE-YEARS DIGITS DEPRECIATION
   3000      SOYD=LIFE*(LIFE+1.)/2.
             ACCUM=0.
             DO 3100 I=1,USEYRS
                DEPREC=((LIFE+1.-I)/SOYD)*(COST-SALV)
                ACCUM=ACCUM+DEPREC
   3100      CONTINUE
C                                    PRINT DEPRECIATION CALCULATIONS
   4000      WRITE(6,140) NUMBER, NAME,PURYR,LIFE,COST,SALV,
         +               METHOD,DEPREC,ACCUM
    140      FORMAT(1X,I10,2X,5A4,2X,I5,11X,F5.0,2X,F10.0,1X,
         +          F10.0,6X,I1,4X,F10.0,4X,F10.0)
             TDEPR=TDEPR+DEPREC
             TACCUM=TACCUM+ACCUM
             GOTO 120
    150   WRITE(6,160) TDEPR,TACCUM
    160   FORMAT(13X,102(1H-),/,13X,5HTOTAL,72X,F10.0,4X,F10.0)
          STOP
          END


input
   1978
   1000100115FORK LIFT TRUCK       1975    10     9000      2000    1
   1000100203CONVEYOR              1976     5     6200       500    3
   1000100409PUNCH PRESS           1969    12    50000      6000    2
   1000200760EXECUTIVE DESK        1972     6     1200       100    2
   1000200843SECRETARIAL DESK      1966    20      400        20    1
   1000500301OSHA PORTA POTTI      1975     5     3350         0    3
   1000600932MOUNTAIN VILLA        1963    40   120000    100000    1
          0                           0     0        0         0    0


output
                          DEPRECIATION INDUSTRIES, INC.

                       ANNUAL DEPRECIATION REPORT FOR 1978

                              YEAR                                          1978        ACCUMULATED
   NUMBER      NAME          PURCHASED    LIFE   COST    SALVAGE   METHOD  DEPRECIATION  DEPRECIATION

1000100115  FORK LIFT TRUCK    1975       10.    9000.   2000.       1        700.         2100.
1000100203  CONVEYOR           1976        5.    6200.    500.       3       1520.         3420.
1000100409  PUNCH PRESS        1969       12.   50000.   6000.       2       1938.        40310.
1000200760  EXECUTIVE DESK     1972        6.    1200.    100.       2         53.         1095.
1000200843  SECRETARIAL DESK   1966       20.     400.     20.       1         19.          228.
1000500301  OSHA PORTA POTTI   1975        5.    3350.      0.       3        670.         2680.
1000600932  MOUNTAIN VILLA     1963       40.  120000. 100000.       1        500.         7500.
            -------------------------------------------------------------------------------------
            TOTAL                                                            5400.        57332.
```

If you look at the program for a while, you can probably figure out how the computed GO TO works.

Let's consider how we used the multiple branch. The depreciation methods were coded 1, 2, or 3. You should notice that these are INTEGERS. They have to be in order for our computed GO TO to work. Look back at the example again. What are the numbers in parentheses? You might recognize them as statement labels. Well, that's what they are. So how does the statement work? When METHOD is 1, the program branches to the first statement label, in our example 1000; when METHOD is 2, the program branches to the second statement label, in our example 2000; and similarly for METHOD 3. If we had more METHODS, we would just continue listing the statement labels in order. Our decision value, METHOD, must be an unsubscripted INTEGER.

If you want to decide to branch on other than integer values, then the computed GO TO may *not* be the statement for you.

Let's look at how we can flowchart our computed GO TO. This might help you determine where you can use it. Figure 7 4 1 shows you two ways to flowchart the computed GO TO. As you can see, one way is fine for a three-way branch, while another would handle an *n*-way branch.

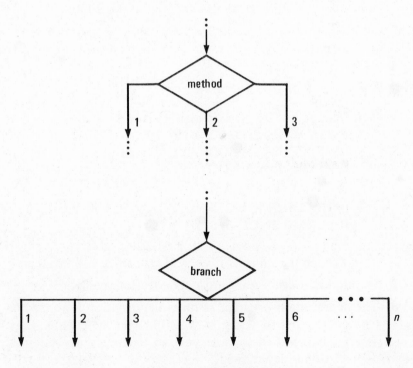

Figure 7 4 1   Flowcharting the Computed GO TO

If you can believe it, there is still *another* way we could do a three-way branch. It's known as the **arithmetic IF** statement. Providing you want to do a branch like that shown in the top of Figure 7 4 1, then the arithmitic IF may be just the statement for you. In this three-branch transfer of control, the choice of one of the three branches depends on whether the value of an arithmetic expression is positive, negative, or zero.

---

arithmetic IF statement

form
    IF (e) s_{neg}, s_{zero}, s_{pos}
    e is an arithmetic expression
    s_{neg}, s_{zero}, and s_{pos} are statement labels

meaning
    computes e and transfers to s_{neg} if e is negative, s_{zero} if e is zero, and s_{pos} if e is positive

examples
```
IF (A) 30,10,20
IF (X - EXP(R*P))  100,300,200
```

Let's consider how we might modify our asset depreciation program to use the arithmetic IF in place of the computed GO TO. All we need to do is change one statement. The computed GO TO would be replaced with the following arithmetic IF:

IF(METHOD−2) 1000, 2000, 3000

So, if you need to do a three-way branch, you have a choice. But, when you're branching in more than three ways, the computed GO TO will do it for you.

EXERCISES 7 4

  1 Write computed GO TO statements that do the same as
     a IF (TYPE .EQ. 1) GO TO 10
        IF (TYPE .EQ. 2) GO TO 20
        IF (TYPE .EQ. 3) GO TO 30
        Assume TYPE is 1, 2, or 3.
     b IF (BRANCH .GT. 2 .AND. BRANCH .LT. 5) GO TO 100
        IF (BRANCH .LT. 6) GO TO 200
        300 . . . . .
        Assume the value of BRANCH is positive and less than 7.

  2 Do exercise 1 again using arithmetic IF statements.

  3 The depreciation program assumes depreciation is applied on the basis of a whole number of years. How would you change the program to handle assets purchased during the year so that only a portion of the annual depreciation is determined?

4 In the last year of the life of an asset, the depreciation is what's left. How would you change the program to calculate depreciation in the last year?

PROBLEMS 7

1 You, Ace Programmer at Ryeland Tech., are asked to print a table of the averages, ranges, and standard deviations of the ages, heights, weights, and number of students from each state. There is one record per student. Summarize at the end of the report by listing the total institution's averages, ranges, and standard deviations. (Don't print 00.0 or the state number if there is no information for that state.)

$$\text{range} = \text{highest} - \text{lowest}$$

$$\text{mean or average} = \frac{\text{total value of items}}{\text{total no. of items}}$$

$$\text{standard deviation} \atop (\text{measure of dispersion}) = \sqrt{\frac{\Sigma x^2 - \frac{(\Sigma x)^2}{n}}{n-1}}$$

Input Design:

STUDENT NUMBER 1–9	NAME 10–31	HOME STATE NUMBER 32–33	AGE 34–35	HEIGHT 36–37	SEX 41	MARITAL STATUS 42

Output Sketch:

STATE NUMBER	NO. OF STUDENTS	RANGES AGE LO–HI	RANGES WEIGHT LO–HI	RANGES HEIGHT LO–HI	AVERAGES AGE	AVERAGES WEIGHT	AVERAGES HEIGHT	STANDARD DEVIATIONS AGE	STANDARD DEVIATIONS HEIGHT	STANDARD DEVIATIONS WEIGHT
01	12	20–40	110–195	60–72	25.3	142.3	67.2	3.2	7.6	10.1
02	8	19–24	100–210	58–70	23.4	147.8	64.7	4.8	8.2	9.7
05	56	18–26	105–227	63–68	22.6	185.3	66.5	5.6	6.5	12.3
.										
.										
51	5	17–19	120–165	64–76	18.1	170.3	72.7	6.1	7.6	13.3
TOTALS		16–62	95–310	56–78	19.7	165.3	66.5	3.9	6.5	9.6

2 Over the past year, your private stock of automobiles has included many cars, some of which were: Shelby 500, Olds 442, VW bug, L-88 Corvette, Z/28 Camaro, and a model T roadster. Needless to say, the gasoline consumption of these vehicles has varied considerably. Since you expect the coming year to be about the same as last, and since you are getting a strong urge to see what sort of gasoline consumption your vehicles will obtain, you decide to put your data processing knowledge to work.

Every time you purchase gasoline, the information is recorded on a card. Since some of the vehicles have horrible gasoline consumption characteristics (and you have a heavy foot), you have developed the "fill-it-up" syndrome for every gasoline purchase.

At the end of the year, you sort your data card file and put it in sequence by data. Then you prepare a set of data cards which includes the initial mileage at the beginning of the year when the car had a full tank of gas. This set of cards includes a description of the auto but the gallons and cost are zero. When you sequence your data cards by date, the cards with the description and beginning miles are at the front of the data deck.

Since you could own up to 20 cars in one year (a small fleet) your program needs to be designed to handle this as a maximum. In your program design, use a table array to keep track of the information on the various autos in your mini-fleet.

Input Data:

data item	description
auto I.D.	XX
date	MMDDYY
gallons	XX.X
cost	XXX.XX
miles reading at fill-up	XXXXX.X
auto description	20 characters

Output Sketch:

1977
GASOLINE CONSUMPTION ANALYSIS

DESCRIPTION	TOTAL GALLONS	TOTAL COST	AVERAGE COST PER GALLON	MILES PER GALLON	MILES TRAVELED
SHELBY 500	572.3	$275.10	48.7	9.05	6,342.2
OLDS 442	440.0	198.75	44.8	9.28	4,085.3
VW 1300	56.0	17.10	31.2	31.40	1,726.9
L-88 CORVETTE	747.4	397.17	39.9	8.23	6,107.8
HONDA 600	25.3	7.11	35.6	54.91	1,397.7

YEARLY SUMMARY INFO.

	19,470.2	$6902.20	35.7	14.01	272,149.6

Complete the input/output designs and make up a set of test data for your program.

3 In your travels around the western United States you decide to record temperature data. Since some of the temperatures are reported in Fahrenheit and some in Celsius, you want a program which will convert the recorded temperature to the other scale. The temperature formulas are:

$$C = (5/9)(F - 32)$$
$$F = (9/5)C + 32$$

Input Design:

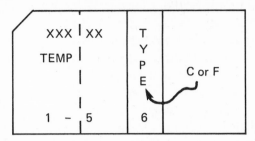

If the temperature type is F, convert to C; if C, convert to F—in either case you want your report to print an appropriate message describing the temperature conditions.

Temperature Conditions	
32° F or less	"frozen"
32° to 45°	"cold"
45° to 60°	"chilly"
60° to 75°	"moderate"
75° to 87°	"warm"
87° to 100°	"hot"
100° to 115°	"scorching"
115° to 135°	"death valley"
135° or more	"scalding"

Output Sketch:

```
        TEMPERATURES
     C        F          CONDITION
   XXX.XX   XXX.XX          WARM
   XXX.XX   XXX.XX          HOT
     ?        ?              ?
   AVERAGE TEMPERATURE:
     C        F
   XXX.XX   XXX.XX
```

4 You are a programmer for MAGNUM, Inc., a computer electronic component manufacturer on the Peninsula. The director of finance has requested a summary report of labor costs involved in each of the company's contracts, by job number, by department, with totals of each job number and contract number, and the total labor costs of all contracts. Since each job has a preassigned number from the PERT and Critical Path charts, you can assume, and should check for, proper ascending sequence of job numbers. Management data in this area has always been a problem.

MAGNUM's finance director is extremely anxious to receive this information and to verify the accuracy of the new cost system. (Spies from the competition are anxious to get their hands on the information, too.)

The cost for each operation (allocated to one of seven departments) is found by multiplying the cost factor by the time factor. If the work code is A–C, use the Regular time factor; if the work code is D–F, use the Nonregular time factor. Round off all costs to the nearest dollar. Assume data to be in ascending order by job number, but check for out of sequence jobs. Display an error message and cancel such jobs since a card out of sequence will give erroneous management information.

Input Data:

data item	cols.	field information
contract number	1–2	
job number	3–5	
department code	6	(from 1–7)
cost factor	7–12	
work code	13	(from A–F)
regular time factor	14–18	XXX.XX
nonregular time factor	19–23	XXX.XX equals decimal portion of an hour, e.g., .50 = 30 minutes

Output Sketch:

CONTRACT NUMBER	JOB NUMBER	\multicolumn{7}{DEPARTMENTS}							TOTALS

```
CONTRACT     JOB              DEPARTMENTS
 NUMBER    NUMBER    1   2   3   4   5   6   7   TOTALS
    1         1     $_  $~  $_  $_  $_  $~  $_   $ _____
              2     __  __  __  __  __  __  __     _____
              3     __  __  __  __  __  __  __     _____
              4     __  __  __  __  __  __  __     _____

                         CONTRACT 1 TOTAL  $ _____

    2         1     __  __  __  __  __  __  __     _____
              2     __  __  __  __  __  __  __     _____
              3     __  __  __  __  __  __  __     _____
              4     __  __  __  __  __  __  __     _____
              5     __  __  __  __  __  __  __     _____

                         CONTRACT 2 TOTAL  $

    3         1     ~   __  __  __  __  __  __     _____
              2     __  ~   ~   ~   __  __  __     _____
              3     __  ~   __  ~   __  __  __     _____

                         CONTRACT 3 TOTAL  $ _____

DEPARTMENT TOTALS              TOTAL LABOR COSTS  $ _____
                       1    2    3    4    5    6    7
                     $~ $~ $~ $~ $~ $~ $~
```

5   Redo problem 6 7 (address labels) but instead of printing name in the format

LAST FIRST Middle Initial

turn the name around so that it prints

FIRST M LAST

6 Write a program which will create an Accounts Receivable Aging Schedule. This schedule will consist of group totals (by account) of all outstanding invoices for each customer, broken down by current, thirty-day, sixty-day, ninety-day and older, and total outstanding balance. As customers remit payments, the amount of the payment and date of payment, along with the number of the invoice to which the payment applies, are punched into a card, as shown below. A payment will not necessarily pay the entire invoice amount; partial payments are often made. For the convenience of the credit department, list the most recent payment.

    The program will be run at the end of each calendar month. Invoices dated from the first of the current month to the end of the month fall into the current category, those dated with last month's date fall into the thirty-day category, the previous month's invoices are sixty-day balances, and any invoices older than that are ninety-day or older balances.

    Prior to running the program, the data check will be sorted into order by

Date—1st sorter pass
Invoice number—2nd sorter pass
Account number—3d sorter pass

Input Designs:

Debit Card

ACCT NO. 1–4	INVOICE NO. 5–9	DATE 10–15	AMOUNT XXX.XX 16–22	NAME 23–50	D 80

Credit Card

ACCT NO. 1–4	INVOICE NO. 5–9	DATE 10–15	AMOUNT XXX.XX 16–22	NAME 23–50	C 80

Output Sketch:

ARA COMPANY, INC.
ACCOUNTS RECEIVABLE AGING SCHEDULE

ACCT NO.	NAME	TOTAL	CURRENT	30 DAY	60 DAY	90 DAY	LAST PAYMENT
X——X	X—X	X—X	X——X	X—X	X—X	X—X	X——X
TOTAL			X——X	X—X	X—X	X—X	X——X

7 The table shown below may be used for computing tax due for any person with an income between $4500 and $5000 and no more than six exemptions. Also given is information regarding six individuals for whom the tax due is to be determined.

Write a program which will READ the tax table and taxpayer information, select from the tax table the correct tax due for each person, then output all taxpayer information plus the tax due.

Prepare an output design so that the output report looks neat and provides all the input information plus the tax due. Develop input designs for the tax table and taxpayer information to meet your needs for input.

TAX TABLE

Income	Exemptions					
	1	2	3	4	5	6
4500–4549	565	430	326	218	116	18
4550–4599	565	430	326	218	116	25
4600–4649	581	444	342	224	130	32
4650–4699	589	451	350	241	137	39
4700–4749	597	459	358	249	144	46
4750–4799	606	463	366	256	151	53
4800–4849	614	474	374	264	159	60
4850–4899	622	482	382	271	166	67
4900–4949	630	490	390	279	174	74
4950–4999	638	497	398	286	181	81

TAXPAYERS

Smith, William "Doc"   Soc. Sec. No. 496-28-5293
224 S. Loomis Street   exemptions: 5
Fort Collins, Colorado   income: $4,510

Walsingham, Louise M.   Soc. Sec. No. 216-70-4318
602 Encino Drive   exemptions: 1
Aptos, California   income: $4,700

Lesley, F. David   Soc. Sec. No. 511-46-8420
211 Cliff Street   exemptions: 3
Solana Beach, California   incqme: $4,580

Minda, Carl David   Soc. Sec. No. 316-43-1124
13402 Shawnee Run Road   exemptions: 2
Cincinnati, Ohio   income: $4,900

8 Suppose a zoologist comes to you with a collection of data. He has made a count of the number of prairie rattlesnakes (Crotalus viridis viridis) found on a square mile of land at various altitudes around Fort Collins, Colorado. The data he has gathered is summarized in the table below.

altitude	number of snakes
5000'	30
5300'	28
5800'	20
6000'	14
6500'	10
7000'	3

He suspects that the number of snakes s at altitude a can be expressed as a linear function

$$s(a) = Da + M$$

He asks you to try to determine from his data what would be reasonable values to take for the coefficients D and M.

Naturally, you want to choose values for D and M so that the observed data deviates as little as possible from the values predicted by your coefficients D and M. In other words you want

$s(5000)$ to be close to 30
$s(5300)$ to be close to 28
$s(5800)$ to be close to 20

One technique that is often used in cases like this is to choose values for D and M which minimize the sum of the squares of the deviations from the observed values. In other words, so that

$$(s(5000) - 30)^2 + (s(5300) - 28)^2 + (s(5800) - 20)^2 + (s(6000)$$
$$- 14)^2 + (s(6500) - 10)^2 + (s(7000) - 3)^2$$

(where $s(a) = Da + M$)

is as small as possible.

Your job is to write a program which READs an integer n from a card, then READs n measurements a_i, s_i from the following n cards, then calculates values for D and M by solving the following pair of linear equations (which solve the least squares problem posed above).

$$\left(\sum_{i=1}^{n} a_i^2 \right) D + \left(\sum_{i=1}^{n} a_i \right) M = \sum_{i=1}^{n} a_i s_i$$

$$\left(\sum_{i=1}^{n} a_i \right) D + nM = \sum_{i=1}^{n} s_i$$

The output from your program should include the values of D and M as well as the value of the square deviation (for the computed values D and M) divided by n, that is

$$\frac{1}{n} \sum_{i=1}^{n} (Da_i - M - s_i)^2$$

9   The 55th Street Whiz Kids (a tough gang) have found it necessary to send messages to one another in secret code. In order to write a message in this secret code, a member must write down the message on a piece of scrap paper. Then under each character (including spaces and punctuation marks), the Whiz Kid places an integer between 0 and 42 according to the following scheme: 0 through 25 for A through Z respectively; 26 through 42 for the characters blank . , – ( ) ' 0 1 2 3 4 5 6 7 8 9 respectively. Then the Whiz Kid adds each pair of numbers and writes the result below the pair with the convention that if the sum is 43 or more, 43 is subtracted from it before writing it down, so that each number written will be between 0 and 42. The numbers are then decoded into characters, again using the above scheme.

Example:

1	written message:	MEET JIM 10 P.M.						
2	integers:	12	04	04	19	26	09	08	12
		26	34	33	26	15	27	12	27
3	added integers:	16	08	23	02	35	17	20	38
		17	24	16	41	42	39	39	
4	coded message:	QIXC2RU5RYQ8966						

Note that the coded message has only 15 characters, whereas the original message has 16. It will always be the case with this code system that the original message has one more character than the coded message. To make it possible to decode their message, the Whiz Kids made an agreement that the original message should always end with a period.

Write a program which will read coded messages from cards in the FORMAT 80A1 and print out the decoded message. You may assume the coded message has fewer than 500 characters and that the end of the coded message will be marked with a slash (/). The slash will be used for no other purpose than to mark the end of the coded message and therefore should not be used in decoding the message. You may use the above message to test your program.

8 SUBPROGRAMS

Chapter Objectives: After studying this chapter, you should be able to:

- Define and describe a subprogram.
- Design modular programs using subprograms.
- Write and use your own FUNCTIONs in programming.
- Write and use SUBROUTINEs in programming.
- Plot data using a line printer.
- Sort data using a simple sort program.
- Generate random numbers when you don't have or can't use RANF.
- Store data in COMMON.

Section 8 1

Introduction

"The code was muddled. There were layers of modification. And no written specifications were available. In other words, it was a normal situation." (*Datamation*, March 1976, p. 112.) How can you help combat the status quo?

> *steps in program design*
>
> 1 *statement of the problem*
> 2 *description of the desired solution in terms of input, computation, and output*
> 3 *refinement of the solution through successive levels of detail*
> 4 *coding of the program in Fortran*

Throughout this book we have emphasized a systematic approach to the development of programs. Surely you have discovered by now that the process doesn't always proceed smoothly. Sometimes problems in coding (step 4 in box) will force you to revise some of the details in your program design (step 3). Sometimes problems with the final program will force you to reconsider the statement of input/output behavior (step 2) or even the entire statement of the problem (step 1). (Review the Big Picture in Section 1 2.) The main advantage of using an organized, top-down approach to programming is that problems in your proposed solution are more likely to come to light before you've invested inordinate amounts of time in the coding phase. Programmers who use a systematic, top-down, patient approach produce correct, useful programs more quickly. Programmers who insist on trying to think directly in Fortran and who leap immediately from step 1 to step 4 simply do not survive in the long run. In this chapter, we will discuss ways of developing and implementing the successive levels of detail indicated in step 3.

The basic idea is to break up a given, large problem into a number of smaller, more manageable subprograms. But that's not a new idea—breaking large problems into units, subunits, subunits of subunits, and so on, in a hierarchical manner is the way we attack a wide range of problems in organization and communication.

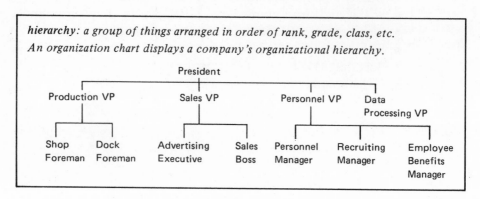

Some people find it helpful to write out something like a table of contents to a book to describe the way they've divided up their problem. Others prefer to draw something that looks like a company's organization chart. Figure 8 1 1 shows an example of the latter way of depicting the hierarchical breakdown of your problem. Such charts are called **HIPO diagrams**. HIPO is an acronym for **Hierarchy plus Input-Process-Output**, which is simply an awkward description of steps 1 through 3 in the box at the beginning of this section.

To use a HIPO diagram like that shown in Figure 8 1 1, you would write a short phrase which describes the problem you want to solve in the top-most box. In this particular case, we see that by solving two additional (simpler) subproblems (labeled Sub A and Sub B), we will be able to solve the main problem. Sub A, in turn, can be solved if we can provide solutions for the subsubproblems called Sub C, Sub D, and Sub E. Of course, in an actual case, we would write short phrases or words describing each subproblem in the boxes, instead of Sub A, Sub B, and so forth.

Don't confuse a HIPO diagram with a flowchart. As we refine the overall problem further, we'll draw a flowchart for each box in the HIPO diagram—the HIPO diagram serves as an overall guide showing how the various parts of our final program fit together. A HIPO diagram has much less detail than a flowchart, and should be expressed in high-level, convenient terms. That is, a HIPO diagram should indicate the way you have thought about the problem, the way you've divided it up. A flowchart, on the other hand, shows the details of your solution to a specific subproblem, and is expressed in terms closer to the final Fortran code.

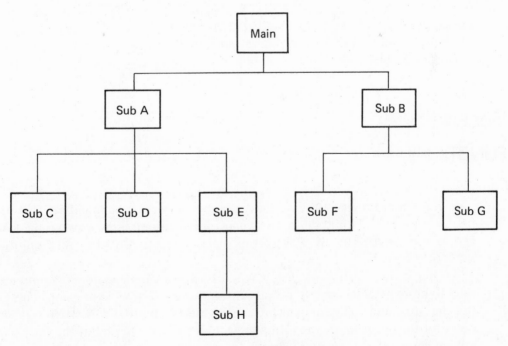

Figure 8 1 1   A HIPO Diagram

One particularly useful way of making the overall organization of your finished program clear, that is, of making your program have the same form as your HIPO chart, is coding each box in the HIPO diagram as a Fortran *subprogram*. There are two different kinds of subprograms, called FUNCTIONs and SUBROUTINEs.

You already know how to use built-in FUNCTIONs like SQRT, INT, MIN0, and so forth, to perform useful subtasks. Besides using built-in FUNCTIONs, you can use FUNCTIONs you design yourself and SUBROUTINEs of your own making to implement a program which you have designed in a hierarchical fashion. Both FUNCTIONs and SUBROUTINEs are lumped together under the term **subprograms** because they play a *subordinate* role, giving details of computations used in other parts of the program. As you have seen, FUNCTIONs are appropriate when a single value is computed by the subprogram, like the maximum of several numbers or the square root of a number. SUBROUTINEs are our choice when the subprogram returns several results each time it is used.

> *subprogram: a complete and separate program which may be referred to by another program*

> *program unit: the main program or a subprogram. Every Fortran program has at least one program unit. All our programs up to now have had exactly one unit, the main program.*

Since you are already familiar with built-in FUNCTIONs, we will discuss the writing of FUNCTION subprograms first. Then we'll deal with SUBROUTINEs. But let's not forget that both FUNCTIONs and SUBROUTINEs are members of the same family—subprograms—and that they're both used to make the program better by breaking it into small, understandable modules.

Divide and conquer!

Section 8 2

FUNCTIONs

If you want to describe the warranty on your new car, you might say something like "it's good for 24,000 miles, two years, or when something goes wrong, *whichever comes first*." That is, the warranty period is equal to the minimum of the three time periods.

As you know, Fortran gives us a way of using a simple word like *minimum* to refer to more detailed computations right in the midst of an expression. This clarifies the program by eliminating clutter. The built-in FUNCTION MIN0 is made to order for the problem of computing the actual warranty period of the car we were talking about. If it took us 57 weeks to drive 24,000 miles, and it took 7 weeks before something went wrong with our car, then these Fortran statements tell us how long our warranty period was:

```
      INTEGER WARPER
      WARPER = MINO(57, 2*52, 7)
      WRITE(6,3000) WARPER
 3000 FORMAT(' WARRANTY LASTED', I4, ' WEEKS')
      STOP
      END
```

output

```
WARRANTY LASTED    7 WEEKS
```

We are not limited to using just the built-in FUNCTIONs—we can define our own, suiting them to our exact needs. But before plunging into the details of defining our own, let's make clear where and how references to FUNCTIONs are used.

When we write MIN0(57, 2*52, 7) or SQRT(2.0) or ABS(−3.14159), we are referring to the FUNCTIONs MIN0, SQRT, and ABS, but more importantly, we are specifying numbers. For example, MIN0(57, 2 * 52, 7) may be viewed as specifying the INTEGER value 7. Since FUNCTION references are values, you may use a FUNCTION reference anywhere that an expression may appear. Thus,

```
WARPER = MINO(57, 2*52, 7)
```

contains a legitimate FUNCTION reference—it makes sense to assign the value of the FUNCTION reference to memory cell WARPER. However,

```
MINO(57, 2*52, 7) = 7
```

is *not* legitimate—MIN0(57, 2*52, 7) is not a memory cell, it is a value.

argument: an "input" to a computation. One very old meaning was related to the word refashioning. *We could say that in SQRT (2.0), the argument 2.0 is "refashioned" into 1.4142 . . .*

Notice that since a FUNCTION-value may be used in any expression, it is possible for a FUNCTION-value to appear as one of the arguments of another FUNCTION-reference. Thus,

```
WARPER = MINO (MINO(24,57), MINO(104,48), 7)
```

is a legal form which, like the examples above, assigns the value 7 to memory cell WARPER.

In Fortran, FUNCTION-values may be of any numeric type or they may be LOGICAL, but they can produce only one value. If you want a subprogram which returns an array of values, use a SUBROUTINE.

Now let's go through an example which shows why and how we might use a FUNCTION that's not built-in. Suppose you are involved in writing a program which needs to compute the sales tax of a given dollar amount. Sales tax computations aren't difficult, and you could put the statements for computing the sales

form

$$f(e_1, e_2, \ldots, e_n)$$

f is the name of a FUNCTION taking n arguments ($n \geqslant 1$)

e is a constant, expression, memory cell, array, FUNCTION name, or SUBROUTINE name (special arrangements are needed for the last two—see EXTERNAL in the index)

meaning

A FUNCTION-value is a single value of numeric or LOGICAL type and may be used in any arithmetic or LOGICAL expression where a constant of that data type may be used

examples

```
Z = SQRT(173.7*R)
X = F(Y**2)
J = LOCSM(A,N) +12
```

tax right in the program wherever you needed them. But since there are several statements involved in the sales tax computation, it would be more convenient to have a FUNCTION designed to do it and to use the FUNCTION when the sales tax is needed.

The following program computes the price of two automobiles, including tax and license.

```
      REAL TAX
      REAL AUTO1, PAINT, TIRES, LIC1, PRICE1
      REAL AUTO2, TRIM, LIC2, PRICE2
      READ(5,1000) AUTO1, PAINT, TIRES, LIC1
 1000 FORMAT(4F10.0)
      PRICE1 = AUTO1 + PAINT + TIRES +
     +          TAX(AUTO1+PAINT+TIRES) + LIC1
      READ(5,1000) AUTO2, TRIM, LIC2
      PRICE2 = AUTO2 + TRIM + TAX(AUTO2+TRIM) + LIC2
      WRITE(6,2000) PRICE1, PRICE2
 2000 FORMAT(' PRICE OF FIRST AUTO IS', F8.2/
     +        ' PRICE OF SECOND IS', F8.2)
      STOP
      END
```

data

```
7685.65    287.00    259.46    109.00
5400.27     56.95     86.50
```

output

```
PRICE OF FIRST AUTO IS 8835.04
PRICE OF SECOND IS 5871.15
```

As you can see, the FUNCTION TAX is used at two points in the program to compute the sales tax on the taxable portions of the total price (the license fee is not taxable). This is typical of situations in which we write FUNCTIONs. The important point is that the same computation must be performed at several points, but on different input values. Thus FUNCTIONs can be used to break the program into manageable pieces. FUNCTIONs are independent program units, external to all other modules of the program. Since a FUNCTION is a separate program, it has its own declarations, memory cells, statement labels, FORMATs, and END. All of these things are local to the FUNCTION. That is, they are automatically kept separate from their counterparts in other program units. Even if your main program and a FUNCTION both have statements labeled 100, the two labels won't be confused. The same goes for memory cells and the other constructs.

Arguments are transmitted from a FUNCTION reference to the FUNCTION. The FUNCTION returns its value via the FUNCTION name. When the FUNCTION-value has been computed and control returns to the calling program, it is as if the FUNCTION reference were replaced by the value the FUNCTION computed. A RETURN statement in a FUNCTION causes the controller to return to the point where the FUNCTION was referenced. Let's look at the following FUNCTION to see how this comes about.

```
        REAL FUNCTION TAX(AMT)
        REAL AMT
        INTEGER CENTS, CUTOFF, TBL(7), T
        DATA CUTOFF/108/
        DATA TBL(1),TBL(2),TBL(3),TBL(4),TBL(5),TBL(6),TBL(7)
      +  / 10  , 22  , 39  , 56  , 73  , 90  , 108 /

C       CONVERT AMT TO CENTS (+0.5 FORCES PROPER ROUND OFF)
        CENTS = INT(100.00*AMT + 0.5)
        IF (CENTS .LE. CUTOFF) GO TO 200
C          COMPUTE 6 PER CENT SALES TAX
        TAX = AINT(6.0*AMT+0.5)/100.00
        RETURN
C       USE TAX TABLE FOR AMOUNTS UNDER $1.08
  200   T=0
  210   IF (CENTS .LE. TBL(T+1))  GO TO 250
        T = T+1
        GO TO 210
  250   TAX = FLOAT(T)/100.00
        RETURN
        END
```

As you can see in the definition of the FUNCTION TAX, before returning, we assign the total tax to the name of the FUNCTION, as if the FUNCTION's name were a memory cell. This is how the FUNCTION gets its value. The value is then transmitted back to the statement that references the FUNCTION. Therefore, throughout the body of the FUNCTION, you may use the name of a FUNCTION as if it were a memory cell. The value of that "memory cell" when a RETURN is encountered becomes the value of the FUNCTION. FUNCTIONs have three parts: header statement, body, and END. The first line of the FUNCTION is its **header**. The last line is the END. The **body** is in between. The header contains the name of the FUNCTION. This name should appear on the left side of the equal sign in an assignment statement located somewhere in the body of the FUNCTION before the RETURN is encountered. We'll spend more time on these pieces of subprograms in the next section on SUBROUTINEs.

FUNCTION statement

forms

$$type \; \text{FUNCTION} \; f(p_1, p_2, \ldots, p_n)$$
$$\text{FUNCTION} \; f(p_1, p_2, \ldots, p_n)$$

type is any data type

f (the FUNCTION name) is an identifier

$p_1, p_2, \ldots, p_n$ (the parameter names) are identifiers

The body of the FUNCTION, that is, the statements between the FUNCTION statement and the corresponding END, must assign a value to the name f and must contain at least one RETURN statement. There must be at least one parameter in the parentheses.

If *type* is omitted, implicit typing takes over.

meaning

The value the FUNCTION computes when invoked is the value of its name when a RETURN statement is executed.

examples

```
REAL FUNCTION F(X)
INTEGER FUNCTION LOCSM(A,N)
FUNCTION G(X,Y,Z)
```

RETURN statement

form

RETURN

meaning

instructs the controller to go back to the point in the calling program where this subprogram was called

examples

```
RETURN
IF (X .EQ. Y)  RETURN
```

EXERCISES 8 2

1 What sequence of values will the REAL memory cell A be given by the following statements using built-in FUNCTIONs?

```
A = ABS(1.0 - 2.0)
A = ABS(A)*4.0
A = SQRT(ABS(2.0-A)*2.0)/2.0
```

2 What is wrong with the following FUNCTION definition?

```
REAL FUNCTION R
R = 2.0
RETURN
END
```

3 What value does FUNCTION TAX return if its argument is 3.49? How about 1.03?

4 What are the values of INT(5.0/3.0 + 0.5), INT(4.0/3.0 + 0.5), and AINT(5.0/2.0 + 0.5)? Do you see why we used similar expressions in the FUNCTION TAX?

5 Write a FUNCTION which duplicates the effect of the built-in FUNCTION ABS.

Section 8 3

SUBROUTINEs

One important use of SUBROUTINEs is to avoid having to write the same sequence of statements over and over again. For example, if you are writing a program that generates a long report, you'd probably want to number the pages. To do this your program needs to keep track of the number of pages printed. Each time a new page is printed, the page counter needs to be updated and its value printed at the upper right-hand corner of the next page of output. In addition, it would be nice to print the title of the report under the page number to insure that different reports don't get scrambled after the pages are burst. This is not a complicated process, but there are several Fortran statements involved, and by putting these statements in a SUBROUTINE we can avoid having to write them at every point in the program where we want to start a new page of output.

> **burst:** *to separate continuous form paper into separate sheets*

Like a FUNCTION, a SUBROUTINE is a separate program. It has its own declarations, memory cells, statement numbers, FORMATs, END statement, and so forth. All of these things are **local** to the SUBROUTINE. That is, they are automatically kept separate from their counterparts in other program units. Even if your main program and a SUBROUTINE both have statements labeled 100, the two labels won't be confused. They are local to their own program units. The same goes for memory cells and the other constructs.

In our example, we need some way to tell the page-numbering SUBROUTINE what the current page number is so that the SUBROUTINE can update the number and print it. Thus, we need some communication between the main program and the SUBROUTINE. We can transmit a memory cell to the SUBROUTINE via an **argument** in a **CALL statement**, the statement which gets the SUBROUTINE into action. Let's take a look at a typical CALL statement.

```
CALL   NEWPGE (PGENUM)
```
key word / SUBROUTINE name \ argument

A CALL statement has three parts: (1) the key word CALL, indicating that a SUBROUTINE is to be used; (2) the name of the SUBROUTINE to be brought into action (NEWPGE in our example); and (3) the argument list (there is only one argument, the INTEGER memory cell PGENUM, in our example, but other SUBROUTINEs may have several arguments).

CALL statement

forms
    CALL $s(a_1, a_2, \ldots, a_n)$
    CALL s

    s is a SUBROUTINE name
    a_i is an argument (i.e., a memory cell name, array name, constant, or expression)

meaning
    performs the computation described by SUBROUTINE s using the information and/or memory cells specified in the arguments

examples
```
CALL SORT (NAMES, N)
CALL AVG(GRD, N, AV)
CALL PRMESS
CALL CMPT(A, 32.0*CAB+1.0, SQRT(C))
```

To perform a CALL statement, the controller does three things: (1) it sets up a linkage so that control can return to the statement following the CALL, (2) it sets up the arguments to be transmitted to the SUBROUTINE, and (3) it transfers to the beginning of the SUBROUTINE to get its next instruction.

Now let's take a look at the SUBROUTINE itself.

```
      SUBROUTINE NEWPGE(PAGE)
      INTEGER PAGE
      PAGE = PAGE+1
      WRITE(6,1000) PAGE
 1000 FORMAT('1', 50X, 'PAGE', I5)
      WRITE(6,1001)
 1001 FORMAT(39X,'WEATHER SYSTEMS, INC.'/
     +        39X,'ANNUAL REPORT--1978'    )
      RETURN
      END
```

The first line of a SUBROUTINE, known as the **header** statement, contains the name of the SUBROUTINE and a list of **formal parameters**. Formal parameters are symbols which will be used in the **body** of the SUBROUTINE (the part between the header statement and the END) to stand for the arguments which will be transmitted via a CALL statement.

The name (NEWPGE) of the SUBROUTINE is placed after the key word SUBROUTINE and followed by the parenthesized list of formal parameters (PAGE). After the header statement come the formal parameter declarations (INTEGER PAGE). Even though these look like normal declaration statements, their effect is quite different. Instead of instructing the compiler to attach names to memory cells or arrays, they tell the compiler what kind of values or structures to expect the formal parameters to be attached to when the SUBROUTINE is called. The first thing the controller does when it begins to perform the statements in a SUBROUTINE is to attach the formal parameter names to the arguments transmitted by the CALL statement. Once that is done, the controller begins to perform the executable statements in the body of the SUBROUTINE. In our example, this amounts to increasing the value of the memory cell attached to the

Subprograms help you break your program into smaller logical chunks. Then you can work on each chunk separately.

formal parameter PAGE. Our CALL would have transmitted the memory cell PGENUM from the main program, hence the first statement would increase the value of PGENUM. It is important to realize that the memory cell itself is transmitted, not just its value. Its value is changed in our SUBROUTINE. Next come the WRITE statements, which put the page number in the upper right-hand corner of the next page and the report title underneath. Finally, the controller encounters the **RETURN instruction**. At this point it uses the linkage established by the CALL to return to the statement immediately following the CALL in the main program. Since every SUBROUTINE is a separate program unit, the compiler must be instructed when to wrap up the compilation of a SUBROUTINE. The END statement is used for this purpose. It must be the last statement in every program unit. In the deck setup, program units are simply placed in sequence, one behind the other (as in Figure 8 3 1).

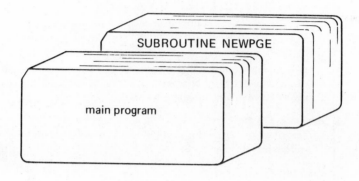

Figure 8 3 1

The following program uses the SUBROUTINE NEWPGE.

```
COMMENT PROGRAM TO WRITE ANNUAL REPORT FOR
C          WEATHER SYSTEMS, INC.
       INTEGER PGENUM, LINCNT, ITEM(6), I, FINIS
       REAL LASTYR, THISYR, CHANGE
C   VARIABLES:
C       PGENUM--CURRENT PAGE NUMBER
C       LINCNT--NUMBER OF LINES PRINTED SO FAR ON THIS PAGE
C       ITEM--DESCRIPTION OF A LINE ITEM
C       LASTYR--LAST YEAR'S DOLLAR AMOUNT FOR THIS ITEM
C       THISYR--THIS YEAR'S DOLLAR AMOUNT
C       CHANGE--INCREASE IN DOLLAR AMOUNT OVER LAST YEAR
C               (NEGATIVE MEANS DECREASE)
       DATA FINIS/3HEND/
       PGENUM = 0
C                                        PRINT INCOME SHEET
C                               HERE'S THE FIRST SUBROUTINE CALL
       CALL NEWPGE(PGENUM)
       WRITE(6,1000)
 1000  FORMAT('0',43X,'INCOME STATEMENT'/)
 10    LINCNT = 0
 100      READ(5,1010) ITEM, LASTYR,THISYR
 1010     FORMAT(6A4,2F10.0)
          IF (ITEM(1) .EQ. FINIS)  GO TO 200
          CHANGE = THISYR-LASTYR
          WRITE(6,1020) ITEM, LASTYR,THISYR,CHANGE
 1020     FORMAT('0',6A4/3F20.2)
          LINCNT = LINCNT+3
          IF (LINCNT .LT. 21)  GO TO 100
```

```
C                                              MOVING TO NEXT PAGE
C                                CALL NEWPGE SUBROUTINE AGAIN
C                                AND GO BACK TO RESET LINE COUNT
        CALL NEWPGE(PGENUM)
        GO TO 10
C                                              PRINT BALANCE SHEET
C                                HERE'S ANOTHER CALL STATEMENT
  200   CALL NEWPGE(PGENUM)
        WRITE(6,2000)
 2000 FORMAT('0',46X,'BALANCE SHEET')
  210   LINCNT = 0
  220     READ(5,1010) ITEM, LASTYR,THISYR
            IF (ITEM(1) .EQ. FINIS)  STOP
            CHANGE = THISYR-LASTYR
            WRITE(6,1020) ITEM, LASTYR,THISYR,CHANGE
            LINCNT = LINCNT+3
            IF (LINCNT .LT. 21)  GO TO 220
C                                              MOVING TO NEXT PAGE
C                                CALL NEWPGE SUBROUTINE AGAIN
C                                AND GO BACK TO RESET LINE COUNT
        CALL NEWPGE(PGENUM)
        GO TO 210
        END
```

data
```
FURNACE SALES--NEW BLDGS   45227.56   52146.35
FURNACE SALES--OLD BLDGS   11235.77   13269.25
FURNACE INSTALLATION      245322.78  287526.97
AIR COND SALES             34258.46   52348.98
AIR COND INSTALLATION     111247.52  164523.27
ATTIC BLOWER SALES          7462.24    6289.42
WINDOW FAN SALES            5212.35    9875.23
ARCHITECTURAL CONSULTING   32428.82   41237.72
------GROSS INCOME        492395.50  627217.19
EXPENDITURES              432115.24  552253.24
******PROFIT               60280.26   74964.95
END
CASH                        1456.52    1875.22
FURNACE INVENTORY           6327.75    5214.74
AIR COND INVENTORY          3244.51    5241.70
FAN AND BLOWER INVENTORY    2153.68    1475.58
MISC. SUPPLIES              1453.01    2401.80
BUILDINGS AND LAND        253000.00  275000.00
------TOTAL ASSETS        267635.47  291209.04
ACCOUNTS PAYABLE            5423.42    6302.08
BANK NOTES                  4521.01    6321.00
MORTGAGE                  175200.24  164010.23
TOTAL LIABILITIES - O.E.  185144.67  176633.31
******OWNER'S EQUITY       82490.80  114575.67
------TOTAL LIABILITIES   267635.47  291209.04
END
```

output

INCOME STATEMENT

FURNACE SALES--NEW BLDGS
    45227.56   52146.35   6918.79

FURNACE SALES--OLD BLDGS
    11235.77   13269.25   2033.48

FURNACE INSTALLATION
   245322.78   287526.97   42204.19

AIR COND SALES
    34258.46   52348.98   18090.52

AIR COND INSTALLATION
   111247.52   164523.27   53275.75

ATTIC BLOWER SALES
     7462.24   6289.42   -1172.82

WINDOW FAN SALES
     5212.35   9875.23   4662.88

ARCHITECTURAL CONSULTING
    32428.82   41237.72   8808.90

------GROSS INCOME
   492395.50   627217.19   134821.69

EXPENDITURES
   432115.24   552253.24   120138.00

******PROFIT
    60280.26   74964.95   14684.69

BALANCE SHEET

CASH
1456.52	1875.22	418.70

FURNACE INVENTORY
6327.75	5214.74	-1113.01

AIR COND INVENTORY
3244.51	5241.70	1997.19

FAN AND BLOWER INVENTORY
2153.68	1475.58	-678.10

MISC. SUPPLIES
1453.01	2401.80	948.79

BUILDINGS AND LAND
253000.00	275000.00	22000.00

------TOTAL ASSETS
267635.47	291209.04	23573.57

ACCOUNTS PAYABLE
5423.42	6302.08	878.66

BANK NOTES
4521.01	6321.00	1799.99

MORTGAGE
175200.24	164010.23	-11190.01

TOTAL LIABILITIES - O.E.
185144.67	176633.31	-8511.36

******OWNER'S EQUITY
82490.80	114575.67	32084.87

------TOTAL LIABILITIES
267635.47	291209.04	23573.57

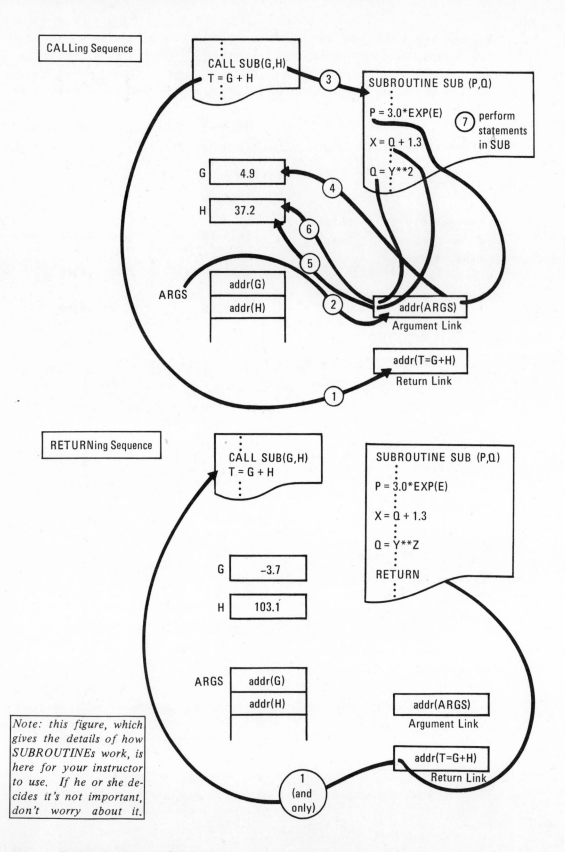

Because SUBROUTINEs are completely separate program units, they are often called **externals**. The consequences of this subprogram independence can be confusing at first. Suppose, for example, that you write a SUBROUTINE AREA which has two REAL parameters, but when you CALL AREA you accidentally use an INTEGER argument.

```
                                    error!
      REAL S
      CALL AREA(2, S)
      WRITE(6,1000) S
 1000 FORMAT(' AREA IS', F5.2)
      STOP
      END

      SUBROUTINE AREA(R, A)
      REAL R, A
      A = 3.14*R**2
      RETURN
      END
```

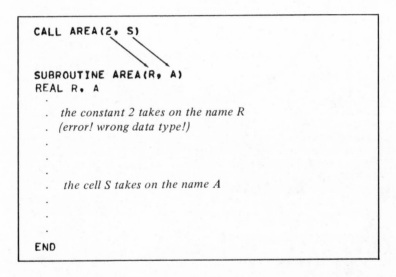

```
      CALL AREA(2, S)



      SUBROUTINE AREA(R, A)
      REAL R, A
        .
        .   the constant 2 takes on the name R
        .   (error! wrong data type!)
        .
        .
        .
        .   the cell S takes on the name A
        .
        .
        .
      END
```

> *Caution—data type: The data type of each argument in a CALL statement must match that of the corresponding parameter in the SUBROUTINE.*

This will cause an error when the computer tries to do the computation in AREA because the INTEGER 2 and the REAL 2.0 are not the same. On most Fortran systems the pattern of 1's and 0's that represents the INTEGER 2 is very close to the pattern that represents the REAL number 0.0. This information might help you track down errors of this nature in case your Fortran system doesn't detect them (most don't). Even so, this kind of error can be exceedingly difficult to find. The moral is to make sure the arguments in CALL statements match the corresponding parameter declarations in the SUBROUTINE.

To illustrate this point further, let's consider a second case. As you know, the arguments in CALL statements may be values (that is, arithmetic or LOGICAL expressions or constants like 2 in the CALL AREA(2,S) above, or they may be memory cell names, or array names. But you must be careful when you write CALL statements: Don't give the SUBROUTINE arguments that it will try to use in illegitimate ways. For example, suppose we had gotten the data types right in our CALL statement above, but had accidentally switched the order of the arguments, as shown below.

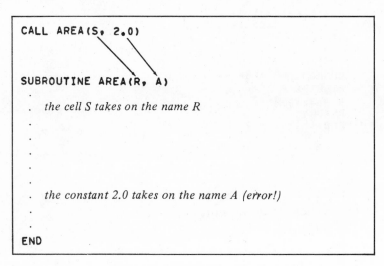

```
CALL AREA(S, 2.0)


SUBROUTINE AREA(R, A)
   .
   .    the cell S takes on the name R
   .
   .
   .
   .
   .    the constant 2.0 takes on the name A (error!)
   .
   .
END
```

```
                            error!
      REAL S
      CALL AREA(S, 2.0)
      WRITE(6,1000) S
 1000 FORMAT(' AREA IS', F5.2)
      STOP
      END

      SUBROUTINE AREA(R, A)
      REAL R, A
      A = 3.14*R**2
      RETURN
      END
```

Then the A in the SUBROUTINE gets linked to the 2.0 in the CALL. But when the SUBROUTINE tries to perform the assignment statement A = 3.14 * R ** 2, it is actually trying to assign a new value to the constant 2.0. Clearly a mistake! The results of such an error vary from one Fortran system to another, but many systems don't give you any warning when this happens, making the mistake very hard to find.

> *Caution—constant arguments: A* SUBROUTINE *must not try to change the value of a parameter which is linked to a constant in a* CALL *statement.*

A third way in which CALL arguments and SUBROUTINE parameters must match is in structure. If a SUBROUTINE parameter is declared as an array, the corresponding argument in a CALL must be an array. The two examples in Figure 8 3 2 illustrate the point. In the program on the left, the SUBROUTINE expects the CALL statement to give it access to a memory cell, and it gets one—the third element in the array A. All is well. In the example on the right, the SUBROUTINE is expecting an array but gets a memory cell instead. Things will go badly there, possibly without warning—again, a difficult error to eliminate from the program once it creeps in. Be careful when CALLing SUBROUTINEs!

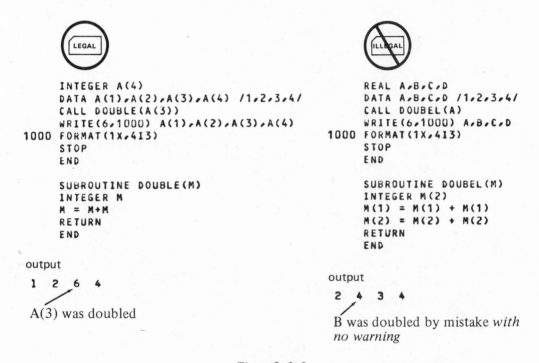

```
        INTEGER A(4)
        DATA A(1),A(2),A(3),A(4) /1,2,3,4/
        CALL DOUBLE(A(3))
        WRITE(6,1000) A(1),A(2),A(3),A(4)
1000    FORMAT(1X,4I3)
        STOP
        END

        SUBROUTINE DOUBLE(M)
        INTEGER M
        M = M+M
        RETURN
        END
```

output

1 2 6 4

A(3) was doubled

```
        REAL A,B,C,D
        DATA A,B,C,D /1,2,3,4/
        CALL DOUBEL(A)
        WRITE(6,1000) A,B,C,D
1000    FORMAT(1X,4I3)
        STOP
        END

        SUBROUTINE DOUBEL(M)
        INTEGER M(2)
        M(1) = M(1) + M(1)
        M(2) = M(2) + M(2)
        RETURN
        END
```

output

2 4 3 4

B was doubled by mistake *with no warning*

Figure 8 3 2

> *Caution—array parameters: If a* SUBROUTINE *parameter is declared to be an array, make sure the* CALL *statement supplies an array for the* SUBROUTINE *to use.*

The matching correspondence between CALL arguments and SUBROUTINE parameters is so crucial that we think one final cautionary example will be helpful. When a SUBROUTINE parameter is declared to be a multidimensional array, the corresponding argument in the CALL statement must be an array of the same shape. If it isn't, problems will ensue. Avoid problems by being careful in CALL statements.

The two CALL statements in Figure 8 3 3 illustrate what can happen. In the first CALL statement, the array R has a 3-by-3 arrangement, and the corresponding parameter in the SUBROUTINE is declared to be a 3-by-3 array, consistent with the argument. The SUBROUTINE puts zeros across the bottom row as it was intended to do. In the second CALL, the argument W is again a 3-by-3 array, but the SUBROUTINE is led to believe its parameter will be a 2-by-2 array. Instead of getting a row of zeros, as expected, we get strange results and no clue as to what went wrong.

The moral is to be careful when CALLing SUBROUTINEs. Know what assumptions the SUBROUTINE will make about its parameters, and make your CALL statements consistent with those assumptions.

```
        INTEGER R(3,3), W(3,3)
        DATA R(1,1),R(1,2),R(1,3) /11,12,13/
        DATA R(2,1),R(2,2),R(2,3) /21,22,23/
        DATA R(3,1),R(3,2),R(3,3) /31,32,33/
        DATA W(1,1),W(1,2) /11,12/
        DATA W(2,1),W(2,2) /21,22/
        CALL ZAPROW(R,3)
        CALL ZAPROW(W,2)
        WRITE(6,1000) R(1,1),R(1,2),R(1,3), W(1,1),W(1,2),
     +                R(2,1),R(2,2),R(2,3), W(2,1),W(2,2),
     +                R(3,1),R(3,2),R(3,3)
 1000   FORMAT(1X,3I3,10X,2I3)
        STOP
        END

        SUBROUTINE ZAPROW(A,N)
        INTEGER N, A(N,N)
        INTEGER C
        C=1
 100    A(N,C) = 0
          C = C+1
          IF (C .LE. N)  GO TO 100
        RETURN
        END
```

output

```
11 12 13          11  0
21 22 23           0 22
 0  0  0
```

Figure 8 2 3   Right and Wrong Ways to CALL

Caution—multidimensional array arguments: When you put a multidimensional array in a CALL statement's argument list, make sure its dimensions are the same as those declared for the corresponding parameter in the SUBROUTINE.

In spite of the difficulties they sometimes cause, SUBROUTINEs are one of the most important and useful features of Fortran. Over the years, people have written programs to do many things. Those that may be applied to many common problems are often written in the form of SUBROUTINEs and saved. At your computer center, no doubt, there is a large collection of SUBROUTINEs already written and available for you to use. Since the means of access to the collection differs from place to place, you will have to consult a local expert. Once you know how to attach these SUBROUTINEs to your program, you can use them simply by writing CALL statements with appropriate arguments. The availability of prepackaged SUBROUTINEs and FUNCTIONs, by itself, would be a good reason to learn how to use SUBROUTINEs. This, along with their use as time-savers in coding, as in the annual report example, should motivate you to become proficient with SUBROUTINEs.

---

*Fortran subprograms are said to be **externals**. As a consequence of this organization, the compiler treats each program unit (i.e., your main program and your subprograms) independently. The END card, which must be the last card of every program unit, tells the compiler to stop compiling one program and to get ready to compile another.*

Things to remember about subprograms

Variable names and statement numbers are not confused between programs.

It is very easy to use subprograms written by someone else.

They can make your program more readable.

You cannot use variables from the calling program merely by using the same names in the subprogram.

The primary difference between FUNCTIONs and SUBROUTINEs is the contexts in which they are used. A FUNCTION returns *one* value; a SUBROUTINE may return *any number* of values (through its arguments). A FUNCTION reference looks like a prefix operator notation; a SUBROUTINE CALL looks more like a transfer of control. Deciding which to use is a matter of taste and convenience.

EXERCISES 8 3

1 Which of the following are legal SUBROUTINE statements? If not, explain why not.

```
SUBROUTINE APPLE(RED,GREEN)
SUBROUTINE PEAR
SUBROUTINE POMEGRANATE(SEED)
SUBROUTINE PIZZA(SMALL, OR, LARGE(ONE))
```

2 Which of the following are legal CALL statements? If not, explain why not.

```
CALL APPLE(1,3HRED)
CALL PEAR
CALL POMEG(RANATE)
CALL PIZZA(SMALL,OR,LARGE(ONE))
```

3   What would the following program print?

```
      INTEGER A, B, C
      CALL SQUARE(3,A)
      CALL SQUARE(4,B)
      CALL SQUARE(5,C)
      WRITE(6,1000) A,B,C
 1000 FORMAT(1X,3I3)
      STOP
      END

      SUBROUTINE SQUARE(NUMBER,SQ)
      INTEGER NUMBER, SQ
      SQ = NUMBER*NUMBER
      RETURN
      END
```

4   What would the following program print?

```
      INTEGER A(3)
      DATA A(1)/3HDOG/, A(2)/3HCAT/, A(3)/3HBAT/
      CALL CHANGE(A,2)
      WRITE(6,1000) A
 1000 FORMAT(' A=',3(1X,A4))
      STOP
      END

      SUBROUTINE CHANGE(ARRAY, INDEX)
      INTEGER ARRAY(3), INDEX
      INTEGER NONE
      DATA NONE/4HNONE/
      ARRAY(INDEX) = NONE
      RETURN
      END
```

Section 8 4

Plotting—An Example Using SUBROUTINEs

It wasn't long after the first printed pages came zooming out of computer line printers that people, perhaps initially attracted by the moving, shifting patterns of program listings, began writing programs which produce two-dimensional patterns for their own sake. Practitioners of **computer graphics** have developed elaborate techniques and can produce a fantastic range of visual effects. There are even contests for computer produced art.

In this section we'll point out a few of the mechanics of plotting—specifically, how to go from an internally stored or generated image to a properly scaled image on the printed page. There are numerous ways of creating images to plot. Ideas include generating lines and boxes with random orientations, generating random subpatterns and sprinkling them around, storing subpatterns (circles, squares, or whatever) and expanding or shrinking and shifting copies of them. It is also fairly simple to write subprograms which will make mirror images of already created subpatterns.

Your computer center may well have more elaborate devices for plotting which will make it possible to create more elaborate, more finely detailed drawings. Fancy gadgetry is no substitute for imagination, though.

The basic idea we will use to draw pictures on the line printer is **discretization,** which means representing something which is continuously, smoothly changing in terms of a small number of specific values. This is necessary because the printer can't print symbols just anywhere on the page; it is neatly organized to print in columns and rows. We must convert any other sort of image into one which has symbols in column and row positions. Conceptually we lay a grid over our image and let each grid square correspond to a character position on the printed page (i.e., some specific row and column). Then we place a symbol on the page for each grid which covers any dark part of the image. Figure 8 4 1 shows a continuous image and three discrete versions of it at different levels of discretization.

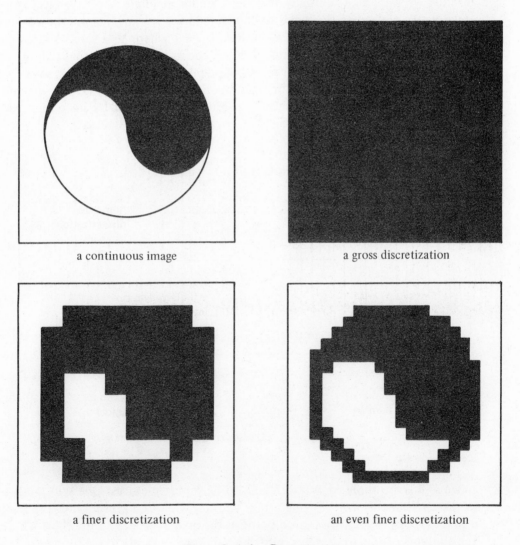

a continuous image   a gross discretization

a finer discretization   an even finer discretization

Figure 8 4 1   Discretization

Probably the most convenient way to deal with the print grid is to use a two-dimensional array. If the image grid has H rows and W columns, then we use a W-by-H two-dimensional INTEGER array to represent the printed page. To begin, we fill the array with blanks. Then we store nonblank symbols (e.g., asterisks) in array positions which correspond to dark spots in the image. The hard part is setting up this correspondence between the image plane and the two-dimensional array. What we need is a way to convert a pair of REAL coordinates (X, Y) in the image plane to a pair of INTEGER subscripts (I, J) in the ranges 1 to H and 1 to W respectively.

First we'll convert X to I. If the left boundary of the image plane corresponds to X = XMIN and the right boundary to X = XMAX, then (X – XMIN)/(XMAX – XMIN) is a number between 0.0 and 1.0. Consequently, INT(W*(X – XMIN)/(XMAX – XMIN)) + 1 is an INTEGER between 1 and W. This is the conversion formula we wanted. Essentially it divides the image plane into W vertical strips of equal width and takes the value I when X is in the Ith strip. Similarly we convert Y to INT(H*(Y – YMIN)/(YMAX – YMIN)) + 1 where YMIN and YMAX correspond to the bottom and top boundaries of the image plane. Actually, if an image point lies exactly on the top or right boundary, we'll have problems, so we won't allow image points on the top or right boundary. This is easy to do—if there are any troublesome points, just shift the grid a tiny amount by increasing XMAX and YMAX.

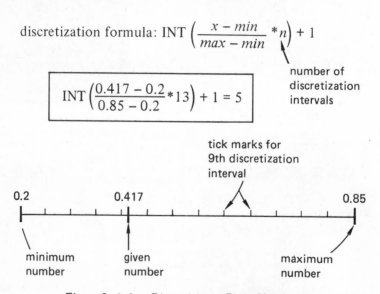

$$\text{discretization formula: INT}\left(\frac{x - min}{max - min} * n\right) + 1$$

number of discretization intervals

$$\text{INT}\left(\frac{0.417 - 0.2}{0.85 - 0.2} * 13\right) + 1 = 5$$

tick marks for 9th discretization interval

0.2   0.417   0.85

minimum number   given number   maximum number

Figure 8 4 2   Discretizing a Given Number

We will write three SUBROUTINEs to help plot pictures. One will put blanks in the two-dimensional plotting array; another will put a symbol into the array at a point corresponding to a given point in the image plane; and the third will print the contents of the array. Thus, plotting a picture amounts to CALLing the blank-out routine, then CALLing the point-plotting routine once for each dark spot in the image, and finally, CALLing the printing routine. These SUBROUTINEs are written below. The only tricky part is the discretization, that is, converting X to I and Y to J, which we've already discussed. Figure 8 4 3 is a HIPO diagram of the process.

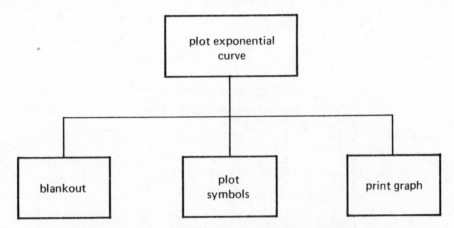

Figure 8 4 3   A HIPO Diagram Indicating the Relationships among the Various Program Units

```
       SUBROUTINE BLKOUT (GRAPH, W,H)
       INTEGER W,H, GRAPH(W,H)
COMMENT:  THIS SUBROUTINE FILLS THE PLOTTING ARRAY "GRAPH"
C         WITH BLANKS
       INTEGER I,J, BLANK
       DATA BLANK/1H /
       J=H
100    I=1
200      GRAPH(I,J) = BLANK
         I = I+1
         IF (I .LE. W)  GO TO 200
       J = J-1
       IF (J .GE. 1)  GO TO 100
       RETURN
       END

       SUBROUTINE PLOT (X,Y, XMIN,XMAX, YMIN,YMAX,
      +                    SYMBOL, GRAPH,W,H)
       REAL X,Y, XMIN,XMAX, YMIN,YMAX
       INTEGER SYMBOL, W,H,GRAPH(W,H)
COMMENT:  THIS SUBROUTINE PUTS "SYMBOL" INTO THE PLOTTING
C         ARRAY "GRAPH" AT A POINT CORRESPONDING TO
C         (X,Y) IN THE IMAGE PLANE
C         THE RANGE OF COORDINATES IS ASSUMED TO BE
C            (XMIN TO XMAX , YMIN TO YMAX)
C         COORDINATES OUTSIDE THIS RANGE WILL NOT BE PLOTTED
       INTEGER I,J
C      DISCRETIZE X AND Y
       I = INT( ((X-XMIN)/(XMAX-XMIN)) * FLOAT(W) ) +1
       J = INT( ((Y-YMIN)/(YMAX-YMIN)) * FLOAT(H) ) +1
C      PUT (X,Y) INTO "GRAPH" (IF IN RANGE)
       IF (I .GE. 1  .AND.
      +    I .LE. W  .AND.
      +    J .GE. 1  .AND.
      +    J .LE. H          ) GRAPH(I,J) = SYMBOL
       RETURN
       END
```

> *The line number J in the plotting routine PRGRPH steps backwards because, according to the discretization formula, large Y-values, which should go near the top of the picture, correspond to large J-values. Therefore, the line numbers which are the largest must be printed first to put them near the top of the page.*

```
      SUBROUTINE PRGRPH (GRAPH,W,H)
      INTEGER W,H, GRAPH(W,H)
COMMENT:  THIS SUBROUTINE PRINTS THE PLOTTING ARRAY "GRAPH"
      INTEGER I,J
      J = H
  100 WRITE(6,1000) (GRAPH(I,J), I=1,W)
      J = J-1
      IF (J .GE. 1)  GO TO 100
      RETURN
 1000 FORMAT(1X, 120A1)
      END

COMMENT:  PLOT THE EXPONENTIAL CURVE
      REAL X, EXP
      INTEGER G(25,15)
      CALL BLKOUT(G,25,15)
      X = -1.0
  100 CALL PLOT (X,EXP(X), -1.0,1.0, 0.0,2.0, 1H*, G,25,15)
      X = X + 0.05
      IF (X .LE. 1.0)  GO TO 100
      CALL PRGRPH (G,25,15)
      STOP
      END
```

output

When plotting with the line printer, you will get better results if you keep in mind that the distance between characters on a line is less than the distance between lines. That is, the plotting device you are using has sharper resolution in the horizontal direction than in the vertical direction. The ratio of these resolutions is about five to three for most line printers. Therefore, in order to avoid distorting your picture, you should divide the image plane into about five parts in the horizontal direction for every three parts in the vertical direction. In other words, the ratio w/h of the width to the height of your plotting array should be about 5/3.

EXERCISES 8 4

1 What would you have to change in SUBROUTINE PRGRPH to make it plot your data instead of the exponential growth curve?

Section 8 5

Sorting—Using Variable Length Arrays

The managers of a marketing and sales research firm have asked us to help them out. Many customers come to their staff with lists of sales figures (usually either monthly or weekly) tabulated over several years. Normally the research firm begins by preparing a year-by-year listing of this data. For each year the sales figures are listed two ways. One is simply a month-by-month (or week-by-week) tabulation of the monthly (or weekly) sales amounts. The other lists the amounts in decreasing order, from the best sales period to the worst. In this way the research firm gets a picture of seasonal effects on the customer's sales.

The research firm's business has grown in recent years and the staff can no longer handle all of it. Consequently they have decided to turn the tabulations over to a computer. The sales figures will be punched on cards, with one group of cards for each year. The first card of each yearly group will have the year and the sales period type (MONTHLY or WEEKLY) punched on it. The remaining cards of the group will have the sales figures (in whole dollars) punched on them. The firm wants us to write a program to print the tabulations in order to save the staff this tedious job.

If you think about it, you will see that this is a relatively simple programming task except for the business of listing the sales figures in order of decreasing sales period. Up to that point it is simply a matter of READing values and printing them. No rearrangement is necessary because they come in chronological order. But in order to print the sales figures in order of decreasing sales periods, we need to rearrange the data. One way to do that is to put the sales figures into an array and, when necessary, to change the order in which they are stored. We will want the output from the program to look something like the sample below. Figure 8 5 1 is a HIPO diagram showing the processes to be performed.

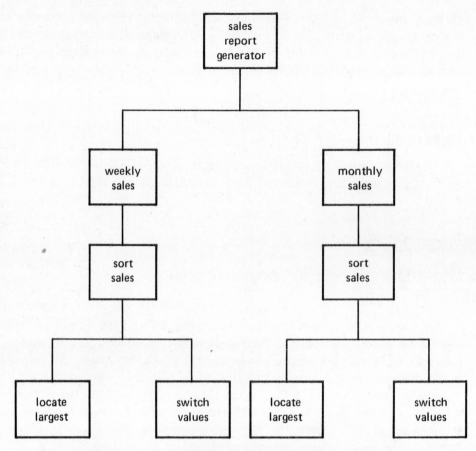

Figure 8 5 1 A HIPO Diagram of the Basic Functions
to Be Performed in Subprograms

```
                    SALES TABULATION
        1976
MONTHLY SALES FIGURES

        CHRONOLOGICAL                    BEST TO WORST
        MONTH        SALES               MONTH        SALES
          1          6472                 12          10428
          2          4103                 10           9342
          3          2001                 11           8497
          4          2422                  1           6472
          5          3501                  6           5402
          6          5402                  7           5117
          7          5117                  8           4322
          8          4322                  2           4103
          9          2173                  5           3501
         10          9342                  4           2422
         11          8497                  9           2173
         12         10428                  3           2001
```

SALES TABULATION

WEEKLY SALES FIGURES

CHRONOLOGICAL			BEST TO WORST	
WEEK	SALES		WEEK	SALES
1	1647		49	2544
2	1500		52	2544
3	1399		45	2422
4	1822		41	2411
5	1021		50	2144
6	1059		43	2134
7	987		44	2111
8	855		51	2066
9	502		48	2032
10	408		46	2031
11	201		40	2011
12	422		42	1955
13	385		47	1902
14	638		4	1822
15	655		1	1647
16	588		25	1621
17	574		24	1534
18	788		2	1500
19	698		23	1422
20	755		39	1422
21	802		3	1399
22	621		29	1354
23	1422		26	1308
24	1534		28	1307
25	1621		30	1238
26	1308		27	1205
27	1205		31	1104
28	1307		6	1059
29	1354		5	1021
30	1238		32	987
31	1104		7	987
32	987		33	855
33	855		8	855
34	445		21	802
35	655		18	788
36	521		20	755
37	411		19	698
38	322		15	655
39	1422		35	655
40	2011		14	638
41	2411		22	621
42	1955		16	588
43	2134		17	574
44	2111		36	521
45	2422		9	502
46	2031		34	445
47	1902		12	422
48	2032		37	411
49	2544		10	408
50	2144		13	385
51	2066		38	322
52	2544		11	201

Because the line printer can't back up to print the columns under BEST TO WORST SALES MONTH, we'll have to store the sales information twice, once in chronological order and once in order of decreasing sales. When we arrange the sales figures in decreasing order, we must also arrange the corresponding month numbers to be printed beside the sales figures. Thus, in addition to the array

---

plan for sales report program

1 *determine year of report*
2 *determine period of report (weekly or monthly)*
3 *process weekly or monthly data (sort and print)*
4 *repeat*

---

storing the sales figures in chronological order, we need a pair of arrays to store the month numbers and sales figures in decreasing order. We'll use a SUBROU-TINE to arrange the data for the columns on the right. We'll call it SORT since it sorts data into a certain order. It will have three parameters: (1) the array containing the sales figures, (2) the array containing the corresponding month numbers, and (3) the number of elements in the arrays (12 or 52). The first two are both input and output parameters (when SORT is CALLed, the first two arguments will contain information in some order and SORT will rearrange the information) and the third is an input parameter.

Study the program below. We'll discuss the SORT subprogram once you understand its purpose.

```
COMMENT:  THIS PROGRAM MAKES SALES REPORT SUMMARIES
          INTEGER YEAR,PERIOD,MONTH
          DATA MONTH/1HM/
C         GET YEAR AND SALES PERIOD FROM FIRST CARD OF GROUP
  100     READ(5,1000) YEAR,PERIOD
 1000     FORMAT(I4,A1)
          IF ( YEAR .EQ. 0 )  STOP
          WRITE(6,1001)
 1001     FORMAT('1',21X, 'SALES TABULATION')
          WRITE(6,1002) YEAR
 1002     FORMAT(1X,I12)
C         CALL APPROPRIATE SUBROUTINE TO HANDLE
C         WEEKLY OR MONTHLY SALES PERIOD.
          IF ( PERIOD'.EQ. MONTH )  GO TO 200
          CALL WEEKLY
          GO TO 100
  200     CALL MNTHLY
          GO TO 100
COMMENT:  THE SUBROUTINES "WEEKLY" AND "MNTHLY" NEED NO
C         INFORMATION FROM THIS PROGRAM. THEREFORE, THEY'VE
C         NO ARGUMENTS.  THEY GET THEIR INFORMATION
C         FROM DATA CARDS AND PRINT THEIR RESULTS.
C         HENCE,  THEY DON'T NEED TO COMMUNICATE VALUES TO
C         OR FROM THE CALLING PROGRAM.
          END
```

```
      SUBROUTINE MNTHLY
      INTEGER SALES(12), MN(12), MNSALE(12), I
      WRITE(6,1000)
1000  FORMAT(' MONTHLY SALES FIGURES'/
     +          '0',11X,'CHRONOLOGICAL',25X,'BEST TO WORST'/
     +          10X,'MONTH',9X,'SALES',18X,'MONTH',9X,'SALES')
      READ(5,1001) SALES
1001  FORMAT(10I6)
C     SAVE SALES FIGURES AND MAKE A LIST OF MONTH NUMBERS
      I = 1
100   MN(I) = I
      MNSALE(I) = SALES(I)
      I = I + 1
      IF ( I .LE. 12 )  GO TO 100
C     SORT INFORMATION ACCORDING TO DECREASING SALES.
      CALL SORT (MNSALE, MN, 12)
C     PRINT REPORT
      I = 1
200   WRITE(6,2000) I,SALES(I),MN(I),MNSALE(I)
2000  FORMAT(1X,I12,I16,18X,I3,I16)
      I = I + 1
      IF ( I .LE. 12 )  GO TO 200
      RETURN
      END


      SUBROUTINE WEEKLY
      INTEGER SALES(52), WK(52), WKSALE(52), I
      WRITE(6,1000)
1000  FORMAT( ' WEEKLY SALES FIGURES'/
     +          '0',11X,'CHRONOLOGICAL',25X,'BEST TO WORST'/
     +          10X,'WEEK ',9X,'SALES',18X,'WEEK ',9X,'SALES')
      READ(5,1001) SALES
1001  FORMAT(10I6)
C     SAVE SALES FIGURES AND MAKE A LIST OF  WEEK NUMBERS
      I = 1
100   WK(I) = I
      WKSALE(I) = SALES(I)
      I = I + 1
      IF ( I .LE. 52 )  GO TO 100
C     SORT INFORMATION ACCORDING TO DECREASING SALES.
      CALL SORT (WKSALE, WK, 52)
C     PRINT REPORT
      I = 1
200   WRITE(6,2000) I,SALES(I),WK(I),WKSALE(I)
2000  FORMAT(1X,I12,I16,18X,I3,I16)
      I = I + 1
      IF ( I .LE. 52 )  GO TO 200
      RETURN
      END
```

Both of the above SUBROUTINEs use the SORT subprogram, but the arguments in the two CALLs are different. Different arrays of different lengths are in the arguments.

Now that the program is written, we must write the SUBROUTINE SORT. The problem of sorting numbers into decreasing order has been studied by many people and there are lots of solutions. Some are better than others. The method we describe here has at least two virtues: it is easy to understand, and it clearly demonstrates the uses of subprograms. We'll have more to say about other methods in the next chapter.

Briefly, the idea is to locate the largest of the numbers and put it on top of the list and then to repeat the same process on the remaining unsorted numbers (from the second to the last). We keep repeating the process on shorter and shorter lists

until finally there are none left. The only tricky part of the process arises from the way in which the numbers are stored, which is in an array. When we find the largest number and want to put it on top of the unsorted portion of the list, we must find something to do with the number currently in the top position. It must go into the unsorted portion of the list, of course, and the natural place to put it is in the position vacated by the largest number. In other words, we interchange the largest number with the number on top of the unsorted portion of the list. Figure 8 5 2 illustrates the method.

The SUBROUTINE below uses a FUNCTION to locate the largest number in the unsorted part of the array and a SUBROUTINE to interchange the largest with the top number. You have already seen techniques for locating the largest number several times, so the FUNCTION should be easy to follow. You haven't seen a technique for switching the values in a pair of memory cells, however, and we'll get to that shortly.

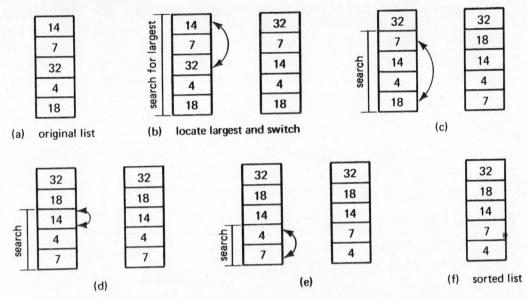

(a) original list   (b) locate largest and switch   (c)

(d)   (e)   (f) sorted list

Figure 8 5 2   Sorting a List of Numbers

You will notice something unusual in the parameter declarations of the following subprograms. The array declarations have subprogram parameters for length declarators. This clearly illustrates the difference between parameter declarations and true declarations. Since parameter declarations describe already existing objects, the compiler is not required to reserve space for them. Consequently, the length of a subprogram parameter array may be specified by one of the variables in the parameter list. (If the array has more than one subscript, then the range of values for any one or all of the subscripts may be specified by variables in the

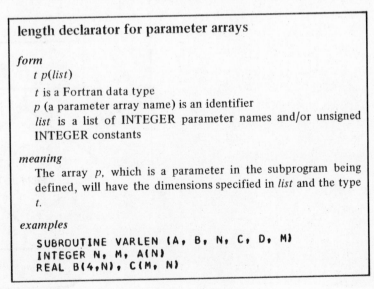

length declarator for parameter arrays

form
   $t\ p(list)$

   t is a Fortran data type
   p (a parameter array name) is an identifier
   list is a list of INTEGER parameter names and/or unsigned INTEGER constants

meaning
   The array p, which is a parameter in the subprogram being defined, will have the dimensions specified in *list* and the type t.

examples
```
SUBROUTINE VARLEN (A, B, N, C, D, M)
INTEGER N, M, A(N)
REAL B(4,N), C(M, N)
```

parameter list.) It is important to realize that this does not mean that any existing array actually has a varying length. All actual array declarations must have a constant length declarator; only parameter array declarations may have variables for length declarators. Furthermore, the value(s) of the parameter(s) declaring the dimension(s) of the array should not be changed by the subprogram because this would imply a change in the length of the actual array given in the argument list in the subprogram reference. No such change is possible.

VERBAL DESCRIPTION

Let TOP be 1.

Start loop:

locate largest element between TOP and end

interchange largest element with TOP element

increase TOP by 1

repeat unless TOP ⩾ length of array

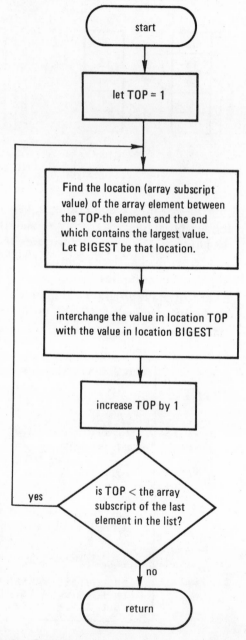

Figure 8 5 3   Sorting

```
      SUBROUTINE SORT (KEYS, OTHER, N)
      INTEGER N, KEYS(N), OTHER(N)
COMMENT:  ARRANGE THE VALUES IN "KEYS" AND "OTHER" INTO
C           DECREASING ORDER ACCORDING TO "KEYS"
      INTEGER TOP, BIGEST
      INTEGER LOCBIG
      TOP = 1
C     FIND LARGEST NUMBER IN "KEY", BETWEEN "TOP" AND "N".
100   BIGEST = LOCBIG(KEYS, TOP, N)
C         INTERCHANGE KEYS(TOP) WITH KEYS(BIGEST)
          CALL SWITCH (KEYS(TOP), KEYS(BIGEST))
C         TO AVOID MESSING UP THE CORRESPONDENCE BETWEEN
C         VALUES IN "KEYS" AND VALUES IN "OTHER", MAKE AN
C         IDENTICAL INTERCHANGE IN "OTHER".
          CALL SWITCH (OTHER(TOP), OTHER(BIGEST))
C         INCREMENT "TOP" TO REFLECT NEW TOP OF UNSORTED
C         PORTION OF ARRAYS.
          TOP = TOP + 1
          IF ( TOP .LT. N )  GO TO 100
      RETURN
      END


      INTEGER FUNCTION LOCBIG (A, FROM, TO)
      INTEGER FROM, TO, A(TO)
COMMENT:  LOCATE THE LARGEST NUMBER IN "A" BETWEEN A(FROM)
C           AND THE END OF THE ARRAY.
      INTEGER I
      LOCBIG = FROM
      I = FROM + 1
100   IF ( I .GT. TO )  RETURN
          IF ( A(I) .GT. A(LOCBIG) )  LOCBIG = I
          I = I + 1
          GO TO 100
      END
```

The subprogram SWITCH, which interchanges the values in a pair of memory cells, requires explanation. It has three steps: (1) the value in the first cell is copied into a third cell so that it won't be lost in step 2, (2) the value of the second cell is copied into the first, and (3) the value in the third cell is copied into the second. If you think about it, you will realize that a two-step process simply won't work.

```
SUBROUTINE SWITCH (A,B)
INTEGER A, B
INTEGER COPYA
COPYA = A
A = B
B = COPYA
RETURN
END
```

Please be sure that you understand how this sorting method works by making up a small example and following it through. We'll want to use the sorting subprogram again.

When our completed program was run using the data cards below, it produced the sales report you saw at the beginning of this section.

```
1976M
  647?   4103   2001   242?   3501   5402   5117   4322   2173   9342
  8497  10428
1976W
  1647   1500   1399   1822   1021   1059    987    855    502    408
   201    422    385    638    655    588    574    788    698    755
   802    621   1422   1534   1621   1308   1205   1307   1354   1238
  1104    987    855    445    655    521    411    322   1422   2011
  2411   1955   2134   ?111   2422   2031   1902   2032   2544   2144
  2066   2544
0000
```

EXERCISES 8 5

1 Which of the following parameter declarations are legal and which aren't? If not, explain why not.

```
SUBROUTINE ONE(A, N,M)
INTEGER M,N, A(N,M)

SUBROUTINE TWO(A,N)
INTEGER N, A(10,N,4)

SUBROUTINE THREE(A,N)
INTEGER N, A(LENGTH)
```

2 What is wrong with the following SUBROUTINE?

```
SUBROUTINE WRONG(A,N)
INTEGER N, A(N)
N = N+1
A(N) = 0
RETURN
END
```

3 What would need to be changed in order to make our SUBROUTINE SORT arrange the numbers into increasing (rather than decreasing) order?

4 What would happen to INTEGER memory cells ONE and TWO if the statement CALL BADSWT (ONE, TWO) were executed?

```
SUBROUTINE BADSWT(A,B)
INTEGER A,B
A = B
B = A
RETURN
END
```

5 What is wrong with the statement CALL BADSWT (1, 2), given the above subprogram?

Section 8 6*

You know what the asterisk means by now.

Random Number Generation

In Chapter 4 we listed RANF as a non-ANSI built-in FUNCTION that produces random numbers. We used this FUNCTION in Chapter 6 to conduct a simple simulation. This was only one of many situations in business computing in which we need to have access to random numbers. If your Fortran compiler doesn't have RANF or something similar built in, chances are your computer center can provide you

Can you know if an event is really random?

with a subprogram which generates a random number each time it is called. Actually, the numbers it generates are usually called "pseudorandom" because they are produced by a deterministic program; every time you start the program over, you get the same sequence of pseudorandom numbers. However, the numbers pass a large number of statistical tests for randomness so that we can say that they act very much like true random numbers, whatever those are.

The pseudorandom numbers are usually uniformly distributed REAL numbers in the range from 0.0 to 1.0 (endpoints *not* included). In other words, the likelihood that a number will fall in a particular subinterval is the same as the likelihood that it will fall in any other subinterval of the same length. (A descriptive, albeit imprecise, way of saying this is: "All numbers between 0.0 and 1.0 are equally likely.") They are generated using the multiplicative congruential method—each new number is obtained from the last by multiplying it by a fixed multiplier and taking the last few digits of the product as the new random number.

It isn't our purpose to dwell on random numbers or random number generators here. We simply want to make sure that you have access to a random number generator since we will use random numbers in later chapters. If you don't have one easily available, you can copy SUBROUTINE RANDOM, which appears below. It has one parameter, an output parameter. When you CALL it, it will store a pseudorandom, uniformly distributed, REAL number in the memory cell you specify as its argument. This number will be greater than 0.0 and less than 1.0.

```
      SUBROUTINE RANDOM (X)
      REAL X
COMMENT:  THIS SUBROUTINE PRODUCES A SAMPLE "X" FROM A
C           UNIFORM DISTRIBUTION  ACROSS THE INTERVAL (0.0,1.0)
C   WARNING!  IF YOU INTEND TO GENERATE MORE THAN A COUPLE
C             THOUSAND RANDOM NUMBERS, USE SOME OTHER ROUTINE.
C           FOR INFORMATION ON HOW WELL THIS TYPE OF RANDOM
C           NUMBER GENERATOR WORKS, SEE 'THE ART OF COMPUTER
C           PROGRAMMING', VOL. 2, D. KNUTH, ADDISON-WESLEY.
      INTEGER MOD
      REAL FLOAT
      INTEGER A, MULT, BASE
      DATA    A/19727/, MULT/25211/, BASE/32768/
      A = MOD(MULT*A, 32768)
      X = FLOAT(A) / FLOAT(BASE)
      RETURN
      END
```

Warning! This routine may not work on computer systems with dynamic allocation or virtual memory. See your local expert.

Often it is very useful to have a FUNCTION which generates a random INTEGER between 1 and some given upper limit, each possible value having the same likelihood. The FUNCTION CHOOSE does this. It uses our SUBROUTINE RANDOM, but it could just as well use any random number generator with similar properties.

```
      INTEGER FUNCTION CHOOSE (N)
      INTEGER N
COMMENT:  THIS FUNCTION CHOOSES, AT RANDOM, ONE OF THE
C         INTEGERS 1, 2, 3, ...., N .
      REAL U
      CALL RANDOM(U)
      CHOOSE = INT(FLOAT(N)*U) +1
      RETURN
      END
```

Section 8 7

The COMMON Statement

Up to now, the only way we've had to communicate values from one program unit to the next was through argument-parameter association. Statements in one subprogram could not affect the memory cells in another unless the memory cells in question were given to the subprogram as arguments. However, that isn't the whole story.

There are times when it is handy for several subprograms to use some of the same memory cells without having to list them as parameters. This can be done by placing the memory cells in a special part of central memory known as a COMMON region. Any program unit can gain access to the memory cells in a COMMON region by including an appropriate COMMON statement in the declaration section. Deciding when to use COMMON regions to communicate values between program units requires a good sense of judgment. Some programmers disavow COMMON regions altogether, but most will use them when several subprograms need access to the same collection of data. A situation like this occurs in the following example.

The Little Beaver Company is in the business of renting trucks. The company currently maintains a fleet of thirteen trucks of four different types: (1) 20-foot bed, enclosed, hydraulic lift gate; (2) 16-foot bed, enclosed, hydraulic lift gate; (3) 5-ton truck, open-slat sides; and (4) three-quarter-ton van.

The company's managers want a weekly summary of the percentage of rented time and total miles driven for each of the four classes of trucks. They plan to use these summaries to help them decide which types of trucks to buy when they decide to augment their fleet.

Our job is to write a computer program to print the statistical summaries. The input to our program will be a collection of time and mileage cards covering the rentals for the week. These cards are filled out by employees at the dispatch desk every time a customer returns a truck that has been rented. Each card will contain four pieces of information: (1) truck ID, columns 1–4, alphameric; (2) truck class, column 5, INTEGER 1, 2, 3, or 4; (3) rental time in half-days, columns 6–8, INTEGER; and (4) miles driven during the rental period, columns 9–13, INTEGER. There will be a blank card at the end so that our program can tell when it has received all the necessary information. A typical data card is diagrammed in Figure 8 7 1.

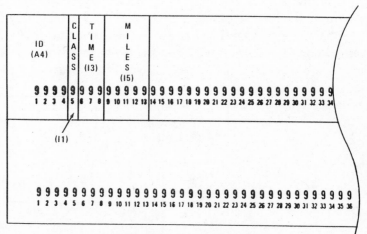

Figure 8 7 1   Data Card

Our program should print a time and mileage summary for each of the four classes of trucks. The time figure should be the percentage of the total available rental time that trucks from this class were rented during this week. This percentage would be the total time (in half-days) that trucks from the class were rented this week divided by the total available time for rental (time available is the number of trucks in the class multiplied by 14, the number of half-days in a week). Of course this ratio must be multiplied by 100 to convert it from a fraction between 0.00 and 1.00 to a percentage between 0 and 100 percent. The mileage figure should be the total miles driven by customers renting trucks for this class. Figure 8 7 2 shows the output design.

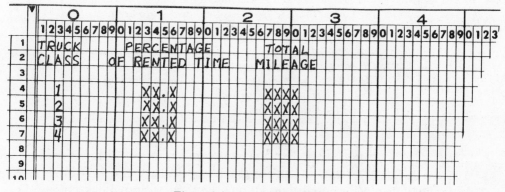

Figure 8 7 2   Output Design

The HIPO diagram in Figure 8 7 3 shows the stages in the process. The subprograms for each stage will need access to the region of memory where the input data will be stored. Therefore, we'll set up a COMMON region to provide this access. We do this by putting a COMMON statement in each of the subprograms.

As you can see in the box, the COMMON statement sets up COMMON regions in memory, the labels of the regions being surrounded by slashes; after each label it names the memory cells to be included in the COMMON area. It is important to remember that the *label* is the only thing which can be directly communicated from one subprogram to another. The names of the individual memory cells within the COMMON area are local to the subprogram and *may* differ from one to another, although people usually choose to make them the same in all subprograms.

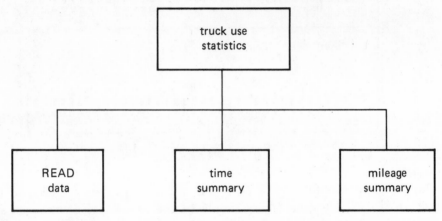

Figure 8 7 3   HIPO Diagram for Program to Print Statistics on Use of Rental Trucks

COMMON *names: Each subprogram (or main program) which uses a* COMMON *region must declare the region with a* COMMON *statement. A* COMMON *region is a collection of contiguous storage units. The names referring to these storage units may be different in different subprograms. It is the* order *of the memory cell and array names in the* COMMON *statement which determines which names will be associated with which storage units.*

COMMON *safety: To be safe, for each* COMMON *region, punch a "*COMMON *deck" of memory cell and array declarations and a single* COMMON *statement. Duplicate the deck for each program unit that uses the* COMMON *region.*

COMMON regions are labeled so that a program can set up more than one region when it is appropriate. In our program we will have two COMMON regions, one to communicate the input data among the three subprograms and another to communicate the available time for rental, by truck class, between the main program and the subprogram which handles the time summary. We have given the first region the label /DATA/ and the second region the label /TIMAVL/ (TIMe AVaiLable). Since these regions have labels, they are known as **labeled COMMON** regions. There is a second type of COMMON region known as **blank COMMON**. This region has no label, and the rules governing it differ from those covering labeled COMMONs. One difference has to do with the declared lengths of the COMMON regions in the various program units. This is discussed below. Other differences will be found in the Fortran reference manual for your computer system, so look there if you need to know.

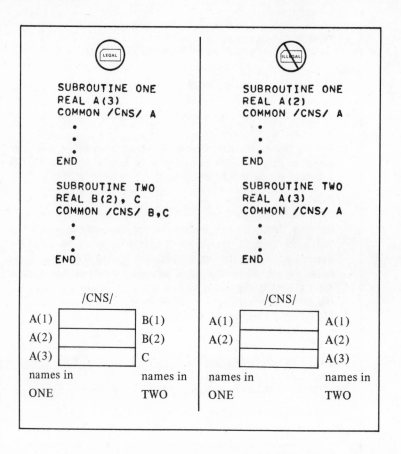

The total number of memory cells in a particular COMMON area must be the same in all the subprograms in which it is declared. The names of the memory cells in the COMMON area don't have to be the same from one subprogram to the next, but the total length of a COMMON area must be the same from one program unit to another. The one exception is with the blank COMMON region. The declared length of blank COMMON need not be the same in every program unit. If it's not, the total length of the blank COMMON area is the maximum of its sizes in the various program units where it is declared.

> *Experienced programmers* sometimes use COMMON *regions to save memory space. This use requires extreme caution to avoid wiping out information you may need later in the computation.*

Now that you are prepared with at least a superficial understanding of the COMMON statement, you should be able to read through the program below to help confirm your knowledge. Review Figures 8 7 1, 8 7 2, and 8 7 3 to remind yourself of the overall plan.

```
COMMENT:  PROGRAM TO PREPARE TIME AND MILEAGE SUMMARIES FOR
C            THE LITTLE BEAVER COMPANY.
C                    "THEY RENT TRUCKS!"
C   VARIABLES:
C        CLASS--1, 2, 3, OR 4
C        NUMTRK(CLASS)--NUMBER OF TRUCKS OF THIS "CLASS"
C        T(CLASS)--NUMBER OF HALF-DAYS AVAILABLE PER WEEK
C                    ON TRUCKS OF THIS "CLASS"
C        PRCNT(CLASS)--PERCENTAGE OF TIME THAT TRUCKS OF THIS
C                    "CLASS" WERE RENTED
C                      (OUTPUT FROM SUBROUTINE "TIMES")
C        DIST(CLASS)--DISTANCE THAT TRUCKS FROM THIS "CLASS"
C                      WERE DRIVEN (OUTPUT FROM "MILES")
      INTEGER NUMTRK(4), CLASS
      REAL T(4)
      COMMON /TIMAVL/ T
      REAL PRCNT(4)
      INTEGER DIST(4)
      DATA NUMTRK(1),NUMTRK(2),NUMTRK(3),NUMTRK(4)/3,4,2,6/
C                                          COMPUTE TIME AVAILABLE
C                                              FOR EACH CLASS
      DO 100 CLASS=1,4
        T(CLASS) = FLOAT(NUMTRK(CLASS))*14.0
  100   CONTINUE
C                                          GET TRUCK USAGE DATA
      CALL GETDAT
C                                          DO TIME SUMMARIES
      CALL TIMES(PRCNT)
C                                          DO MILEAGE SUMMARIES
      CALL MILES(DIST)
C                                          PRINT STATISTICS
      WRITE(6,2000)(CLASS,PRCNT(CLASS),DIST(CLASS)  ,
     +                                    CLASS = 1,4)
 2000 FORMAT('1TRUCK      PERCENTAGE       TOTAL'/
     +        ' CLASS    OF RENTED TIME    MILEAGE'//
     +        (I4,F13.1,I14)                        )
      STOP
      END


      SUBROUTINE GETDAT
C   VARIABLES:
C        N--NUMBER OF RENTAL CARDS
C        CLASS(I)--CLASS OF TRUCK ON I-TH RENTAL CARD
C        RENTIM(I)--TIME RECORDED ON I-TH RENTAL CARD
C        MILAGE(I)--MILEAGE RECORDED ON I-TH RENTAL CARD
C        MAXRNT--LIMIT ON NUMBER OF RENTAL CARDS
      INTEGER N, CLASS(100), RENTIM(100), MILAGE(100)
      COMMON /DATA/ N,CLASS,RENTIM,MILAGE
      INTEGER ID,FINIS,MAXRNT
      DATA FINIS/4H    /, MAXRNT/100/
      N=0
  100 READ(5,1000) ID,CLASS(N+1),RENTIM(N+1),MILAGE(N+1)
 1000 FORMAT(A4,I1,I3,I5)
      IF (ID .EQ. FINIS) RETURN
      IF (CLASS(N+1).GE.1 .AND. CLASS(N+1).LE.4) GO TO 110
        WRITE(6,1090)ID,CLASS(N+1),RENTIM(N+1),MILAGE(N+1)
 1090   FORMAT('0ILLEGAL CLASS ON DATA CARD SHOWN BELOW'/
     +          1X,A4,I1,I3,I5, 15X,'CARD IGNORED')
        GO TO 120
  110   N = N+1
  120 IF (N .LT. MAXRNT) GO TO 100
      WRITE(6,9000) MAXRNT
 9000 FORMAT(' PROGRAM CAN HANDLE ONLY',I4,' RENTAL CARDS')
      RETURN
      END
```

```
            SUBROUTINE TIMES(PRCNT)
            REAL PRCNT(4)
C                       --OUTPUT PARAMETER.  SEE MAIN PROGRAM
C   VARIABLES:
C       /DATA/--SEE SUBROUTINE "GETDAT"
C       /TIMAVL/--SEE MAIN PROGRAM
C       TOTIM(K)--TOTAL RENTAL TIME ON TRUCKS FROM CLASS K
            INTEGER N, CLASS(100), RENTIM(100), MILAGE(100)
            COMMON /DATA/ N,CLASS,RENTIM,MILAGE
            REAL T(4)
            COMMON /TIMAVL/ T
            INTEGER TOTTIM(4), I,K
C                                    COMPUTE TOTAL TIME RENTED
C                                          FOR EACH CLASS
            DO 100 K=1,4
  100       TOTTIM(K) = 0
            DO 110 I=1,N
            K = CLASS(I)
            TOTTIM(K) = TOTTIM(K) + RENTIM(I)
  110       CONTINUE
C                                    COMPUTE PERCENTAGE
C                                          OF TIME IN USE
            DO 200 K=1,4
            PRCNT(K) = (FLOAT(TOTTIM(K))*100.0)/T(K)
  200       CONTINUE
            RETURN
            END


            SUBROUTINE MILES(DIST)
            INTEGER DIST(4)
C                       --OUTPUT PARAMETER.  SEE MAIN PROGRAM.
C   VARIABLES:
C       /DATA/--SEE SUBROUTINE "GETDAT"
            INTEGER N, CLASS(100), RENTIM(100), MILAGE(100)
            COMMON /DATA/ N,CLASS,RENTIM,MILAGE
            INTEGER I,K
C                                    COMPUTE TOTAL MILEAGE
C                                          FOR EACH CLASS
            DO 100 K=1,4
  100       DIST(K) = 0
            DO 110 I=1,N
            K = CLASS(I)
            DIST(K) = DIST(K) + MILAGE(I)
  110       CONTINUE
            RETURN
            END


data
    G3472  3   697
    XC274 12  2445
    XO071 12  3498
    G3472  8  1253
    ST774  8  2511
    TX291  4  1324
    Y2253 12  4582
    RE514  6  2113
    ST774  5   972
```

output

TRUCK CLASS	PERCENTAGE OF RENTED TIME	TOTAL MILEAGE
1	38.1	4822
2	19.6	1950
3	42.9	4582
4	36.9	8041

EXERCISES 8 7

1 Describe the correspondence between memory cells in the following SUB-ROUTINEs.

```
SUBROUTINE ONE
REAL A(3), B, C(2)
COMMON /BLK1/A,B    /BLK2/C
A(2) = 1.0
C(1) = 1.0
RETURN
END

SUBROUTINE TWO
REAL B(3), C, D(2)
COMMON /BLK1/C,B    /BLK2/D
B(2) = 2.0
C = 2.0
RETURN
END

SUBROUTINE THREE
REAL Q(4), R, S
COMMON /BLK1/Q     /BLK2/R,S
Q(1) = 3.0
Q(2) = 3.0
Q(3) = 3.0
Q(4) = 3.0
R = 3.0
S = 3.0
RETURN
END
```

2 The following program calls the SUBROUTINEs of exercise 1. What does it print?

```
      REAL A,B,C,D, E,F
      COMMON /BLK1/A,B,C,D    /BLK2/E,F
      CALL THREE
      CALL TWO
      CALL ONE
      WRITE(6,1000) A,B,C,D, E,F
 1000 FORMAT(1X,6F10.1)
      STOP
      END
```

Section 8 8

Subprograms as Arguments to Subprograms

On occasion you may wish to define a FUNCTION or SUBROUTINE which accepts yet another subprogram as one of its arguments. One very common use of this is in subprograms which accept a FUNCTION from your program and then do something useful for you with it. Typical tasks are (1) plotting out its values over some range, (2) finding where your FUNCTION has maxima and minima, and (3) computing the area under your FUNCTION. Subprograms which do these things are no doubt available at your computer center.

You will recall from Sections 2 and 3 that FUNCTIONs and SUBROUTINEs are said to be **external** subprograms because their definitions lie wholly without the program from which they are called and because they are compiled separately and independently from the main program and from each other. This means that when the compiler is dealing with one program unit, it doesn't look at other program units to decide if a particular identifier refers to a memory cell or to another program unit.

Let's examine the problem carefully. Suppose we have a SUBROUTINE called PLOT which accepts as arguments F (the FUNCTION whose values we want plotted), LIM1 and LIM2 (describing the range over which values are to be plotted), and DELTA (the stepsize).

```
      SUBROUTINE PLOT (F, LIM1,LIM2, DELTA)
      REAL F, LIM1,LIM2, DELTA
      REAL STEP, Y
      INTEGER POINT, I, BLANK, STAR
      DATA BLANK/1H /,  STAR/1H*/
      STEP = LIM1
100   Y = F(STEP)
      POINT = MAX0(1,MIN0(113,INT(10.0*Y)+49))
      WRITE(6,1000) (BLANK, I=1,POINT), STAR
1000  FORMAT(1X, 120A1)
      STEP = STEP+DELTA
      IF (STEP .LE. LIM2)  GO TO 100
      RETURN
      END
```

Look at statement 100. The form of the expression F(STEP) indicates that F is either an array or a FUNCTION. It can't be an array; if it were, there would be a declaration to that effect. Therefore, F must be a FUNCTION, and when SUB-ROUTINE PLOT is called, it will be informed of the FUNCTION's name. No problem here.

Now let's go to another program unit and look at a statement which CALLs SUBROUTINE PLOT. Suppose we want to plot out the values taken by the built-in FUNCTION ALOG10 (base 10 logarithm). We might write

```
   CALL PLOT (ALOG10,1.0,10.0,1.0)
```

and hope that that would do the trick. However, "ALOG10" looks as if it could be a memory cell name. The only way for the compiler to tell that it is supposed to be a FUNCTION name is to look into SUBROUTINE PLOT and see how it uses its third argument. But the compiler doesn't look at SUBROUTINE PLOT while it is compiling the program containing the CALL. To solve the dilemma we must inform the compiler that ALOG10 stands for the FUNCTION called ALOG10, not a memory cell of that name. An EXTERNAL statement gives the compiler this information.

```
EXTERNAL ALOG10
```

If our main program makes several references to SUBROUTINE PLOT, say

```
EXTERNAL ALOG10, EXP, SIN
REAL      ALOG10, EXP, SIN
CALL PLOT (ALOG10,1.0,10.0,1.0)
CALL PLOT (SIN, -3.0, 3.0, 0.5)
CALL PLOT (EXP, -1.0, 0.0, 0.1)
STOP
END
```

output

then we must inform the compiler that ALOG10, EXP, and SIN are all names of external FUNCTIONs:

```
EXTERNAL ALOG10, EXP, SIN
```

We've seen an example where a FUNCTION name was an argument for a SUBROUTINE. Other combinations (e.g., a SUBROUTINE name as an argument for a FUNCTION) follow the same rules. Here's an example where a FUNCTION receives the name of another FUNCTION as an argument.

Suppose we have a number of FUNCTIONs we're trying out and we know (since we're going to divide by the result) that if any of our FUNCTIONs return the value 0, we're in trouble. For added safety we could define another FUNCTION called ZERCHK (ZERo CHecK) to protect us. Our main program is outlined below.

```
          .
          .
          .
      INTEGER FN1, FN2, FN3, X, Y, ZERCHK
      EXTERNAL FN1, FN2, FN3
          .
          .
          .
COMMENT:  TRY FN1, BUT BE CAREFUL
      Y1 = 100/ZERCHK(X,FN1)
COMMENT:  TRY FN2, BUT BE CAREFUL
      Y2 = 100/ZERCHK(X,FN2)
COMMENT:  TRY FN3, BUT BE CAREFUL
      Y3 = 100/ZERCHK(X,FN3)
          .
          .
          .
      END
```

We want ZERCHK to try out the FUNCTION and test the result to protect us from zero.

```
      INTEGER FUNCTION ZERCHK(ARG,FUNCT)
      INTEGER ARG, FUNCT
COMMENT:  COMPUTE THE VALUE OF "FUNCT"
      ZERCHK = FUNCT(ARG)
COMMENT:  TEST FOR ZERO
      IF (ZERCHK .NE. 0)  RETURN
COMMENT:  IT WAS ZERO, NOTIFY AND SAVE THE DAY
      WRITE(6,1000) ARG
 1000 FORMAT(' WITH ARGUMENT', I8,
     +          ' THE VALUE OF THE FUNCTION IS 0--BEWARE')
      ZERCHK = 1
      RETURN
      END
```

EXERCISES 8 8

1 Where must the EXTERNAL statement appear?
   a in the subprogram to warn it that one of its arguments is another subprogram
   b in your job control cards so that the compiler can figure out the necessary communication among subprograms
   c in the executive washroom

2 Would your program's performance be affected if you used EXTERNAL statements to declare every subprogram you reference?

PROBLEMS 8

1   Write and test a SUBROUTINE that accepts an array of people's nick-names and that returns the name which comes first alphabetically and the one which comes last. Of course, the SUBROUTINE must also be told how many names are in the list.

2   Do a problem from Chapter 4 or 6, perhaps one you have already done, making use of FUNCTIONs and SUBROUTINEs and any other technique you can think of to make your program more clearly organized.

3   Write a FUNCTION called PV which has three parameters, AMOUNT, INTRST, and PERIOD, and which returns the present value of a future AMOUNT of money at the interest rate INTRST per period in the number of periods PERIOD.
    Remember:

$$\text{present value (PV)} = \frac{\text{amount}}{(1 + \text{interest})^{\text{periods}}}$$

4   Write a FUNCTION called COMPND which has three parameters, AMOUNT, INTRST, and PERIOD, and which returns the future value of an AMOUNT at the interest rate INTRST per period at the end of PERIOD periods.
    Remember:

$$\text{future amount} = \text{amount} (1 + \text{interest rate})^{\text{periods}}$$

5   Redo the asset depreciation program of Chapter 7, making each depreciation method a SUBROUTINE.

6   Two cars are traveling down the highway at 55 mph, with the second car 70 feet behind the first. The first car suddenly slams on its brakes. Will the second car be able to stop in time to avoid ramming into the first? It will if its driver is able to slam on the brakes before the car has traveled 70 feet (right?). The time it takes the second driver to apply the brakes after seeing the brake lights on the car ahead is called the **reaction time**. People's reaction times depend on a number of factors, such as how tired they are, how distracted they are, how drunk they are, etc., so it seems reasonable to model the reaction time as if it were a random variable.
    Assume the driver's reaction time is a (uniform) random number between 0.5 and 1.0 second, i.e., is computed as

$$\text{react. time} = (1.0 + V)/2.0$$

where V comes from CALL RANDOM(V). Given the reaction time, you can compute the distance the second car travels and from that, tell whether or not there was a wreck.
    Write a program that simulates 100 emergency braking situations and outputs the 100 different distances, the number of wrecks and the number of "close calls." If the second car stops less than one foot from the first but doesn't hit it, that's a close call.

7 If the numbers produced by SUBROUTINE RANDOM (Section 8 6) were actually uniformly distributed between 0.0 and 1.0, and if we take a large sample, the average value should be 1/2 and the sample standard deviation should be $\sqrt{(1/12)}$. Test it to see how close it comes.

Write a FUNCTION MEAN that accepts two inputs, one an array of REAL values and one an INTEGER that specifies how many values are in the array. MEAN should return a REAL value that is the sample mean of the values in the input array.

$$\text{mean} = \frac{\sum_{i=1}^{n} x_i}{n}$$

Write a FUNCTION STDDEV that returns the standard deviation of the values in the array it receives.

$$\text{sample std. dev.} = \sqrt{\frac{n \sum_{i=1}^{n} x_i^2 - \left(\sum_{i=1}^{n} x_i\right)^2}{n(n-1)}}$$

Use the two FUNCTIONs to test RANDOM. Generate 100 RANDOM numbers, and print out their mean and standard deviation. Then generate 200 RANDOM numbers and output their mean and standard deviation. Then 300, 400, . . ., 1000. How close are the means and standard deviations to 1/2 and $\sqrt{(1/12)}$?

8 Suppose you were running a pizza parlor and you wanted to figure out how many waitresses/waiters you should hire. If you have too few, then customers will have to wait a long time to be served and you'll lose business, but if you have too many, then you'll lose money paying them. You decide to simulate the process. You estimate that every minute the odds are 50/50 that a new customer will come in and that it takes three minutes of a waitress's time to serve each customer. Your program should simulate the arrival of 1000 customers and should print out the total amount of time customers spend waiting and the amount of time waitresses/waiters spend waiting. Try your program with one, two, and three waitresses/waiters to see how many it would be best to have.

Here are some hints about how you could write the program:

a Have one main loop which corresponds to what happens each successive minute.

b Have memory cells which keep track of the following things:
   □ How many customers are waiting: CWAIT
   □ How many waitresses/waiters are waiting: WWAIT
   □ How many waitresses/waiters have just started waiting on a customer: WWAITO

□ How many waiters/waitresses have been waiting on a customer for one minute: WWAIT1
□ How many waiters/waitresses have been waiting on a customer for two minutes: WWAIT2
□ How much (total) time customers have spent waiting: CTIME
□ How much (total) time waitresses/waiters have spent waiting: WTIME

VERBAL DESCRIPTION

Initialize.

Simulate one minute:
    Account for arriving customers.
    Update status of waitresses.
    Serve customers (as many as possible).
    Account for time customers and/or waitresses have spent waiting during this minute.

Repeat (i.e., simulate next minute) unless it's closing time.

Print results.

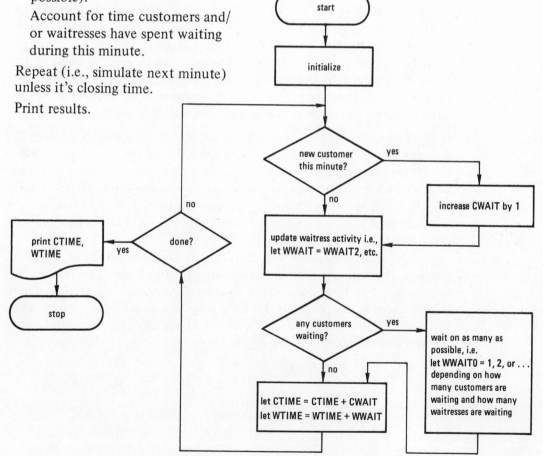

9 If you are familiar with vectors, write a program to convert a given vector
to a unit vector in the same direction. Assume each card contains the
dimension (i.e., number of components) of the vector (INTEGER) followed by the components of the vector (REALs). You may assume the
dimension is less than 100. The termination card will contain the vector
0.0 of dimension 1. (Don't try to convert it to a unit vector!)

The unit vector in the same direction as $(x_1, x_2, \ldots, x_n)$ is $(u_1, u_2, \ldots, u_n)$, where

$$u_k = x_k/r$$

and $r = \sqrt{(x_1{}^2 + x_2{}^2 + \ldots + x_n{}^2)}$

Print the vector and the corresponding unit vector.

10 Write a program to compute the cosine of the angle between two given
vectors. Assume each data card will contain the dimension of the two vectors involved (INTEGER) followed by the components of the one, and
finally the components of the other. Assume the dimension is less than
100. The termination card will contain 1,0.0,0.0. If $(u_1, \ldots, u_n)$ and
$(v_1, \ldots, v_n)$ are the unit vectors in the same direction as the given vectors
x and y, respectively, then the cosine of the angle between the two given
vectors is $u_1 v_1 + u_2 v_2 + \ldots + u_n v_n$. A formula in problem 9 shows the
relation between a given vector and the corresponding unit vector.

11 Write a program to do the matching for a computer dating service. The
dating service's questionnaires have statements and the applicant indicates
his degree of agreement with each question on a scale of one to five. Thus
each data card will contain the name of an applicant (up to 28 characters),
sex (M or F), and responses to the questionnaire (20 INTEGERs). The
last data card will contain the phrase NO MORE APPLICANTS. You may
assume there are no more than 100 applicants.

Match each person with the two most compatible people of the opposite sex. As a measure of compatibility, use the cosine of the angle between their two response vectors; the larger the cosine, the more compatible the couple (see problem 10 for a way to compute the cosine). Your
program's output should be a list of the applicants along with the names
of their two guaranteed dates, e.g.,

```
JOHN DOE       DATES MARY SLATE
               AND ALICE HILL

JANE FLUG      DATES ROGER WHIMSBY
               AND JOE THORNTOR
```

12 Problem 11 has a feature which wouldn't be acceptable to a real computer dating service. If one person is particularly compatible, he or she will receive the names of two dates, but may be listed as a good date on *many* people's lists. The whole thing could get out of balance with almost everybody trying to date a few highly compatible people. Do problem 10 so that no one person is listed for more than six other people. Print *all* the dates a person involved in, not just has own two optimal matches as before. Now another problem arises. You may have to refund some participants' money because in some cases there may not be enough suitable matches to go around. Print a polite apology to those who come up short.

If you feel especially ambitious, dress up the input and output of this problem to include addresses and phone numbers.

9 SOME APPLICATIONS

Chapter Objectives: After studying this chapter, you should be able to:

- Describe a financial planning model.
- Write programs to project financial statements such as income statements, balance sheet, and cashflow statements.
- Write programs which sort arrays using an index.
- Describe the binary search procedure.
- Write programs which locate desired values in an array using a binary search.

Section 9 1

Introduction

We've looked at a number of business problems so far. Some of them have been simple while others have been pretty complex. In this chapter we'll look at three problems in some detail. First, we'll explore a **corporate financial model**, a way of projecting financial statements. In this problem, we'll show you how you can develop a rather complex management model with a relatively limited knowledge of computer programming. Then we'll look at two problems which occur so often that people have spent a great deal of time inventing and comparing alternative algorithms to solve them. You'll get some ideas about how to compare different algorithms. Our first algorithm is **sorting**, or, manipulating an array of values so the values wind up in order. The second algorithm is that of **searching**, or looking in an array for a particular stored value. You've seen solutions to both of these algorithms in earlier parts of the book; here you'll see some solutions which are better.

Section 9 2

Corporate Financial Models—What If?

The managers of businesses plot and scheme the future of their organizations by planning. They formulate business strategy and policy by developing alternative scenarios or views of their businesses several years in the future. To effectively evaluate various strategies, these managers must look at the impact or result of any strategy on the "bottom line," the financial performance of the businesses. They use pro forma or projected financial statements to analyze the effect of different strategies. They can then pick the strategy which best meets the goals and objectives of their firm. The typical pro forma financial statements which managers want to look at are an income statement, a balance sheet, and a cashflow statement.

> *scenario*: a description of what a business might be like in the future assuming certain events will happen.

> *financial planning model*: a bunch of equations used to project financial accounts or planning items. Frequently, they are grouped into pro forma income statements, balance sheets, and cashflow statements.

Let's look at a typical business and see how we might use the computer to make pro forma financial statements. Herbert Buckskin, the president of Future Industries, uses a five-year financial plan to determine company strategy and develop annual policy action plans. Herbie has a staff of financial analysts prepare five-year projections of Future Industries' income statement and balance sheet. These pro forma financial statements evaluate different alternatives for the company. Recently, Herbie has found the finance staff slow in responding to changes he requests in these statements. Several different statements are usually required for Herbie and his vice-presidents to determine the most realistic and desirable course for Future Industries.

The other day Herbie was talking with Clem Sodgras, the vice-president for finance, about some ideas he had on the future of Future Industries. Clem told Herbie, "This evaluation of alternatives wouldn't take so much time if you weren't always changing your mind. You want to know 'what if' sales increase or 'what if' selling expenses decrease! We no more than get one set of statements calculated and you make a change. So, it's back to the calculator for another week. As you know, this keeps three analysts busy for six months of the year. Then you have the nerve to complain about how slow we are at developing the projected statements."

"I agree," said President Herbie, "and I wish you'd do those statements faster. I find it difficult to be imaginative when it takes so long to evaluate one alternative. I'd like to evaluate even more alternatives."

"Oh, no," responded Clem. "How do you expect me to do it? Hire three more analysts?"

"You know, Clem," said Herbie, "we have that computer in your department which produces all those management reports. Why can't you do these projections on it?"

With that, Clem scratched his head and walked back to his office. What should he do?

After a couple of days, Clem called Shirley Analist, his crack computer systems analyst, into his office. They discussed the problem and Clem assigned Shirley to study it. Shirley worked diligently for several weeks. She was able to put together a financial model which would simulate the impact of different alternatives on the company's financial statements. When Herbie wanted to look at different "what if" situations, Shirley could make a few simple changes to the input data of the model. And *presto*, the computer would grind out all the calculations in a few minutes. The program was reviewed for Clem and Herbie's approval. Herbie was ecstatic. His imagination conjured up all kinds of "what if" situations. He couldn't wait to use it. Herbie gave his immediate approval.

The program was designed to use historical data of Future Industries as a basis for making the projections. But President Herbie could change any of the historically derived relationships to reflect his ideas of what the future might be like. He could use his subjective judgment and intuition in looking at alternative future scenarios.

We might consider our planning situation as shown in Figure 9 2 1. The corporate financial model aids us in evaluating the "what ifs." That's not to say it wouldn't be of great value in analyzing the historical data or determining "what

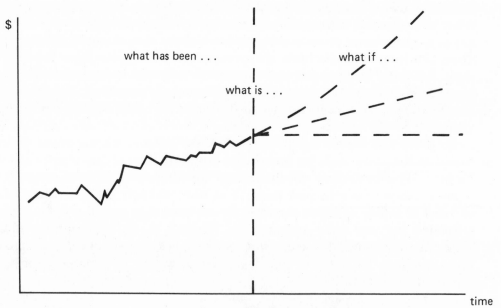

Figure 9 2 1   The Planning Situation

is"; in fact, we would want to do just that before we got on with making pro forma statements. Financial ratios and regression equations are often used to specify historical relationships.

Pro forma financial statements are a collection of financial accounts or planning items. We must figure out a way to calculate each account so we can project it into the future. The method used to calculate each account or item is known as a **relationship**. Many financial accounts are related to one another. Some of these relationships are accounting identities since they follow generally accepted accounting principles in their calculation. For example, cost of goods sold is related to sales. Retained earnings is the retained earnings for the previous period plus the net to retained earning this period.

After a lot of diligent effort, Shirley Analist was able to come up with the relationships and identities to calculate the pro forma income statement and balance sheet for President Herbie. Shirley's effort resulted in the methods of computation for the income statement, shown in Figure 9 2 2, and for the balance sheet,

$$\text{Sales}_t = (\text{sales}_{t-1}) * (\text{growth rate sales})$$

$$\text{Cost of goods sold}_t = (\text{sales}_t) * (\text{percent CGS}_t)$$

$$\text{Gross profit}_t = (\text{sales}_t) - (\text{cost of goods sold}_t)$$

$$\text{Administrative expense}_t = (\text{sales}_t) * (\text{percent AE})$$

$$\text{Selling expense}_t = (\text{sales}_t) * (\text{percent SE})$$

$$\text{Depreciation}_t = (\text{net fixed assets}_{t-1}) * (\text{percent DEP}_t)$$

$$\text{Miscellaneous}_t = \text{constant}$$

$$\text{Total expense}_t = (\text{administrative expense}_t) + (\text{selling expense}_t) + (\text{depreciation}_t) + (\text{miscellaneous}_t)$$

$$\text{Income before interest and taxes}_t = (\text{gross profit}_t) - (\text{total expense}_t)$$

$$\text{Interest expense}_t = (\text{notes payable}_{t-1}) * (\text{percent NP}) + (\text{long-term debt}_{t-1}) * (\text{percent LTD})$$

$$\text{Income before taxes}_t = (\text{income before interest and taxes}_t) - (\text{interest expense}_t)$$

$$\text{Taxes}_t = (\text{income before taxes}_t) * (\text{tax rate})$$

$$\text{Net income}_t = (\text{income before taxes}_t) - (\text{taxes}_t)$$

$$\text{Dividends}_t = (\text{net income}_t) * (\text{dividend payout rate})$$

$$\text{Net to retained earnings}_t = (\text{net income}_t) - (\text{dividends}_t)$$

Figure 9 2 2   Income Statement: Methods of Computation

shown in Figure 9 2 3. In both of these illustrations, the subscript *t* is used to indicate time. These methods of computation are the *conceptual* corporate financial model for Future Industries. For many business managers, executives and presidents, the conceptual model is the most difficult part of building the overall model. This, of course, is exactly where they should use their time and the computer lets them do it.

ASSETS

$\text{Cash}_t = (\text{total assets}_t) - (\text{net fixed assets}_t) - (\text{inventory}_t) - (\text{accounts receivable}_t)$

$\text{Accounts receivable}_t = (\text{sales}_t) * (\text{percent A/R})$

$\text{Inventory}_t = (\text{inventory}_{t-1}) * (\text{growth rate INV})$

$\text{Total current assets}_t = (\text{cash}_t) + (\text{accounts receivable}_t) + (\text{inventory}_t)$

$\text{Net fixed assets}_t = [(\text{net fixed assets}_{t-1}) - (\text{depreciation}_t)] * (\text{growth rate NFA})$

$\text{Total assets}_t = (\text{total assets}_{t-1}) + (\text{net to retained earnings}_t)$

LIABILITIES

$\text{Accounts payable}_t = (\text{sales}_t) * (\text{percent AP})$

$\text{Taxes payable}_t = (\text{sales}_t) * (\text{percent TP})$

$\text{Notes payable}_t = \text{constant}$

$\text{Total current liabilities}_t = (\text{accounts payable}_t) + (\text{taxes payable}_t) + (\text{notes payable}_t)$

$\text{Long-term debt}_t = (\text{long-term debt}_{t-1}) - (\text{long-term debt payment})$

$\text{Common stock}_t = \text{constant}$

$\text{Retained earnings}_t = (\text{total liabilities}_t) - (\text{accounts payable}_t) - (\text{taxes payable}_t) - (\text{notes payable}_t) - (\text{long-term debt}_t) - (\text{common stock}_t)$

$\text{Total liabilities}_t = (\text{total liabilities}_{t-1}) + (\text{net to retained earnings}_t)$

Figure 9 2 3   Balance Sheet: Methods of Computation

---

conceptual model: the accounting identities and relationships, which describe how financial accounts or planning items are to be calculated in preparing pro forma statements, form the conceptual model. It contains many of the assumptions of the financial model.

In addition to the methods of computation, Shirley got Future's income statement and balance sheet for 1978. These are shown in Figures 9 2 4 and 9 2 5. Shirley worked with Clem and President Herbie to come up with the management planning assumptions shown in Figure 9 2 6. The assumptions were based on an analysis of historical data and on their "best guesses" or judgment of the future. Shirley programmed the financial model which follows.

FUTURE INDUSTRIES, INC.
1978 INCOME STATEMENT

Sales	$1,000,000
Cost of goods sold	750,000
Gross profit	$ 250,000
Expenses:	
Administrative	$ 30,000
Selling	40,000
Depreciation	31,300
Miscellaneous	10,000
Total expenses	$ 111,300
Income before interest and taxes	138,700
Interest expense	$ 18,850
Income before taxes	119,850
Taxes	59,925
Net income	$ 59,925
Dividends	$ 29,962
Net to retained earnings	29,963

Figure 9 2 4   1978 Income Statement

FUTURE INDUSTRIES, INC.
1978 BALANCE SHEET
(year ending)

ASSETS	
Cash	$ 40,000
Accounts receivable	180,000
Inventory	200,000
Total current assets	$ 420,000
Net fixed assets	360,000
Total assets	$ 780,000
LIABILITIES	
Accounts payable	$ 100,000
Taxes payable	50,000
Notes payable	80,000
Total current liabilities	$ 230,000
Long-term debt	150,000
Common stock	200,000
Retained earnings	200,000
Total liabilities	$ 780,000

Figure 9 2 5   1978 Balance Sheet

Sales growth rate = 7% per year

Cost of goods sold percent = 75% decreasing 1% per year.

Administrative percent = 3%

Selling expense percent = 4%

Depreciation percent = 10%

Notes payable interest rate = 10% annual rate
   (simple interest not compounded during year)

Long-term debt interest rate = 7% annual rate
   (simple interest not compounded during year)

Tax rate = 50%

Dividended payout rate = 50%

Accounts receivable percent = 18%

Inventory growth rate = 5% per year

Net fixed assets growth rate = 15% per year

Accounts payable percent = 10%

Taxes payable percent = 5%

Long-term debt payment = $5,000 per year

Figure 9 2 6   Management Planning Assumptions

```
COMMENT: FUTURE INDUSTRIES CORPORATE FINANCIAL MODEL
        INTEGER DATE(2),YEAR(6),I,T,PAGE
        REAL SALES(6),CGSOLD(6),GRPROF(6),ADMIN(6),SELL(6)
        REAL DEPREC(6),MISC(6),TOTEXP(6),IBIT(6),INTRST(6)
        REAL IBT(6),TAXES(6),INCOME(6),DIVID(6),NETRE(6)
        REAL CASH(6),ACCREC(6),INVENT(6),TCASET(6),NFASET(6)
        REAL TASSET(6),ACCPAY(6),TAXPAY(6),NOTPAY(6)
        REAL TCLIAB(6),LTDEBT(6),CSTOCK(6),RETEAR(6),TLIAB(6)
        REAL SALEGR,CGSGR,CCGSGR
        REAL ADMPC,SELLPC,DEPRPC,NPIR,LTDIR,TAXRAT,DIVPAR
        REAL ARECPC,INVGR,NFAGR,APAYPC,TAXPPC,LTDPAY
        READ(5,100) (DATE(I),I=1,2), YEAR(1)
    100 FORMAT(2A4,3X,I4)
        READ(5,110) SALES(1),CGSOLD(1),GRPROF(1),ADMIN(1),
       1            SELL(1),DEPREC(1),MISC(1),TOTEXP(1),
       2            IBIT(1),INTRST(1),IBT(1),TAXES(1),
       3            INCOME(1),DIVID(1),NETRE(1),CASH(1),
       4            ACCREC(1),INVENT(1),TCASET(1),NFASET(1),
       5            TASSET(1),ACCPAY(1),TAXPAY(1),NOTPAY(1),
       6            TCLIAB(1),LTDEBT(1),CSTOCK(1),RETEAR(1),
       7            TLIAB(1)
    110 FORMAT(7F10.0)
        READ(5,120) SALEGR,CGSGR,CCGSGR,ADMPC,SELLPC,DEPRPC,
       1            NPIR,LTDIR,TAXRAT,DIVPAR,ARECPC,INVGR,
       2            NFAGR,APAYPC,TAXPPC,LTDPAY
    120 FORMAT(15F5.2,/,F10.0)
C                                       HERE'S THE CALCULATIONS
        DO 1000 T=2,6
          YEAR(T)=YEAR(T-1)+1
```

```
C                                     HERE'S THE INCOME STATEMENT
              SALES(T)=SALES(T-1)*(1.0+SALEGR)
              CGSGR= CGSGR-CCGSGR
              CGSOLD(T)=SALES(T)*CGSGR
              GRPROF(T)=SALES(T)-CGSOLD(T)
              ADMIN(T)=SALES(T)*ADMPC
              SELL(T)=SALES(T)*SELLPC
              DEPREC(T)=NFASET(T-1)*DEPRPC
              MISC(T)=MISC(T-1)
              TOTEXP(T)=ADMIN(T)+SELL(T)+DEPREC(T)+MISC(T)
              IBIT(T)=GRPROF(T)-TOTEXP(T)
              INTRST(T)=NOTPAY(T-1)*NPIR+LTDEBT(T-1)*LTDIR
              IBT(T)=IBIT(T)-INTRST(T)
              TAXES(T)=IBT(T)*TAXRAT
              INCOME(T)=IBT(T)-TAXES(T)
              DIVID(T)=INCOME(T)*DIVPAR
              NETRE(T)=INCOME(T)-DIVID(T)
C                                            HERE'S THE ASSETS
              TASSET(T)=TASSET(T-1)+NETRE(T)
              NFASET(T)=(NFASET(T-1)-DEPREC(T))*(1.0+NFAGR)
              INVENT(T)=INVENT(T-1)*(1.0+INVGR)
              ACCREC(T)=SALES(T)*ARECPC
              CASH(T)=TASSET(T)-NFASET(T)-INVENT(T)-ACCREC(T)
              TCASET(T)=CASH(T)+ACCREC(T)+INVENT(T)
C                                           HERE'S THE LIABILITIES
              ACCPAY(T)=SALES(T)*APAYPC
              TAXPAY(T)=SALES(T)*TAXPPC
              NOTPAY(T)=NOTPAY(T-1)
              TCLIAB(T)=ACCPAY(T)+TAXPAY(T)+NOTPAY(T)
              LTDEBT(T)=LTDEBT(T-1)-LTDPAY
              CSTOCK(T)=CSTOCK(T-1)
              TLIAB(T)=TLIAB(T-1)+NETRE(T)
              RETEAR(T)=TLIAB(T)-TCLIAB(T)-LTDEBT(T)-CSTOCK(T)
    1000      CONTINUE
C                                          WE'RE DONE CALCULATING
C                                          NOW, WRITE OUT THE REPORT
          PAGE=1
          WRITE(6,200) DATE,PAGE
      200 FORMAT(1H1,3X,2A4,110X,4HPAGE,I2)
          WRITE(6,201)
      201 FORMAT(1H ,/,53X,32HFUTURE INDUSTRIES CORPORATE PLAN)
          WRITE(6,202)
      202 FORMAT(58X,22H7 PERCENT SALES GROWTH)
          WRITE(6,203)
      203 FORMAT(56X,26HPRO FORMA INCOME STATEMENT)
          WRITE(6,204)
      204 FORMAT(1H ,/,40X,41(1H-),4HYEAR,41(1H-))
          WRITE(6,205) YEAR
      205 FORMAT(4X,11HDESCRIPTION,18X,6(11X,I4))
          WRITE(6,206) SALES
      206 FORMAT(1H ,/,4X,5HSALES,27X,6(4X,1H$,F10.0))
          WRITE(6,207) CGSOLD
      207 FORMAT(6X,18HCOST OF GOODS SOLD,12X,6(5X,F10.0))
          WRITE(6,208)
      208 FORMAT(36X,6(4X,11H-----------))
          WRITE(6,209) GRPROF
      209 FORMAT(4X,12HGROSS PROFIT,20X,6(4X,1H$,F10.0))
          WRITE(6,210)
      210 FORMAT(4X,8HEXPENSES)
          WRITE(6,211) ADMIN
```

```
211 FORMAT(6X,14HADMINISTRATIVE,16X,6(4X,1H$,F10.0))
    WRITE(6,212) SELL
212 FORMAT(6X,7HSELLING,23X,6(5X,F10.0))
    WRITE(6,213) DEPREC
213 FORMAT(6X,12HDEPRECIATION,18X,6(5X,F10.0))
    WRITE(6,214) MISC
214 FORMAT(6X,13HMISCELLANEOUS,17X,6(5X,F10.0))
    WRITE(6,208)
    WRITE(6,215) TOTEXP
215 FORMAT(4X,14HTOTAL EXPENSES,18X,6(4X,1H$,F10.0))
    WRITE(6,216) IBIT
216 FORMAT(1H ,/,4X,32HINCOME BEFORE INTEREST AND TAXES,
   1        6(4X,1H$,F10.0))
    WRITE(6,217) INTRST
217 FORMAT(4X,16HINTEREST EXPENSE,16X,6(5X,F10.0))
    WRITE(6,218) IBT
218 FORMAT(4X,19HINCOME BEFORE TAXES,13X,6(5X,F10.0))
    WRITE(6,219) TAXES
219 FORMAT(4X,5HTAXES,27X,6(5X,F10.0))
    WRITE(6,208)
    WRITE(6,220) INCOME
220 FORMAT(4X,10HNET INCOME,22X,6(4X,1H$,F10.0))
    WRITE(6,240)
    WRITE(6,221) DIVID
221 FORMAT(4X,9HDIVIDENDS,23X,6(4X,1H$,F10.0))
    WRITE(6,222) NETRE
222 FORMAT(4X,24HNET TO RETAINED EARNINGS, 8X,
   1        6(4X,1H$,F10.0))
    PAGE=2
    WRITE(6,200) DATE,PAGE
    WRITE(6,201)
    WRITE(6,202)
    WRITE(6,223)
223 FORMAT(58X,23HPRO FORMA BALANCE SHEET)
    WRITE(6,204)
    WRITE(6,205) YEAR
    WRITE(6,224)
224 FORMAT(1H ,/,4X,6HASSETS)
    WRITE(6,225) CASH
225 FORMAT(9X,4HCASH,23X,6(4X,1H$,F10.0))
    WRITE(6,226) ACCREC
226 FORMAT(9X,19HACCOUNTS RECEIVABLE,, 8X,6(5X,F10.0))
    WRITE(6,227) INVENT
227 FORMAT(9X,9HINVENTORY,18X,6(5X,F10.0))
    WRITE(6,208)
    WRITE(6,228) TCASET
228 FORMAT(6X,20HTOTAL CURRENT ASSETS,10X,
   1        6(4X,1H$,F10.0))
    WRITE(6,229) NFASET
229 FORMAT(1H ,/,6X,16HNET FIXED ASSETS,14X,
   1        6(4X,1H$,F10.0))
    WRITE(6,208)
    WRITE(6,230) TASSET
230 FORMAT(6X,12HTOTAL ASSETS,18X,6(4X,1H$,F10.0))
    WRITE(6,240)
    WRITE(6,231)
231 FORMAT(1H ,/,4X,11HLIABILITIES)
    WRITE(6,232) ACCPAY
232 FORMAT(9X,16HACCOUNTS PAYABLE,11X,6(4X,1H$,F10.0))
    WRITE(6,233) TAXPAY
233 FORMAT(9X,13HTAXES PAYABLE,14X,6(5X,F10.0))
    WRITE(6,234) NOTPAY
```

```
234 FORMAT(9X,13HNOTES PAYABLE,14X,6(5X,F10.0))
    WRITE(6,208)
    WRITE(6,235) TCLIAB
235 FORMAT(6X,25HTOTAL CURRENT LIABILITIES,,5X,
   1        6(4X,1H$,F10.0))
    WRITE(6,236) LTDEBT
236 FORMAT(1H ,/,6X,14HLONG-TERM DEBT,16X,
   1        6(4X,1H$,F10.0))
    WRITE(6,237) CSTOCK
237 FORMAT(6X,12HCOMMON STOCK,18X,6(5X,F10.0))
    WRITE(6,238) RETEAR
238 FORMAT(6X,17HRETAINED EARNINGS,13X,6(5X,F10.0))
    WRITE(6,208)
    WRITE(6,239) TLIAB
239 FORMAT(6X,17HTOTAL LIABILITIES,13X,6(4X,1H$,F10.0))
    WRITE(6,240)
240 FORMAT(36X,6(4X,11H===========))
    STOP
    END
```

input

```
10/21/79    1978                                                                            1
    1000000      750000     250000        30000      40000      31300      10000            2
     111300      138700      18850       119850      59925      59925      29962            3
      29963       40000     180000       200000     420000     360000     780000           4
     100000       50000      80000       230000     150000     200000     200000           5
     780000                                                                                6
    07    75   01    03    04    10    10    07    50    50    18    05    15    10    05    7
       5000                                                                                 8
```

Record 1

DATE MM / DD / YY	NOT USED	BASE YEAR	SALES

Record 2

TOTAL EXPENSES	COST OF GOODS SOLD	GROSS PROFIT	ADMINISTRATIVE EXPENSES	SELLING EXPENSES	DEPRECIATION EXPENSES	MISCELLANEOUS EXPENSES

Record 3

NET TO RETAINED EARNINGS	INCOME BEFORE INTEREST AND TAXES	INTEREST EXPENSE	INCOME BEFORE TAXES	TAXES	NET INCOME	DIVIDENDS

Record 4

ACCOUNTS PAYABLE	CASH	ACCOUNTS RECEIVABLE	INVENTORY	TOTAL CURRENT ASSETS	NET FIXED ASSETS	TOTAL ASSETS

Record 5

TOTAL LIABILITIES	TAXES PAYABLE	NOTES PAYABLE	TOTAL CURRENT LIABILITIES	LONG-TERM DEBT	COMMON STOCK	RETAINED EARNINGS

Record 6

Record 7

SALES GROWTH RATE	COST OF GOODS SOLD %	COST OF GOODS SOLD CHANGE %	ADMIN %	SELLING %	DEPRECIA-TION %	NOTES PAYABLE INTEREST RATE	LONG-TERM DEBT INTEREST RATE	TAX RATE	DIVIDEND PAYOUT RATE	ACCOUNTS RECEIVABLE %	INVENTORY GROWTH RATE	NET FIXED ASSETS GROWTH RATE	ACCOUNTS PAYABLE %	TAXES PAYABLE %

Record 8

LONG-TERM DEBT PAYMENT

FUTURE INDUSTRIES CORPORATE PLAN
7 PERCENT SALES GROWTH
PRO FORMA INCOME STATEMENT

DESCRIPTION	1978	1979	1980	1981	1982	1983
SALES	$ 1000000.	$ 1070000.	$ 1144900.	$ 1225043.	$ 1310796.	$ 1402552.
COST OF GOODS SOLD	750000.	791800.	835777.	882031.	930665.	981786.
GROSS PROFIT	$ 250000.	$ 278200.	$ 309123.	$ 343012.	$ 380131.	$ 420766.
EXPENSES						
ADMINISTRATIVE	$ 30000.	$ 32100.	$ 34347.	$ 36751.	$ 39324.	$ 42077.
SELLING	40000.	42800.	45798.	49002.	52432.	56102.
DEPRECIATION	31300.	36000.	37260.	38564.	39914.	41311.
MISCELLANEOUS	10000.	10000.	10000.	10000.	10000.	10000.
TOTAL EXPENSES	$ 111300.	$ 120900.	$ 127403.	$ 134317.	$ 141670.	$ 149489.
INCOME BEFORE INTEREST AND TAXES	$ 138700.	$ 157300.	$ 181720.	$ 208695.	$ 238461.	$ 271276.
INTEREST EXPENSE	18850.	18500.	18150.	17800.	17450.	17100.
INCOME BEFORE TAXES	119850.	138800.	163570.	190895.	221011.	254176.
TAXES	59925.	69400.	81785.	95447.	110506.	127088.
NET INCOME	$ 59925.	$ 69400.	$ 81785.	$ 95447.	$ 110506.	$ 127088.
DIVIDENDS	$ 29962.	$ 34700.	$ 40893.	$ 47724.	$ 55253.	$ 63544.
NET TO RETAINED EARNINGS	$ 29963.	$ 34700.	$ 40893.	$ 47724.	$ 55253.	$ 63544.

FUTURE INDUSTRIES CORPORATE PLAN
7 PERCENT SALES GROWTH
PRO FORMA BALANCE SHEET

DESCRIPTION	1978	1979	1980	1981	1982	1983
ASSETS						
CASH	$ 40000.	$ 39500.	$ 43370.	$ 52145.	$ 66416.	$ 86830.
ACCOUNTS RECEIVABLE	180000.	192600.	206082.	220508.	235943.	252459.
INVENTORY	200000.	210000.	220500.	231525.	243101.	255256.
TOTAL CURRENT ASSETS	$ 420000.	$ 442100.	$ 469952.	$ 504178.	$ 545461.	$ 594546.
NET FIXED ASSETS	$ 360000.	$ 372600.	$ 385641.	$ 399138.	$ 413108.	$ 427567.
TOTAL ASSETS	$ 780000.	$ 814700.	$ 855593.	$ 903316.	$ 958569.	$ 1022113.
LIABILITIES						
ACCOUNTS PAYABLE	$ 100000.	$ 107000.	$ 114490.	$ 122504.	$ 131080.	$ 140255.
TAXES PAYABLE	50000.	53500.	57245.	61252.	65540.	70128.
NOTES PAYABLE	80000.	80000.	80000.	80000.	80000.	80000.
TOTAL CURRENT LIABILITIES	$ 230000.	$ 240500.	$ 251735.	$ 263756.	$ 276619.	$ 290383.
LONG-TERM DEBT	$ 150000.	$ 145000.	$ 140000.	$ 135000.	$ 130000.	$ 125000.
COMMON STOCK	200000.	200000.	200000.	200000.	200000.	200000.
RETAINED EARNINGS	200000.	229200.	263858.	304560.	351950.	406730.
TOTAL LIABILITIES	$ 780000.	$ 814700.	$ 855593.	$ 903316.	$ 958569.	$ 1022113.

------YEAR------

In the above program, T is used to indicate the year or time period. You might notice that Shirley has used arrays containing six elements to do the five-year projection. T equal to 1 is the base year of 1978. Shirley then projected five years from this base. Look at the program; you should be able to see where the methods of computation have been included in the program. The only tricky parts to the program are that the cash account and total current assets account are the last ones calculated in the assets section of the balance sheet and retained earnings is the dead last item calculated in the balance sheet. If you think about these equations, you'll see that other items have to be calculated first in order to do these. Another thing you might notice about Shirley's program is that the projection was calculated year-by-year, rather than planning item–by–item. For some items it doesn't matter, but for others it's crucial to the projections.

The projection of corporate financial data is done so frequently that some companies have developed special problem-oriented programming languages to do these kinds of projections. They are known as financial planning languages, planning and budgeting languages, and planning model generators. The input into one of these modeling languages includes not only the data, as in the program above, but also the methods of computation. They're even easier to use than Shirley's program.

EXERCISES 9 2

1 Financial planning models can be used to evaluate "what if" situations. Change the assumption on sales growth rate from 7 percent to 9 percent and run the program. Compare your results to those Shirley got for President Herbie.

2 Change some other management planning assumptions and run the program. Compare your results. This sure is easier than using your calculator on each "what if," isn't it?

3 Shirley's program READs the entire current income statement and balance sheet. Which of these items could be calculated in the program?

Section 9 3
Sorting—Arranging Several Arrays at Once

In Section 8 5 we discussed a problem in which a pair of arrays needed to be rearranged in a particular order. The arrangement was based on the values in only one of the arrays, but since elements in corresponding positions in the arrays had to be *kept* in corresponding positions, whenever we moved an element of one array, we had to make a similar change in the other array.

Let's look at another sorting problem. What we want to do is print a list of personal statistics records (name, age, weight, and height from each of several persons) in order by weight, from lightest to heaviest.

> **problem statement:** *Arrange a list of personal statistics records in order of increasing weight. Each personal statistics record will consist of a name, age, weight, and height.*

The input for the program will be a bunch of these personal statistics records, one to a card, followed by a terminal record containing the signal name END so that we'll know when we've reached the end of the records. We want the output to be the same list of records rearranged so that the weights are in order from lightest to heaviest.

> **input/output description**
>
> input: (a) one personal statistics record for each person, consisting of name, age, weight, and height;
> (b) terminal record with END in the name field
>
> computation: arrange the records by weights, lightest to heaviest
>
> output: list of all input personal statistics records in order of increasing weight

A first stab at designing our program is shown below. Since we've had a lot of experience with input and output loops of the kind we'll need here, there's not much point in spending time analyzing those processes here. The sorting process is the one we need to look at carefully.

> **personal statistics sorting algorithm**
> 1 bring records into memory
> 2 compute arrangement by weight
> 3 print records

It is nearly always the case in a sorting problem that more than one array is involved. The example in this section involves four arrays, but the sorting subprogram we'll write will be useful for sorting, simultaneously, *any* number of corresponding arrays. The sorting process will be the same as in Section 8 5, but instead of rearranging the arrays themselves, we'll simply build an **index** which will tell us how they should be arranged. The first entry in the index will tell us where to find the array elements which come first in the ordering, the second entry will tell us

> **index:** *a list of numbers telling us how to arrange another list in alphabetical order; the first entry in index tells us which element in the list goes first, the second index entry tells us which goes second, and so on*

where to find the elements which should come second, and so on. Figure 9 3 1 pictures an index for some arrays containing the names, ages, weights, and heights of a group of children which we want to arrange in order from lightest to heaviest.

	names	ages	weights	heights	index	
1	BOB	5	45	46	3	(AMY lightest)
2	TED	6	39	45	4	(JOY 2nd)
3	AMY	3	27	32	5	(SUE 3rd)
4	JOY	4	31	36	2	(TED 4th)
5	SUE	5	33	38	1	(BOB heaviest)

Figure 9 3 1

The index will tell us what order the elements should come in. Our subprogram won't rearrange the arrays themselves so it won't need to know how many arrays are involved. All it will need to know is what values are in the array containing the **keys**, the values we want in increasing order. From that it can build the index, which will tell us what order to take the array elements in. We'll use a technique that can be used in conjunction with almost any sorting algorithm.

> **keys:** *a list of values which we want to know how to arrange in some particular order (e.g., increasing order)*

In the beginning, we set up the index as if the array were already in the correct order; that is, the index will have the entries 1, 2, 3, 4, and so on, to begin with. Then we rearrange the index until it correctly orders the keys. The trick is that we always refer to the keys *through the index*. Instead of referring to the *i*th key, we refer to the key designated by the *i*th entry in the index. If the keys array is called KEYS and the index array is called INDEX, then instead of referring to KEYS(I), we refer to KEYS(INDEX(I)). Whenever we want to interchange a pair of keys, we interchange the corresponding *index* entries (not the keys themselves). Since we are referring to the keys through the index anyway, it will be as if we had interchanged the pair of keys. Perhaps this is best explained pictorially, as in Figures 9 3 2, 9 3 3, and 9 3 4.

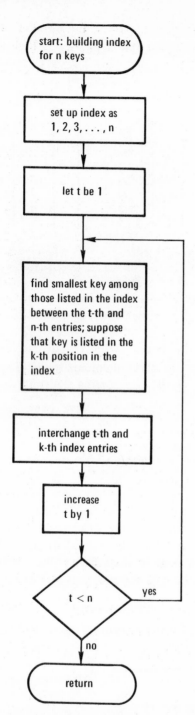

VERBAL DESCRIPTION

Set up index.

Find largest element in bottom section of array.

Interchange largest element with top element in bottom section.

Decrease size of bottom section.

Repeat unless bottom section contains only one element.

Figure 9 3 2   Sorting Algorithm

The subprogram below prepares an index for a list of keys in the way described by the flowchart of Figure 9 3 2. It has two input parameters: KEYS, an array of values we want to arrange in increasing order; and N, the number of values in the array KEYS. It has one output parameter, INDEX, an array which will tell us how to arrange the KEYS.

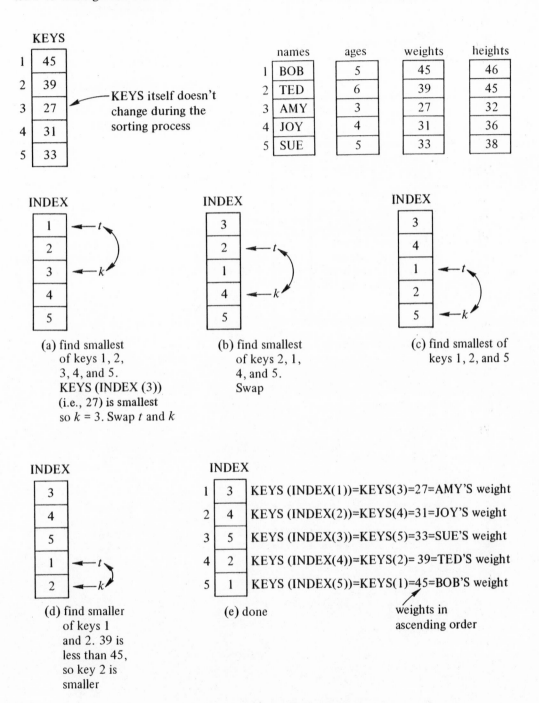

(a) find smallest
of keys 1, 2,
3, 4, and 5.
KEYS (INDEX (3))
(i.e., 27) is smallest
so $k = 3$. Swap t and k

(b) find smallest
of keys 2, 1,
4, and 5.
Swap

(c) find smallest of
keys 1, 2, and 5

(d) find smaller
of keys 1
and 2. 39 is
less than 45,
so key 2 is
smaller

(e) done

KEYS (INDEX(1))=KEYS(3)=27=AMY'S weight
KEYS (INDEX(2))=KEYS(4)=31=JOY'S weight
KEYS (INDEX(3))=KEYS(5)=33=SUE'S weight
KEYS (INDEX(4))=KEYS(2)= 39=TED'S weight
KEYS (INDEX(5))=KEYS(1)=45=BOB'S weight

weights in
ascending order

Figure 9 3 3   Arranging an Index

```
        SUBROUTINE INDSRT (KEYS, INDEX, N)
        INTEGER N, KEYS(N), INDEX(N)
COMMENT:  THIS SUBROUTINE PERFORMS AN INDEX SORT.
C         IT FILLS THE ARRAY "INDEX" WITH VALUES WHICH TELL
C         US HOW TO ARRANGE THE ARRAY "KEYS" IN INCREASING
C         ORDER.
C       INPUT:
C         KEYS--AN ARRAY OF INTEGERS
C         N--THE NUMBER OF ENTRIES IN KEYS
C       OUTPUT:
C         INDEX--AN ARRAY CONTAINING ALL THE INTEGERS
C                 BETWEEN 1 AND N ARRANGED SO THAT
C                 KEYS(INDEX(1)).LE.KEYS(INDEX(2)).LE. ...
C                 ETC.  UP TO KEYS(INDEX(N))
        INTEGER TOP, SM, LOCSM, NLESS1
C       INITIALIZE INDEX
        DO 50 TOP=1,N
  50      INDEX(TOP)=TOP
C       SORT
        NLESS1 = N-1
        DO 100 TOP=1,NLESS1
          SM = LOCSM(KEYS,INDEX, TOP, N)
          CALL SWITCH(INDEX(SM),INDEX(TOP))
C                                       NOTICE!  AT THIS POINT
C                       KEYS(INDEX(I)) .LE. KEYS(INDEX(I+1))
C                       FOR EACH I FROM 1 TO TOP, INCLUSIVE
 100      CONTINUE
        RETURN
        END

        INTEGER FUNCTION LOCSM (KEYS,INDEX, FROM,TO)
        INTEGER FROM, TO, KEYS(TO), INDEX(TO)
COMMENT:  LOCATE THE SMALLEST VALUE
C       INPUT:
C         KEYS--AS IN SUBROUTINE INDSRT
C         INDEX--AN ARRAY CONTAINING THE INTEGERS BETWEEN
C                 1 AND "TO" (SCRAMBLED)
C         FROM--AN INTEGER BETWEEN 1 AND "TO"
C         TO--THE NUMBER OF ENTRIES IN KEYS AND INDEX
C       OUTPUT:
C         LOCSM--KEYS(INDEX(LOCSM)).LE.KEYS(INDEX(I))
C                 FOR EACH I BETWEEN "FROM" AND "TO"
        INTEGER I
        LOCSM=FROM
        DO 100 I=FROM,TO
          IF (KEYS(INDEX(I)).LT.KEYS(INDEX(LOCSM))) LOCSM=I
C                                       NOTICE!  AT THIS POINT
C                       KEYS(INDEX(LOCSM)).LE.KEYS(INDEX(J))
C               FOR EACH J BETWEEN "FROM" AND "I", INCLUSIVE
 100      CONTINUE
        RETURN
        END

        SUBROUTINE SWITCH (A,B)
        INTEGER A,B
        INTEGER COPYA
        COPYA = A
        A = B
        B = COPYA
        RETURN
        END
```

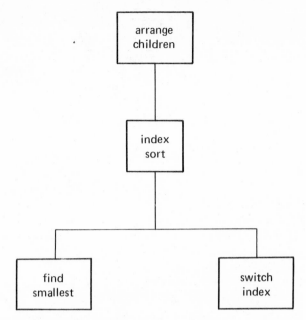

Figure 9 3 4 HIPO Diagram for Program to List Children
in Order by Weight and Age

We can use INDSRT to solve the problem of printing our list of children's
names (along with their ages and weights) in order of their weights. All we need to
do, once the information is stored in the arrays, is CALL our SUBROUTINE.
We use the array that stores their weights as our argument, and provide an array
to be used for an index. Then we will be able to print the arrays in the proper
order by using the index. While we're at it, we may as well sort the arrays again
so that we can also print the lists in order of increasing age. That will just involve
another CALL to the SUBROUTINE.

```
COMMENT:   THIS PROGRAM READS A LIST OF CHILDREN'S NAMES,
C          AGES, WEIGHTS, AND HEIGHTS FROM CARDS, THEN PRINTS
C          THE LIST TWICE.  ONCE IN THE ORDER OF INCREASING
C          WEIGHT, THEN ONCE IN ORDER OF INCREASING AGE.
       INTEGER NAME(100), AGE(100), WGT(100), HGT(100)
       INTEGER N, I, X(100), FINIS
       DATA FINIS/3HEND/
C                                              STORE THE DATA
       N=0
 100   READ(5,1000) NAME(N+1),AGE(N+1),WGT(N+1),HGT(N+1)
1000 FORMAT(A3, 3I3)
       IF (NAME(N+1) .EQ. FINIS)  GO TO 200
       N = N+1
       GO TO 100
C                                       FIRST SORT ON WEIGHTS
 200   CALL INDSRT(WGT,X,N)
       WRITE(6,2000)
2000 FORMAT('0CHILDREN BY INCREASING WEIGHT'/
      +          ' NAME       AGE      WEIGHT      HEIGHT')
       WRITE(6,3000) (NAME(X(I)),AGE(X(I)),WGT(X(I)),
      +                       HGT(X(I)), I=1,N)
3000 FORMAT(' ',A3,3I10)
```

```
C                                              NOW SORT ON AGES
        CALL INDSRT(AGE,X,N)
        WRITE(6,4000)
   4000 FORMAT('0CHILDREN BY INCREASING AGE'/
       +        ' NAME       AGE      WEIGHT      HEIGHT')
        WRITE(6,3000) (NAME(X(I)),AGE(X(I)),WGT(X(I)),
       +                       HGT(X(I)), I=1,N)
        STOP
        END
```

data
```
    BOB   5  45  46
    TED   6  39  45
    AMY   3  27  32
    JOY   4  31  36
    SUE   5  33  38
    END
```

output
```
    CHILDREN BY INCREASING WEIGHT
    NAME       AGE      WEIGHT      HEIGHT
    AMY         3         27          32
    JOY         4         31          36
    SUE         5         33          38
    TED         6         39          45
    BOB         5         45          46

    CHILDREN BY INCREASING AGE
    NAME       AGE      WEIGHT      HEIGHT
    AMY         3         27          32
    JOY         4         31          36
    BOB         5         45          46
    SUE         5         33          38
    TED         6         39          45
```

---

nonstandard subscripts

Many of the subscripts used in this program, like the X(I) in
NAME*(X(I)), are not ANSI standard subscripts. The standards
require that expressions in subscripts be one of the following
forms.*

k

v *c and k are unsigned*

$v - k$ INTEGER *constants*

$v + k$

$c*v$ *v is an unsubscripted*
                               INTEGER *memory cell name*

$c*v - k$

$c*v + k$

*To make our program fit the standards, we would need to declare
an* INTEGER *memory cell and assign it the value X(I) whenever
necessary. Thus the last* WRITE *statement in the program would
be written:*

```
        DO 310 I=1,N
            J = X(I)
   310      WRITE(6,3010) NAME(J),AGE(J),WGT(J),HGT(J)
```

---

266 Fortran for Business People

1 What statements would you add to the final program of this section so that it also prints the lists of children's names in alphabetical order?

2 What statements could you add to the program to make certain it didn't try to READ more cards than it had room for in its arrays?

3 The arrays are declared to be of length 100 in the program. But the array parameters in INDSRT are declared to be of length N, where N is one of the parameters. When INDSRT is CALLed, the parameter indicating the length of the arrays won't have a value equal to the actual declared array length. Do you think this should cause an error? Why or why not?

Section 9 4

Searching—Finding a Data Value

Our problem here is how to store numbers in an array if you are going to have to look up specific ones later. One place the problem arises is in assembling, maintaining, and using files of information about people (data banks). In Section 9 3 we saw a way of using several arrays, one for each type of information. There we let the subscripts link the various pieces of information together—for example, letting the ith memory cell in each array correspond to the information stored about the ith person. For example, suppose we want a file of information to help prepare paychecks. For each person, we'd need to record (1) a social security number, (2) an hourly wage, (3) the number of income tax deductions claimed, and (4) the type of company health insurance carried, if any. If there are not more than 2000 employees, we'd declare the arrays

```
INTEGER SOCSEC(2000), HRWAGE(2000), DEDUCS(2000)
INTEGER INSURE(2000)
```

and the first part of our "data bank" might look like Figure 9 4 1.

	SOCSEC		HRWAGE		DEDUCS		INSURE
1	275307041	1	375	1	2	1	N
2	444226810	2	425	2	1	2	S
3	721337726	3	326	3	5	3	F
	⋮		⋮	4	⋮		⋮

Figure 9 4 1

The information stored about the second person is that her social security number is 444226810, her hourly wage is $4.25, she has claimed one deduction, and it is .TRUE. that she carries the company health insurance for single people. (Note that we've stored wages as INTEGERs instead of REALs so that we don't have to worry about round-off errors.)

Now when the records showing how many hours each person worked this week come in, we must find the information stored about that person to be able to compute his or her pay for the week. Suppose one such record is

soc-sec-no = 721337726   hrs worked = 36.5

As we have things set up, we would have to search in the SOCSEC array until we found an entry with the value 721337726. We would find it in SOCSEC(3), so we would know that the information about this person is stored in HRWAGE(3), DEDUCS(3), and INSURE(3). In this case, that wouldn't take much effort, but on the average we would have to look through about half of the employees before we found the one we wanted. There is a much faster way. Suppose that we stored things so that the person's social security number *was the array subscript value of the memory cells where that person's records were stored.* Then if memory cell ID contained a particular person's social security number, the cells

HRWAGE(ID), DEDUCS(ID) and INSURE(ID)

would contain the information we want. This way, no matter whom we're looking for, once we know the social security number, we can immediately find the desired information.

No doubt you can see the trouble with our scheme. It requires that the arrays be as long as the largest possible social security number! If we had only 2000 employees, we'd still need 999,999,999 memory cells in each array, even though 999,997,999 of them wouldn't be used for anything. Inserting new records and retrieving old ones is very fast and easy, but the memory requirements are simply unacceptable.

"Aha!" you may say. "Why not just give each employee a number between 1 and 2000?" Then we could use the same technique but would need only 2000 spaces in each array.

That solution is also unacceptable because it would mean that each employee would have to learn an employee number (and a number for the bank, the savings and loan, and every organization that wanted to use this efficient and convenient—for the computer—way of storing information). That's just the sort of thing that makes people say that computers are dehumanizing.

The only acceptable way of utilizing a data bank such as we're describing is a combination of the techniques we've described—give everybody a small number, but never let them know it. Instead, store an array which makes the correspondence between a social security number (or, even better, a name) and the number you want to use internally. To find a person's records, first locate the social security number, then use the corresponding element in the internal number array to retrieve the records. If you turn back a few pages, you'll see that this is equivalent to the way we started! Thus, no matter how much information you want to store about each person, the only acceptable ways of accessing that information involve looking up a number (or name) in an array.

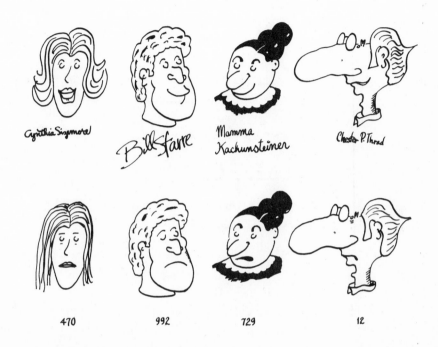

Now that we've resigned ourselves to the fact that we must look in an array to locate the information we want, let's concentrate on that problem. The most obvious way is the simple one we already mentioned. Look at the contents of the first memory cell and see if that's the one we want. If so, then we're done. If not, we'll look at the second, and so on. We'll call this a **sequential search**. Figure 9 4 2 describes the process, assuming the array we're searching is named PEOPLE and the value we're looking for is PERSON.

This algorithm will work fine as long as PERSON really is in the array PEOPLE somewhere. If there's been a typing error, or PERSON represents a new employee, then the algorithm gets into trouble because it doesn't check to make sure it doesn't keep going past the end of the array. As long as we're going to fix *that*, let's change it so that if PERSON doesn't appear in the array, we'll make a new entry. Let the memory cell NENTRY store the number of entries (people's names or numbers) stored in the array.

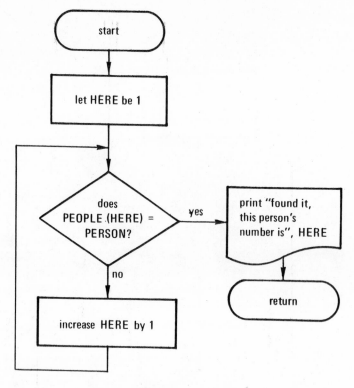

Figure 9 4 2

Making a new entry is very easy. We just add 1 to NENTRY since there's now one more person stored and then stick in PERSON (see Figure 9 4 3). If there are NENTRY people, then finding a PERSON takes NENTRY/2 steps on the average. If the PERSON isn't in the array, it takes NENTRY steps to discover that fact. Sequential search is very easy, but it can take a long time even on a very fast computer. For instance, if there are 10,000 people on a company's payroll, it would take

$$\underbrace{10,000}_{\substack{\text{number of} \\ \text{searches}}} \qquad * \qquad \underbrace{10,000/2}_{\substack{\text{average steps} \\ \text{per search}}} = 50,000,000 \text{ steps}$$

to find the information needed to compute all the paychecks.

There is a situation that we're all familiar with that is very similar to the one we're facing. Suppose you are given someone's name and a phone book and are asked to find that person's phone number. If the phone book listings were in no particular order, you'd have to carry out the sequential search algorithm to find the name you're looking for! Except in a very small town, that would be a horrendous task. Fortunately, the phone company has had the good sense to put the listings in alphabetical order so that you have some hope of finding the name

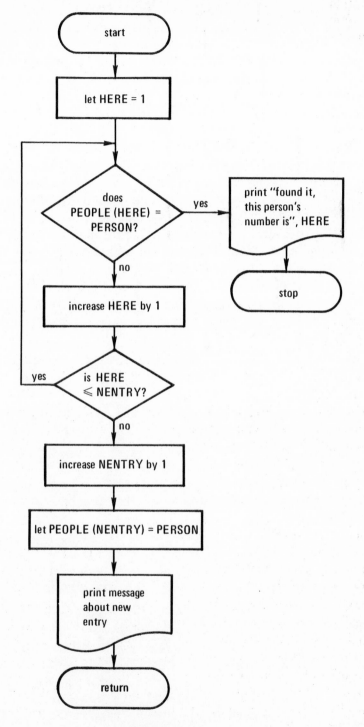

Figure 9 4 3

you want (or discovering that it's not listed) before your eyes fall out. Obviously, it would be faster to find an entry in an array if the array were arranged in a nice order. If the array is in increasing order, we can use the following algorithm, which is related to the way you look up a number in a phone book.

We'll use two variables, one called LOW, which stores an array index value that we know is lower than the place we want, and a memory cell HIGH, which is higher than the place we want. Before we look anywhere, we know that 0 is lower than the place we want, and the NENTRY + 1 must be higher than the place we want. Then we'll start looking. Since we don't yet know anything except that the place we want is somewhere in between LOW and HIGH, we might as well look in the *middle*, guessing that the place we want is just as likely to be in the first half of the array as the last half. The middle value is, of course, PEOPLE((LOW + HIGH)/2). Maybe that's the value we wanted. If so, we've finished. If *not*, then we can tell if the value we wanted is before the middle or after the middle just by comparing the value PERSON to the value PEOPLE((LOW + HIGH)/2). If PER-SON is not equal to PEOPLE((LOW + HIGH)/2) then we know that if PERSON appears at all, it (1) lies *above* the middle or (2) lies *below* the middle. In either case we continue the process, changing the value of LOW in the first case or HIGH in case (2). If LOW and HIGH ever get so close together that there are no entries

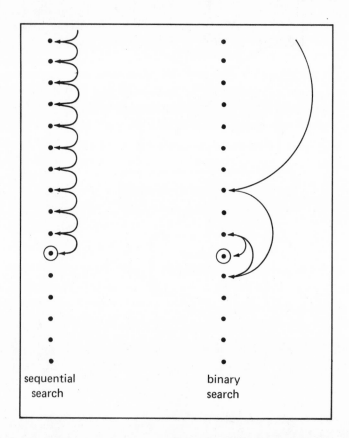

sequential
search

binary
search

between them, we know that PERSON wasn't in the array at all! We call this kind of search **binary search** because at each step we eliminate about one half of the alternatives. The flowchart in Figure 9 4 4 describes the search more precisely.

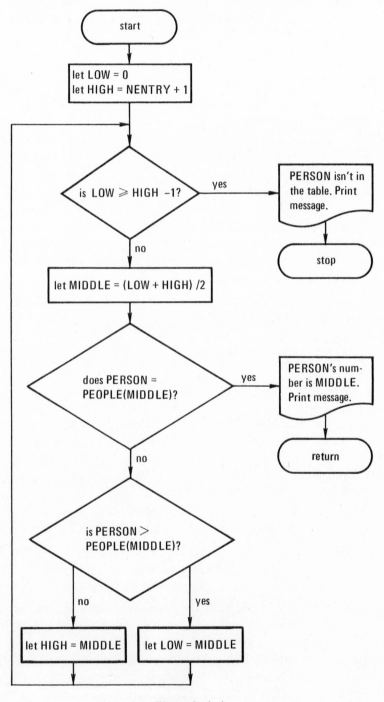

Figure 9 4 4

```
        SUBROUTINE BINARY(PERSON,PEOPLE,NENTRY,HERE)
        INTEGER PERSON, NENTRY, PEOPLE(100), HERE
COMMENT:   BINARY SEARCH ALGORITHM TO  FIND "PERSON" IN THE
C          ARRAY "PEOPLE" .
C             IF "PERSON" IS NOT FOUND, IT IS INSERTED.
        INTEGER LOW, HIGH, MIDDLE, SHIFT
C       IF "PERSON" IS IN THE ARRAY, IT MUST BE BETWEEN
C       THE FIRST AND LAST POSITION IN THE ARRAY.
        LOW = 0
        HIGH = NENTRY + 1
C       ARE "LOW" AND "HIGH" TOO CLOSE TOGETHER?
  10    IF ( LOW .GE. HIGH-1 )  GO TO 200
C          LOOK IN THE MIDDLE
           MIDDLE = (LOW+HIGH)/2
C          EXIT IF FOUND
        IF ( PERSON .EQ. PEOPLE(MIDDLE) )  GO TO 100
C          PROCEED IN TOP OR BOTTOM HALF OF ARRAY
           IF ( PERSON .GT. PEOPLE(MIDDLE) )  GO TO 20
           HIGH = MIDDLE
           GO TO 10
  20       LOW = MIDDLE
           GO TO 10
C
C       FOUND IT...RETURN ITS POSITION
 100    HERE = MIDDLE
        RETURN
C
C       NOT PRESENT.. INSERT IT
 200    SHIFT = NENTRY
 210    PEOPLE(SHIFT+1) = PEOPLE(SHIFT)
        SHIFT = SHIFT - 1
        IF ( SHIFT .GE. LOW+1 )  GO TO 210
        NENTRY = NENTRY + 1
        PEOPLE(LOW+1) = PERSON
        HERE = LOW +1
        RETURN
        END
```

Since we eliminate about half of the alternatives each time around the loop, after one time there are NENTRY/2 alternatives left, after two times there are NENTRY/(2*2) left, after three times there are NENTRY/(2*2*2) left, and after n times there are NENTRY/2^n left. We stop if there can't be more than one alternative left, that is when NENTRY/2^n $\leq$ 1. Solving for n, we find that the most steps it could ever take is $n = \log_2$ (NENTRY). Now to look up the information to compute the payroll for our company of 10,000, it takes no more than

$$10,000 \quad * \quad \log_2 (10,000) \quad = \quad 133,000 \text{ steps}$$

number of   maximum time

searches   per search

which is many, many fewer than the number required by the sequential method.

While the binary search method is much better for looking things *up* than the sequential method, it's a little worse when we have to put a new person into the array. In the sequential scheme, to put in a new person, we just stick the number (or name) in at the bottom. In the binary scheme we must insert the new person in the right place so that the array stays in order.

If you look at the binary search flowchart (Figure 9 4 4), you'll see that when we discover that PERSON doesn't appear in the array, we at least know where it should be—it should be at position LOW + 1. All we need to do then is to slide all entries after LOW down one position and then stick in PERSON. On the average, that will take NENTRY/2 steps. Here's a complete binary search routine. It takes an array called PEOPLE as an argument along with a PERSON to look for, and it returns the position of PERSON in the array if it found it, or the position of PERSON after PERSON was inserted.

There are yet more algorithms for searching an array or sorting data. They make use of schemes such as **hash coding** and **binary trees**, to name a couple. Some are compromises between speed and the amount of memory you'll allow your program to use. There is no doubt some absolute limit to how good an algorithm can be for searching or sorting on current digital computers. Computer scientists work for ever better algorithms to search and sort faster and more efficiently. If you are interested in the race for better algorithms, you might check your library for some references.

EXERCISES 9 4

1 Try the following game to convince yourself of the speed of the binary search strategy. Pick a number between 1 and 1000. See how many guesses a friend makes before he gets the number if after each guess you tell him whether his guess was "high" or "low." The binary search algorithm guarantees that you will find the answer in ten or fewer guesses.

PROBLEMS 9

1 After President Herbie received the pro forma income statement and balance sheet from Shirley, he was so elated he gave Shirley a raise. Then he asked Shirley to do a cashflow statement for Future Industries. Shirley has put together the planning assumption given below for the cashflow statement. Your job, if you want to remain a loyal employee of Future, is to write a program to project cashflow for five years or twelve months, your choice. Design your own inputs and outputs. It would be nice if you followed the design formats Shirley used for the income statement and balance sheet. Shirley would be pleased. Make up your own test data; be realistic. You'll need to specify beginning or base values and the growth rates or percent changes, as Shirley did.

CASHFLOW RELATIONSHIPS:

$$\text{Cash balance, beginning}_t = \text{Cash balance, ending}_{t-1}$$
$$\text{Sales}_t = \text{sales}_{t-1} * \text{sales growth rate}$$

Cash receipts:

$$\text{Cash sales}_t = \text{sales}_t * \text{percent cash sales}$$

Credit sale collections (current period)$_t$ = Sales *
(1 − percent cash sales) * (Percent credit sale paid
in current period)
Credit sales collections (previous period)$_t$ = Sales$_{t-1}$ *
(1 − percent cash sales) * (1 − percent credit sales paid
in current period)
Other cash receipts$_t$ = other cash receipts$_{t-1}$ * other
cash receipts growth rate
Total cash receipts$_t$ = cash sales$_t$ + credit sale collections
(current period)$_t$ + credit sale collections
(previous period)$_t$ + other cash receipts$_t$
Total cash available$_t$ = cash balance, beginning$_t$ +
total cash receipts$_t$

Cash disbursements:
Purchases$_t$ = sales$_t$ * percent purchases of sales
Payroll$_t$ = payroll$_{t-1}$ * percent payroll increase
Income taxes$_t$ = sales$_t$ * percent income tax of sales
Dividends$_t$ = constant
Other expenses$_t$ = sales$_t$ * percent other expenses
Total cash disbursements$_t$ = purchases$_t$ + payroll$_t$ +
income taxes$_t$ + dividends$_t$ + other expenses$_t$
Cash balance, ending$_t$ = total cash available$_t$ −
total cash disbursements$_t$

As you can see, some of the accounts in our cashflow, such as dividends and taxes, are closely related to the income statement. You might want to try to add the cashflow statement to the income and balance sheet program of Future Industries. Then you could obtain cash receipts and disbursements from the income statement or balance sheet. If you aren't sure of the relationships, make up some that seem reasonable to you.

2　READ a value for m (the number of grades for each student). READ in m grades for each student, compute each student's average, and store the average grades in a one-dimensional array. Arrange the array of average grades in descending order and write out the ordered array. Finally, calculate and WRITE (with appropriate labeling) the number of average scores which fall in each of the percentile groups 1 to 10, 11 to 20, . . ., 91 to 100.

3　Compare the sorting method of Section 8 5 with the **bubble sort** (described below) by generating 100 random numbers, sorting them each way, and counting how many times each routine compares pairs of numbers.

　　The bubble sort works like this: Go through the array one spot at a time, comparing the current element with the next and reversing their order if the first is larger than the second. Keep doing this until you have gone completely through the array. The largest value is now at the bottom of the array. Now go through the array again, but stop before the last array location is reached, since it's already in order. Keep making passes through the array, stopping one location closer to the top of the array each time, until you make one complete pass which requires no reversals. At that point you're finished—the array is in order.

Print out the original numbers, the sorted numbers, and the number of comparisons made by the two different sorting methods. Implement the two methods in separate SUBROUTINEs.

4 Write a program which assigns grades. The input will be a bunch of cards, each containing a student's name and five scores. Your program should compute each student's average score and PRINT each student's name, average score, and letter grade. Compute the letter grade by the time-honored formula below.

$$90–100 \quad A$$
$$80–89 \quad B$$
$$70–79 \quad C$$
$$60–69 \quad F$$

5 A certain company rents time on five of its machines. Each time a machine is used, the customer turns in a time card. At the first of each month the company sends out bills for the use of the machines for the past month.

The rates on the machines are different for different customers and for different time periods during the day. Therefore, your first input will be ten price cards, each card specifying a price code (00–09) and the cost per hour for the price code.

Compute a bill for each customer which includes the following information:

customer number
machine number
total hours and total costs for each machine used by the customer
total cost for the customer

The time cards for the month are sorted by customer number but not by machine and contain the following information:

customer number (XXXXXXX)
price code (XX)
machine number (1, 2, 3, 4, or 5)
time in (XX.XX)
time out (XX.XX)

Assume the time is given to the nearest hundredth of an hour on the 24-hour clock (e.g., 20.25 means 8:15 p.m.). (Thanks to Ed Noyce for this problem.)

6 Bicycle Registration

You are a programmer for a progressive college town that has a great deal of bicycle thievery. The town council decides to require everyone to register his or her bicycle so that there will be some chance of restoring captured stolen bikes to their original owners. Your job, should you decide to accept it, is to write a program which maintains and searches the data on bicycles. Your program must accept data cards of two different types:

new registrations

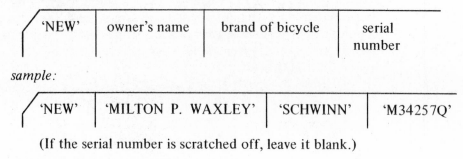

| 'NEW' | owner's name | brand of bicycle | serial number |

sample:

| 'NEW' | 'MILTON P. WAXLEY' | 'SCHWINN' | 'M34257Q' |

(If the serial number is scratched off, leave it blank.)

found bicycles

| 'OLD' | brand of bicycle | serial number |

Obviously, if a 'NEW' card comes in, you just add the information in. If an 'OLD' card comes in, there are two different situations. First, if the serial number of the recovered bike is known, you search the data and if such a bike has been registered, you print the owner's name (so she or he can be notified). Second, if the serial number has been scratched off, your program should print the names of everyone who owns that type of bike so they can be asked if the recovered bike is theirs. (Do not assume that the 'NEW' and 'OLD' cards have been separated.)

7

Each of the following data cards has three pieces of information: the name of a football player, his number, and his weight. Write a program to read and print the arrays in four different orders. First in the original order, second in alphabetical order using the players' last names, third in order of their numbers, and fourth in order of their weights. (Hint: Use INDSRT from Section 9 3.)

Data:

SQUARE, JOHNNY	27	170
DUDA, PAUL	31	200
JULIANA, PAT	9	180
BLACKFORD, BOB	5	183
WILSON, MIKE	25	197

CASWELL, GERALD	95	240
DRISCOLL, MARK	8	175
BABICH, FRED	80	220
BATTLE, GREG	46	195
MONTGOMERY, CHARLES	63	255
ST. CLAIR, STEVE	87	195
STEWART, GUY	18	170
MOSS, JESSE	19	190
O'ROURKE, DAN	22	190

8 Bank Accounts

Write a program which creates and keeps track of bank accounts for up to 20 people. For each person, keep track of (a) the person's name, (b) the balance in his account, and (c) the number of withdrawals or deposits. A deposit will correspond to a data card such as

'MARY MOONY'   +303.02

and a withdrawal will correspond to a card like

'CAPT. BEEFHEART'   −2.00

Each time your program reads a card, check to see if there is an account for that person, and if not, create a new entry. If there already is an account, add or subtract the deposit or withdrawal and add 1 to the number of transactions. After there are no more data cards to read, your program should print the information it has compiled about each account.

Data:

FRANK FEEBLES	+ 100.00
RALPH WILLIAMS	+1901.74
RALPH WILLIAMS	+2794.25
BETTY FURNACE	+ 3.01
RALPH WILLIAMS	+ 470.00
HARRY IGNAZ	+ 25.00
FRANK FEEBLES	− 35.00
JESS UNRUH	+ 11.00
HAROLD STASSEN	+ 342.00
RALPH WILLIAMS	− 400.00
JESS UNRUH	−5243.00
MINNEY MOOS	+ 35.75
RALPH WILLIAMS	+7500.20
WAYNE ASPINALL	− .06
BETTY FURNACE	+ 3.01

HINT: Use several one-dimensional arrays to keep track of the accounts so that after the first three cards have been read, the arrays look like the following:

	NAME		BAL		TRANS
1	FRANK FEEBLES		100.00		1
2	RALPH WILLIAMS		4695.99		2
3					
4					

9 Write a program which produces an array of shuffled cards, represented as the INTEGERs 1, 2, . . ., 52. If you establish an appropriate correspondence between INTEGERs and cards, you can compute the card's suit and denomination with expressions like (CARD − 1)/13 and MOD(CARD,13).

VERBAL DESCRIPTION

Start with 52 cards in your hand.

Choose a card from your hand at random and place it on the table (in a stack).

Repeat step 2 until you run out of cards in your hand.

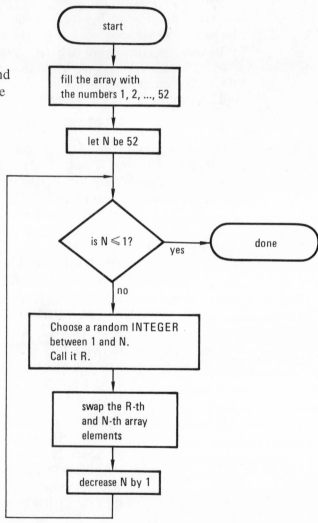

Shuffle Algorithm

Write the shuffling algorithm as a SUBROU-
TINE, and use it to shuffle a deck of cards. Print
the shuffled deck one card at a time. If the jack of
any suit comes up, use the FORMAT carriage
control character + to "SLAP!" the jack.

KING OF CLUBS
TEN OF HEARTS
SEVEN OF HEARTS
FOUR OF SPADES
JACK OF CLUBS
NINE OF SPADES
QUEEN OF SPADES

10 Design and write a program which deals a random bridge hand and displays it in the usual bridge notation.

NORTH
S: K J 3
H:
D: A Q 7 4
C: K Q 10 9 4 2

WEST
S: A 5 4
H: 8 7 4 3 2
D: K 9 6
C: A 7

EAST
S: Q 10 7 6
H: 10 5
D: J 10 5 3 2
C: 6 3

SOUTH
S: 9 8 2
H: A K Q J 9 6
D: 8
C: J 8 5

Use SUBROUTINE SHUFFLE from problem 9 to shuffle the deck.

11 Write an INTEGER FUNCTION GOREN which takes a bridge hand as
an argument (i.e., an array of 13 INTEGERs that represent cards, as in
problems 9 and 10 above) and returns the Goren point value of the hand.

12 Write programs for two or more hash coding storage schemes and compare their behavior. A discussion of such schemes may be found in

Harold S. Stone, *Introduction to Computer Organization and Data
Structure,* McGraw-Hill, 1972, Chapter 11.

Some specific hash coding schemes are in

J. R. Bell, "The quadratic quotient method: a hash code eliminating secondary clustering," *Comm ACM.* vol. 13, no. 2, 1940, pp. 107–109.

J. R. Bell and C. H. Kaman, "The linear quotient hash code," *Comm ACM*, vol. 13, no. 11, 1970, pp. 675–677.

W. D. Maurer, "An improved hash code for scatter storage," *Comm ACM*, vol. 11, no. 1, 1968, pp. 35–38.

R. Morris, "Scatter storage techniques," *Comm ACM.* vol. 11, no. 1, 1968, pp. 38–44.

13 If you are interested in the searching problem, do some reading on AVL trees. The following articles will give you a start.

G. M. Adel'son-Velskii and E. M. Landis, "An algorithm for the organization of information," *Dokl. Akad. Nank CCCP, Mathemat.,* vol. 146, no. 2, 1962, pp. 263–266.

Caxton C. Foster, "Information storage and retrieval using AVL trees," *Proc. ACM Nat'l Conf.,* 1965, pp. 192–205.

14 If you are interested in sorting, do some reading on the subject. The following references will give you a start.

C. A. R. Hoare, "Quicksort," *Comm ACM*, vol. 4, no. 7, 1961, p. 321.

R. W. Floyd, "Tree sort," *Comm ACM*, vol. 7, no. 12, 1964, p. 701.

R. Sedgewick, "Quicksort," Computer Science Dept. Technical Report STAN–CS–75–492, Stanford Univ.

15 Find someone who does a lot of sorting and ask what technique he or she is using. If it's not one of the fast methods you learned of in problem 14, compare his or her method to those by timing the methods on the type of data he or she uses. (The methods of problem 14 are about as fast as any sorting techniques known on random data, but in special situations other techniques may be faster.)

10 ON-LINE PROGRAMMING

Chapter Objectives: After studying this chapter, you should be able to:

- Define and describe on-line programming, interactive processing, and time-sharing.
- Write and execute programs at a computer terminal operating on-line.
- Solve a simple break-even problem with the computer.
- Write and execute interactive computer problems.
- Solve an economic order quantity problem with the computer.
- Create and access data files on-line or in the batch mode of processing.

Section 10 1

Introduction

So far, you've used cards to punch your program and data on. However, there are other ways to enter programs and data into the computer and get your results back. In this chapter, we are going to explore how to use a terminal for both input and output. The kind of terminal we are referring to has a keyboard similar to a typewriter or keypunch. Your program and data are entered via a keyboard, but, rather than punching holes in cards as a keypunch does, the terminal transmits to the computer. Similarly, your output from the computer will be sent back to your terminal. When you can communicate with the computer in this manner, it's known as **on-line** processing.

> *on-line: when you can enter and send data directly from a terminal to the computer or receive output directly from the computer to your terminal, your terminal is on-line to the computer. You are doing on-line processing.*

Terminals come in a number of different shapes, sizes, colors, and forms. We are concerned primarily with the typewriter-like terminals, sometimes called Teletypes, but our examples also apply to CRTs. CRT stands for cathode ray tube, and as you probably know, it's essentially like the screen on a television. In fact, some companies sell keyboard units which connect to TV sets and make computer terminals out of them. The big difference between the Teletype and CRT is that the Teletype writes your input and output on paper so you can tear it off and take it with you. Your local expert would call this paper output a **hardcopy**. The CRT doesn't produce a hardcopy unless it has some kind of special attachment. We will show you how you can run your programs on either Teletypes or CRT terminals, but our examples are from the Teletype variety since we needed to take them to the publisher so he could put them in this book.

Most computers can have more than one terminal connected to them and operating at one time. A large computer might have as many as 500 terminals hooked up and operating simultaneously. This way of using a computer is known as **time-sharing**. The computer would not process all 500 programs in its central processor at the same time; however, it would appear to you at your terminal that you were the only one using the computer.

> **time-sharing:** *the use of a single computer by a number of people simultaneously. Each user shares the time the computer works on his/her job with other users. The use of the computer by others is not apparent to you at your terminal.*

When you are working with a terminal, you can run your programs in either the batch or interactive mode. In the batch mode, you prepare a source program and your data and then tell the computer to compile your program and execute it with your data. This is the same process as with cards, except, of course, you don't have the cards. With an interactive program, you don't prepare any data to submit with your program. When your program is executing, it stops and waits for you to enter your data before it continues executing. The ability to do this opens all kinds of doors for imaginative computing responsive to the needs of today's managers.

Section 10 2

Programming with Terminals

Let's look at how you might enter and execute a program at a terminal by considering an example which calculates a simple break-even volume. The equation for calculating the break-even volume is

$$\text{units} = \frac{\text{fixed cost}}{\text{price} - \text{variable cost}}$$

where UNITS is the break-even volume, PRICE is the selling price per unit, and VARIABLE COST is the variable cost per unit. The program to calculate the break-even volume is shown below.

```
00100 COMMENT: ON-LINE BREAK-EVEN PROGRAM
00110       REAL PRICE,FCOST,VCOST,UNITS
00120       PRICE=10.
00130       FCOST=125000.
00140       VCOST=7.50
00150       UNITS=FCOST/(PRICE-VCOST)
00160       WRITE(6,100) UNITS
00170   100 FORMAT(4X,24HTHE BREAK-EVEN VOLUME IS,F8.0,
00175     1       6H UNITS)
00180       STOP
00190       END
```

output
```
THE BREAK-EVEN VOLUME IS  50000. UNITS
```

When you look at the program, the first thing you should notice that's different is the line number appearing at the left of each statement. The rest of the program looks just like the others we entered on cards. In fact, except for those line numbers, this program is completely ANSI. The biggest thing you need to keep straight in on-line programs is that line numbers and statement labels are two completely different things. You can see that by looking at line 170, which has statement label 100. Not all on-line systems use line numbers. You should check with your local expert to see if you need them or not.

Line numbers are of great help when you want to change a statement in your program. On most systems all you need to do is retype the line with its line number. The computer will put the retyped line in the right place. Also, if you need to insert a statement, you just use a line number that has a value between the two line numbers of the statements where you want to insert it. For example, if we wanted to insert a comment just before the equation, we could do it like this:

```
00155 COMMENT: HERE'S THE BREAK-EVEN EQUATION
```

If we wanted to change the price and rerun the program, we could do it like this:

```
00120       PRICE=12.00
```

If your computer doesn't let you use line numbers, then you'll have to find out the method used on your system from your local expert. Line numbering depends on the computer; however, our Fortran program still follows ANSI rules.

When Fortran programs are entered on cards, you need to put some extra cards with the source program and data deck to tell the computer you have a Fortran program and where your program ends and your data starts. These extra cards are called job control cards, sometimes called JCL for short (Job Control Language). Most likely, you found out about JCL cards from your local expert. These cards depend on the particular computer used. They bear no relation to the ANSI standards for Fortran.

When you are computing on-line, how do you tell the computer you have a

Fortran program or that you want to compile and execute the program? You need to use the job control commands for *your particular computer.* For example, a JCL command like FORTRAN might get you the Fortran compiler; LIST could cause a listing of your program to be printed on your terminal; and RUN might command the computer to execute your program.

Another problem that comes up when you're programming on-line is you can't take your program with you when you're done. Oh, sure, you can take a listing, but you'd have to retype the program the next time you wanted to use it or work on it. If we actually had to do that, nobody would want to program on-line. It'd be a real pain in the neck. With cards, this was no problem because you could take the card deck with you, work on it, and then resubmit the deck the next time. So, what can you do when you're programming on-line? Most computers have JCL commands such as OLD, NEW, SAVE, and UNSAVE. These tell the computer you want to enter a completely NEW program, work on an OLD program that you told the computer to SAVE or store the last time you were on the computer, or UNSAVE or erase a program you don't need stored in the computer any longer.

The JCL commands for your computer may be a little different, but you should have ones to do each of these things. You'll probably learn there are many others. Since it's not our mission to cover this myriad of commands, we'll leave these for you to explore for your computer now that you know they exist and the general functions they perform.

Now, back to our program. You should notice that in entering the program we have put statement labels and statements in the same positions on each line as if we were entering them on a card. That is, C for comment is in column 1, statement labels are in columns 1 through 5, and the statements are in columns 7 through 72. Some on-line Fortran compilers let you deviate from these rules. However, to follow ANSI Fortran, we have put them in the same columns.

Another thing you need to find out from your local expert is how to do something called **log-on** and **log-off**. Log-on lets you identify yourself as a legitimate user of the computer. If you can't log-on, then you might as well forget everything else, because there's no way you're going to be able to run your Fortran program, whether it's in ANSI Fortran or not. The log-on procedure usually replaces the very first card in the deck you submitted to the card reader. This first card was probably called a **job-card**. It let your program run on your computer. Well, log-on does the same thing as that job card did. When you're all done at the terminal, the last thing you do before you hit the off switch on the terminal is to log-off. This is similar to the computer finishing reading the very last card in your card deck, which was probably a JCL card.

On-line programming is winning over many experienced programmers who for some time have felt that cards were the only way to go for large programs. There is a general feeling that by entering and debugging programs on-line, the elapsed time from beginning to end of a programming project can be substantially reduced. This is true for programs that will operate in the batch mode once they become operational, as well as for programs normally executed on-line.

EXERCISES 10 2

1 Locate a computer terminal that you can use. Find out how to turn it on and the JCL you need to know to log-on and to enter and run an ANSI Fortran program.

2 For practice, enter and execute the break-even program. Change the price and rerun it. It sure is easy to make changes, isn't it?

Section 10 3

Interactive Programming

Many management uses of the computer in businesses require the retrieval of management information. Interactive computer programs are great aids in these kinds of computer applications. An interactive application most everyone has heard about, seen, or used is the airline reservation system. In this system, an airline representative can find out flight information, make reservations, cancel reservations, and so on. To do this, the computer displays messages on a CRT. The agent then responds to the message or question by entering data into a computer. In this manner, a conversation takes place between the computer and the agent. For this reason, interactive computing is sometimes called conversational computing.

> *interactive: the execution of a program in which the program requests input data and/or decisions from the user during program execution. Interactive computing is frequently performed using an on-line terminal in a time-sharing environment.*

Imagine what the airline reservation system would be like if a card reader and line printer were used instead of a CRT. The agent would go to a keypunch and punch up a card; the card would be taken to the card reader and read into the computer; a message would be written on the line printer; the agent would read it and go back to the keypunch and start the cycle over again. Do you think the reservation system would be practical if it had to be operated like this?

Suppose you would like to write a Fortran program which would let you converse with the computer and enter data as the computer requested it. Can we write such programs in ANSI Fortran? Well, as you have probably guessed by now, we most certainly can.

Let's look at a program which calculates the economic order quantity (EOQ) for purchasing items for use in a manufacturing process or for sale in a merchandising operation. We'd like to enter the values of our variable in the EOQ equation and then let the computer calculate our ordering policy, which is the EOQ and the frequency at which we should order. The EOQ equations are:

$$EOQ = \sqrt{\frac{2 \times \text{order cost} \times \text{demand}}{\text{holding cost}}}$$

$$T = \frac{EOQ}{\text{demand}}$$

```
00100 COMMENT: ECONOMIC ORDER QUANTITY CALCULATION
00110 C      DEMAND = DEMAND PER YEAR IN UNITS
00120 C      HOLD   = ANNUAL UNIT HOLDING COST
00130 C      ORDER  = ORDERING COST PER ORDER PROCESSED
00140        REAL DEMAND,HOLD,ORDER,EOQ,TIME
00150        READ(5,100) DEMAND
00160    100 FORMAT(F10.0)
00170        READ(5,100) HOLD
00180        READ(5,100) ORDER
00190 C                                        CALCULATE EOQ
00200        EOQ=SQRT((2.0*ORDER*DEMAND)/HOLD)
00210 C                            CALCULATE ORDER FREQUENCY
00220        TIME=EOQ/DEMAND*12.
00230        WRITE(6,110) EOQ,TIME
00240    110 FORMAT(/,1X,30HTHE ECOMONIC ORDER QUANTITY IS,
00250   1         F8.1,7H UNITS.,/,1X,14HRE-ORDER EVERY,
00260   2         F6.1,8H MONTHS.)
00270        STOP
00280.       END
```

When you execute the program, what happens? Every time a READ statement is encountered, the computer prints a "?" and waits for you to enter a number. Here's the execution of the program.

```
? 2500.
? .30
? 15.

     THE ECOMONIC ORDER QUANTITY IS    500.0 UNITS.
     RE-ORDER EVERY    2.4 MONTHS.
```

How did you know the computer wanted you to enter demand, holding cost, price per unit, and ordering cost in that particular order? To find out, you had to look back at a listing of your program. This works pretty well as long as you don't have a very complex program. It certainly wouldn't do for the airline reservation system. Could you imagine a reservation agent reading through a program listing while you were waiting to make a reservation? What a pain! What we need to do is fix our program so it tells you what data is to be entered before it stops to let you enter it. How can we do it? Think about the dialog or conversation you'd like to have with the computer. First, the computer should write out a message that you can easily understand. Then, it should print a "?" and wait patiently for your answer. That means you WRITE the message and then READ the input response. For each item to be entered, we'll use the WRITE, READ statement combination. As you can see, this doesn't require any new statements—just the combined use of a couple of old familiar statements.

The EOQ program now looks like this:

```
00100 COMMENT: ECONOMIC ORDER QUANTITY CALCULATION
00110 C      DEMAND = DEMAND PER YEAR IN UNITS
00120 C      HOLD   = ANNUAL UNIT HOLDING COST
00130 C      ORDER  = ORDERING COST PER ORDER PROCESSED
00140        REAL DEMAND,HOLD,ORDER,EOQ,TIME
00150        WRITE(6,200)
00160    200 FORMAT(1X,30HENTER DEMAND IN UNITS PER YEAR)
00170        READ(5,100) DEMAND
00180    100 FORMAT(F10.0)
00190        WRITE(6,210)
00200    210 FORMAT(1X,25HENTER ANNUAL HOLDING COST)
00210        READ(5,100) HOLD
00220        WRITE(6,220)
00230    220 FORMAT(1X,29HENTER ORDERING COST PER ORDER)
00240        READ(5,100) ORDER
00250 C                                    CALCULATE EOQ
00260        EOQ=SQRT((2.0*ORDER*DEMAND)/HOLD)
00270 C                          CALCULATE ORDER FREQUENCY
00280        TIME=EOQ/DEMAND*12.
00290        WRITE(6,110) EOQ,TIME
00300    110 FORMAT(/,1X,30HTHE ECOMONIC ORDER QUANTITY IS,
00310   1         F8.1,7H UNITS.,/,1X,14HRE-ORDER EVERY,
00315   2         F6.1,8H MONTHS.)
00320        STOP
00330        END
```

And, execution of the program produces these results:

```
 ENTER DEMAND IN UNITS PER YEAR
 ? 2500.
 ENTER ANNUAL HOLDING COST
 ? .30
 ENTER ORDERING COST PER ORDER
 ? 15.

 THE ECOMONIC ORDER QUANTITY IS   500.0 UNITS.
 RE-ORDER EVERY   2.4 MONTHS.
```

The EOQ program prints out messages for each data item to be entered. What other kinds of messages could be printed? Well, really anything you want. Using the basic concept we've just shown you, it's possible to write complex interactive programs to be executed at computer terminals. Not only can these programs tell you what data to enter, they can also provide you with other instructions on how to use the program. That way, when you are running the program and can't remember how to use it, you don't have to go find a manual that describes how to use the program. All you need to do is answer a question such as "DO YOU WANT INSTRUCTIONS?" and the computer will print them out for you. This feature can be a lot of help to people who use canned programs. Now, you can write this kind of interactive program.

Look back at the last EOQ program. We entered each data item with a READ statement. Suppose you'd like to enter all the data with one READ. How could you do it? You might change the program so it has one READ, like this:

```
00100 COMMENT: ECONOMIC ORDER QUANTITY CALCULATION
00110 C     DEMAND = DEMAND PER YEAR IN UNITS
00120 C     HOLD   = ANNUAL UNIT HOLDING COST
00130 C     ORDER  = ORDERING COST PER ORDER PROCESSED
00140       REAL DEMAND,HOLD,ORDER,EOQ,TIME
00150       WRITE(6,200)
00160   200 FORMAT(1X,28HENTER DEMAND, HOLDING COST, ,
00170     1        13HORDERING COST)
00180       READ(5,100) DEMAND,HOLD,ORDER
00190   100 FORMAT(3F10.0)
00200 C                                        CALCULATE EOQ
00210       EOQ=SQRT((2.0*ORDER*DEMAND)/HOLD)
00220 C                            CALCULATE ORDER FREQUENCY
00230       TIME=EOQ/DEMAND*12.
00240       WRITE(6,110) EOQ,TIME
00250   110 FORMAT(/,1X,30HTHE ECOMONIC ORDER QUANTITY IS,
00260     1         F8.1,7H UNITS.,/,1X,14HRE-ORDER EVERY,
00270     2         F6.1,8H MONTHS.)
00280       STOP
00290       END
```

When you try to run the program, you'll encounter a slight problem from the formatted READ. DEMAND is entered in positions 1–10, HOLD in 11–20, and ORDER in 21–30. You might be thinking, so what? Well, most terminals don't have an indicator which tells you what position you're typing in. So, you need to very carefully count to avoid entering data in the wrong position or column. When the program is run with one READ, the result is:

```
ENTER DEMAND, HOLDING COST, ORDERING COST
? 2500.     .30        15.

THE ECOMONIC ORDER QUANTITY IS   500.0 UNITS.
RE-ORDER EVERY   2.4 MONTHS.
```

and we had to count positions to get the data in the right place. Now, you can see why we used three READ statements and entered a decimal point with each data item in the first two versions of the program. If you use formatted READs on a terminal, there is no way to get around counting positions except by entering one item at a time.

Does ANSI Fortran provide a way to get around this dilemma? No, it sure doesn't. However, it's something that people want to do so often that most Fortran compilers which can be operated from a terminal have a means to circumvent the difficulty. It's known as **free-format**. And, not only can you use free-format

---

READ statement (free-format) non-ANSI

forms
    READ, *list*   ⎫
      or   ⎬ check with your local expert
    READ*, *list*   ⎭
    READ(*unit*,*) *list*
    list is an input list
    unit is an unsigned INTEGER constant or unsubscripted INTEGER memory cell

---

```
┌─────────────────────────────────────────────────────────────────┐
│                                                                   │
│  PRINT/WRITE statements (free-format) non-ANSI                    │
│                                                                   │
│                                                                   │
│  forms                                                            │
│      PRINT, list    ⎫                                             │
│          or         ⎬  check with your local expert               │
│      PRINT*, list   ⎭                                             │
│      WRITE (unit,*) list                                          │
│      list is an output list                                       │
│      unit is an unsigned INTEGER constant or unsubscripted        │
│      INTEGER memory cell                                          │
│                                                                   │
└─────────────────────────────────────────────────────────────────┘
```

on input, you can also use it on output. This feature is not limited to terminal-oriented Fortran compilers and you just may find that you can do it this way in batch processing with cards as well.

With the free-format READ statement, you can enter as many data items as you'd like on one line. The items are separated by commas. You can usually mix free-format and formatted READs and WRITEs/PRINTs in your program. So, if you want to do a free-format READ and then format your output, you can in the same program. Let's redo the EOQ program using free-format READs.

```
00100 COMMENT: ECONOMIC ORDER QUANTITY CALCULATION
00110 C     DEMAND = DEMAND PER YEAR IN UNITS
00120 C     HOLD   = ANNUAL UNIT HOLDING COST
00130 C     ORDER  = ORDERING COST PER ORDER PROCESSED
00140       REAL DEMAND,HOLD,ORDER,EOQ,TIME
00150       WRITE(6,200)
00160   200 FORMAT(1X,28HENTER DEMAND, HOLDING COST, ,
00170     1        13HORDERING COST)
00180 C                              HERE'S THE FREE-FORMAT READ
00190       READ(5,*) DEMAND,HOLD,ORDER
00200 C                                    CALCULATE EOQ
00210       EOQ=SQRT((2.0*ORDER*DEMAND)/HOLD)
00220 C                              CALCULATE ORDER FREQUENCY
00230       TIME=EOQ/DEMAND*12.
00240       WRITE(6,110) EOQ,TIME
00250   110 FORMAT(/,1X,30HTHE ECOMONIC ORDER QUANTITY IS,
00260     1        F8.1,7H UNITS.,/,1X,14HRE-ORDER EVERY,
00270     2        F6.1,8H MONTHS.)
00280       STOP
00290       END
```

When you run the program, the input and output are:

```
 ENTER DEMAND, HOLDING COST, ORDERING COST
? 2500,.30,15

 THE ECOMONIC ORDER QUANTITY IS   500.0 UNITS.
 RE-ORDER EVERY   2.4 MONTHS.
```

```
┌─────────────────────────────────────────────────────────────────┐
│  Caution—free-format: when free-formats are used with alpha-      │
│  numeric data, some Fortran compilers require the data to be en-  │
│  closed in quotes, and some don't. But, when you use an ANSI      │
│  FORMAT you don't need to enclose your data in quotes.            │
└─────────────────────────────────────────────────────────────────┘
```

Remember, free-formats are non-ANSI, and they may cause you some usually minor problems as you go from one computer system to another. If you really want to play it safe, stick to ANSI Fortran. You may have to enter one data item at a time to keep things simple with ANSI, but by now you should be aware of what you gain or lose by doing so.

EXERCISES 10 3

1 Change the EOQ program so it prints instructions. Make up instructions which you feel are appropriate.

2 Change the EOQ program so it uses only free-format READs and WRITE/PRINTs.

Section 10 4

Data Files

The on-line programs we've considered so far have gotten their data values either in assignment statements or from your input at the keyboard during execution. There is another way to input data. You can create a data file and then have your program read the data from that file when the program is run. The data file is very similar to the data deck when you used card input. The difference, of course, is that it's not stored on cards but on some other medium. Since you are familiar with inputting data on cards, let's look at how we can build a data file at a terminal and then READ it into a Fortran program. Although we're going to see how you create the data file at a terminal, it is possible to punch the data on cards, read the cards into the computer with the card reader, and store the data in a file. Then you could go to the nearest terminal and run your program. This works really well when you have a big bunch of data to input and then need to make a few minor changes to it as you process the data through your program several times. This situation occurs frequently in doing statistical data analyses, such as the cross-tabs in the questionnaire analysis of Chapter 7.

Creating data files at the terminal or with a data deck is quite frequently a non-Fortran process. It is commonly done with job control or some similar language. As a result you'll need to check with your local expert to find out how to do it on your computer.

Suppose you wanted to calculate the break-even volume for a number of different products. Rather than revising the program in Section 10 2 and rerunning it each time, you'll store the data in a file. Then you go to the terminal and after gaining access to the computer, you build this data file:

```
NEW,BEDATA
```

```
00100          12.       50000.         8.25
00110          11.25   1650000.         7.
00120          20.       100000.        16.96
00130          42.50     750000.        35.25
00140          89.95     850000.        76.05
00150           3.89       1500.         3.22
00160           1.38       5600.         0.93
00170           0.00          0.         0.0
```

We've named our data file BEDATA. As you can see, we've used line numbers for entering each record. That way, if we made a mistake, it would be easy to go back and fix it. Remember, naming files and numbering lines depends on your specific computer. Since we don't want the line numbers as part of our data, we ask our local expert how to recopy the file and get rid of them. After chopping off the line numbers, our data file looks like this:

```
    12.       50000.         8.25
    11.25   1650000.         7.
    20.       100000.        16.96
    42.50     750000.        35.25
    89.95     850000.        76.05
     3.89       1500.         3.22
     1.38       5600.         0.93
     0.00          0.         0.0
```

As you can see, each line in the data file looks like a data card. To make sure our data file doesn't get erased, we might use a job control command such as SAVE to make sure it's stored somewhere in the computer for future use. Next, we can run our revised break-even program using the data file. You might tell the computer GET, TAPE5 = BEDATA and then run your program.

```
00100          REAL PRICE,FCOST,VCOST,UNITS
00110          WRITE(6,70)
00120       70 FORMAT(7X,5HPRICE,5X,10HFIXED COST,5X,
00130        1        13HVARIABLE COST,5X,5HUNITS)
00140       80 READ(5,90) PRICE,FCOST,VCOST
00150       90 FORMAT(3F10.0)
00160          IF (PRICE.EQ.0.0) GOTO 900
00170          UNITS=FCOST/(PRICE-VCOST)
00180          WRITE(6,100) PRICE,FCOST,VCOST,UNITS
00190      100 FORMAT(2X,F10.2,4X,F10.0,5X,F10.2,5X,F10.0)
00200          GOTO 80
00210      900 STOP
00220          END
```

output

PRICE	FIXED COST	VARIABLE COST	UNITS
12.00	50000.	8.25	13333.
11.25	1650000.	7.00	388235.
20.00	100000.	16.96	32895.
42.50	750000.	35.25	103448.
89.95	850000.	76.05	61151.
3.89	1500.	3.22	2239.
1.38	5600.	.93	12444.

This program did *not* use any new Fortran concepts. It does show you how Fortran programs can be used to READ data files that are created at a terminal using a different processor than the Fortran compiler. Many computer installations contain a variety of processors that can be used with your data in conjunction with your Fortran program. Our purpose is not to give you all the gory details about these processors, but merely to indicate they exist and that your computer may have some of them. You'll need to hunt up your local expert to find out what's available and how to use them. Enough of this; let's get back to writing programs in Fortran.

We've been primarily concerned with the card reader, the line printer, and the terminal. These are only three of many I/O devices which may be hung on a computer. There are many other kinds of I/O equipment—card punches, paper tapes, magnetic tapes, disks, drums, plotters, and so on. Each kind of device has different advantages in terms of speed and convenience which we'll not dwell on here.

peripheral device: any piece of hardware (other than the controller or memory) which is connected to a computer

Because of the great variety of I/O devices (some or all of which may be present at any particular computer center), it would be difficult for Fortran to provide different I/O statements for each device. Instead, as you already know, devices are assigned numbers, and your READ and WRITE statements specify the peripheral device you wish to use by including a unit number. Since *the correspondence between numbers and devices is not standardized,* you will have to ask a local expert for the information. Often the number 5 identifies the card reader, 6 the line printer, and 7 the card punch. Beyond that, there is not even a hint of common usage. You'll have to find out from your local expert how to communicate your use of unit numbers to your program since this may be part of either your Fortran program or job control language depending on your particular compiler.

The Fortran input and output statements we have been dealing with have always involved a *conversion.* As we have used them so far, input statements convert character strings (taken from our data cards or terminal) into INTEGERs, REALs, or whatever type is specified in the FORMAT. An output statement performs the reverse conversion from a representation of data in memory to a character string (normally printed on paper). The I/O devices, as we've used them, store information in a form very different from the way it would be stored in memory cells. This is quite natural, of course, because we have been using I/O devices primarily as a means of communication between human and computer.

However, I/O devices can be used as an extension of the computer's memory as well as a means of communication. When an I/O device is used for this purpose, the information on the I/O device might just as well be stored in essentially the same form as it would be stored in memory cells since that would avoid the conversion process. This is the reason for **unformatted I/O statements.** We use the word *unformatted* to mean that the form in which the data is stored in the I/O device is left up to the computing system being used, and hence is not specified by a FORMAT statement. Most computing systems choose a format essentially like the one used in representing data in memory cells, so that the I/O process involves very little computation. *Don't confuse this with free-format I/O, which we use as a means of communication with the computer. Free-format I/O makes the conversion between your input and the computer's internal representations according to a compiler-supplied format.*

Since unformatted I/O statements are used primarily to extend the computer's memory, the unit designated by an unformatted output statement should write records which can be read by a similar input device. The line printer, for example, would be an inappropriate unit for an unformatted I/O statement because the computer couldn't read the values back into its memory and the output would be wasted. When the data is written out, it is written as a data file. The data file is then read back into your program as you specify it in the program.

In order to use I/O devices as extended memory, you must be able to position the I/O device at records in your data file (e.g., at the beginning of the information or back one record). For this reason the REWIND and BACKSPACE statements are provided. The REWIND statement positions the I/O device at the beginning of the first record written in the file on the device. An unformatted record is a set of values written by a single unformatted WRITE statement. The BACKSPACE statement positions the I/O device at the beginning of the record just previous to the one at which it is currently positioned. An I/O device, when stopped, is always positioned at the beginning of a record, and a READ statement must READ a whole record, even if some of the values in the record are not used in your program.

Another I/O statement is used to mark the end of your data file. The ENDFILE statement puts a special mark, called an end-of-file (EOF) mark, on the I/O unit specified. This mark terminates the series of records contained in your file on the unit up to that point. Since many versions of Fortran provide a way to detect this special mark, it provides a way to insure that your program does not try to READ

---

unformatted I/O statement

forms

    READ (*u*) *list*
    WRITE (*u*) *list*

    u is a unit number
    list is an I/O list

meaning

    READs or WRITEs the values of the memory cells in *list* on unit *u* without changing their representation

examples

```
READ(10) X, (T(I), I=1,N)
WRITE(N) R,P,G
```

```
┌─────────────────────────────────────────────────────────────────┐
│                                                                   │
│  unit positioning statements                                      │
│                                                                   │
│  form                                                             │
│      REWIND u                                                     │
│                                                                   │
│  meaning                                                          │
│      position unit u at beginning of first record                 │
│                                                                   │
│  form                                                             │
│      BACKSPACE u                                                  │
│                                                                   │
│  meaning                                                          │
│      position unit u at beginning of the immediately previous     │
│      record.                                                      │
│                                                                   │
│  form                                                             │
│      ENDFILE u                                                    │
│                                                                   │
│  meaning                                                          │
│      place an end-of-file mark on unit u at the current position  │
│                                                                   │
│  examples                                                         │
│      BACKSPACE  10                                                │
│      BACKSPACE  N                                                 │
│      REWIND  10                                                   │
│      REWIND  N                                                    │
│      ENDFILE  10                                                  │
│      ENDFILE  N                                                   │
│                                                                   │
└─────────────────────────────────────────────────────────────────┘
```

data which you haven't written on the I/O unit. End-of-file marks are often used to separate logical blocks of information or data files on I/O storage media (especially magnetic tape).

Most manufacturers provide additional (non-ANSI) direct access I/O statements, some allowing very useful and elegant manipulation of mass storage files. Since there is no standard notation, you'll have to dig the information out of the manuals provided by the manufacturers or ask your local experts for advice on where to find out how to use these features.

EXERCISES 10 4

1 Find out about the different kinds of peripheral equipment available at your computer center. Perhaps some of it would be of great use to you.

PROBLEMS 10

Go back to the previous chapters and find some problems that you think would make good interactive programs. Change your input design as necessary and write the programs as interactive programs and execute them at a terminal.

11 THIS COMPUTING TOOL

Chapter Objectives: When you have finished this chapter, you will have completed this book. You should be able to discuss your understanding of:

- The computer as a tool for business.
- Some limitations of the computer.
- Fear of the computer.
- Who's responsible for what computers do or don't do.
- Errors in program results.
- Tight code.
- The future of computers or "where do we go from here?"

This is the computer age, so they say. Man couldn't have gotten to the moon if it hadn't been for computers. Computers are giant brains, capable of making flawless, logical decisions in incomprehensibly small fractions of a second. Computers are controlling us, dehumanizing us. "Computer designed" means "better." Computers never make mistakes and they never go on strike. You put data into a computer and it gives you answers. Computers write paychecks; computers run assembly lines; computers control inventories; they "keep the books" for many companies. Computers draw pictures and write music; computers play chess; computers control airplanes and missiles; they keep tabs on your every credit transaction, phone call, and suspicious move. Computers are good; computers are evil.

Perhaps these "media" notions about computers seem hopelessly at odds with the view of computers you have seen in this book. At least *we* think they are different. Perhaps a few words about the way we think of computers will help you come to your own conclusions about what computers are or should be or can be. . . .

We think that computers are (1) useful tools and (2) fun. The second point is, of course, very subjective, and we certainly don't mean to imply that learning the intricacies of Fortran FORMAT statements or reading floods of obscure error messages is particularly enjoyable. We just mean that wracking our brains to describe some process, programming our description, and seeing the consequences of our program is enjoyable. It's fun to play around with programs, seeing large changes in the program's behavior with seemingly tiny changes in its exact form.

We see computers as tools just as people see mathematics as a tool, that is, as something external to yourself which can be used to help you do something useful or fun. Computer programs can be used as models of processes that go on in the real world. For example, an architect could write a computer program to study the effects of wind loads on a building being designed; a financial analyst could use the computer to manage a portfolio of stocks and bonds; an industrial engineer could write a computer program to describe the way an assembly line operates. The program doesn't replace the reality of the process under study any more than writing a mathematical equation to describe customer buying habits replaces sales to customers. A computer program is easier to change and experiment with than a real building, an advertising campaign or a bankruptcy, but it can't really replace them—it *can* be used to help understand them.

An important issue here is that if we view computers as tools, then we have no more reason to trust the results we get than we do with any other tool. No theory or analysis becomes more (or less) true because it was done on a computer (or adding machine, slide rule, or abacus).

Another issue is that viewing computers as tools says nothing about their limitations. If you want to ask, "Is it possible for a computer to be the world chess champion?" we would have to say that we don't see why not. No master-level chess playing programs exist today, but there's no known reason why one could not be written. Such questions are really questions about *algorithms*, not computers, because any general-purpose computer can, theoretically, carry out anything that is computable.

OK. If what we say is true, then why have you heard about all the troubles with computers? Why are we increasingly discovering that, say, a mistake in our credit card bill can go unfixed for months, piling up spurious interest charges? Why do we get answers like "I'm really sorry you're having trouble, but your account is on the computer." No doubt someone you know has had some sort of "computer trouble."

Yes, you might say, it's true that the problem shows up when someone in an organization puts too much faith in something just because it came out of a computer, but *if the computer weren't there, it couldn't have happened to begin with.* Hah! *Not so,* we would say.

> The thing to fear is not that computers are gods; the thing to fear is people who think that computers are gods.

A well-known fact is that what the computer does is determined by its program, which was written by a human. Ultimately, the people who are responsible are the ones who set up a business, determine where their data comes from, how it is to be manipulated, and what is to be done with the results. It doesn't matter that it was a computer that printed out an erroneous credit balance. The same wrong results could have been produced by humans; the problem is in the structure of the business organization. Perhaps computers have made things worse because they are a new, modern gadget that can easily be blamed for the errors of a faulty business.

There are a number of lessons to be learned about good programming from all the bad programming we come into contact with daily. For instance, it should be clear to you that a few simple IF statements could immediately halt such absurdities as sending someone an erroneous utility bill for one million dollars. The only reasonable way to program is to admit that there are going to be errors, and to put in tests and controls for them. In the case of billing programs, any bill that is much different from the average should be detected and set aside for a person to check.

Another bad practice that arises is getting carried away in writing efficient programs. You have probably run into someone who delights in telling you obscure facts like, "Hey, our machine can do a fixed point add in 1.632 microseconds and it takes 10.924 to do a multiply but only .964 to do a shift, so instead of

```
10   ENDPT = 2*NORMAL
```

like you've got and understand, it would be faster to do

```
10   ENDPT = NORMAL + NORMAL
```

and even faster to do

```
10   ENDPT = SHL(NORMAL, 1)
```

and while you're at it, why are you using such long variable names? The scanner has to grind through all those things and, man, that takes time—why not

```
10   E = SHL(N,1)
```

and then you've got all those *comments* in there! Get them out, they just waste time. Listen to me and I'll have you writing *tight code!*"

> *avoid obscure abbreviations! Programmers tend to fall into this sort of thing, perhaps because early programming languages (like Fortran) require such short memory cell names.*

> *"I'm going down to SFOF to get an RFP for the EVA PEX," he said clearly.*

Let's analyze what you can save by the above suggestions for writing "tight code." If you write the statement using the shift, you'll save 10 millionths of a second of computer time every time the statement is executed. At that rate, you would save only one second of computer time even if the statement were executed 100,000 times, an unlikely possibility. Although you might save a fraction of a second of machine time, you would almost certainly *lose* a substantial amount of human time because your program would be harder to understand and, hence, harder to debug.

This problem can be circumvented if programmers would keep in mind the principle that their programs should be understandable not only to themselves and their computer, but also *to other people*. The point is that saving a little time on one statement is rarely worth it. The primary idea behind higher-level languages is that they have a degree of machine independence, that they can be shared by different people using different machines. Use them to *your* advantage.

Enough of this.

So far, computers have been extensively employed by the military, widely employed by technologically sophisticated industries, and used for accounting and record keeping by most other large businesses. Certainly these sorts of uses of large-scale computing will continue to grow, hopefully to yield increases in productivity and an improved quality of life. In the future, we expect that computers will make steady inroads into our everyday business and personal lives. To us, the

pocket calculators, the barroom "pong" games, and terminals in the boardroom are portents of a dramatic domestication of computers. Now that computers are getting into the hands of the kid on the corner, the crackpot inventor, the lemonade stand tycoon, watch out! It will be fun. The technology for producing small, inexpensive computers already exists. What is currently lacking is just the sort of thing this book is about—programs to do interesting tasks. It is clear that computer hardware will continue to undergo revolutionary decreases in size and cost, while the salaries of programmers increase. What will continue to be necessary is new programs for businesses. With the understanding of programming concepts you've received from this book, you should be in good shape to cope with and help apply computers in the businesses of the future.

ANSWERS TO EXERCISES

ANSWERS TO EXERCISES 1 3

1   algorithm   d
      compiler   e
      flowchart   a
      Fortran   c
      module   b

2   Making "Pineapple Sliders"—Verbal Description

Sift together
      1 cup all purpose flour
      1 tsp. baking powder
      1/4 tsp. salt

In a separate bowl mix together (with wire whip)
      2 eggs
      1/2 cup granulated sugar
      1/2 cup brown sugar

Add
      1 tsp. vanilla
      1/2 cup chopped walnuts
      1 8 oz. can, crushed, unsweetened pineapple (drained)

Slowly add the flour mixture and blend thoroughly.

Bake in a slightly greased 8" square aluminum pan for 30 minutes at 350°.

Cool on rack for 5 minutes and cut into bars.

Roll in confectioner's sugar while warm.

"Pineapple Sliders" courtesy of C. M. Drotos.

Making "Pineapple Sliders" – Flowchart

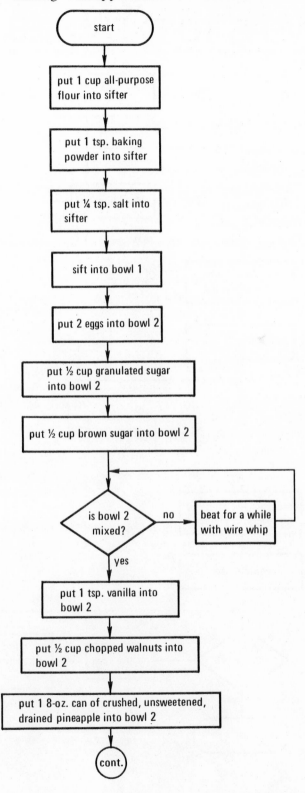

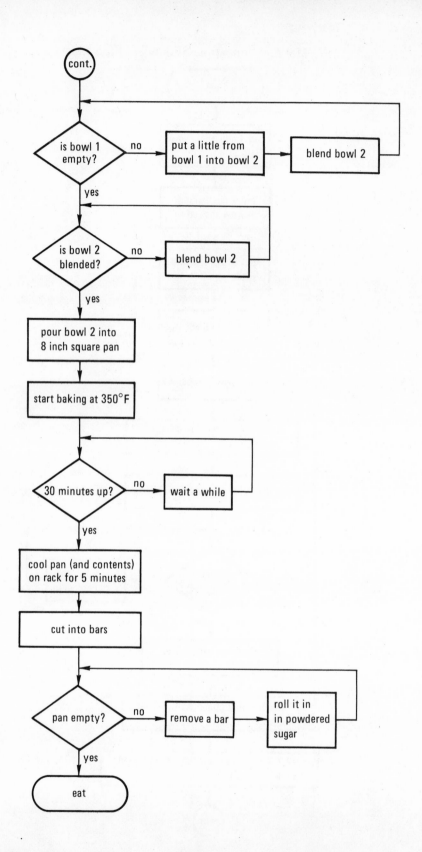

3 controller: executes statements of program

memory: cells in which instructions and data are stored

I/O: provides for communication between human and computer

4 The memory cell is a device which stores information; its name allows us to locate it for purposes of examining or changing its contents; its value is what's in it at a given point in time.

ANSWERS TO EXERCISES 1 5

1 Add the following statement between STATEMENT 1 and STATEMENT 2

STATEMENT 1.5   Look at the value in memory cell YEARS. If it is less than zero, stop.

2 We will need several memory cells: SUM to store the running total of the numbers, N to keep track of the number of numbers, NUM to store the numbers, one at a time, and ST1, ST2, . . . , ST9 in which to store the statements.

card number	memory cell which stores this statement	statement
1	ST1	Store 0 in SUM
2	ST2	Store 0 in N
3	ST3	Remove top card from the card reader stack; copy the number on it into NUM. Discard the card. (If there were no cards, get next instruction from ST7.)
4	ST4	Look at the values in NUM and SUM, add them together, and store the result in SUM.
5	ST5	Look at the value in N, add 1 and store the result in N.
6	ST6	Get your next instruction from ST3.
7	ST7	Look at the values in SUM and N, divide the former by the latter, and store the result in SUM.
8	ST8	Send the string "AVERAGE IS", followed by the number in SUM to the printer.
9	ST9	Stop.
10	none	Comment: End of program. Now comes the data.
11	none	14
12	none	17
13	none	3
14	none	-4
15	none	8

3 We will need several memory cells: LONGEST to store the longest name seen, NAME to store the names on the cards, one at a time, and ST1, ST2, . . . , ST6 to store the statements of the program.

card number	memory cell which stores the statement	statement
1	ST1	Remove the top card from the card reader stack and copy the character string on it into LONGEST. Discard the card.
2	ST2	Remove the top card from the card reader stack and copy the value on it into NAME. Discard the card. (If there were no cards on the card reader stack, get your next instruction from ST5.)
3	ST3	Look at the strings in LONGEST and NAME and copy the longer one into LONGEST.
4	ST4	Get your next instruction from ST2.
5	ST5	Send the string "THE LONGEST NAME IS", followed by the value of LONGEST, to the printer.
6	ST6	Stop
7	none	Comment: End of program. Now comes the data.
8	none	J E Birk
9	none	D E Farmer
10	none	P Das
11	none	P G McCrea
12	none	C C Cheung
13	none	D L Milgram

ANSWERS TO EXERCISES 2 1

1 23SKIDOO is illegal because it starts with a digit.
SKIDOO23, FLIMFLAM, TONY THE TIGER and FORTRAN are illegal because they have more than six characters.
SALE3, TORQUE and JUICE are legal memory cell names.

2 INTEGER VERYLONG is illegal because the memory cell name is too long.
INTERGER Q is illegal because INTEGER is misspelled.
REAL A, 149.2 is illegal because 149.2 is not a memory cell name.

3 INTEGER AJAX,FOAM.

4 The REALs are 41.7, 692.0, and −896.721.

ANSWERS TO EXERCISES 2 2

1 A and B are 10 and 2, respectively.

2 Memory cell B takes on the values 24, 3, and −38 at successive points in time (B contains only one of the values at a time, of course).

3 −AT = 2 and CAT + DOG = FIGHT are illegal because their left hand sides are expressions rather than memory cell names. CAT + DOG − 3, of course, is hopelessly illegal since it doesn't even have an assignment operator.

4 SOUP contains, at successive points in time, the values 15, 61, 1, 2, and 0.

5
```
INTEGER FIRST
FIRST = 2
FIRST = FIRST*4
FIRST = FIRST + 1
```

ANSWERS TO EXERCISES 2 3

1 The second is illegal because it contains expressions and constants instead of just memory cell names. The third one is illegal because it has no unit number or FORMAT number. The last one is illegal because it has a comma immediately after the parenthesis.

2 70.40*bb*12

ANSWERS TO EXERCISES 2 4

1 a 80
   b 80
   c 80
   d Same as the number of cards in the deck.

2 *data*

$$1.25$$
$$4.27$$
$$27.92$$
$$132.00$$
$$9.42$$
$$-237.26$$
$$0.0$$

output

NEW BALANCE IS*b*$*bb*64.90

3 READ(5,3000) A+B,2 is illegal because A+B and 2 are values, not memory cell names.

WRITE(6,4000),A is illegal because the comma before the A is improper.

```
4          INTEGER A,B,C,D,S
           READ(5,1000) A,B,C,D
     1000  FORMAT(I3,I3,I3,I3)
           S=A+B+C+D
           WRITE(6,2000) S
     200   FORMAT(' ',I4)
           STOP
           END
```

data
```
10 15  7 10
```

output
```
   42
```

ANSWERS TO EXERCISES 3 2

1 It corresponds to a statement label.

2 The first two statements are OK.

   The third statement contains the illegal relation .EG.

   The fourth statement contains the illegal relation .SGT.

   The last statement lacks parentheses and has an illegal comma. It should look like this

```
   IF (Y .EQ. 0) GO TO 20
```

3
```
           REAL BALNCE, TRANS
           READ(5,1000)BALNCE
     1000  FORMAT(F7.0)
     20    READ(5,1000) TRANS
           IF (TRANS .EQ. 0) GO TO 30
           BALNCE=BALNCE-TRANS
           GO TO 20
     30    WRITE(6,2000) BALNCE
     2000  FORMAT(' ',F7.2)
           STOP
           END
```

data
```
   456.03
   78.36
   -25.39
   45.22
   -75.42
   0.0
```

output
```
   433.26
```

1   `IF (PRICE .GT. 999.0)   GO TO 20`

  Note: It's unwise to test for exact equality of REALs because they are represented to limited precision.

2 Both of the loops in the flowchart in Figure 1 3 3 are in the post-test form. The smaller loop happens to be contained in the larger loop, but that's OK. It's an example of a **nested loop**, which we'll cover next (Section 3 4).

    The smaller loop in the flowchart in Figure 1 5 1 is in the pre-test form (the test is "is the value stored in YEARS zero?"). The other loop is neither a pre-test nor a post-test loop. It's a **no-test loop**, that is, an infinite loop. If we wanted to run this program on a real computer instead of the simulated computer we used in Section 1 5, obviously we should change it to some kind of conditional loop.

3
```
      INTEGER FIVES
      FIVES=0
10    FIVES=FIVES+5
      WRITE(6,1000) FIVES
1000  FORMAT(I15)
      IF (FIVES .LT. 100) GO TO 10
      STOP
      END
```

output
```
        5
       10
       15
       20
       25
       30
       35
       40
       45
       50
       55
       60
       65
       70
       75
       80
       85
       90
       95
      100
```

4 Change the loop as shown below.

```
        .
        .
        .
     N=0.0
     SUM=0.00
     READ(5,1000) PRICE,WGT
10   SUM = SUM + PRICE/WGT
     N = N + 1.0
     READ(5,1000) PRICE,WGT
     IF (PRICE .GT. 0.00) GO TO 10
        .
        .
        .
```

ANSWERS TO EXERCISES 3 4

1 The inner loop in the knitting algorithm is "1st row: K2, P2, repeat from
* across"; the inner loop in the bank balance program is the one which
READs the old balance and transactions. The outer loop in the knitting
algorithm is the repetition of the first row until 60 inches; the outer loop
in the bank balance program is the one which begins by READing the
social security number and ends by printing the new balance.

2 `IF (PRICE*QTY .GE. LIMIT)  PRICE = PRICE*(1.0-DSCNT)`

Writing it this way not only is shorter, but seems clearer. Do you agree?

3
```
        INTEGER SOCSEC
        REAL BALNCE,TRANS
100     READ(5,1000) SOCSEC
1000    FORMAT(I9)
        IF (SOCSEC .LT. 0) STOP
        WRITE(6,1010)SOCSEC
1010    FORMAT('0SOCIAL SECURITY NUMBER: ',I10)
        READ(5,1020) BALNCE
1020    FORMAT(F20.0)
        WRITE(6,1030) BALNCE
1030    FORMAT('  $',F7.2,' PREVIOUS BALANCE')
        WRITE(6,1040)
1040    FORMAT(' TRANSACTIONS')
200     READ(5,1020) TRANS
        IF (TRANS .EQ. 0.0)  GO TO 300
        BALNCE = BALNCE - TRANS
        IF (TRANS .GT. 0.0)  GO TO 210
        TRANS = -TRANS
        WRITE(6,2001) TRANS
2001    FORMAT('  $', F7.2, ' DEPOSIT')
        GO TO 200
210     WRITE(6,2010) TRANS
2010    FORMAT('  $', F7.2, ' CHECK')
        GO TO 200
300     WRITE(6,3000) BALNCE
3000    FORMAT(10X,'NEW BALANCE:   $', F7.2)
        GO TO 100
        END
```

data

```
276407566
456.32
 22.96
 33.54
-291.55
 54.39
 0.0
175504244
332.53
 22.03
-329.41
 22.11
 0.0
        -1
```

output

```
SOCIAL SECURITY NUMBER:  276407566
   $ 456.32 PREVIOUS BALANCE
TRANSACTIONS
   $  22.96 CHECK
   $  33.54 CHECK
   $ 291.55 DEPOSIT
   $  54.39 CHECK
        NEW BALANCE:   $ 636.96

SOCIAL SECURITY NUMBER:  175504244
   $ 332.53 PREVIOUS BALANCE
TRANSACTIONS
   $  22.03 CHECK
   $ 329.41 DEPOSIT
   $  22.11 CHECK
        NEW BALANCE:   $ 617.80
```

ANSWERS TO EXERCISES 4 2

1 12 + 2 and 4 * 2 are INTEGER expressions; the term constant is restricted to values involving no computations and no memory cells.

12.75, 1.0, −127.5, are REAL constants. The others are INTEGER constants.

2 2 and +2 are INTEGER constants

−2.01E3.2 and 300E30. contain illegal decimal point shift factors

The others are legitimate REAL constants.

3 Here are some possibilities:

+1.0   1.0   1.00   1.0E+0   0.001E+3   0.001E3   10.0E−1

ANSWERS TO EXERCISES 4 3

1 a PRINC*RATE**1.06
  b CAR*TER/PEA/NUT
  c can't be done without parentheses
  d COST + COST*STAX + COST*FEDTAX − BRIBE

2 The expression is evaluated like 0−1**2. Since exponentiations are performed before subtractions, the result is −1.

3 The possible values are 0, 4, 6, and 7. Here are some of the ways of adding parentheses to get those values:

  (6 + 2)/8/4 equals (8)/8/4 equals 1/4 equals 0
  (6 + 2)/(8/4) equals (8)/(2) equals 4
  6 + (2/8/4) equals 6 + (0/4) equals 6
  6 + 2/(8/4) equals 6 + 2/(2) equals 7.

4 The program works fine if N happens to be 1, and it's a disaster otherwise. If N has any value over 1, the statement

```
AVERGE = (1/N)*SUM
```

stores 0.0 in AVERGE. Probably the best way to correct this flaw is to convert the values in SUM and N to the equivalent REALs before computing AVERGE. So, change

```
REAL AVERGE
```

to

```
REAL AVERGE, RSUM, RN
```

and replace

```
AVERGE = (1/N)*SUM
```

by these three statements:

```
RSUM = SUM
RN = N
AVERGE = (1.0/RN)*RSUM
```

ANSWERS TO EXERCISES 4 4

1 2.0
  −2
  3
  1.0
  3.0
  21.0

2 No. $\tan(x) = \dfrac{\sin(x)}{\cos(x)}$

ANSWERS TO EXERCISES 4 5

1
```
INTEGER NICKS,CENTS
NICKS=CENTS/5
```

2   4.175   goes into   BAR4
       3.2   goes into   BAR3
       0.96   goes into   BAR0
     −2.98   goes into   no BAR, but terminates loop
    496.1   goes into   no BAR, but evokes an error message

What bar do you go into?

ANSWERS TO EXERCISES 4 6

1
```
      IF (TOTAL .GT. 0 .AND.  TOTAL .LT. 10)  STOP
30    ...
```

2
```
      IF (TOTAL .GT. 10 .OR. TOTAL .LT. 0)  STOP
30    ...
```

3
```
COMMENT: PROGRAM TO DETERMINE THE COST OF
C          HEALTH INSURANCE FOR AN EMPLOYEE OF
C          ARCHETYPAL SYSTEMS, INC.
       INTEGER EMPNO,HEALTH,MATERN,MAJOR
       REAL INSUR
  900  READ(5,1000) EMPNO,HEALTH,MATERN,MAJOR
 1000  FORMAT(I10,3I1)
       IF (EMPNO.EQ.0) STOP
C                                          HERE'S THE DECISION TABLE
       INSUR=0.
       IF (HEALTH.EQ.1) INSUR=10.
       IF (HEALTH.EQ.2) INSUR=17.
       IF (HEALTH.EQ.3) INSUR=25.
       IF (INSUR.EQ.0) GOTO 1200
       IF (HEALTH.EQ.1.AND.MATERN.EQ.1) INSUR=INSUR+4.
       IF (HEALTH.EQ.2.AND.MATERN.EQ.1) INSUR=INSUR+5.
       IF (HEALTH.EQ.3.AND.MATERN.EQ.1) INSUR=INSUR+5.
       IF (HEALTH.EQ.1.AND.MATERN.EQ.1.AND.MAJOR.EQ.1)
      +                              INSUR=INSUR+2.
       IF (HEALTH.EQ.2.AND.MATERN.EQ.1.AND.MAJOR.EQ.1)
      +                              INSUR=INSUR+3.
       IF (HEALTH.EQ.3.AND.MATERN.EQ.1.AND.MAJOR.EQ.1)
      +                              INSUR=INSUR+3.
       WRITE(6,1100) EMPNO,INSUR
 1100  FORMAT('EMPLOYEE ',I10,' INSURANCE ',F6.2)
       GOTO 900
 1200  WRITE(6,1300) EMPNO
 1300  FORMAT('EMPLOYEE ',I10,' INCORRECT INSURANCE CLASS.')
       GOTO 900
       END
```

```
data
  0012936784310
  0100938762211
  0293007564410
  0694381792111
  0769573214311
  0836475313210
  0911289742000
  0936583218110
  0000000000000
```

```
output
    EMPLOYEE    12936784 INSURANCE   30.00
    EMPLOYEE   100938762 INSURANCE   25.00
    EMPLOYEE   293007564 INCORRECT   INSURANCE CLASS.
    EMPLOYEE   694381792 INSURANCE   16.00
    EMPLOYEE   769573214 INSURANCE   33.00
    EMPLOYEE   836475313 INSURANCE   22.00
    EMPLOYEE   911289742 INCORRECT   INSURANCE CLASS.
    EMPLOYEE   936583218 INSURANCE   14.00
```

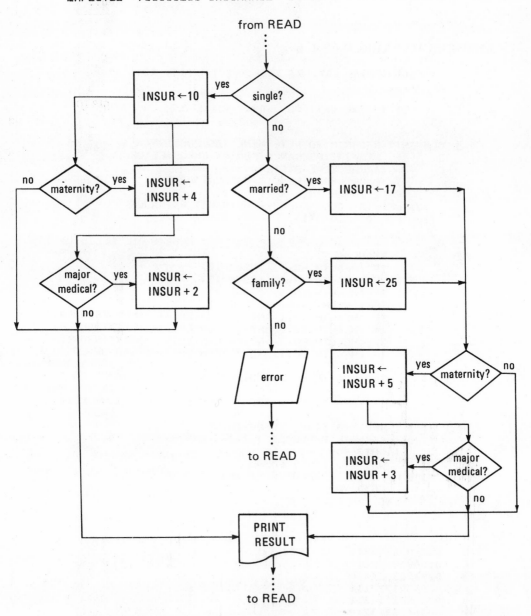

It's usually easier to use the decision table. All you need to do is select the appropriate rule and the actions are specified for you. It's harder to overlook a condition or action with the decision table. With some practice a programmer can go directly from a decision table to the program. Don't worry about using a few extra IF statements. The idea is to make the logic easy to follow rather than saving one or two Fortran program statements. But you have a choice, so use the method that works best for you.

ANSWERS TO EXERCISES 4 7

1 We would have to alter the DATA statement so that NAMES1 is initialized to 4HJONE and so that NAMES2 is initialized to 1HS. Also, it would be only fair to change FORMAT 2000 so it says JONES instead of SMITH.

2
```
      INTEGER COL1,COL2,COL3,COL4,COL5,DOLLAR
      DATA DOLLAR/1H$/
      READ(5,1000) COL1,COL2,COL3,COL4,COL5
 1000 FORMAT(5A1)
      IF (COL1 .EQ. DOLLAR) GO TO 100
      IF (COL2 .EQ. DOLLAR) GO TO 100
      IF (COL3 .EQ. DOLLAR) GO TO 100
      IF (COL4 .EQ. DOLLAR) GO TO 100
      IF (COL5 .EQ. DOLLAR) GO TO 100
      WRITE(6,2000)
 2000 FORMAT(' NOPE')
      STOP
  100 WRITE(6,3000)
 3000 FORMAT(' YES, THERE WAS A $ SIGN')
      STOP
      END
```

data
48.23

output
NOPE

3 Yes. (It's true that there is *no* Exercise 3 in Section 4 7, but we thought that since there are a few exercises we don't give answers for, it's only fair we give a few answers we don't have exercises for.)

ANSWERS TO EXERCISES 4 8

1 a REAL, F5.3 or INTEGER, I3
   b INTEGER, I1
   c INTEGER, rAw
      where r and w depend on the length of the names and your computer system
   d REAL, F15.2

2 FORMAT 1000 is equivalent to ('*b*', 3I3, F12.2) which has a different effect from FORMAT 1001. The other pairs leave identical effects.

3 You can put it anywhere you want as long as it contains a decimal point.

4 It describes a data card with 120 columns (most have only 80).

5 Two numbers per card in the two fields, columns 1–10, and columns 11–20.

6 One solution is: `6000 FORMAT (A2,18X,3(F10.0,10)`

7 A +6.02E+23

  B +60.2E+230   too large on most systems (overflow)

8 A = bb123400.0bA = b.123E+06bA = bbb.1E+06

9
```
      WRITE(6,7000)
7000 FORMAT('1'/100('  FORMAT IS A TRICKY LANGUAGE'/))
```
Note: This will start on the second line of a page.

10
```
IN FIRST PLACE WAS BO
THERE WERE 2 TIED FOR IT

IN SECOND PLACE WAS MO
THERE WERE
```
(*Note*: Here's a place where gobbling up the FORMAT to the next data descriptor has an undesirable result.)

ANSWERS TO EXERCISES 6 1

1 `REAL A(10)`	legal
`INTEGER A(13-2)`	illegal; no computation allowed in length declarator
`INTEGER A(I)`	illegal; no variable allowed in length declarator
`REAL A(150), BOK(3472)`	legal
`REAL X(15.0)`	illegal; length declarator must be INTEGER

2 If the values in memory cells I and J are the same and that value is a legal subscript for B, then B(I) and B(J) denote the same cell.

3 `B(3) = B(I)`	legal; but since I has the value 3, nothing is changed
`B(I) = B(I-1)`	legal; changes value of B(3) to value contained in B(2)
`B(J) = B(2*I)`	legal; changes value of B(7) to value contained in B(6)
`B(2*I) = B(J+4)`	illegal; B(J + 4) refers to B(11), which doesn't exist
`B(4) = B(J-1) + B(I*J-21)`	illegal; B(I*J−21) refers to B(0), which doesn't exist
`B(1.7) = 0`	illegal; REAL subscripts aren't allowed

4 No arrays would be needed, as shown in the program below.

```
COMMENT--PROGRAM TO LIST THE WESTERN STATES, THEIR
C          SALES TAX RATES, AND THE AVERAGE RATE OVER THE
C          WESTERN STATES.
       REAL T,SUM,AVE
       INTEGER S,N
C
       SUM=0.0
       N=0
 100   READ(5,1000) S,T
 1000  FORMAT(A2,F7.0)
        WRITE(6,1010) S,T
 1010    FORMAT(' ',A2,F7.3)
        SUM=SUM+T
        N=N+1
        IF (N .LT. 11) GO TO 100
C
       AVE=SUM/11.0
C
       WRITE(6,2000) AVE
 2000  FORMAT('0AVERAGE WESTERN STATES SALES TAX IS',
      +                                     F7.3)
       STOP
       END
```

data

```
WA 0.045
ID 0.03
MT 0.00
OR 0.04
WY 0.03
CA 0.06
NV 0.03
UT 0.04
CO 0.03
AZ 0.04
NM 0.04
```

output

```
WA  0.045
ID  0.03
MT  0.00
OR  0.04
WY  0.03
CA  0.06
NV  0.03
UT  0.04
CO  0.03
AZ  0.04
NM  0.04

AVERAGE WESTERN STATES SALES TAX IS   .035
```

ANSWERS TO EXERCISES 6 2

1 We need 12 cells in the arrays because the information on the "**" card will have to be stored somewhere. Since there will be up to 11 response cards, we need a twelfth cell to include the information from the "**" card.

2 Change the STORE DATA and COMPUTE AVERAGE sections of the program as shown below.

```
C       STORE DATA
        SUM=0.0
        N=0
100     READ(5,1000) S(N+1),T(N+1)
1000    FORMAT(A2,F7.0)
            IF (S(N+1) .EQ. FIN)  GO TO 200
            SUM=SUM+S(N+1)
            GO TO 100
200     AVE=SUM/N
```

3 Since N will be zero when the computer reaches the COMPUTE AVER-AGE section of the program the computer will attempt to divide by zero, resulting in an error. To avoid this, change the statements between statements 200 and 210 in the program to the ones below.

```
200  IF (N .NE. 0) GO TO 205
        WRITE(6,2000)
2000    FORMAT(' NO DATA FOR TAX PROGRAM')
        STOP
205  SUM=0.0
     K=1
```

4 Increase the length of the arrays S and T to 51. That's all!

5 The program will try to use nonexistent array elements. Change the statement GO TO 100 in the STORE DATA section of the program to the following sequence of statements.

```
     IF (N .LE. 11) GO TO 100
        N=N-1
        WRITE(6,2009) N
2009    FORMAT(' ONLY',I3,' RESPONSE CARDS ALLOWED FOR.'/)
```

6
```
     COMMENT--PROGRAM TO LIST THE WESTERN STATES WITH
     C        BELOW AVERAGE SALES TAX RATES.
              INTEGER S1,S2,S3,S4,S5,S6,S7,S8,S9,S10,S11
              REAL T1,T2,T3,T4,T5,T6,T7,T8,T9,T10,T11,SUM,AVE
              INTEGER FIN
              DATA FIN/2H**/
     C
     C        SET ALL TAX RATES TO ZERO INITIALLY SO THAT UNUSED
     C        CELLS WILL NOT CONTRIBUTE TO SUM IN STATEMENT 200.
              DATA T1,T2,T3,T4,T5,T6,T7,T8,T9,T10,T11/11*0.0/
```

```
C
C       STORE DATA AND ACCUMULATE SUM
        SUM=0.0
        N=0
        READ(5,1000) S1,T1
 1000   FORMAT(A2,F7.0)
        IF (S1 .EQ. FIN) GO TO 200
        N=N+1
        READ(5,1000) S2,T2
        IF (S2 .EQ. FIN) GO TO 200
        N=N+1
        READ(5,1000) S3,T3
        IF (S3 .EQ. FIN) GO TO 200
        N=N+1
        READ(5,1000) S4,T4
        IF (S4 .EQ. FIN) GO TO 200
        N=N+1
        READ(5,1000) S5,T5
        IF (S5 .EQ. FIN) GO TO 200
        N=N+1
        READ(5,1000) S6,T6
        IF (S6 .EQ. FIN) GO TO 200
        N=N+1
        READ(5,1000) S7,T7
        IF (S7 .EQ. FIN) GO TO 200
        N=N+1
        READ(5,1000) S8,T8
        IF (S8 .EQ. FIN) GO TO 200
        N=N+1
        READ(5,1000) S9,T9
        IF (S9 .EQ. FIN) GO TO 200
        N=N+1
        READ(5,1000) S10,T10
        IF (S10 .EQ. FIN) GO TO 200
        N=N+1
        READ(5,1000) S11,T1
        IF (S11 .EQ. FIN) GO TO 200
        N=N+1
C
  200   AVE=(T1+T2+T3+T4+T5+T6+T7+T8+T9+T10+T11)/N
C
        WRITE(6,2000)
 2000   FORMAT(' STATES WITH BELOW AVERAGE SALES TAX'/)
        IF (T1  .LE. AVE  .AND. N .GE. 1 ) WRITE(6,2010) S1
        IF (T2  .LE. AVE  .AND. N .GE. 2 ) WRITE(6,2010) S2
        IF (T3  .LE. AVE  .AND. N .GE. 3 ) WRITE(6,2010) S3
        IF (T4  .LE. AVE  .AND. N .GE. 4 ) WRITE(6,2010) S4
        IF (T5  .LE. AVE  .AND. N .GE. 5 ) WRITE(6,2010) S5
        IF (T6  .LE. AVE  .AND. N .GE. 6 ) WRITE(6,2010) S6
        IF (T7  .LE. AVE  .AND. N .GE. 7 ) WRITE(6,2010) S7
        IF (T8  .LE. AVE  .AND. N .GE. 8 ) WRITE(6,2010) S8
        IF (T9  .LE. AVE  .AND. N .GE. 9 ) WRITE(6,2010) S9
        IF (T10 .LE. AVE  .AND. N .GE. 10) WRITE(6,2010) S10
        IF (T11 .LE. AVE  .AND. N .GE. 11) WRITE(6,2010) S11
 2010   FORMAT(' ',A2)
        STOP
        END
```

data
```
WA 0.045
ID 0.03
MT 0.00
OR 0.04
WY 0.03
CA 0.06
NV 0.03
UT 0.04
CO 0.03
AZ 0.04
NM 0.04
**
```

output
```
STATES WITH BELOW AVERAGE SALES TAX

ID
MT
WY
NV
CO
NM
```

Imagine changing this program to handle all 50 states!

```
7   COMMENT:  MAKE A BAR GRAPH FROM DISTANCE DATA.
          INTEGER BAR(6), NUMB
          REAL DIST
    C     INITIALIZE BAR HEIGHTHS
          NUMB = 1
    5     BAR(NUMB) = 0
            NUMB = NUMB+1
            IF (NUMB .LE. 6)  GO TO 5
    C     READ DISTANCES AND ACCUMULATE BAR SUMS
    10    READ(5,1000) DIST
    1000 FORMAT(F10.0)
            IF (DIST .LT. 0.0)  GO TO 200
    C     DROP FRACTIONAL PART TO DETERMINE BAR SUM AFFECTED
          NUMB = DIST
    C     INCREMENT APPROPRIATE BAR COUNTER
          IF (NUMB .LE. 5)  GO TO 30
            WRITE(6,2009) DIST
    2009    FORMAT(' DISTANCE', F7.1, ' IS OUT OF RANGE.')
            GO TO 10
    30      BAR(NUMB+1) = BAR(NUMB+1) + 1
            GO TO 10
    C     PRINT RESULTS
    200   WRITE(6,2000)
    2000 FORMAT('1BAR    HEIGHT')
          NUMB = 0
    210   WRITE(6,2100) NUMB, BAR(NUMB+1)
    2100 FORMAT(' ', I2, I7)
            NUMB = NUMB+1
            IF (NUMB .LE. 5)  GO TO 210
          STOP
          END
```

data

```
1.9
0.4
0.9
3.9
17.5
2.8
4.5
4.1
3.2
5.8
6.9
4.5
3.7
2.9
5.2
-1.0
```

output

```
DISTANCE   17.5 IS OUT OF RANGE
DISTANCE    6.9 IS OUT OF RANGE

BAR    HEIGHT
 0       2
 1       1
 2       2
 3       3
 4       3
 5       2
```

ANSWERS TO EXERCISES 6 5

```
1          INTEGER PEOPLE(12), CARS, N
      C                                          INITIALIZE COUNTERS
           N = 1
     100   PEOPLE(N) = 0
           N = N+1
           IF (N .LE. 12) GO TO 100
      C                                          SIMULATE ARRIVALS
           CARS = 1
     200   N = INT(RANF(0.0)*12.0) + 1
      C                                            A CAR WITH
      C                                    "N" PEOPLE HAS ARRIVED
           PEOPLE(N) = PEOPLE(N) + 1
           CARS = CARS + 1
           IF (CARS .LE. 100)  GO TO 200
      C                                          PRINT RESULTS
           N = 1
     300   WRITE(6,3000) PEOPLE(N), N
    3000   FORMAT(1X,I3, ' CARS ARRIVED WITH', I3, ' PERSON(S)')
           N = N+1
           IF (N .LE. 12) GO TO 300
           STOP
           END
```

output

```
 5 CARS ARRIVED WITH  1 PERSON(S)
 9 CARS ARRIVED WITH  2 PERSON(S)
 6 CARS ARRIVED WITH  3 PERSON(S)
10 CARS ARRIVED WITH  4 PERSON(S)
 6 CARS ARRIVED WITH  5 PERSON(S)
 9 CARS ARRIVED WITH  6 PERSON(S)
 9 CARS ARRIVED WITH  7 PERSON(S)
12 CARS ARRIVED WITH  8 PERSON(S)
 8 CARS ARRIVED WITH  9 PERSON(S)
 8 CARS ARRIVED WITH 10 PERSON(S)
 9 CARS ARRIVED WITH 11 PERSON(S)
 9 CARS ARRIVED WITH 12 PERSON(S)
```

```
2   COMMENT:  PROGRAM TO SIMULATE THE ARRIVAL OF 100 CARS
    C           ON DOLLAR-A-CAR NIGHT
          INTEGER PEOPLE(7), CARS, N
    C                                        INITIALIZE COUNTERS
          N = 1
    100   PEOPLE(N) = 0
          N = N+1
          IF (N .LE. 7)  GO TO 100
    C                                        SIMULATE ARRIVALS
          CARS = 1
    200   N = INT(RANF(0.0)*7.0)
    C                                          A CAR WITH
    C                                    "N" PEOPLE HAS ARRIVED
          PEOPLE(N+1) = PEOPLE(N+1) + 1
          CARS = CARS + 1
          IF (CARS .LE. 100)  GO TO 200
    C                                        PRINT RESULTS
          N = 0
    300   WRITE(6,3000) PEOPLE(N+1), N
    3000  FORMAT(1X,I3, ' CARS ARRIVED WITH', I2, ' PERSON(S)')
          N = N+1
          IF (N .LE. 6)  GO TO 300
          STOP
          END
```

output

```
13 CARS ARRIVED WITH 0 PERSON(S)
12 CARS ARRIVED WITH 1 PERSON(S)
12 CARS ARRIVED WITH 2 PERSON(S)
13 CARS ARRIVED WITH 3 PERSON(S)
21 CARS ARRIVED WITH 4 PERSON(S)
13 CARS ARRIVED WITH 5 PERSON(S)
16 CARS ARRIVED WITH 6 PERSON(S)
```

You can't have an array subscript of zero so PEOPLE(1) is used to indicate zero people, PEOPLE(2) for 1 person, PEOPLE(3) for 2 people, and so on. How can a car have no people in it? The dog was driving. . . . Or else you might interpret it to mean that many cars didn't arrive. There are other interpretations. We'll leave those for you to explore if you're interested.

ANSWERS TO EXERCISES 6 6

1 `INTEGER A(100,3), B(3,100),I`   legal; declares two INTEGER arrays A and B

    `REAL QRT(3,49)`   legal; declares a REAL array QRT

    `REAL X(N,100)`   illegal; length declarators must be constants

2 `A(4,2) = 0`   legal
    `B(4,2) = 0`   illegal; 4 is too large
    `A(3,50) = 0`   illegal; 50 is too large
    `I = 10`   legal

3 Replace this part of the program

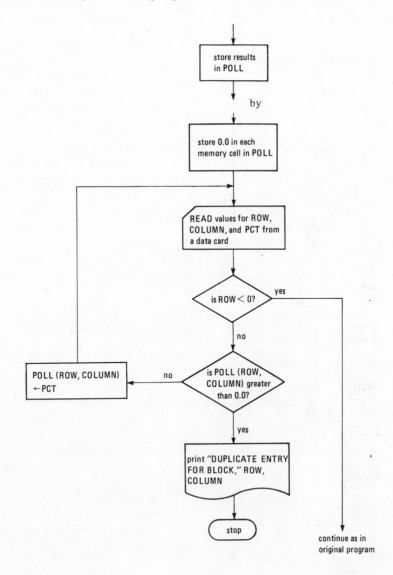

```
1    READ(5,5000) A(1),A(2),A(3),A(4)
     WRITE(6,1000) A(4),A(6),A(8),A(10),A(12)
     WRITE(6,3000) A(2),A(6),A(10)
     READ(5,2000) B(1,1),B(2,1),B(3,1),B(4,1),
    +             B(1,2),B(2,2),B(3,2),B(4,2)
     WRITE(6,4000) Q,R, S,B(3,1),A(1), S,B(3,2),A(2), BC,
    +             A(1),A(2),A(3),A(4)

2    WRITE(6,1000) (A(I), I=1,5)
     WRITE(6,1000) (A(I), I=2,10,2)

     READ(5,2000) ( (B(I,J), I=2,3), J=1,3)
                              or
     READ(5,2000) (B(2,J),B(3,J), J=1,3)
```

3
```
WRITE(6,2000) (A(J), J=1,N-1)
```
N−1 is illegal; expressions not allowed as implied do list parameters

```
READ(5,7000) (J,A(J), J=1,N)
```
implied do list parameters may not be changed while the list is being used. This READ would change J by giving it a value from a data card

```
WRITE(6,1000) (A(J), J=1,C(N))
```
C(N) is illegal; only constants and *simple* INTEGER variables may be parameters in implied do lists

4 Trouble. We should test for that case too. Here's one way.

```
300    THISB=BAR(NUMB+1)
       IF (THISB .LE. 0) GO TO 310
304    IF (THISB .LE. 60 ) GO TO 308
C          MORE THAN 60 ITEMS IN THIS BAR.
       WRITE(6,3000) NUMB,(XCH,COUNT=1,60)
       THISB=THISB-60
       GO TO 304
C          BETWEEN 1 AND 60 ITEMS
308    WRITE(6,3000) NUMB,(XCH,COUNT=1,THISB)
3000   FORMAT(' BAR',I1,':',100A1)
       GO TO 400
C          NO ITEMS AT ALL.
310    WRITE(6,3000) NUMB
400    NUMB=NUMB+1
       IF (NUMB .LE. 5) GO TO 300
       STOP
       END
```

This makes fat bars if there are more than 60 items in a bar, like this:

```
BAR0:XXXXXXXXXXXXXXXXXXXXXXXXXXXXXXXXXXX
BAR1:XXXXXXXXXXXXXXXXXXXXXXXXXXXXXXXXXXXXXXXXXXXXXXXXXXXXXXXXXXXXX
BAR2:XXXXXXXXXXXXXXXXXXXXXXXXXXXXXXXXXXXXXXXXXXXXXXXXXXXXXXXXXXXXXX
BAR2:XXXXXXXXXXXXXXXXXXXXXXXXXXXXXXXXXXXXXXXXXXXXXXXXXXXXXXXXXXXXXX
BAR2:X
BAR3:XXXXXXXXXXXXXXXXXXXXXXXXXXXXXXXXXXXXXXXXXXXXXXXXXXXXXXXXXXXXXX
BAR3:XXXXXXXXXXXXXXXXXXXXXXXXXXXXXXXXXXXXXXXXXXXXXXXXXXXXXXXXXXXXXX
BAR3:XXXXXXXXXXXXXXXXXXXXXXXXXXXXXXXXXX
BAR4:XXXXXXXXXXXXXXXXXXXXXXXXXXXXXXXXXXXXXXXXXXXXXXXXXXXXXXXXXXXXXX
BAR4:XXXXXXXXXXXXXXXXXXXXXXXXXXXXXXXXXXXXXXXXXXXXXXXXXXXXXXXXXXXXXX
BAR4:XXXXXXXXXXXXXXXXXXXXXXXXXXXXXXXXXXXXXXXXXXXXXXXXXXXXXXXXXXXXXX
BAR4:XXXXXXXXXXXXXXXXXXXXXXXXXXXXXXXXXXXXXXXXXXXXXXXX
BAR5:XXXXXXXXXXXXXXXXXXXXXXXXXXXXXXXXXXXXXXXXXXXXXXXXXXXXXXX
```

```
5      WRITE(6,3000) NUMB, (NUMB, COUNT=1,THISB)
    3000 FORMAT(' BAR', I1, ':', 100I1)
```

ANSWERS TO EXERCISES 6 8

```
1  COMMENT---THIS PROGRAM CALCULATES INSURANCE PERMIUMS BY
   C          LOOKING UP AN INSURANCE RATE IN A TABLE
             INTEGER M,F,A,B,C,MAXAGE(8),IAGE,JSEX,KJOB,NAME(5)
             INTEGER AGE,SEX,JOB
             INTEGER TOTAL,INSRD,UNINSR
             REAL RATE(8,2,3),INSUR,AMOUNT,PREM
             DATA M,F,A,B,C/1HM,1HF,1HA,1HB,1HC/
             DATA TOTAL,INSRD,UNINSR/3*0/
                             .
                             .
                             .
                             .
   C                                              READ APPLICANT
      100 READ(5,1200) (NAME(I),I=1,5),AGE,SEX,JOB,INSUR
     1200 FORMAT(5A4,I2,2A1,F4.1)
             IF (AGE.EQ.99) GOTO 600
             TOTAL=TOTAL+1
   C                     CHECK APPLICANT'S AGE FOR INSURABILITY
                             .
                             .
                             .
                             .
   C                                     PRINT DATA FOR APPLICANT
             WRITE(6,1600) (NAME(I),I=1,5),AGE,SEX,JOB,
     +                     RATE(IAGE,JSEX,KJOB),AMOUNT,PREM
     1600    FORMAT(1X,5A4,3X,I2,3X,A1,4X,A1,3X,1H$,F6.2,5X,1H$,
     +           F8.0,5X,1H$,F7.2)
             INSRD=INSRD+1
             GOTO 100
      600 UNINSR=TOTAL-INSRD
             WRITE(6,1650) TOTAL,INSRD,UNINSR
     1650 FORMAT(//,1X,26HTOTAL APPLICANTS PROCESSED ,I3,/,
     +           1X,17HNUMBER QUALIFYING ,I3,/,
     +           1X,18HNUMBER UNINSURABLE ,I3,//)
   C                                          PRINT RATE TABLE
                             .
                             .
                             .
```

output

NAME	AGE	SEX	JOB	RATE	INSURANCE	PREMIUM
JOHN Q. SMITH	48	M	B	$ 29.50	$ 16400.	$ 483.80
PAUL B. BUNYON	24	M	C	$ 24.00	$ 20000.	$ 480.00
CLARA P. MONROE	55	F	A	$ 30.50	$ 6000.	$ 183.00
DUSTY O. RHODE		JOB CLASS ERROR				
JANE G. DOWNS	42	F	B	$ 24.50	$ 11900.	$ 291.55
JIMMY P. STARTER	52	M	C	$ 35.00	$ 40000.	$1400.00
CANDY A. SWEET		SEX ERROR				
JAMES C. MOORE	36	M	A	$ 24.00	$ 50000.	$1200.00
BILLIE T. KIDD	19	F	A	$ 19.00	$ 15000.	$ 285.00
CHEVY C. FORD	62					UNINSURABLE
JUNIOR S. FRYE	15					UNINSURABLE

TOTAL APPLICANTS PROCESSED 11
NUMBER QUALIFYING 7
NUMBER UNINSURABLE 4

```
    2    COMMENT--THIS PROGRAM CALCULATES INSURANCE PERMIUMS BY
         C          LOOKING UP AN INSURANCE RATE IN A TABLE
                INTEGER M,F,A,B,C,MAXAGE(8),IAGE,JSEX,KJOB,NAME(5)
                INTEGER AGE,SEX,JOB
                INTEGER TOTAL,INSRD,UNINSR
                REAL RATE(8,2,3),INSUR,AMOUNT,PREM
                DATA M,F,A,B,C/1HM,1HF,1HA,1HB,1HC/
                DATA TOTAL,INSRD,UNINSR,SEXERR,JOBERR/5*0/
                                  .
                                  .
                                  .
                                  .
         C                              CHECK SEX AND JOB CLASS CODE
         C                              HERE'S THE CHANGE FOR
         C                              BOTH A SEX AND JOB ERROR
                SEXERR=1
                JOBERR=1
                IF ((SEX.EQ.M).OR.(SEX.EQ.F)) SEXERR=0
                IF ((JOB.EQ.A).OR.(JOB.EQ.B).OR.(JOB.EQ.C)) JOBERR=0
                IF ((SEXERR.EQ.0).AND.(JOBERR.EQ.0)) GOTO 500
                IF (SEXERR.EQ.0) GOTO 400
                WRITE(6,1400) (NAME(I),I=1,5)
         1400   FORMAT(1X,5A4,8X,9HSEX ERROR )
                IF (JOBERR.EQ.1) WRITE(6,1450)
         1450   FORMAT(29X,15HJOB CLASS ERROR)
                GOTO 100
          400   WRITE(6,1500) (NAME(I),I=1,5)
         1500   FORMAT(1X,5A4,8X,15HJOB CLASS ERROR )
                GOTO 100
         C                        FIND SEX SUBSCRIPT FOR RATE TABLE
          500   IF (SEX.EQ.M) JSEX=1
                IF (SEX.EQ.F) JSEX=2
         C                    FIND JOB CLASS SUBSCRIPT FOR RATE TABLE
                                  .
                                  .
                                  .
                                  .
```

data

```
        JOHN Q. SMITH        48MB16.4
        PAUL B. BUNYON       24MC20.0
        CLARA P. MONROE      55UD 6.0
        DUSTY O. RHODE       31MD24.5
        JANE G. DOWNS        42FB11.9
        JIMMY P. STARTER     52MC40.0
        CANDY A. SWEET       26UC12.4
        JAMES C. MOORE       36MA50.0
        BILLIE T. KIDD       19FA15.0
        CHEVY C. FORD        62MA20.0
        JUNIOR S. FRYE       15MA 5.0
                             99
```

output

NAME	AGE	SEX	JOB	RATE	INSURANCE	PREMIUM
JOHN Q. SMITH	48	M	B	$ 29.50	$ 16400.	$ 483.80
PAUL B. BUNYON	24	M	C	$ 24.00	$ 20000.	$ 480.00
CLARA P. MONROE		SEX ERROR				
		JOB CLASS ERROR				
DUSTY O. RHODE		JOB CLASS ERROR				
JANE G. DOWNS	42	F	B	$ 24.50	$ 11900.	$ 291.55
JIMMY P. STARTER	52	M	C	$ 35.00	$ 40000.	$1400.00
CANDY A. SWEET		SEX ERROR				
JAMES C. MOORE	36	M	A	$ 24.00	$ 50000.	$1200.00
BILLIE T. KIDD	19	F	A	$ 19.00	$ 15000.	$ 285.00
CHEVY C. FORD	62					UNINSURABLE
JUNIOR S. FRYE	15					UNINSURABLE

```
TOTAL APPLICANTS PROCESSED 11
NUMBER QUALIFYING  6
NUMBER UNINSURABLE  5
```

```
    3  COMMENT--THIS PROGRAM CALCULATES INSURANCE PREMIUMS BY
       C        LOOKING UP AN INSURANCE RATE IN A TABLE
               INTEGER M,F,A,B,C,MAXAGE(8),IAGE,JSEX,KJOB,NAME(5)
               INTEGER AGE,SEX,JOB
               INTEGER TOTAL,INSRD,UNINSR
               REAL RATE(8,2,3),INSUR,AMOUNT,PREM
               REAL TINSUR,TRATE,AVGINS,AVGRAT
               DATA M,F,A,B,C/1HM,1HF,1HA,1HB,1HC/
               DATA TOTAL,INSRD,UNINSR,SEXERR,JOBERR/5*0/
               DATA TINSUR,TRATE/2*0.0/
                                      .
                                      .
                                      .
                                      .
                                      .
       C                            PRINT DATA FOR APPLICANT
               WRITE(6,1600) (NAME(I),I=1,5),AGE,SEX,JOB,
              +               RATE(IAGE,JSEX,KJOB),AMOUNT,PREM
        1600   FORMAT(1X,5A4,3X,I2,3X,A1,4X,A1,3X,1H$,F6.2,5X,1H$,
              +        F8.0,5X,1H ,F7.2)
               TINSUR=TINSUR+AMOUNT
               TRATE=TRATE+RATE(IAGE,JSEX,KJOB)
               INSRD=INSRD+1
               GOTO 100
         600   UNINSR=TOTAL-INSRD
               WRITE(6,1650) TOTAL,INSRD,UNINSR
        1650   FORMAT(//,1X,26HTOTAL APPLICANTS PROCESSED ,I3,/,
              +        1X,17HNUMBER QUALIFYING ,I3,/,
              +        1X,18HNUMBER UNINSURABLE ,I3,/)
```

```
C                                          HERE'S THE CALCULATION OF
C                             THE AVERAGE AMOUNT OF INSURANCE
C                                              AND THE AVERAGE RATE
        AVGINS=TINSUR/INSRD
        AVGRAT=TRATE/INSRD
        WRITE(6,1680) AVGINS,AVGRAT
   1680 FORMAT(1X,19HAVERAGE INSURANCE $,F8.0,/,
       +        1X,24HAVERAGE INSURANCE RATE $,F7.2,//)
C                                             PRINT RATE TABLE
                              .
                              .
                              .
                              .
                              .
```

output

NAME	AGE	SEX	JOB	RATE	INSURANCE	PREMIUM
JOHN Q. SMITH	48	M	B	$ 29.50	$ 16400.	483.80
PAUL B. BUNYON	24	M	C	$ 24.00	$ 20000.	480.00
CLARA P. MONROE	55	F	A	$ 30.50	$ 6000.	183.00
DUSTY O. RHODE		JOB CLASS ERROR				
JANE G. DOWNS	42	F	B	$ 24.50	$ 11900.	291.55
JIMMY F. STARTER	52	M	C	$ 35.00	$ 40000.	1400.00
CANDY A. SWEET		SEX ERROR				
JAMES C. MOORE	36	M	A	$ 24.00	$ 50000.	1200.00
BILLIE T. KIDD	19	F	A	$ 19.00	$ 15000.	285.00
CHEVY C. FORD	62					UNINSURABLE
JUNIOR S. FRYE	15					UNINSURABLE

```
TOTAL APPLICANTS PROCESSED 11
NUMBER QUALIFYING  7
NUMBER UNINSURABLE  4

AVERAGE INSURANCE $  22757.
AVERAGE INSURANCE RATE $  26.64
```

ANSWERS TO EXERCISES 7 1

1 a
```
        INTEGER FIVES
        DO 10 FIVES = 5,100,5
        WRITE(6,1000) FIVES
   1000 FORMAT(I15)
   10   CONTINUE
          .
          .
          .
```

b
```
        DO 10 I=1,N
        PV = 1.0/(1.0+RATE)**I
        WRITE(6,1001) I,PV
   10   CONTINUE
          .
          .
          .
```

```
        C          DO 100 HOT=99,108,1
                       BODYT = (HOT-BODYT)/BODYT + BODYT
           100         CONTINUE
                          .
                          .
                          .
```

2    $1 AT 8%

```
     YEAR   PRESENT
             VALUE
        1     .92593
        2     .85734
```

3   In no way.

4   The IF statement includes an illegal transfer of control into the range of the DO-loop.

5   Eight, as near as we can tell.

ANSWERS TO EXERCISES 7 2

1   Chapter 3:

   None of the loops were counting loops, so DO-loops aren't appropriate.

   Section 6 1:

   The first program has no loops at all. Both the READ loop and the WRITE loop in the last program are counting loops and could be written profitably as DO-loops.

   Section 6 2:

   The loop which computes the average and the WRITE loop are counting loops and would make good DO-loops. The READ loop, on the other hand, is not a counting loop. It's termination condition doesn't test the loop index (N) against a predetermined count.

   Section 6 5:

   All the loops in the simulation program would make good DO-loops.

   Section 6 6:

   All the loops in the political poll program are counting loops and are, therefore, good candidates for DO-loops.

   Section 6 7:

   The READ loop in the bar graph program is not a counting loop because its termination condition does not depend on N reaching a predetermined count. The WRITE loop, however, is a counting loop and would make a good DO-loop.

   Section 6 8:

   The main loop (from statement 100 up to just before 600) is not a counting loop, so wouldn't make a good DO-loop.

2 Change all references to memory cell MAXIM to MINIM. Change the COMMENTs appropriately, and most important, change the IF statement in the range of the DO-loop to

```
IF (SALES(HERE) .GE. MINIM)   GO TO 300
```

3 Add an INTEGER memory cell NUMB, then use these statements (or their equivalents):

```
COMMENT:   THERE'S BEEN ONLY ONE ELEMENT SO FAR, SO IT (THE
C          FIRST ELEMENT) IS THE LARGEST, AND THE CURRENT
C          MAXIMUM HAS BEEN ENCOUNTERED ONLY ONCE.
       MAXIM = SALES(1)
       NUMB = 1
C
C          SEARCH THE OTHER ELEMENTS IN "SALES" FOR LARGER
C          VALUES, KEEPING TRACK OF THE NUMBER OF TIMES THE
C          CURRENT MAXIMUM HAS BEEN ENCOUNTERED.
       DO 300 HERE=2,N
          IF (SALES(HERE) .LT. MAXIM)   GO TO 300
          IF (SALES(HERE) .GT. MAXIM)   GO TO 200
C          CURRENT MAXIMUM ENCOUNTERED AGAIN.
          NUMB = NUMB+1
          GO TO 300
C          FOUND A LARGER VALUE.  UPDATE.
  200     MAXIM = SALES(HERE)
          NUMB = 1
  300     CONTINUE
```

ANSWERS TO EXERCISES 7 3

1 (6I1, 1X, 3I1)

2
```
C                                THIS DOES THE FREQUENCY COUNT
       DO 100 Q=1,NUMBER
         READ(5,IFORM) (RESPON(I),I=1,NQ)
         DO 100 I=1,NQ
           IF ((RESPON(I).EQ.0).OR.(RESPON(I).GT.MXCODE(I)))
     +       GOTO 100
C                    HERE'S THE STATEMENT FOR FEMALES AGE 20-39
           IF ((RESPON(1).NE.2).AND.(RESPON(2).NE.2)) GOTO 100
           J=RESPON(I)
           TALLY(I,J)=TALLY(I,J)+1
  100      CONTINUE
                            .
                            .
                            .
```

3
```
C                                THIS DOES THE FREQUENCY COUNT
       DO 100 Q=1,NUMBER
         READ(5,IFORM) (RESPON(I),I=1,NQ)
         DO 100 I=1,NQ
           IF ((RESPON(I).EQ.0).OR.(RESPON(I).GT.MXCODE(I)))
     +       GOTO 100
C                     HERE'S THE STATEMENT FOR PROFESSIONALS
           IF (RESPON(4).NE.6) GOTO 100
           J=RESPON(I)
           TALLY(I,J)=TALLY(I,J)+1
  100      CONTINUE
```

4 One possible answer is to change DO-loop 100 as shown below.

```
      DO 120 Q=1,NUMBER
        READ(5,IFORM) (RESPON(I), I=1,Q)
        DO 110 I=1,NQ
          IF (RESPON(I) .EQ. 0  .AND.
     +        RESPON(I) .GT. MXCODE(I))  GO TO 109
          J = RESPON(I)
          TALLY(I,J) = TALLY(I,J) + 1
          GO TO 110
C                                              INVALID RESPONSE
109       WRITE(6,1090) I,Q
1090      FORMAT(' RESPONSE',I3,' ON QUESTIONNAIRE',I3
     +           ' WAS MISSING OR INVALID.')
110       CONTINUE
120     CONTINUE
```

ANSWERS TO EXERCISES 7 4

1 a `GO TO (10,20,30), TYPE`

  b `GO TO (200,200,100,100,200,300), BRANCH`

2 `IF (TYPE-2) 10,20,30`

3 To your input data you would need to add PURDAY, the day of the year from 1 to 365 on which the asset was purchased. If it was purchased during the year, then the depreciation value is multiplied by

$$\left(1 - \frac{PURDAY}{365}\right).$$

4 If the asset ends its useful life during the year, the depreciation for the year is the value left to depreciate. This is calculated by cost − salvage value − accumulated depreciation. We'll let you revise the program.

ANSWERS TO EXERCISES 8 2

1 Memory cell A will take the values 1.0, 4.0, and then 1.0 again. (We're pretty sure that last 1.0 is correct.)

2 A FUNCTION must have at least one parameter.

3 TAX (3.49) is 0.21; TAX (1.03) is 0.06.

4 2, 1, and 3.0. The expression rounds the result to the nearest whole number. In computing taxes we wanted to round, not truncate.

5
```
REAL FUNCTION OURABS(A)
REAL A
OURABS = A
IF (OURABS .LT. 0.0)  OURABS = -OURABS
RETURN
END
```

ANSWERS TO EXERCISES 8 3

1 The first two are legal.

   The third is illegal. The name POMEGRANATE is too long.

   The fourth is illegal. A parameter must be listed by name only. If it is an array, the parameter declarations will say so. If it is only a memory cell, it doesn't need a subscript.

2 They are all legal.

3 It would print the line

       9   **16**   **25**

4 It would print

   ```
   A= DOG  NONE BAT
   ```

ANSWERS TO EXERCISES 8 4

1 You wouldn't have to change SUBROUTINE PRGRPH at all. It plots out whatever graph it's sent as an argument. You *would* have to change the main program, altering it so that it made a CALL to SUBROUTINE PLOT for every one of your data points.

   Suppose you have punched your data on cards, with one (x,y) pair per card. Suppose that your data includes x values between 0 and 10 and y values between 0 and 5. Then this program could be used to plot your data.

   ```
   COMMENT:  PLOT MY DATA
         REAL X,Y
         INTEGER G(25,15)
         CALL BLKOUT(G,25,15)
    10   READ(5,1000) X,Y
    1000    FORMAT(2F10.5)
         IF (X .LT. 0.0)  GO TO 20
         CALL PLOT(X,Y, 0.0,10.0, 0.0,5.0, 1H+, G,25,15)
         GO TO 10
   C                                    GRAPH IS FINISHED.  PRINT.
    20   CALL PRGRPH(G,25,15)
         STOP
         END
   ```

ANSWERS TO EXERCISES 8 5

1 ONE: legal

   TWO: legal

   THREE: illegal—LENGTH isn't in the parameter list of the SUBROUTINE THREE, so it can't be used as an array size declarator in the SUBROUTINE's parameter declaration section.

2 It is illegal to change the value of an array size declarator. Thus, the statement N=N+1 is illegal in this context.

3   Change the FUNCTION LOCBIG so that the second IF statement becomes
    ```
    IF (A(I) .LT. A(LOCBIG)) LOCBIG = I
    ```
    It would also be nice, although not strictly necessary, to change the name of the FUNCTION (and all references to it) to LOCSM since it now LOCates the SMallest element in the array.

4   After execution of the CALL statement, the cells ONE and TWO would both have whatever value TWO had before execution of the CALL statement.

5   The statement CALL BADSWT (1,2) lists two *constant* values as arguments, yet the SUBROUTINE BADSWT *changes* the values of the arguments given to it. It is immoral to change the value of a constant (according to the standards of ANSI).

ANSWERS TO EXERCISES 8 7

1

	ONE	TWO	THREE

BLK1

A(1)	C	Q(1)
A(2)	B(1)	Q(2)
A(3)	B(2)	Q(3)
B	B(3)	Q(4)

BLK2

C(1)	D(1)	R
C(2)	D(2)	S

2   It will print the values of A, B, C, D, E, and F, which will be 2.0, 1.0, 2.0, 3.0, 1.0, and 3.0, respectively.

ANSWERS TO EXERCISES 8 8

1   None of the answers is correct. The EXTERNAL statement appears in the program unit which has a subprogram reference in which an argument is the name of another subprogram.

2   It wouldn't hurt anything.

ANSWERS TO EXERCISES 9 2

1 Here are some values for 1983 that you can use to check or validate your results.

Net income $ 142736
Total assets $1042265

3 All the 1978 values could be calculated *except*

Sales   Long-term debt
Net fixed assets   Inventory
Notes payable   Total assets
                 Total liabilities

These can be used with the planning assumptions to calculate all the other values. You might notice that those items which use an amount from a previous period (i.e., $t - 1$) can't be calculated. They must be input.

ANSWERS TO EXERCISES 9 3

1
```
COMMENT:  NOW SORT ON NAMES
       CALL  INDSRT(NAME,X,N)
       WRITE(6,5000)
 5000 FORMAT('0CHILDREN IN ALPHABETICAL ORDER'/
      +          ' NAME        AGE      WEIGHT      HEIGHT')
  410  WRITE(6,3000) (NAME(X(I)),AGE(X(I)),WGT(X(I)),
      +                              HGT(X(I)), I=1,N)
```

2 Put a test to assure that N never gets larger than 100 (the length of our arrays) in the loop that READs in the data.

3 No, it won't cause an error. As long as N does not exceed the actual declared length of the array (100 here), the SUBROUTINE can just use the lower parts of the array (up to position N) with no problem. However, this can cause unexpected problems when the array is multidimensional.

ANSWERS TO EXERCISES 10 3

```
1 00100 COMMENT: ECONOMIC ORDER QUANTITY CALCULATION
  00110 C     DEMAND = DEMAND PER YEAR IN UNITS
  00120 C     HOLD   = ANNUAL UNIT HOLDING COST
  00130 C     ORDER  = ORDERING COST PER ORDER PROCESSED
  00140       REAL DEMAND,HOLD,ORDER,EOQ,TIME
  00150 C                        HERE ARE THE INSTRUCTIONS
  00160       WRITE(6,100)
  00170   100 FORMAT(1X,14HINSTRUCTIONS--,/,1X,
  00180      1        36HTHIS PROGRAM CALCULATES THE ECONOMIC,
  00190      2        /,1X,
  00200      3        35HORDER QUANTITY AND THE TIME BETWEEN,
  00210      4        /,1X,
  00220      5        27HORDERS IN MONTHS. YOU ENTER,/,6X,
  00230      6        31H(1)THE DEMAND PER YEAR IN UNITS,/,6X,
  00240      7        37H(2)THE ANNUAL HOLDING COST IN DOLLARS,
  00250      8        4H AND,/,6X,
  00260      9        32H(3)THE COST PER ORDER IN DOLLARS,/,1X,
  00270      A        27HWHEN ASKED BY THE COMPUTER.,//)
  00280       WRITE(6,200)
  00290   200 FORMAT(1X,28HENTER DEMAND, HOLDING COST, ,
  00300      1        13HORDERING COST)
  00310 C                        HERE'S THE FREE-FORMAT READ
  00320       READ(5,*) DEMAND,HOLD,ORDER
  00330 C                        CALCULATE EOQ
  00340       EOQ=SQRT((2.0*ORDER*DEMAND)/HOLD)
  00350 C                        CALCULATE ORDER FREQUENCY
  00360       TIME=EOQ/DEMAND*12.
  00370       WRITE(6,110) EOQ,TIME
  00380   110 FORMAT(/,1X,30HTHE ECOMONIC ORDER QUANTITY IS,
  00390      1        F8.1,7H UNITS.,/,1X,14HRE-ORDER EVERY,
  00400      2        F6.1,8H MONTHS.)
  00410       STOP
  00420       END
```

output

```
INSTRUCTIONS--
THIS PROGRAM CALCULATES THE ECONOMIC
ORDER QUANTITY AND THE TIME BETWEEN
ORDERS IN MONTHS. YOU ENTER
       (1)THE DEMAND PER YEAR IN UNITS
       (2)THE ANNUAL HOLDING COST IN DOLLARS AND
       (3)THE COST PER ORDER IN DOLLARS
WHEN ASKED BY THE COMPUTER.


ENTER DEMAND, HOLDING COST, ORDERING COST
? 2500,.3,15

THE ECONOMIC ORDER QUANTITY IS   500.0 UNITS.
RE-ORDER EVERY   2.4 MONTHS.
```

```
2  00100  COMMENT: ECONOMIC ORDER QUANTITY CALCULATION
   00110 C      DEMAND = DEMAND PER YEAR IN UNITS
   00120 C      HOLD   = ANNUAL UNIT HOLDING COST
   00130 C      ORDER  = ORDERING COST PER ORDER PROCESSED
   00140        REAL DEMAND,HOLD,ORDER,EOQ,TIME
   00150 C                        HERE'S A FREE-FORMAT PRINT
   00160        PRINT *, 'ENTER DEMAND, HOLDING COST, ORDERING',
   00170        PRINT *, 'COST'
   00180 C                        HERE'S THE FREE-FORMAT READ
   00190        READ *, DEMAND,HOLD,ORDER
   00200 C                                  CALCULATE EOQ
   00210        EOQ=SQRT((2.0*ORDER*DEMAND)/HOLD)
   00220 C                        CALCULATE ORDER FREQUENCY
   00230        TIME=EOQ/DEMAND*12.
   00240 C                        HERE'S HOW YOU SKIP TWO LINES
   00250        PRINT *
   00260        PRINT *
   00270 C                        HERE'S A FREE-FORMAT PRINT
   00280        PRINT *, 'THE ECONOMIC ORDER QUANTITY IS ',EOQ,
   00290       +          ' UNITS.'
   00300        PRINT *, 'RE-ORDER EVERY ',TIME,' MONTHS.'
   00310        STOP
   00320        END
```

output

```
   ENTER DEMAND, HOLDING COST, ORDERING  COST
? 2500,.3,15


   THE ECONOMIC ORDER QUANTITY IS 500. UNITS.
   RE-ORDER EVERY 2.4 MONTHS.
```

INDEX

```
************************************************************

C                    QUICK REFERENCE INDEX

C  USING THE QUICK REFERENCE INDEX
C     SCAN THIS INDEX FOR THE TYPE OF STATEMENT YOU WANT.
C     SEEING IT IN PRINT MAY ANSWER YOUR QUESTIONS.
C     IF NOT, USE THE PAGE NUMBER TO FIND MORE INFORMATION.


C
C  TYPICAL STATEMENT                                    PAGE NO.
C
C  SPECIFICATION STATEMENTS
       INTEGER A, B, PARTNO, AMT                          25
       REAL PRINC, BAL, RATE                              25
       REAL X(25), Y(15,100)                              127,139
       END                                                38
       SUBROUTINE ACCT(ASSET, LIAB, N)                    203
       REAL FUNCTION ANNUIT(P, R, Y)                      200
       DATA X/1.4/, A,B/3HCAT,3HDOG/                      96
C
C  ASSIGNMENT AND I/O STATEMENTS
       N = 1                                              27
       QWKREF = THANKS**DDM                               27
       BASE = SQRT(AREA)/HT                               80
       V = SUMSQ/(N-1) - SUM**2/(N*(N-1))                 74
       READ(5,1000) A, B, C                               41
       READ(5,1000, END=999) A, B, C                      55
  1000 FORMAT(2F10.0, I3)                                 41,100
       WRITE(6,2000) A, B, C                              31
  2000 FORMAT(' DIMENSIONS ', 2G11.4/                     99,101
      +        25X, 'PART NUMBER ', I4)                   36
       READ(5,3000) (X(I), Y(I), I=1,N)                   144
  3000 FORMAT(2F10.0)                                     41,103
       WRITE(6,4000) (TITLE(I),I=1,10),                   144
      +              ((D(I,J),J=1,8), I=1,N)              144,103
  4000 FORMAT('1', 20X, 10A4/                             34,93
      +        (1X,8G20.6)      )                         100,103
       READ(9) ARRAY                                      145,295
       WRITE(NT) XARRAY, YARRAY                           145,295
       ENDFILE NT                                         296
       REWIND NT                                          296
       BACKSPACE 9                                        296
C
C  CONTROL STATEMENTS
       STOP                                               38
       GO TO 100                                          49
       IF (N .LT. 1000)  GO TO 10                         51
       IF (X.GT.A .AND. X.LT.B) CALL PLOT(X)              89
       IF (X .GT. 10.32)  Y=X-10.32                       59
       GO TO (10,20,50,30,400), JTH                       183
       CALL SUBR(R*B, 5HFINIS, A)                         202
       Y = F(X)                                           198
       T = ALOG(ALOG(X))                                  80,98
       RETURN                                             200
       DO 100 I=1,N                                       166
  100  CONTINUE                                           165

************************************************************
```
                              †
                             342